Forthcoming Books in the Dove on Fundraising Series:

Conducting a Successful Major Gifts and Planned Giving Program
Conducting a Successful Development Services Program

Books Currently Available in the Dove on Fundraising Series:

Conducting a Successful Capital Campaign, 2nd Edition
Conducting a Successful Fundraising Program

Other Nonprofit Resources from Jossey-Bass:

CPR for Nonprofits, *Alvin Reiss*
The Five Strategies for Fundraising Success, *Mal Warwick*
Team-Based Fundraising Step by Step, *Mim Carlson and Cheryl Clarke*
Listening to Your Donors, *Bruce Campbell*
The Insider's Guide to Grantmaking, *Joel J. Orosz*
How Foundations Work, *Dennis P. McIlnay*
Winning Grants Step By Step, *Mim Carlson*
The Fundraising Planner: A Working Model for Raising the Dollars You Need, *Terry and Doug Schaff*
The Jossey-Bass Guide to Strategic Communications for Nonprofits, *Kathleen Bonk, Henry Griggs, Emily Tynes*
Marketing Nonprofit Programs and Services, *Douglas B Herron*
Transforming Fundraising: A Practical Guide to Evaluating and Strengthening Fundraising to Grow with Change, *Judith Nichols*
Achieving Excellence in Fund Raising, *Henry A. Rosso and Associates*
The Grantwriter's Start-Up Kit, *Creed C. Black, Tom Ezell, Rhonda Ritchie*
Secrets of Successful Grantsmanship, *Susan L. Golden*

CONDUCTING A SUCCESSFUL ANNUAL GIVING PROGRAM

The Dove on Fundraising Series is a library of premier resource guides that combine practical instruction with real-world examples. In response to the ever-changing challenges nonprofits face, Kent E. Dove, The Indiana University Foundation, and Jossey-Bass have come together to develop and advance professional standards for fundraisers everywhere. Built on the successful fundraising model developed by veteran fundraiser and series editor Kent Dove, these publications provide a flexible campaign-based approach that recognizes fundraising as both a science and an art.

Clustered around the comprehensive *Conducting a Successful Fundraising Program,* each publication examines a key aspect of fundraising, and all authors bring years of experience and knowledge to their topics. Together, these guides present an integrated framework validated by research and practical results. **The Dove on Fundraising Series** seeks to provide nonprofit leaders, fundraisers, consultants, and students with not only time-tested principles, but also successful examples, strategies, and publications that readers can use to shape their own development programs.

CONDUCTING A SUCCESSFUL ANNUAL GIVING PROGRAM

A Comprehensive Guide and Resource

Kent E. Dove
Jeffrey A. Lindauer
Carolyn P. Madvig

JOSSEY-BASS
A Wiley Company
San Francisco

Published by Jossey-Bass
A Wiley Imprint
989 Market Street, San Francisco, CA 94103-1741   www.josseybass.com

The *Discover Art Inside & Out* brochure cover in Resource 8 is reprinted by courtesy of Indianapolis Museum of Art, Indianapolis, Indiana, USA. The cover features *Near Arles*, 1888, by Paul Gauguin, French (1848–1903), oil on canvas, $36 \times 28\frac{1}{2}$ inches. IMA44.10 Indianapolis Museum of Art. Gift in memory of William Ray Adams.

The *Corporate Partner Program: Gifts and Collaborations* brochure cover in Resource 8 is reprinted by courtesy of Indianapolis Museum of Art. Indianapolis, Indiana, USA.

Readers should be aware that Internet Web sites offered as citations and/or sources for further information may have changed or disappeared between the time this was written and when it is read.

Jossey-Bass books and products are available through most bookstores. To contact Jossey-Bass directly call our Customer Care Department within the U.S. at 800-956-7739, outside the U.S. at 317-572-3986, or fax 317-572-4002.

Jossey-Bass also publishes its books in a variety of electronic formats. Some content that appears in print may not be available in electronic books.

Library of Congress Cataloging-in-Publication Data

Dove, Kent E., date.
   Conducting a successful annual giving program: a comprehensive guide and resource / Kent E. Dove, Jeffrey A. Lindauer, Carolyn P. Madvig.—1st ed.
         p.   cm.
Includes bibliographical references and index.
   ISBN 0–7879–5649-X
   1. Fund raising. 2. Nonprofit organizations—Finance.
   3. Charities—Finance. I. Lindauer, Jeffrey A., date. II. Madvig, Carolyn P., date. III. Title.
   HV41.2 .D678 2001
   658.15'224—dc21

                                                                                    00-013120

FIRST EDITION
HB Printing   10 9 8 7 6 5 4 3

CONTENTS

Preface   xi

Acknowledgments   xv

The Authors   xvii

PART ONE: PLANNING AND IMPLEMENTING YOUR ANNUAL GIVING PROGRAM   1

Tables, Figures, and Exhibits in Part One   3

Introduction: Defining the Annual Campaign   7

Preparing for the Annual Campaign

1. Developing an Annual Giving Plan   11

2. Segmenting Appeals   32

3. Testing and Statistical Analysis   50

Elements of the Annual Campaign

4. Implementing a Direct Mail Campaign   60

5. Sponsoring Special Events   87

6. Telemarketing Your Cause   95

7. Soliciting Funds in Person   123

The Annual Fund in Action

8. Key Program Roles and Responsibilities   139

9. Working with Volunteers   153

10. Promotions, Communications, and Marketing   164

11. Gift Administration and Donor Appreciation   179

12. Closing the Campaign and Moving Forward   194

PART TWO: THE ANNUAL FUND RESOURCE GUIDE   201

Resource Guide Contents   203

Preparing for the Annual Campaign

1. Stanford Law School Direct Appeal Program   207

2. Annual Fund Solicitation Calendar   215

3. Web Site Examples   219

Elements of the Annual Campaign

4. Annual Fund–Capital Campaign Combined
   Strategic Goals and Calendar   223

5. Corporate Campaign Plan   229

6. Corporate Matching Gift Companies   243

7. Corporate Matching Gift Guidelines and Application Form   257

The Annual Fund in Action

8. Membership Program with Benefits   265

9. University Annual Fund Analysis   273

10. Annual Fund Survey   277

11. Direct Mail Solicitation Package   281

12. Gala Event Invitation and Program   291

13. Sales and Raffle Event Promotion   301

14. "A-Thon" Event Packages   305

15. "A-Thon" Team Captain's Kit and Supplies   313

16. Entertainment and Show Publicity Pieces   337

17. Outing Registration Letter and Materials   349

18. Special Events Planning Checklists   355

19. Sample Telemarketing Script for Lapsed Donors   375

20. Telemarketing Objection Packet   379

21. Code of Ethics Samples   381

22. Fundraising Guidebook   391

23. Case Statement Examples   409

24. Newsletter Sample   421

25. Gift Receipt Templates   431

26. Gift Agreement Template   439

27. Post-Campaign Assessment Report   443

28. Final Report   451

References   485

Index   487

To my talented coworkers at the Indiana University Foundation,
the best annual and special gifts staff anywhere;
to my wonderful parents;
to my husband, Don, my love and best friend;
and to my son, Ian, the light of my life.

—Carolyn P. Madvig

To Angie, Jordan, and Kaylea: Thank you for understanding
and allowing me the time to work on this book.
And to all members of the Indiana University Foundation
annual fund team, past and present—I could not ask
for a better group of people to work with.

—Jeffrey A. Lindauer

PREFACE

What started as a sprint is turning into a marathon. First there was *Conducting a Successful Capital Campaign*. Then came *Conducting a Successful Fundraising Program*. Now it is *Conducting a Successful Annual Giving Program*. In fact, Jossey-Bass and I have agreed to a series of books, with at least two more to come: one on major gifts and planned giving programs and the other on development services (prospect research, prospect management programs, special events, gift administration, information services, and stewardship and donor recognition).

Because virtually every nonprofit organization conducts an annual giving program, this book holds special importance. The annual fund requires more immediate attention and specialized expertise than many people realize. These can only be gained through active, daily participation in an annual giving program. Fortunately, two of America's foremost annual giving professionals call Indiana University home too. They have agreed to join me in the preparation of *Conducting a Successful Annual Giving Program*, and I am delighted to introduce them.

Carolyn P. Madvig and Jeffrey A. Lindauer are an unlikely pair, especially if you buy first impressions. Carolyn is quiet, always smiling, and pleasant, a behind-the-scenes manager and motivator who comes by her management talents naturally. Her father was in management with a major corporation, and she grew up in a home where managing people and process were topics of frequent discussion. Jeff is living proof that what you see is not always what you get. The odds of finding him in a coat and tie are about as good as his actually winning money on one of his frequent Las Vegas junkets. He is witty and funny, and irreverent in an innocent way. Jeff loves to perform and does it well; Carolyn will do just about anything to avoid the limelight. Carolyn is a soccer mom. She really is. Her husband is a soccer coach and her son a soccer player. Jeff is a couch potato. He really is. He is also one of the leading authorities on nonprofit telemarketing and direct mail. Jeff began as a student caller at Indiana University and continued with the program, joining the staff after graduation. A decade later he manages a model state-of-the-art program.

They work so well together because both are passionate about their work. Both set the performance bar very high and will accept nothing short of their expectations. Although it does not show, both are extremely competitive. Neither likes to lose, and neither is ever totally satisfied with the results. Both are inquisitive and willing to try new ideas and take risks, albeit calculated risks, and are constantly pushing the envelope.

Both are highly analytical when you talk to them about their program; they may tell you what they think or believe, but they will also tell you what they know. They know because they evaluate and reevaluate, and test, and analyze everything they do. And the respect they have for each other means, among other things, they can disagree while looking for agreement without harm being done to their relationship.

As you read this book, I know you will come to have the same respect, possibly even awe, I have for them. As fundraising enters the twenty-first century, I am pleased to join them to share a new level of comprehensive thought on the most basic and most primary of all fundraising efforts, the annual giving program.

Audience

Conducting a Successful Annual Giving Program is written for two primary audiences. First, it is intended to serve as a constant companion to those who work actively on annual funds in service to the more than 730,000 registered nonprofit organizations in the United States, for the countless others that are not registered, and for friends and colleagues outside the United States who engage in annual fund appeals. Staff, board members, leaders, and volunteers can all benefit from this book. The second intended audience is students. The book is written to serve as a textbook too. One of the aims of this book and its companion pieces, now being produced as part of this Jossey-Bass series, is to serve as an encouragement to the teaching of the subject of fundraising in educational settings across the country.

Overview of the Contents

This book is designed to follow logically and sequentially the path of the annual giving program from the earliest days of planning through the victory celebration at the end of the campaign, and coming back full circle to the beginning of the next year's annual giving program.

Chapter One discusses planning the program and some of the major considerations that affect decisions. Readers will see that everything stems from the demographic profile of the organization and its prospect pool.

Chapter Two follows closely as it discusses market segmentation and the dramatic difference that is made when a nonprofit thoughtfully, systematically, and intelligently deciphers its market and designs appropriate programs using applicable techniques to reach its target audiences. Those who enjoy annual fund success understand that one size does not fit all.

Chapter Three brings to focus the importance of testing results and making adjustments in the program based on what is known rather than what is thought or believed. It precedes four chapters that each in turn discuss the primary techniques used in the annual fund.

Direct mail, the most often used form of solicitation, is the subject of Chapter Four. Design of the outer envelope, solicitation piece, response device, response envelope, and enclosures is covered. The chapter concludes with an evaluation of two direct mail solicitations.

Chapter Five discusses special events used for fundraising purposes. A key is allowing enough time for proper planning and attention to every detail. Checklists are included to aid those using this popular and versatile technique.

Telemarketing is the subject of Chapter Six. The thorough discussion covers planning a calling program, choosing callers, training callers, conducting the calling session itself, and tracking results.

Personal solicitation is covered in Chapter Seven. This thorough chapter discusses researching, rating, and assigning prospects and then walks the reader through the process of preparing for and then making a face-to-face solicitation. It also addresses the importance of ethical behavior and conduct in the field of fundraising.

Chapters Eight and Nine discuss the role of volunteers—board members, key leaders, and the body of volunteers who are the lifeblood of philanthropy. The nuts-and-bolts discussion covers every possible subject.

Chapter Ten addresses promotion, communications, and marketing. The important pieces of literature that sustain the annual fund are covered, as is the need for a communications plan and a marketing program.

Receiving and handling gifts, accounting and reporting to donors, and donor relations and stewardship are the topics of Chapter Eleven, a behind-the-scenes look at these subjects.

The text concludes in Chapter Twelve where celebrating, or saving, the victory is discussed, the need to produce final reports is addressed, and looking to next year's campaign is stressed.

The text concludes at the end of Chapter Twelve, but the book does not end there. Part Two contains the Annual Fund Resource Guide. One of the aims of this book is to provide a visual aid to support each of the major points addressed in the text. This feature, common to the books in this series, not only tells readers how to do things but also shows them how. Too often busy people do not have time to begin a task with a blank piece of paper. They like something to look at to guide them, something that they can quickly and easily adopt or adapt. This is our goal. We hope we reached it.

Bloomington, Indiana   Kent E. Dove
April 2001

ACKNOWLEDGMENTS

This book and the others in this series took a large, team effort. Space does not permit mentioning everyone who assisted, but there are some who must be mentioned by name.

The board of directors of the Indiana University Foundation and Curtis R. Simic, its president, deserve special mention. The board approved this enterprise with the full understanding that it would take time, energy, effort, and resources from very busy people who are responsible for conducting a $100 million-a-year program on a daily basis. The board believes the project is worthwhile for what it promises to share with the larger nonprofit community, and there is a commitment on the part of everyone at Indiana University to encourage best practices in fundraising whenever possible. Without board permission, we could not have done this. We thank the board members for their support.

Two people whose names will appear nowhere else did the laborious, tedious task of word processing, and constantly revising, the text. Connie Daugherty assists both Carolyn and me. In addition, she made time for this project. We use a lot of student help at the Indiana University Foundation. We like to help students who are working their way through school, and there are a myriad of tasks we could not get done without their assistance. Occasionally an outstanding worker appears at our door. Stacey Austin is one such person. I do not know her plans after graduation, but some nonprofit should enlist her. She is a great worker, and she can truthfully say she has read this book and *Conducting a Successful Fundraising Program* several times over.

This book, like the others in the series, is resource rich. At the risk of offending some whose names are not cited here, I mention a few of the people who were especially helpful as we gathered the more than one hundred exhibits and resources reproduced in the book: Steve Bonchek, Harmony School Education Center; Helen Brenneman, Penn State University; Julie Daily, Tulip Trace Council of Girl Scouts, Inc.; Susan Lyons, Bloomington (Indiana) Hospital Foundation; Melanie McKenzie, Greater Victoria Hospitals Foundation; Kimberly Ruff, Amethyst House; Martin Shell, Stanford Law School; Margaret Skidmore, Museum of Fine Arts, Houston; Jim Smith, United Way of Central Indiana; Peg Stice, United Way of Bloomington and Monroe County (Indiana); and Faye Wightman, British Colombia's Children's Hospital.

As always, there is the editorial team for the Nonprofit and Public Management Series at Jossey-Bass to thank. On this book, three new faces joined the team: Johanna Vondeling, associate editor; Ocean Howell, assistant editor; and Mariana Raykov, production editor. Welcome and thank you to all three. Dorothy Hearst, editor, remains interested and involved too, although further removed now as she continues to grow in her responsibilities at Jossey-Bass. I now receive far less of her time, but she is still there when needed.

Thanks to everyone for their support, encouragement, and understanding. We will be back soon with another book in this series. Two more are already in process.

—K.E.D.

THE AUTHORS

KENT E. DOVE is the author of *Conducting a Successful Capital Campaign* (second edition, Jossey-Bass, 1999), proclaimed as the leading guide to planning and implementing a capital campaign, and the recently released *Conducting a Successful Fundraising Program: A Comprehensive Guide and Resource* (Jossey-Bass, 2001).

Dove's career began shortly after his graduation from Indiana University when he joined the Indiana University Foundation staff as a publications writer. He also directed annual giving programs for several of the university's professional schools. Over the next decade he moved to progressively responsible positions at other institutions—director of annual giving, assistant director of development, director of development—leading to his appointment as vice president of development, coordinating the offices of development, alumni relations, public relations, and government relations. Six years later he was counsel to and resident director of the largest capital campaign for a public university in America while also serving as a consultant to the largest campaign ever undertaken in Canada to that point in time. Described as "the preeminent fundraising practitioner working in America today," his career spans five decades.

He currently serves as vice president for development at the IU Foundation, where he returned in 1993 to serve as executive director of capital campaigns to manage a six-year, $350 million endowment campaign for Indiana University Bloomington, the largest campaign ever undertaken by the university. The campaign surpassed its goal in the summer of 1999 with $373 million raised more than a year ahead of schedule. It concluded on December 31, 2000, more than $100 million over goal. He was named vice president for development in 1997, and in 1999 the Council for Advancement and Support of Education (CASE) recognized Indiana University with its highest award of excellence for overall fundraising performance for the period 1993–1998.

Dove previously held educational fundraising management positions at Rice University, the University of California–Berkeley, Drake University, the University of Alabama, Northwestern University, the University of Tennessee Center for the Health Sciences, and West Virginia University.

From June 1989 to December 1993 he operated Kent E. Dove & Associates, a small firm designed and organized to offer highly personal, specialized attention to a select client base. His areas of interest are assessment of institutional development programs, institutional planning, market surveys, management and supervision of capital campaigns, staff and board training, and management of nonprofit organizations.

Dove has served three terms on the CASE Educational Fund Raising Committee and one term on the board of directors of the Association of Fundraising Professionals (formerly, National Society of Fund Raising Executives). In 1986 he received the CASE Steuben Glass Apple Award for Outstanding Teaching.

JEFFREY A. LINDAUER received his B.S. degree in public affairs from Indiana University's School of Public and Environmental Affairs in 1992. Throughout college, he worked at the Indiana University Foundation as a student caller and student manager and eventually as assistant director of the Telefund program. Upon graduation, he joined the staff on a full-time basis as associate director of the Telefund. After serving as director of the Telefund and director of annual giving and regional campus services, Jeff was promoted to the position of executive director of special gifts and annual giving programs in April 2001. He is the coauthor (with Kent Dove and Carolyn Madvig) of the chapter in *Conducting a Successful Fundraising Program* focusing on annual giving programs.

CAROLYN P. MADVIG received her B.A. degree in English from Monmouth College (Illinois) in 1985. After working in the admissions office at her alma mater, she moved to a similar position at Indiana University Bloomington. In April 1990 she changed her focus from student recruitment to fundraising when she was named director of the Telefund at the Indiana University Foundation. Over the past ten years she has held a variety of progressively responsible positions within the IU Foundation, including director of annual giving and director of special gifts and annual giving programs. In April 2001 she was promoted to the post of executive director for development administration and services. She is the coauthor (with Kent Dove and Jeffrey Lindauer) of the chapter on annual giving programs in *Conducting a Successful Fundraising Program*.

CONDUCTING A SUCCESSFUL
ANNUAL GIVING PROGRAM

PART ONE

PLANNING AND IMPLEMENTING YOUR ANNUAL GIVING PROGRAM

TABLES, FIGURES, AND EXHIBITS
IN PART ONE

Tables

1.1   Standards of Giving Chart for an Annual Campaign
        with a Goal of $100,000 with a Less-Proven Prospect Pool   16

1.2   Standards of Giving Chart for an Annual Campaign
        with a Goal of $1 Million with a Less-Proven Prospect Pool   16

1.3   Standards of Giving Chart for an Annual Campaign
        with a Goal of $100,000 with a Proven Prospect Pool   17

1.4   Standards of Giving Chart for an Annual Campaign
        with a Goal of $1 Million with a Proven Prospect Pool   17

1.5   Continuous Lifetime Giving Program: Broad Outline   19

2.1   Segmenting Donors into Nine Demographic Groups   34

3.1   Sample Donor Upgrade Report   58

3.2   Sample Donor Retention Report   59

Figures

1.1   Individual Continuous Lifetime Giving Track   20

2.1   University of British Columbia Donor Base Comparison   36

3.1   Annual Fund Growth   57

Exhibits

1.1   United Way Menu Reply Card   21

1.2   Sample Day School Annual Fund Calendar   23

1.3   Electronic Funds Transfer Fact Sheet   27

1.4   Penn State's Annual Fund On-Line Form   28

2.1   United Way–Lilly Endowment Challenge Gift   38

2.2   Donor Solicitation Letter   39

2.3   Nondonor Solicitation Letter   40

2.4   Faculty-Staff Solicitation   48

3.1   Two Letters: Personalization Versus Nonpersonalization   54

4.1   Sample Segmentation Letter: GVHF   64

4.2   Sample Segmentation Letter: Penn State   66

4.3   Direct Mail Envelope   69

4.4   Response Devices   71

4.5   Solicitation Package for Fairfield Country Day
School Annual Fund   77

4.6   Solicitation Package for Penn State Library   83

6.1   Sample Recruitment Ads   99

6.2   Fact Sheet for Telemarketers, Kelley School of Business,
Indiana University   100

6.3   Sample Reasons for Prospects to Give   103

6.4   Pre–Call Notification Mailing   106

6.5   Positive Dollar Asks   108

6.6   Pledge Confirmation Script   109

6.7   Prospect Data Form   111

6.8   Bonus Sheet for Callers   112

6.9   Coaching Evaluation Form   114

6.10   Caller Statistics, Indiana University Telefund   116

6.11   Program Statistics, Indiana University Telefund   119

7.1   Vicky's Bookmarks   128

7.2   Donors' Bill of Rights   138

8.1   Volunteer Job Description for Team Chair   143

8.2   Volunteer Job Description for Leadership Giving Chair   144

10.1   Sample Organization Fact Sheets   165

11.1   Annual Campaign Budget Report   181

11.2   Campaign Progress Report Form   183

11.3   Prospect Status Summary Report Form   184

11.4   Gift Receipt   186

11.5   Donor Recognition at Various Giving Levels   193

INTRODUCTION

Defining the Annual Campaign

Any gifts that can reasonably be expected to recur on a regular, periodic basis to support or sustain the operating budget of a nonprofit organization can be defined as annual gifts. These gifts are sought more to help meet annual operating budgets and generally to sustain nonprofits with gaps between their projected needs and projected revenues from other income sources. Virtually all nonprofits derive their operating budgets from a variety of sources—tuition, fees, contracts, grants—and supplement these revenues with private support. Fundraising takes two standard forms: the annual giving program, or annual fund, and the capital campaign. Over the past quarter-century the standard definition of both forms has expanded, but the basic terms remain in common usage today, and there is no indication that either will disappear from the lexicon of fundraising anytime soon.

The traditional annual fund was characterized by nonprofits seeking one gift from a donor during a given twelve-month period, the period being based on either the organization's fiscal year or, more commonly, the calendar year. It truly sought an "annual" gift. Today, contributed sources of sustaining or operating funds often come from a comprehensive approach that encourages multiple donations from supporters throughout the year rather than "annual" gifts. Today's comprehensive approach includes frequent mailings to mail-responsive supporters; grants for operating funds; sponsorships for performances, activities, and events; personal solicitations; special events; telemarketing; membership drives;

and other fundraising strategies distinctive to a particular organization. Today's broader definition of annual giving is a shorthand, familiar expression for operating funds. It no longer implies one gift per year from each donor but rather describes the organization's annual plan for obtaining and renewing donors.

Typically, annual giving is the primary source for bringing in new donors to the organization, as well as renewing donors up to a certain level—usually $1,000 to $5,000 per year. *Annual fund* is an apt name for the process, which occurs on a yearly basis and provides the support necessary to fund annual budgets and provide ongoing services.

The annual fund is the foundation of all other fundraising efforts. If one thinks of fundraising as a pyramid, the annual fund is the base of that pyramid, bringing in smaller dollars but the largest number of donors. The goal is to create the habit of philanthropy: to work hard in getting the first gift and then continuing to provide compelling reasons for future, increasing gifts, until a few donors identify themselves as serious major gift prospects. Every annual fund should work closely with major and planned giving programs. In essence, the annual fund is in the business of identifying the major donors of the future.

Major gifts are defined as the top 10 to 20 percent of gifts received by an organization that produce 70 to 80 percent or more of its gift income. In larger organizations, it is not unusual to see a major gift defined as $50,000 to $100,000. For smaller and newer organizations, major gifts may be defined as $2,500 to $5,000 or more. For institutions between the two extremes—the majority of all nonprofits—the definition of a major gift will range from $5,000 to $50,000 or more based on individual circumstance. A *lead gift* is one that serves to establish a trend for giving by others believed to be capable of making gifts at the same level. It is possible to secure lead gifts in the major, special, and general division of the gift table. However, most commonly, lead gifts are associated with the top gift, or gifts, to an organization. To satisfy this definition, lead gifts need to represent a gift of 10 percent or more of the campaign goal. A *nucleus gift* is a gift received at the earliest stages of the campaign, usually a major or lead gift, and most often given by an institutional insider (a board member or previous major donor). Nucleus gifts collectively provide a nucleus fund to create a giving momentum to launch a campaign. All are commonly referred to as major gifts and often referred to as key gifts too, particularly in the annual fund context.

Most nonprofits also consider the annual fund the mass marketing arm of their organization because it is the vehicle through which the majority of supporters make contributions, with most gifts coming through mail or telephone appeals or as a result of special events. Special events are widely and heavily used by many smaller nonprofits to raise operating funds, and increasingly technology will also be a factor. For larger annual gifts, face-to-face solicitation remains the preferred method.

Why is it important to have an annual fund? After all, assuming an organization has a sufficient major donor base to pursue a major gift strategy, it can get funding much more quickly by contacting just a few individuals and asking them to make significant gifts. To employ only this approach is extremely shortsighted, however, and can cause significant problems in the long run if the donor base is not continually expanded and properly maintained.

Prospect is used throughout this book to describe in general, familiar terms anyone who has the financial ability to give, as well as an interest, demonstrated or anticipated, in making a contribution. Chapter Seven contains a more specific, differentiated definition, often used to describe potential major gift donors. A prospect pool is the number of names to be included in a specific, or segmented, appeal or approach. For a general appeal or approach, the donor pool equals the number of names in the organization's database. Programs, even those that focus on larger gifts, need a steady stream of new prospects to ensure the pipeline does not run dry. To have annual fund success, an organization needs to be visionary and look not only at what is available today but also at how it is discovering and encouraging its major donors of the future.

A good annual fund incorporates the following components:

- *A personal touch.* As fundraising efforts continue to increase and nonprofits proliferate, people become increasingly discerning, and "Dear Friend" mass approaches will not work as they once did. It has become important to incorporate as much personalization as possible into a program, from personalized salutations to having as much information about the individual available as possible when making telephone calls.
- *Prospect and donor interests.* In order to draw in adequate prospects, an organization needs to keep each prospect's interests in mind at all times. Staff need to think not as much about what the organization needs but about what would make an investment in their organization appealing to prospects. Perhaps it is allowing a designation in honor of a specific individual; perhaps the ask should come from a peer rather than a national volunteer; perhaps the appeal should recognize a specific segment of an organization rather than the more conventional and typical appeal on behalf of the overall organization. All of these are effective ways in which to keep the prospect's interests uppermost in the process.
- *A solid overall plan, as well as a method for evaluating returns.* These components help determine that the staff's initial instincts were on target.
- *Research and good judgment* to ascertain potential market segments to target, thus improving overall results. It is important to follow up on efforts with statistical analysis in order to confirm that instincts about a particular segment are correct. Remember, "You are not your audience"!

Stewardship and good planning are vital to the idea of a continuous lifetime giving program, a concept that more and more annual funds are adopting. This change in thinking involves ensuring that you are looking at the long term as well as the short term when planning an annual fund. What are you doing to move your current annual donors up the ladder? What strategies can you employ that will prove most advantageous to your program? By keeping these questions uppermost in your mind, the maximum possible benefit can be attained, both now and in the future. Remain tuned in to the needs, requests, and desires of your donors, and adapt your program accordingly. Such special efforts will go far toward encouraging initial contributions and ensuring continued allegiance over time.

CHAPTER ONE

DEVELOPING AN ANNUAL GIVING PLAN

Strong preparation is key to planning a successful annual fund. Institutions that are poorly prepared will find they need to slow their pace or postpone campaigns until they acquire the necessary strength or the situation has changed to the point where the campaign can proceed. Failure to consider these factors and contingencies can place the campaign at risk and may predestine its failure. Thus, undertaking an annual fund begins by establishing a strong plan. It realistically determines where the program stands today as well as where the organization would like to be and how it can get there.

Setting goals is an important part of this process. The goals need to be a stretch but should also be attainable. (Unattainable goals are counterproductive.) Goals should also be quantifiable, so that the nonprofit will know how well it is moving toward achieving them. Most important, the goals need to be communicated to and understood by all of the key players.

Fundraising is a goal-driven process. The goal consists of organizational priorities expressed in terms of both needs and dollars needed. These goals are arrived at through the planning process and are considered part of the nonprofit's overall budget, including projected expenditures and income from all sources. The process almost always includes a time line or deadline. For the annual giving program, the time line is generally one year.

The term most commonly used to describe and frame fundraising programs is *campaign*. A campaign is an organized (there is a structure), intentional (there is a plan), systematic (volunteer enlistment and prospect cultivation and solicitation are top down), strategic (movement and progress are plotted) approach to fundraising stated publicly in priorities to be met and dollars to be raised in a specific period of time. Not all aspects of fundraising are campaign bound, however. Planned giving, research, donor relations and stewardship, gift and account administration, and corporation and foundation relations to a large extent are examples of fundraising activities that are ongoing and guided more by donors' timing and decisions than driven by institutional agendas and time lines. But the annual fund virtually by definition is always properly described as a campaign.

Determining the Case for Support

Writing a case statement for the organization is the first step. A case statement identifies what the organization is and what the campaign is about, in addition to the needs being met through the campaign. Typically, the case statement also points out what the benefit to donors is in participating, even if that is as simple as the satisfaction of being helpful. As the rationale for the development efforts, the statement must be compelling and persuasive, as well as carefully researched.

Following the case statement, organizations typically complete a twelve- to eighteen-month marketing plan that defines and predetermines the message to be provided to prospects and other publics. (See Chapter Ten.)

It is very important when putting together the campaign plan that sustains the marketing and communications plans to be certain that progress toward the goal is reviewed at least quarterly so that course corrections can be made—for example, calling more or different prospects or sending out an additional mailing if necessary. Stanford Law School does this in its operating plan (see Resource 1).

Setting Annual Fund Goals

The following elements can help to determine the appropriate level for annual goals:

- Location of the organization
- Age of the organization
- Caliber of the constituency
- Range of the institution's giving programs
- Size and geographical distribution of the constituency
- Previous fundraising success

- Quality of the program and impact of its services
- State of the economy
- Competing and conflicting campaigns
- Favorable or unfavorable publicity
- Most important, size and quality of the organization's prospect pool

A giving chart or gifts table can be particularly helpful when completing planning of this type. Although this chart is most commonly thought of in terms of its uses during a capital campaign, it is in fact a necessary element of any fundraising effort, large or small, annual or capital. Important to volunteers, donors, and staff alike, the gifts table can and should serve several functions throughout the course of any campaign:

- It indicates the number and size of the various gifts that will be needed to reach the goal.
- It serves as a reality test, especially with the board and the major donors from whom leadership gifts are expected.
- Once firmly established, it defines the goals that must be met in order for the campaign to succeed. (It is also to be hoped that the gifts table will raise the sights of prospective donors.)
- It establishes specific guidelines for volunteers to use in patterns of gift solicitation.
- It is an essential management tool, providing the purest and truest indicator of progress to date in any campaign.
- It is a valuable evaluation tool after the campaign.

The mathematical construction of a gifts chart for the annual fund closely parallels that of a capital campaign. Ten percent of the donors will need to give 60 percent of the goal, the next 20 percent of donors will need to give another 20 percent of the goal, and the remaining 70 percent of donors will give the remaining 20 percent of the goal.

If an organization has a prospect pool of 1,000 names, its rate of participation is 20 percent, and the goal is $100,000, then the organization will receive 200 gifts. Ten percent, or 20 donors, need to give $60,000. That averages to $3,000 a donor, but gifts in a range never all hit the average. The next 40 donors will give $20,000, and the remaining 140 donors will give the remaining $20,000. These are the realistic expectations that guide the development of an annual giving goal.

Setting the annual fund goal encompasses the following considerations:

- The pattern (size and number) of gifts received the previous year and the pattern (size and number) of gifts needed to achieve this year's goal, with a determination as to whether the size of the prospect pool has grown (or declined)

- A determination of how many of last year's donors can be upgraded
- Any additional programmatic initiatives that can be undertaken to strengthen the current effort
- A decision as to whether the additional use of techniques (two mailings instead of one, for instance) might yield better-than-average results
- An acknowledgment of other current institutional fundraising programs, such as a capital campaign, and their relative priority and importance

At times nonprofits arrive at their annual fund goal by projecting income and expenses and, assuming the expenses are greater, set the fundraising goal at the difference between the two numbers. This is foolish, even dangerous, thinking, and never a way to predict accurately what an annual fund can accomplish.

All things being equal and in a stable fundraising environment, annual growth of 6 to 10 percent can reasonably be projected in a favorable economic environment. Growth projections beyond this must be validated in light of the factors already cited. Goals projecting slightly less modest growth of 3 to 5 percent may be entirely reasonable too, given the age and maturity of the annual giving program when considered in combination with other factors.

Jim Smith (personal communication, July 30, 1999) describes the United Way of Central Indiana's goal-setting process this way:

> We call it "potential based" as opposed to "need based." The process begins with a detailed analysis of the previous campaign, looking particularly at average gift and rate of participation in participating companies. (Workplace campaigns account for about 55 percent of this United Way's campaign.) Based on growth in the previous campaign and areas where the potential for growth remains the greatest, a range of percentages—high, medium, low—is presented to the volunteer campaign leadership. During this time, personal calls are being made on the chief executive officer of the top fifty companies to enlist their continuing support and to get their input on how much their own company campaigns might (or might not) grow in the coming year. In June, the campaign volunteer leadership, known as the Campaign Cabinet, determine their recommendation for the goal, with that recommendation being presented to the full board of directors for approval in August.

Jessica White (personal communication, July 28, 1999) has this to say about the Indianapolis Children's Museum:

> The development department constructs a goal based on the projects we will be doing for the next year and what we know of our prospects. We try to make this realistic yet challenging. This is then matched with what the museum's

marketing plan will be for the year. This applies mainly to securing sponsor-ships that need to be marketed. The budget is then submitted to our budget committee, who review it along with earned revenue budgets and expense cate-gories. As you might guess, there are always more expenses than revenue, and so adjustments are made. If programs are dropped, we make sure that develop-ment is in the loop so that the associated revenue is also cut. Sometimes we are asked to increase the goal. If that is done, it is a negotiated process between myself and the budget committee to ensure that the final number is realistic.

Two Types of Gift Tables

Construction of a gift table that will produce the established dollar goal is predi-cated on certain mathematical principles that emphasize the need for a few donors to provide proportionally more of the goal based on their ability to do so. Gift charts constructed using a uniform expectation for all donors will prove to be gen-erally unworkable.

A Workable Gift Table

Tables 1.1 through 1.4 illustrate the size and number of gifts needed to achieve success in annual funds with goals of $100,000 and $1 million, respectively. They show that it matters significantly how proven the potential donor pool is. Prospect pools populated with more current donors, more frequent donors, and larger donors hold more promise than do suspects with less-proven histories; therefore, it takes more names in the database in the latter situation to provide the gifts needed to meet a goal. In testing a goal against these standards, the questions are simple: Does the organization have donors capable and willing to give the amounts needed in the numbers needed at each level? And does it have a large enough prospect pool to support such a goal?

Giving patterns differ somewhat by type of nonprofit organization. Public television stations do not rely heavily on personal solicitations. Their distribution of gifts tends to be very broad based, with few major gifts (other than program underwriting that is often secured by staff). Similarly, many social service agencies receive their operating funds largely through grants and contracts. Some may also have a direct mail program but no experience with personal solicitations. Churches and religious organizations similarly have special needs and strategies such as pledges and envelope programs. And arts organizations have the oppor-tunity to secure sponsorships and underwriting for their performances and exhi-bitions. All of these examples tend to skew a typical distribution pattern. The broad-based appeals cited tend to flatten it; sponsorship-driven programs tend to rely more heavily on a key gift or a few big gifts.

TABLE 1.1. STANDARDS OF GIVING CHART FOR AN ANNUAL CAMPAIGN WITH A GOAL OF $100,000 WITH A LESS-PROVEN PROSPECT POOL.

Gift Range	Donors Needed	Prospects[a] (Ratio)	Total
10% of Donors = 60% of Goal			
$5,000	2	14 (7:1)	$10,000
2,500	6	42 (7:1)	15,000
1,000	18	108 (6:1)	18,000
500	34	170 (5:1)	17,000
20% of Donors = 20% of Goal			
250	48	192 (4:1)	12,000
100	80	240 (3:1)	8,000
70% of Donors = 20% of Goal			
Less than 100	412	1,236 (3:1)	20,000
			$100,000

[a]Total prospect pool: 2,002.

TABLE 1.2. STANDARDS OF GIVING CHART FOR AN ANNUAL CAMPAIGN WITH A GOAL OF $1 MILLION WITH A LESS-PROVEN PROSPECT POOL.

Gift Range	Donors Needed	Prospects[a] (Ratio)	Total
10% of Donors = 60% of Goal			
$50,000	2	14 (7:1)	$100,000
25,000	6	42 (7:1)	150,000
10,000	18	108 (6:1)	180,000
5,000	34	170 (5:1)	170,000
20% of Donors = 20% of Goal			
2,500	48	192 (4:1)	120,000
1,000	80	240 (3:1)	80,000
70% of Donors = 20% of Goal			
Less than 1,000	412	1,236 (3:1)	200,000
			$1,000,000

[a]Total prospect pool: 2,002.

TABLE 1.3. STANDARDS OF GIVING CHART FOR AN ANNUAL CAMPAIGN WITH A GOAL OF $100,000 WITH A PROVEN PROSPECT POOL.

Gift Range	Donors Needed	Prospects[a] (Ratio)	Total
10% of Donors = 60% of Goal			
$5,000	2	8 (4:1)	$10,000
2,500	6	24 (4:1)	15,000
1,000	18	54 (3:1)	18,000
500	34	102 (3:1)	17,000
20% of Donors = 20% of Goal			
250	48	96 (2:1)	12,000
100	80	160 (2:1)	8,000
70% of Donors = 20% of Goal			
Less than $100	412	824 (2:1)	20,000
			$100,000

[a]Total prospect pool: 1,258.

TABLE 1.4. STANDARDS OF GIVING CHART FOR AN ANNUAL CAMPAIGN WITH A GOAL OF $1 MILLION WITH A PROVEN PROSPECT POOL.

Gift Range	Donors Needed	Prospects[a] (Ratio)	Total
10% of Donors = 60% of Goal			
$50,000	2	8 (4:1)	$100,000
25,000	6	24 (4:1)	150,000
10,000	18	54 (3:1)	180,000
5,000	34	203 (3:1)	170,000
20% of Donors = 20% of Goal			
2,500	48	96 (2:1)	120,000
1,000	80	160 (2:1)	80,000
70% of Donors = 20% of Goal			
Less than 1,000	412	824 (2:1)	200,000
			$1,000,000

[a]Total prospect pool: 1,258.

An Unworkable Gift Table

One of the most common fallacies regarding gift ranges and distribution patterns is the notion that an annual fund campaign can succeed if everyone in the constituency gives the same amount. For the purpose of illustration, this theory suggests that a campaign with a prospect universe of 1,000 possible donors can achieve a $1 million goal by having each prospect give $1,000. It never works. Why? This type of approach is not fair or equitable to donors. Wealth is not distributed democratically in society. If all are asked to make gifts that are "generous within their own means," each donor will not be expected to give the same amount; much will be expected of a few, and many more will be expected to do as much as they can. Not only will everyone not give the same amount to any given campaign, many will choose to give nothing at all. In addition, this approach limits the amount asked from those who could give more, and donors seldom give more than they are asked to give.

The Big Picture: Continuous Lifetime Giving

Increasingly development professionals are realizing the full scope of the word *development*. *Development* by definition means not just working with those who are ready to make a gift today, but also cultivating and developing prospects who may make a large future gift. Whereas past emphasis has centered on the three- to five-year cultivation that typically leads to a major gift, current thought broadens and deepens that relationship. *Continuous lifetime giving* is a term that defines this long-term and ongoing relationship between a prospect or donor and the organization. (See Table 1.5.)

An effective continuous lifetime giving program usually begins when a prospect is first involved with an organization. (See Figure 1.1.) For hospitals, this can occur when a patient first receives treatment or when friends and relatives visit in the hospital and are interested in expressing appreciation or simply learning more about the services available. For educational institutions, it means working with current students through student alumni, student government, student activity, or student philanthropic organizations. For other nonprofits, it should mean identifying those who use their services early in the process (for example, through guest books and mailing lists) and ensuring that those prospects are included in information sharing about the organization early and often. Think big when defining this potential audience. You never know who may be interested in supporting the organization's efforts, and long-term relationships, which inevitably garner the best results, all must have a starting point.

TABLE 1.5. CONTINUOUS LIFETIME GIVING PROGRAM: BROAD OUTLINE.

Type of Giving	Age of Prospects										
	20–25	25–30	30–35	35–40	40–45	45–50	50–55	55–60	60–65	65–70	70+
Annual gifts											
less than $1,000	X	X	X	X	X	X	X	X	X	X	X
$1,000–4,999			X	X	X	X	X	X	X	X	X
$5,000–24,999					X	X	X	X	X	X	X
$25,000+							X	X	X	X	X
Special gifts											
Programs, events (e.g., reunions)			X		X			X		X	
Major and planned gifts						X	X	X	X	X	X
Wills and bequests								X	X	X	X
Capital gifts							X	X	X	X	X

FIGURE 1.1. INDIVIDUAL CONTINUOUS LIFETIME GIVING TRACK.

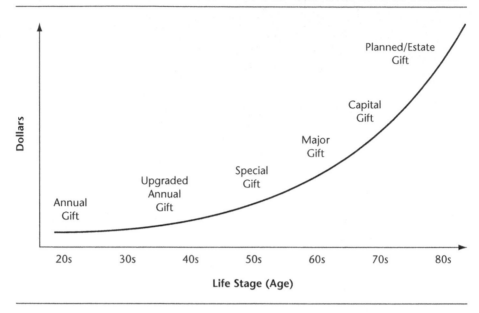

Widening the Base Through Partnerships

One way for small nonprofits to throw the net wider than might otherwise be possible is through partnerships with other nonprofits that share common goals. Perhaps the most obvious example of this approach is that employed by United Way agencies. Here, agencies with similar nonprofit backgrounds and common goals of serving their communities can approach a large, potentially receptive audience together. Donors have the opportunity to be introduced to new services and the option of splitting their gift among many United Way recipient organizations (see the reply card in Exhibit 1.1). The ease of the approach is pleasing to the donor, and the combined effort allows even small organizations to participate. Once a donor checks an organization's name, the first step toward building a long-term relationship has been taken.

Another example of how this can work within one organization is the partnership between a university fundraising program and the alumni association. Both touch the lives of current students in some way, and each has the goal of maintaining contact with students after graduation. While the alumni office typically seeks memberships and the fundraising program is looking for donations, a combined effort can be mutually productive.

EXHIBIT 1.1. UNITED WAY MENU REPLY CARD.

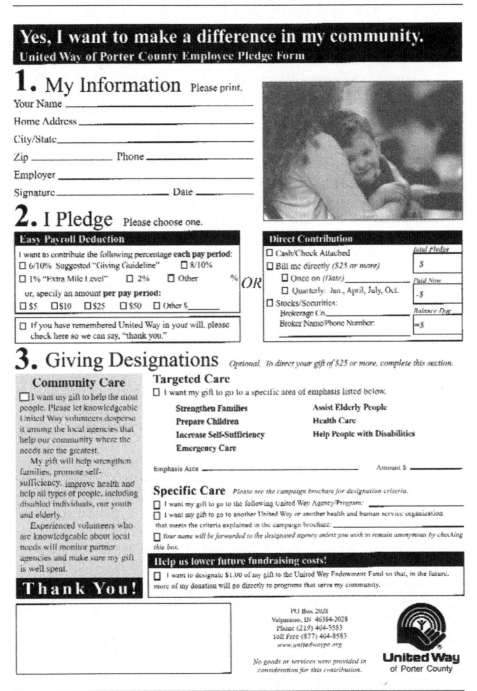

Yes, I want to make a difference in my community.
United Way of Porter County Employee Pledge Form

1. My Information Please print.

Your Name _____

Home Address _____

City/State _____

Zip _____ Phone _____

Employer _____

Signature _____ Date _____

2. I Pledge Please choose one.

Easy Payroll Deduction

I want to contribute the following percentage **each pay period:**

☐ 6/10% Suggested "Giving Guideline" ☐ 8/10%

☐ 1% "Extra Mile Level" ☐ 2% ☐ Other ____%

or, specify an amount **per pay period:**

☐ $5 ☐ $10 ☐ $25 ☐ $50 ☐ Other $_____

☐ If you have remembered United Way in your will, please check here so we can say, "thank you."

OR

Direct Contribution

☐ Cash/Check Attached

☐ Bill me directly *($25 or more)*

   ☐ Once on *(Date)*

   ☐ Quarterly: Jan., April, July, Oct.

☐ Stocks/Securities:

   Brokerage Co. _____

   Broker Name/Phone Number: _____

Total Pledge

$ _____

Paid Now

- $ _____

Balance Due

= $ _____

3. Giving Designations *Optional. To direct your gift of $25 or more, complete this section.*

Community Care

☐ I want my gift to help the most people. Please let knowledgeable United Way volunteers disperse it among the local agencies that help our community where the needs are the greatest.

My gift will help strengthen families, promote self-sufficiency, improve health and help all types of people, including disabled individuals, our youth and elderly.

Experienced volunteers who are knowledgeable about local needs will monitor partner agencies and make sure my gift is well spent.

Thank You!

Targeted Care

☐ I want my gift to go to a specific area of emphasis listed below.

Strengthen Families	**Assist Elderly People**
Prepare Children	**Health Care**
Increase Self-Sufficiency	**Help People with Disabilities**
Emergency Care	

Emphasis Area _____ Amount $ _____

Specific Care *Please see the campaign brochure for designation criteria.*

☐ I want my gift to go to the following United Way Agency/Program: _____

☐ I want my gift to go to another United Way or another health and human service organization that meets the criteria explained in the campaign brochure: _____

☐ *Your name will be forwarded to the designated agency unless you wish to remain anonymous by checking this box.*

Help us lower future fundraising costs!

☐ I want to designate $1.00 of my gift to the United Way Endowment Fund so that, in the future, more of my donation will go directly to programs that serve my community.

PO Box 2028
Valparaiso, IN 46384-2028
Phone (219) 464-3583
Toll Free (877) 464-8583
www.unitedwaype.org

*No goods or services were provided in
consideration for this contribution.*

United Way of Porter County

The Indiana University (IU) Foundation, for instance, works closely with the IU Alumni Association and other IU offices in implementing its Continuous Life-time Involvement Program (CLIP). Representatives from each of these offices coordinate activities that appeal to everyone from current students to fiftieth reunion classes. The group understands that maintaining involvement is key to a prospect's willingness to begin and maintain a long-term relationship with an orga-nization. A specific example of their partnership at work is providing graduates with a lifetime e-mail account. This allows IU to keep accurate records on alumni, thus providing potential for contact after graduation, while providing a valuable service to the alumni. All parties are winners.

A continuous lifetime involvement model can work for any nonprofit. All that is needed is a way to identify new prospects and the wherewithal, discipline, and determination to follow those prospects throughout a long-term relationship with the organization. A fundraising appeal must be sure to target the particular phase the prospect appears to have reached. Remember that most first-time donors entering the cycle will be donors to the annual fund.

A continuous model program needs to be a part of a bigger overall plan. More than anything else, it is a way of thinking not only about the present but also about the future, targeting appeals to programs and giving levels that make the most sense for the potential donors. When a prospect reaches the next life stage, the appeal should change accordingly. By keeping appeals fresh and topi-cal, as well as forming a long-term relationship, organizations are able to keep their very best donors throughout their lives.

Planning an Annual Fund Solicitation Calendar

The most common vehicle to use when putting together an annual fund plan is a solicitation calendar (see Exhibit 1.2 and Resource 2). It shows all efforts to be made, in order and by completion date, the follow-up evaluation that will occur, and by what standard success will be measured. It is essential to have such a plan in place in order to capture information that will be vital to future success.

In connection with solicitation calendars, note that what is planned today will be the basis on which future calendars are built. You should therefore commit seri-ous time to thinking about what is to happen over not just the next twelve months but also the next five or even ten years. This type of time commitment now will ensure that the base laid will be a good foundation rather than a false start that needs to be rebuilt later.

A calendar can be extremely simple or very complex, depending on the orga-nization represented. For some small nonprofits, the entire solicitation cycle may take only one month and consist of one mailing and a special event. At a slightly

EXHIBIT 1.2. SAMPLE DAY SCHOOL ANNUAL FUND CALENDAR.

FAIRFIELD COUNTRY DAY SCHOOL
ANNUAL FUND 2000 CALENDAR

June 1999	Concept meeting with designers to discuss Annual Fund brochure and stationery
July 1999	First-draft text and rough photos to designers
	Choose and order Annual Fund premium
	Choose and order Bronson Society premium
August 1999	Final brochure design to printer
September 1999	Brochure delivery from printer
	Brochure mailed to all constituents
October 1999	New Parent letter mailed
	First Annual Fund Parent Volunteer Committee Meeting (orientation/training)
	First *Solicitor Performance Analysis* sent to volunteer callers at end of month.
November 1999	Bronson Society cocktail party (1998–99 Annual Fund donors—$2,000+)
	Annual Report sent with Annual Fund envelope insert
December 1999	End-of-year Non-Donor letter to Current Parents and New Parents
	End-of-Year LYBUNT letter (all other constituents)
February 2000	SYBUNT letter to donors who have given within the last three years
	NON-DONOR letter to all Current and New Parents
	Follow-up calls by Parent Volunteer Committee
May 2000	Spring Alumni Newsletter with Annual Fund "ad" and response envelope mailed
	Annual Fund mailing sent to all Grandparents (timed to go out three weeks after Grandparents' and Special Friends' Day)
	Thank you dinner for parent volunteers at headmaster's home
June 2000	"Time Is Running Out" mailing to all constituents: Non-Donor Current and New Parents/Grandparents, all LYBUNTs, and 3-yr. SYBUNTs
	Concept meeting with designers for 2000–01 brochure design
July 2000	Close books; reconcile totals with Business Office
	Analyze giving percentages by constituent group
	Copy for 2000–01 brochure to designers

Note: LYBUNT stands for "last year but unfortunately not this year," used to describe a donor renewal prospect. SYBUNT stands for "some year but unfortunately not this year," used to describe a lapsed donor prospect.

more involved level, an organization might send out two mailings, one in the spring and another in the fall, and hold one or two special events to attract new donors (see Exhibit 1.1). For larger nonprofits, a more complex calendar becomes necessary, with three to four annual mailings and personal and corporate solicitations. At its most complicated, a calendar could be a year-round chronicle of activities such as an ongoing mail and telephone program, as well as several special events (see Resource 1).

Quality of Prospects

Two sets of critical variables need to be thoughtfully and thoroughly considered: the prospect pool and the fundraising techniques.

Current Prospect Pool

Typically, annual giving programs concentrate on three specific giving patterns:

- Current donors—those who gave in the current year
- Lapsed donors—those who have given previously but not yet this year
- Nondonors—those who have never made a gift to the organization

Depending on the mode of contact, varying rates of success will be achieved with these different groups of prospects.

Donors who have given recently, have made larger gifts in the past, or have made multiple past gifts are the most responsive groups to solicit. These have indicated with their ongoing support that they understand the organization's mission and are willing to make a contribution in order to support its endeavors. This is one area where it often makes most sense to send a mailing as a first attempt at renewal. With the cost of a mailing significantly less than a call and because these prospects may have fewer questions about the program (since they are already supporting it, and you will have done a good job of keeping them involved through newsletters, honor rolls, and other ways), a mailing can be a highly effective way for donors to continue to make gifts.

Reclaiming donors who gave more than twenty-four months ago or who previously made only one or two small gifts is a different situation. These are individuals who at one time supported the cause, however briefly, but have since made a presumably conscious decision to cease that support. A mailing, a telephone call, or both can do the job of requesting a continuation of their past support going forward.

The most difficult process is convincing current nondonors to make their first gift to the organization. It may take several attempts to persuade prospects that their support is warranted, and increased targeting of each appeal can be an effective method to achieve success. It is important to spend adequate time and effort on donor acquisition, despite the comparatively modest returns. Otherwise, the annual giving cycle is compromised.

Annual Giving Techniques

The second variable has to do with consideration of applicable fundraising techniques. Direct mail is an important component of most annual fund programs. Although it is not as effective as other methods of solicitation, its relatively low cost for community-based nonprofits continues to make it productive. Mail programs to nondonors, in particular, can be an effective way to gain future donors, especially if the organization has a compelling case or a specific event to capitalize on (perhaps it is celebrating its twenty-fifth year of service). Mailings to nondonors may generate only a 1 to 2 percent response rate. All too often, those embarking on a mail program concentrate on the number of prospects mailed to, saying, "If I mail to 100 prospects, and each of them just gives $25, I'll meet my goal of $2,500!" In actuality, only 1 or 2 individuals of those 100 prospects will come through with a gift, and the gross income from the mail effort will be a paltry $50.

Telemarketing continues to be a vital part of any annual fund program. Although not everyone is comfortable giving over the telephone, telemarketing is still very successful, particularly with younger prospects. Telephone calls can be a way of converting nondonors, and this is often the better approach than mail, even though the initial cost is higher. The major reason for the improved success over direct mail is the dialogue that occurs between the prospect and the caller; the caller has an opportunity to tell the person more about the project in question and to answer any objections that the person raises to giving.

As a result, telemarketing is an important tool for any annual fund effort. Proper planning, training, and execution are all necessities for a successful telephone program. With today's proliferation of telemarketers, nonprofits may see slight reductions in the efficiency of telemarketing, but it remains an effective way of acquiring new donors as well as of renewing past donors. It offers an opportunity to gain support, interact with donors, receive feedback, and educate prospective donors. It is also a terrific time to update records and build friendships with those who support the organization's cause.

Special events by definition raise money because of a specific activity. Funds may be raised prior to the event, as well as during the event, but the event itself is the focus of the fundraising activity. Special events are often labor intensive and, when all factors are considered, not particularly efficient or effective ways to raise money if the raising of funds is the organization's primary goal. This is not to say that some events are not highly successful fundraisers. Some are. Indeed, for some organizations, their primary special event each year is a signature event that defines the organization in the public's eye and raises a significant portion of its annual gift income.

Beyond the raising of money are the other major purposes of special events. Often publicity is the main benefit. Events can call attention to an organization at a critical point in its life. Too, events can bring new friends and potential donors to the organization. Most organizations, however, have no built-in ability to attract and continually expand the potential donor pool. If interest and information lead to involvement, the special event is a distinctive setting that provides opportunity for one or both to occur.

Sometimes a personal, face-to-face contact is the most productive method, and the result can be expected to make such a contact worthwhile and cost-effective. Increasingly, annual fund programs are expanding to take on a face-to-face element with specific groups of prospects who seem to warrant such individualized attention.

If, for instance, a new donor is identified through a telemarketing program and he or she is willing to make a significant contribution with very little persuasion, there may be some real merit in having a follow-up thank-you come from a staff member with face-to-face responsibilities or from a volunteer. The logic here is that any prospect who can make such a gift with little hesitation is likely to be a good prospect for larger contributions.

Such a thank-you is the first step in an ongoing relationship that will likely bear fruit in future years, when the ask could come in person rather than by mail or telephone. Likely prospects for this kind of special attention include current donors who make above-average gifts to the organization and young prospects who have the capacity to inherit or, because of their profession, have wealth on their own.

Making Giving Easy

However people give to the annual fund, it remains very important to ensure that making a gift is easy for them. It is vital to give the donor a variety of options to contribute, including installments, credit card gifts, and automatic bank withdrawal options (Exhibit 1.3 is an example of the last approach). A recent trend in giving, particularly as credit card companies have developed advantage cards, is for donors to use their cards to make charitable contributions. As consumers become more comfortable with the idea of sharing their credit card numbers on-line, more and more donors will become at ease with the idea of making gifts on-line. (See Chapter

Four.) All organizations should pay close attention to developing this area in response to donor wishes because this is a trend that will only increase.

Web sites have become increasingly prevalent, with the options to make gifts on-line often included. (See Exhibit 1.4.) The challenge with many of these sites is to accomplish the objective of being technologically advanced, while at the same time continuing to emphasize the sort of personal attention that is key to

EXHIBIT 1.3. ELECTRONIC FUNDS TRANSFER FACT SHEET.

E.F.T. FACT SHEET

Total Pledge Amount	Amount per Month
$2,500	$209
$1,500	$125
$1,000	$84
$500	$42
$250	$21
$120	$10
$100	$9
$60	$5

What is an E.F.T.?

- It means Electronic Funds Transfer, also known as the Penn State Transfer.
- A way for alumni to give to Penn State academics through an automatic deduction from their checking account.

What are some benefits for using the E.F.T. option?

- The E.F.T. allows you to make a larger gift more manageable and shows a record of continuous support.
- It costs less for you AND for Penn State, maximizing the impact of your gift.
- You control your monthly gift. You can increase it, decrease it, or cancel it simply by calling Penn State's Office of Annual Giving (1-888-800-9163) or contacting your local bank.
- If you are involved in making an E.F.T. gift, Penn State recognizes this as your annual support and no longer solicits you by phone or mail for the duration of the E.F.T.

How the E.F.T. process works?

- Alumni commit to a specific monthly amount, which is confirmed by a supervisor.
- Lion Line sends pledge letter and authorization form to prospects, which includes a prepaid reply envelope.
- The alumni then return the authorization form with a voided check.
- Within two months, they will see the deduction on their monthly bank statement as a gift to Penn State.
- At the end of the year, the alumni will receive a receipt thanking them for their total gift amount. This receipt can be used for tax purposes as well as matching gift purposes.

Note: Used with permission from Penn State University.

EXHIBIT 1.4. PENN STATE'S ANNUAL FUND ON-LINE FORM (PARTIAL).

Giving *Online*

Yes, I Want to Make a Gift Now Using My Credit Card!

Making a gift to Penn State electronically is now quick, easy and safe. With our secure server, all of the data on the form, including credit card information, is safely submitted to our gift recording department for processing. You should receive an e-mail confirmation of your gift shortly. If you are making a pledge payment, please enter your pledge number below.

All Fields marked with * are required

Date:	01/29/2001		
SSN:	*	**Grad Year:**	
Last Name:	*	**First Name:** *	
Maiden Name:			
Spouse - Full Name:		**Spouse Grad Year:**	
Address:	*		
Address (line 2):			
City:	*	**State/Province:** *	
Zip Code (or Postal):	*	**Country:**	
Email Address:	*		
Day Phone:	*	**Evening Phone:**	

Please charge my: * [▾] * Account Number: [ ]

Note: Used with permission from Penn State University.

development. It can, however, be done, as evidenced by both Stanford University and the British Columbia Children's Hospital Foundation. (See Resource 3.)

The annual fund plan needs to be well thought out and based on a solid set of what the organization feels will be most successful with its particular prospects. Depending on the audience, try a mailing first, and if there is no response within a designated length of time, follow up with a telephone call—or try the reverse if that seems to be the better approach.

If it is the organization's first year to have an annual fund or if it is simply time to have a baseline year, mailing to or calling all prospects provides an opportunity to have a control group analysis that will determine segments to target in the future.

Timing Issues

It is important to keep some specific facts in mind when preparing a solicitation calendar. For instance, large universities need to coordinate efforts not only within the development office but also with the university's alumni association, specific school efforts, and other departments. Remember that prospects tend to view all material from the organization's many separate offices and divisions as coming from the same source. Thus, all parties should try to coordinate efforts in order to maximize results.

Even smaller organizations find it important to consider timing issues. Most solicitations, particularly mailings, go out toward the end of the calendar year, when the organization runs the risk of being lost in a sea of donor options. The best approach may be to send a mailing that goes out in September or October, still near the end of the year but perhaps being the first giving option that many prospects see. Also, organizations that benefit from public proclamations, such as National Heart Month, do well in timing appeals to arrive when their visibility is at its best. Some experts suggest that certain months of the year are best for fund-raising, but all times of year can be effective, depending on the audience. It is more important to have a good, high-quality solicitation than to restrict efforts to one particular time on the calendar.

A solicitation calendar, which typically covers twelve to eighteen months, sets out the following information (see Exhibit 1.2 and Resource 1):

- Which segments of the population to target
- What approaches to use (for example, telephone, mail, personal solicitation)
- What steps will occur should a prospect not respond to the first appeal
- A clear and concise opportunity to plan in such a way as to avoid duplication or oversolicitation

Multiple Gifts to the Campaign

Mention of the word *oversolicitation* begs the question, "How often should a donor be approached in one year?" Traditional wisdom holds that such appeals should cease immediately upon receipt of an individual's gift for that year. Recent data, however, suggest strongly that such a moratorium on subsequent appeals may not be necessary. The very best of donors, those with the greatest loyalty to the organization, may support a variety of designations within a single year if asked appropriately. Today this is accepted and common practice within annual giving programs.

There are three keys to success with this approach. The first key consists of coordination and good timing. Good, solid coordination is essential. It will appear that you do not know what you are doing if you send a prospect two appeals for two different purposes within a short period of time. After having received and thanked the individual for one gift, it can be acceptable to pursue the same prospect for a gift to another fund, or an additional gift to the same fund, but appropriate timing is essential for success.

The second key is distinctly different appeals. Usually, the second appeal, if it is to be successful, needs to be for something different—something additional that this prospect is likely to be interested in supporting. For example, if the first appeal is to support a battered women's shelter, the subsequent approach might be for money to purchase business clothes for the women at the shelter as they strike out on their own. Or one mailing to support a university's biology department could be followed by another appeal by the marching band of which the prospect was a member while in school. Another option is to invite the donor to a special event that has a contribution associated with attendance. In this way, the donor can make an additional gift and enjoy the event at the same time.

The third key is to be up-front about past gifts. It is a breach of your relationship with the donor not to make it clear that this donor has already given to the organization this year and that this gift would be an additional commitment, although to a different recipient designation. Simply say, "We are so grateful for your past gift to _____. It has made such a difference to our program, and we count you among our most generous donors. It is this group that we are contacting about a special, growing need."

With these keys in mind, multiple gifts from annual donors are easily possible.

How does an organization choose which segment to target? In some smaller organizations, it may be as simple as splitting a direct mail appeal into two groups: never-givers and past donors. Even this simple segmentation is significant and will reap rewards. The never-giver letter might acknowledge that the prospect has not given and could employ slightly less conventional methods to garner first-time support, such as humor or a premium. The letter sent to current donors, however, needs to say thank-you, as well as to indicate why continued support is vital. By making even such a simple segmentation, the recipients of the letters will feel far more as if they have received a letter that is personal in nature—the first step toward intriguing a prospect enough to read the item.

There are varying schools of thought as to which type of solicitation should typically come first in a solicitation year. Many development professionals begin by using the letter. A mailing typically has a far lower response rate than a telephone call or a face-to-face solicitation, but it is also significantly less expensive than these alternatives. As a result, it can be productive to start first with a mailing that will skim those prospects most likely to contribute or renew past gifts. For those who have not responded to the letter after two to three months, a telephone call can be the next logical step. Although telephone calls are more expensive than letters, the response rate of prospects who receive a call is often much higher than that of a mailing, making the extra expense worthwhile. Special events can be worked in to the mix too, particularly with nondonors. When current techniques are not working, introduce a new one.

Yet for other constituencies, such as past donors who have responded positively to telephone asks, it can make sense to make the first attempt by telephone. In cases such as this, long-term habits can be difficult to change, and a letter can be used as an effective follow-up instead. Simply use the letter as a vehicle to approach those whom you were unable to reach by telephone. Indicate your disappointment at having missed them, and tell them of this chance to respond and still be part of this year's fund. Thus, which approach is used and in what order is very much dependent on the audience.

It can also depend on the goal of the contact. A personal approach can be particularly effective when attempting to upgrade current larger donors, for instance. At a certain point, donors who have progressed through the continuous lifetime involvement program and have established a habit of philanthropy are ready for the next step: a face-to-face solicitation. If the organization's annual fund is relatively young, such an effort might occur with long-term donors of relatively small amounts. As the annual fund becomes more established, it should be completing its job of moving donors through the giving pyramid, thus saving the face-to-face approaches for donors who have reached a more significant level.

CHAPTER TWO

SEGMENTING APPEALS

Chapter One introduced the most basic types of segmentation: those based on donor status. There are, however, a significant number of other ways to identify prospects. Given that fundraising programs are essentially as good as the known prospects, finding good prospects requires significant and continuing attention.

The most obvious prospects are those who are clearly connected to the cause. Beyond current donors, this may include any group of individuals with whom the organization has a strong connection—for example, users of its services, current and past employees, community-based corporations or foundations, and individuals who have attended a special event.

Some organizations have no logical prospect pool or only a small pool or one with prospects with limited financial ability. In those cases, list buying is the recommended option. List services can provide names, addresses, and sometimes even telephone numbers for prospects who have already expressed interest in similar organizations, prospects who live in the organization's geographic area, or other segments that seem to be particularly appropriate to the situation.

The most significant misstep related to list buying is purchasing a list from a less-than-reputable dealer. In this case, the list may have some of the following shortcomings:

- Prospects who have specifically requested that they no longer be contacted
- Prospects who are only tangentially related to the organization's mission, thus proving to be of little use
- Out-of-date addresses and telephone numbers
- Names of deceased prospects (the worst-case scenario)

Nevertheless, there are plenty of reputable companies to help define a strong list—a company that will serve your needs well and confirm that the relationship you have entered into is worthwhile. You can find these companies by checking with other nonprofits in your community or in your cause area. Many are also listed in the Yellow Pages or can be found on the Web. In all cases, it is important to check references closely.

Another option is to contact an organization with similar goals as your own. It may be possible to orchestrate a trade—one in which each organization ends up with more prospects by trading names. The key to this approach is being certain that the names on the lists being traded will not take exception to being shared with other nonprofits. This is no small point: a prospect who feels a breach of trust is likely lost for good.

Be certain not to overlook obvious options as well. Potentially viable segments include faculty and staff, grateful patients, parents of current students, current service users, and vendors. A special event can generate many new names too.

The Importance of Timeliness

An important part of any prospecting program is confirming as close as possible to the solicitation itself that the information on prospects is accurate. This should not be a necessary step if you have used a reputable list-buying service, but if you are using your own list, investment in such a process can be very worthwhile. One rather startling statistic alone demonstrates why it is vital to update your lists periodically: 20 to 25 percent of prospect bases move each year.

Typically, telephone and address look-up vendors charge on the basis of each name or address change confirmed. The amount charged per find varies with the depth of the research needed to track an individual's new address. The most logical and least expensive place to start is with the national change-of-address information data provided by the U.S. Postal Service. Other options include very specific searches based on information such as social security numbers or warranty card information.

Generally, lists should be updated at least every two years. If funds are available or the population is particularly mobile, it can be quite worthwhile to complete a telephone or address look-up every year or even every six months. Typically, investment in an exercise such as this easily pays for itself in better reach rates and additional dollars given.

Segmenting and Targeting for Maximum Effectiveness

Given a list of prospects, the next step is to segment the list to best advantage. Having the largest prospect list that is reasonably possible should parlay into significant benefits for the organization, but it is by tailoring appeals to different parts of that audience that an organization can truly maximize results.

There are a number of good ways to segment prospect populations—for example, demographically by age, gender, location, profession, donor type, or something else. Consider age. By segmenting a population into separate decades, specific references can be made to matters of interest to that age group. And the more personal the appeal is, the more likely it is to succeed. Table 2.1 demonstrates one possible segmentation, whereby the organization differentiates on the basis of three factors: age, income level, and marital status. Any or all of these could be effective categories for delineating the prospect pool.

To carry the example of targeting specific age segments a step further, consider a health care nonprofit that wants to raise money for medical research. The solicitation letter for fifty to sixty year olds might specifically reference diseases

TABLE 2.1. SEGMENTING DONORS INTO NINE DEMOGRAPHIC GROUPS.

Group	Age	Income Level	Marital Status
1	under 45	under $75,000	N.A.
2	under 45	over $75,000	N.A.
3	45–65	under $75,000	single
4	45–65	under $75,000	married
5	45–65	over $75,000	single
6	45–65	over $75,000	married
7	over 65	under $75,000	single
8	over 65	under $75,000	married
9	over 65	over $75,000	N.A.

Note: N.A., not applicable.

that were common in the 1940s and 1950s (during the recipients' youth) that have since been cured as a result of medical research, or it might point to diseases that are now prevalent in their age group. With a younger group, twenty to thirty year olds, perhaps the focus might be on cancer cure rates in the 1970s and 1980s compared to today. Segmentation allows an organization to make a specific and personal appeal, which is more likely to garner a positive response than a general appeal. And it lets you ask those who are older for more, based on age, income, and net worth.

Reports on progress can also be done by segments, thus enabling better measurement of the effectiveness of appeals, as well as potential segments for future efforts. The graph in Figure 2.1 makes particularly visible comparisons by clearly delineating comparisons of new, lapsed, and annual renewal donors. Reports can be particularly effective when they compare progress toward goal or to the prior year's results.

Regardless of the segment, nonprofits will likely find an increasing interest on the part of prospects to learn specifics regarding the designation of their gifts. During the solicitation, it needs to be clear how important their gifts are, and good stewardship informs donors how and where their contribution is used. In addition, any solicitation will be most effective if it is bold and confident and expresses enthusiasm about the cause at hand. This method is the most likely to break through the proliferation of calls and letters received and truly stand out from the rest. Those who are unable to provide this information are at a disadvantage.

The Annual Fund During a Capital Campaign

Planning and coordinating a solicitation calendar during a capital campaign can be particularly important. Most capital campaigns run for three to five years, and organizations cannot afford to let the annual fund lapse or focus on campaign gifts exclusively. Indeed, to do so is dangerous, for what will bring the annual fund back to life once the campaign is complete? As a result, extra attention needs to be paid to the idea of coordinating the calendar in such a way that donors can be approached in support of both efforts.

The key to making such an approach effective is to identify clearly for prospects the difference between their ongoing annual fund contribution and any extra gift that they may choose to make on behalf of the campaign. This should be an integral part of all mail and telephone efforts in order to avoid any confusion or resentment on the part of prospects. If this situation is handled well, however, it can be a real opportunity to increase giving from donors who might have otherwise stayed at a smaller plateau. (See Resource 4.)

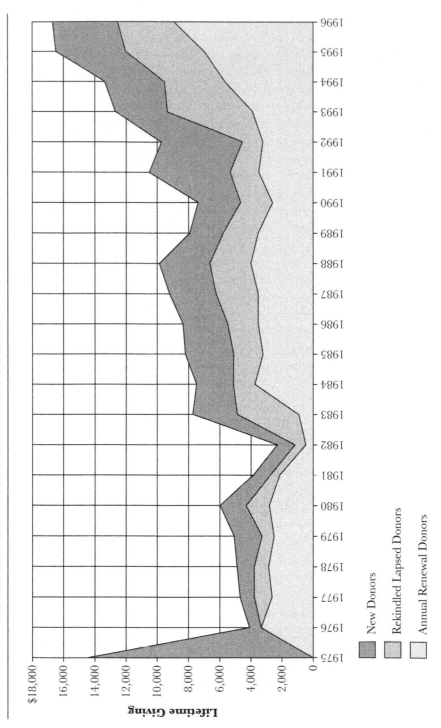

FIGURE 2.1. UNIVERSITY OF BRITISH COLUMBIA DONOR BASE COMPARISON.

Y-axis: Lifetime Giving — $18,000; 16,000; 14,000; 12,000; 10,000; 8,000; 6,000; 4,000; 2,000; 0

X-axis: 1975 1976 1977 1978 1979 1980 1981 1982 1983 1984 1985 1986 1987 1988 1989 1990 1991 1992 1993 1994 1995 1996

New Donors

Rekindled Lapsed Donors

Annual Renewal Donors

Source: Go Direct Marketing, Inc. Research & Analysis, 12/10/97.

Challenge Gifts

Never underestimate the power of a challenge gift: North Americans love the "buy one, get one free" concept, and the ability to leverage a gift is an irresistible temptation for many. (See Exhibit 2.1.) Obviously, a one-to-one match (every dollar that the donor gives is matched by another dollar) is more appealing than a one-to-two challenge (a dollar is given for every two dollars contributed by the donor), but even if the match is diluted by a factor of two, it can still be very helpful. Challenges presenting a less than a one-to-two incentive usually see their influence fall off significantly, and a richer challenge (two-to-one) greatly adds to the match's attractiveness.

Margaret Skidmore (personal communication, May 2000), associate director and director of development for the Museum of Fine Arts, Houston, reports that one donor annually provides a substantial matching gift that is used up to the limit of the grant to increase current donors' giving and encourage new gifts. The challenge is structured to assist the museum both to renew and increase its donor base and to increase annual support levels from current donors.

A donor in support of a local effort on behalf of the American Diabetes Association recently provided a $1,000 challenge grant to coworkers, thereby increasing the company's support threefold from one year to the next.

And Steve Bonchek, executive director of Harmony School Education Center in Bloomington, Indiana (personal communication, April 2000), reports a one-time grant of $100,000 from a New York–based foundation "to strengthen Harmony School's core, its teachers and students." It is a one-to-one match, and all gifts made qualify to meet the match. Shortly after it received this grant, the Lilly Endowment, through the Community Foundation of Bloomington and Monroe County, provided another challenge grant (see Exhibits 2.2 and 2.3). Harmony School met both matches.

In situations like the last two, the intention is to both retain and increase the size of current gifts and to encourage both equally. However, if the nonprofit is particularly interested in increasing its donor pool while still paying attention to its current donors, a two-for-one match for new gifts and a one-for-one match for increases on gifts is a successful way of promoting and emphasizing one aspect of the annual giving program without neglecting others.

Corporate Campaigns

The large majority of nonprofits conduct a corporate campaign as a part of the annual fund. This is another form of segmentation in that it brings together prospects who share a common bond, a common purpose, or common characteristics

EXHIBIT 2.1 UNITED WAY–LILLY ENDOWMENT CHALLENGE GIFT.

Solutions For People
UNITED WAY OF CENTRAL INDIANA

2000
CHALLENGE MATCH
CATEGORIES

Lilly Endowment Inc. has generously agreed to match
dollar-for-dollar all contributions in the following categories
up to the amount listed.

New Key Club Members	$ 600,000
10 Percent or More Increase for Existing Key Club Members**	$ 250,000
New Alexis de Tocqueville Society Members (or increased gift**)	$ 150,000
New Corporate and Employee Campaigns	$ 200,000
Increase of both Corporate Gifts and Employee Campaigns at Pacesetter Companies**	$ 200,000
First-Time Gifts from Individuals (minimum gift – $52)	$ 50,000
New or Increased Corporate or Employee Campaigns in the High Technology Sector**	$ 50,000
TOTAL	$1,500,000

**Only the increased dollars are matched

United Way of Central Indiana
3901 N. Meridian Street
P.O. Box 88409
Indianapolis, IN 46208-0409
(317) 920-1400

Hamilton County Service Center
942 North Tenth Street
Noblesville, IN 46060-0678
(317) 773-1498

United Way Center For Human Services
500 South Polk Street
Greenwood, Indiana 46143
(317) 888-1498

Serving Boone, Hamilton, Hancock, Hendricks, Marion and Morgan counties
e-mail: community@uwci.org   website: www.uwci.org

EXHIBIT 2.2. DONOR SOLICITATION LETTER.

Harmony School Education Center
P.O. Box 1787
Bloomington, IN 47402
(812) 334-8349
Fax (812) 333-3435

April 14, 1999

Dear Friends:

Thank you for supporting us with your contribution several months ago. I now have both good news and "bad" news for you. The good news is that Harmony has been selected as a Community Partner by the Community Foundation of Bloomington and Monroe County. This means that Harmony will receive a $200,000 grant from The Lilly Endowment. The "bad" news is that we need your help again so soon after our last request because the Lilly grant is a CHALLENGE grant, and we must raise $100,000 by May 14th to receive it! Because it is an "all or nothing" challenge we again ask you to consider a contribution. So far we have raised $65,000 of the $100,000 we need.

In addition, The Lilly Endowment will add $25,000 to Harmony's $100,000 to set up a permanent endowment at the Community Foundation. The $200,000 from Lilly will be used on much needed repairs for our 1926 building (most likely first replacing our 1926 boiler). The $125,000 endowment will go toward supporting "the mission and purpose of Harmony School." Your tax-deductible donation will genuinely be a "gift that will keep on giving" because this endowment will forever contribute 5% per year to the school. I hope you can help.

I am including an article about another recent grant Harmony received which will allow us to reflect on our work at Harmony while we continue to help other schools.

Sincerely,

Steve Bonchek,
Director

Source: Harmony School Education Center. Printed with permission.

EXHIBIT 2.3. NONDONOR SOLICITATION LETTER.

Harmony School Education Center
P.O. Box 1787
Bloomington, IN 47402
(812) 334-8349
Fax (812) 333-3435

April 14, 1999

Dear Friends:

I was sorry that when I wrote to you last December, you were unable to make a contribution. However, now I am less disappointed because I need your help raising $100,000 by May 14th. You see, Harmony has been selected as a Community Partner by the Community Foundation of Bloomington and Monroe County. This means that Harmony will receive a $200,000 grant from The Lilly Endowment if we raise $100,000 by May 14th. Because it is an "all or nothing" CHALLENGE grant we again ask you to consider a contribution. So far we have raised $65,000 of the $100,000 we need.

In addition, The Lilly Endowment will add $25,000 to Harmony's $100,000 to set up a permanent endowment at the Community Foundation. The $200,000 from Lilly will be used on much-needed repairs for our 1926 building (most likely first replacing our 1926 boiler). The $125,000 endowment will go toward supporting "the mission and purpose of Harmony School." Your tax-deductible donation will genuinely be a "gift that will keep on giving" because this endowment will forever contribute 5% per year to the school. I hope you can help.

I am including an article about another recent grant Harmony received which will allow us to reflect on our work at Harmony while we continue to help other schools.

Sincerely,

Steve Bonchek,
Director

Source: Harmony School Education Center. Printed with permission.

(such as their workplace). This appeal can be integrated into the overall community solicitation or conducted as a separate campaign within the campaign. (See Resource 5.) Most community-based nonprofits have no staff to devote to such an endeavor and therefore rely heavily, if not exclusively, on volunteers. Even when there is a staff presence, the solicitation calls are still best made by a peer from the community who has likely responded to those being called on when called on by them in the past.

According to William L. Taylor Jr. (personal communication, July 1999), businesses and corporations give "to established reputations and quality; to well designed and convincing cases that present vision, not problems, solutions, not needs; to ideas that advance the community; and to solicitors who are peers and whom they cannot turn down." For nonprofits that fit this model, corporations can be a significant resource. It is easy to understand why local family-owned businesses and small and midsized companies in a community support the community. But what about larger businesses, publicly held ones, and those with multiple facility sites or personnel centers?

Richard K. Dupree, executive director of development at Indiana University's Kelley School of Business, and Tracy A. Connelly, director of corporate and foundation relations at the Kelley School of Business (personal communication, July 1999), say that businesses, corporations, and corporate foundations give to what they know. They know their local communities, local and state institutions, and local nonprofit organizations. They also know their business and its needs.

Businesses and corporations give in a variety of ways and for a variety of reasons. Increasingly, larger corporations have an objective to carry out with their nonprofit organization partners. A corporation that wants to combat illiteracy might donate cash to organize and deliver workshops for children at risk. It might also encourage volunteerism by its employees to serve as role models and mentors to the children and might provide a corporate van to transport children to and from a workshop.

Primary Methods of Giving

Cash, in-kind equipment and services, volunteerism, pro bono services, and facilities usage are just a few of the ways that corporations and foundations accomplish philanthropy.

Outright Gift. Outright gifts are of the most benefit to the organization in that they represent actual income, or cash in hand, as the result of a specific solicitation. Although it is important for annual funds to offer the option of giving in many ways, outright gifts are truly the lifeblood of any annual fund.

Corporate Matching Gifts. In the year 2000, approximately one thousand companies in the United States offered matching gift programs. (See Resource 6.) Originally offered to recognize and reward employees' personal giving through the incentive of the match and the appeal of letting employees direct corporate giving toward their individual interests, these programs have proven very popular. (See Resource 7.) Indeed, because of the tremendous demands on funds available to provide matches, a number of companies are now making changes to their programs—for example:

1. Leveling out the incentives. Three-to-one and two-to-one matches were more prevalent in the past. One-to-one is the norm today.
2. Putting ceilings or lowering existing ceilings on amounts they will match per individual donor.
3. Becoming more selective in the kinds of designations they will let employees place on gifts. Historically, companies let the match follow the employee's gift designation. Now more companies are limiting the scope of what they will match in order to track corporate priorities more closely. Some are not matching certain types of gifts at all (for example, gifts to college athletic programs). And virtually all companies choose not to give to religious organizations or to organizations they deem controversial.

Volunteerism. Corporations are becoming more supportive of volunteerism programs. Although the growth is hard to quantify and varies by industry, some studies suggest that it has more than doubled in the past five years. This approach is an excellent way for nonprofits without a ready-made way of identifying new prospects to bring additional people into their realm of influence.

In-Kind Gifts. In-kind gifts represent about 25 percent of all corporate contributions, according to the Conference Board (Tillman, 1998). Pharmaceutical companies, office equipment manufacturers, and manufacturers of scientific and photographic equipment and computers are among the industry leaders in this form of giving.

Pro Bono Services. The giving of time is a practice often used by professionals and professional groups, such as lawyers, doctors, and accountants. Companies also do this by loaning executives for a specified period of time to assist in an area of need for the organization.

Facilities. In addition, a growing number of companies are opening up meeting rooms and other facilities at no cost for use by nonprofits.

Cause-Related Marketing

Other trends in corporate support of nonprofits straddle the line between philanthropy and advertising (Wasow, 1998). Cause-related marketing is defined as a partnership between a for-profit company and a nonprofit organization that increases the company's sales while raising money and visibility for the cause (Tri-Media, 2000). It is potentially a profitable revenue source for nonprofit organizations and enjoys a place of growing prominence as a result of changes in consumer expectations of the businesses they frequent and businesses now appreciating that they have a role to play in the wider community. It presents an opportunity for businesses to address business and social issues simultaneously. It also gives nonprofits an opportunity to leverage their philanthropic image and raise additional funds without having to create additional infrastructure. This is especially important to small nonprofits that lack sufficient staff support or a substantial volunteer base.

One of the earliest examples of cause-related marketing is American Express's relationship with a San Francisco arts organization in the early 1980s. American Express donated a nickel every time a consumer used its card and donated two dollars for each new American Express member. The program raised over $3 million in three months. Perhaps the most storied cause-related marketing program was another American Express effort: the restoration of Ellis Island in New York Harbor. In both cases, American Express increased its business, raised its profile, created a favorable public image, and substantially benefited the entities with which it paired. Two currently active cause-related marketing programs that are well known and long-running are McDonalds's support of Ronald McDonald Houses and the National Football League's tie-in with the United Way.

Beyond raising money, cause-related marketing can also raise awareness. In the 1990s Hanes and *Glamour* magazine underwrote a program to promote breast health awareness. Cosponsored by the National Cancer Institute, American College of Obstetricians and Gynecologists, and the American Health Foundation, informational inserts about mammograms were printed to be included with 120 million pairs of Hanes pantyhose. This effort increased the education level about breast cancer, and Hanes and *Glamour* were perceived as companies that care about their customers.

A third benefit that can be derived beyond gifts and publicity is in-kind services that may be performed. In Bloomington, Indiana, General Electric employees painted Hanna House, a temporary home for women with unplanned pregnancies; Eli Lilly and Company employees build Habitat for Humanity homes in Indianapolis; and Bloomington's Monroe County Bank participates in a "Day of Caring" sponsored by the local United Way, when employees annually visit a community organization and assist with painting, clean-up, and many fix-up chores. Similar stories proliferate in every part of the country today.

Companies that participate in cause-related marketing realize these benefits:

- It differentiates the company from other businesses.
- It increases customer loyalty.
- It builds business while building the community.
- It increases social responsibility.
- It increases sales.
- It develops new customers.
- It allows targeting of specific consumers.
- It enhances corporate image.
- It develops employee citizenship and improves employee relations.
- It generates positive media coverage.
- It raises funds and increases contributions.

There are advantages for the nonprofit too:

- It widens exposure for the nonprofit's missions or cause.
- It increases the involvement of people in the community, region, or nation.
- It develops new donors, volunteers, and leaders.

Jaci Thiede, director of analytical services at the Indiana University Foundation, identifies three key success factors:

Choose your business partner. Look for natural relationships with companies that have a similar interest to your mission. Does a certain company give time and money to your organization? Does its customer base have a tie to your organization?

Partner with a reputable and professional business. Your organization's image is at stake. Make sure the company you are considering partnering with is stable, and research the efficacy of past cause-related marketing campaigns it has done.

Develop a written contract. Include in the written contract corporate and charity goals, goods and services to be offered, geographic area to be covered, and dates for starting and ending the campaign. Also spell out specifics with a thorough understanding of creative specifications, including uses of logos, names, and images. Address accounting details, including how funds will be accounted for, what portion of sales will be given to charity, who will track revenue and how it will be tracked, who will distribute funds, and when funds will be distributed.

Potential Difficulties

A poorly executed cause-related marketing campaign can damage the reputation of both the company and the nonprofit. A poorly chosen business partner can have lasting negative effects on the nonprofit's image. And there can also be obstacles for a nonprofit. Often there will be a lack of resources—time, funds, and staff—to devote to the effort. There is the fear of failure and the concern over a damaged reputation. Even if the campaign is successful, there can be a fear of depleted energy and resources as a result of making the effort. Ironically, there can be a fear of success as well. Some board members and staff will be concerned about protecting the nonprofit status of the organization, of not venturing into new territories and exploring expanded ways of thinking about philanthropy.

Sponsorships

Sponsorships closely resemble cause-related marketing programs in their purpose but not their nature. Sponsoring organizations tend to be passive partners rather than active ones. They typically underwrite or help to underwrite events, programs, exhibitions, and performances. Mention in a printed program or other literature promoting the event, passive signage displayed during the event, recognition from the dais, preferred seating, host receptions, and similar activities are typical ways in which sponsors are recognized. Arts and cultural organizations increasingly are relying on sponsorships. They are a growing staple in the overall budget and fund-raising plans of these organizations.

The discussion about cause-related marketing—its pluses and minuses and the considerations it causes a nonprofit to address—is relevant to any sponsorship decision.

Charity at Home

Most businesses and corporations prefer to give to organizations located in the same geographical area where they are located or have operating locations, for a number of reasons:

- They know the organization and its leadership. They may have read about it in the newspaper or attended events it sponsored, or corporate executives may serve on the organization's board.
- They feel a sense of obligation to the community in which they are located and do business.

- They want to reinvest in the community to help meet short- and long-term business or community objectives (for example, workforce development, neighborhood improvement, or diversity).
- They can more easily monitor the impact of their giving by visiting the organization and meeting with local organizational leaders.
- They can effect change within a narrower focus rather than spreading philanthropic dollars more thinly across wide areas.
- The goodwill gesture and public relations impact of their philanthropy are vastly increased by employees, customers, suppliers, and community members who know the corporation.

Researching Corporations

In smaller communities and with community-based organizations, there is often neither the need nor the wherewithal to do research on prospects. They are already well known to the peer solicitor. Too, even when there are larger corporations in the community, the local manager usually has latitude without checking with headquarters to make gifts in smaller amounts ($5,000 and less). There are, however, some occasions when research is needed or desired.

According to Kathy K. Wilson (personal communication, 1998), research on corporate prospects needs to address two vital questions:

- How financially healthy is the business?
- How has the corporation supported the institution in the past, and why would it want to give support again?

It is more important to fulfill the corporation's need than to fund the institution. The company's responsibility is to its shareholders, its employees, and its customers, not to the nonprofit community except to the extent that the nonprofit helps it meet its responsibilities.

Other research options include many on-line databases. Fee-based services on the Internet that provide excellent financial information on corporations include Dialog, Lexis/Nexis, and Dun & Bradstreet. CD-ROM and print-based sources include *The Directory of Corporation Affiliations*. Many of these CD-ROM and book resources are available at local libraries.

Concludes Taylor (1998), "In every business, there are key players who make decisions and they are swayed by the same considerations any individual of means is—reputation of the institution, fiscal probity, a convincing case, and, preeminently, who solicits. As competition increases, the peer volunteer committed and well versed becomes ever more the trump card in the deck. We all have good causes, and good institutions; but who believes in us, and is willing to 'turn to' for us makes all the difference. This is old news, but every day proves it out more and more."

Other Segmentation Possibilities

Although the market segments already discussed cover most nonprofits' large general constituencies, there are three additional commonly used options to explore: in-house campaigns, membership campaigns, and gift clubs and donor societies.

In-House Annual Fund Campaigns

Giving begins at home. In many cases, those who work for a nonprofit are those most invested in its success and are excellent prospects for the annual fund. Not only will these donors provide additional revenues for the organization; it is important to show others that those working for a nonprofit believe in its mission and invest in its success. Individual donors, corporations, and foundations will see this as a major impetus to make gifts of their own to the organization. (See Exhibit 2.4.)

Membership Campaigns

Individuals interested in receiving benefits as a result of their gift will be more interested in a membership in an organization. While being careful of Internal Revenue Service (IRS) regulations and other tax implications (see Chapter Eleven), annual fund programs can capitalize on this desire by implementing membership campaigns. (See Resource 8.) Members then may join benefactors in receiving invitations to special events, newsletters, decals, or other benefits. Membership may be the key to enticing the prospective donor to write his or her first check.

Membership drives include a tangible benefit that results in a portion of the gift equal to the benefit being subtracted from the amount of the total gift qualifying for IRS credit. Donors may receive anything from minimal tokens to appropriate recognition and special services (for example, assistance in getting tickets, purchases, and preferred seating, inclusion in special activities, and invitations to join in prestigious events and occasions).

Memberships drives are the backbone of many community-based nonprofits' annual giving efforts. To many nonprofits, these drives represent their core constituency in the same way alumni are the core constituent group for an educational institution or a grateful patient group is a core base for a hospital. Advantages of memberships to the nonprofit beyond generating revenue include

EXHIBIT 2.4. FACULTY-STAFF SOLICITATION.

Faculty and Staff

Dear Colleague,

Throughout its long history, Indiana University has pursued academic excellence. Faculty and staff have united with alumni and friends in this goal, and their efforts have paid off as IU has grown to enjoy worldwide recognition for its outstanding academic programs.

For staff and faculty, the achievements of the University reflect each person's contribution and commitment to a quality educational experience at IU. That is why we agreed to be a part of another important effort—one that is essential to everything we do as a university. As co-chairs of the first-ever Faculty and Staff Annual Fund campaign, we believe that our colleagues have an opportunity to make a different, but equally important, contribution to the University through their private support.

The Faculty and Staff Annual Fund is about raising money to help the University in all of its areas of need. Gifts to the Annual Fund will provide necessary funds to programs and services for many essential extras that are not built into an annual budget. We have all seen firsthand the positive effect of private support in the classroom, the laboratory, in research or administration, and in technical services and office support. Computer resources and upgrades, faculty and student support, scholarships, fellowships, and program operating funds have all been made available through the Annual Fund at one time or another.

Now we invite you to join us with a gift to the college or program of your choice. Through your contribution, you will be joining a tremendous effort of more than 96,000 donors including many generous faculty and staff whose annual gifts are already contributing to a stronger future for Indiana University. Enclosed is a pledge form that can be used to make your gift. When completing the form, please remember that your gift can be applied to any area that you wish to support.

The faculty and staff of Indiana University are a special group of people with a strong tradition of pride and support. Together, we can continue to lead Indiana University toward an even brighter future.

Yours sincerely,

James Capshew
History and Philosophy of Science
College of Arts and Sciences

Rex Stockton
Counseling and Educational Psychology
School of Education

greater visibility and recognition in the community, an expanded prospect base, an involvement vehicle that can effectively occupy many volunteers, and a way to solidify the understanding of its mission where the nonprofit lives and serves.

Gift Clubs and Donor Societies

Beyond memberships, gift clubs and donor societies are corollary techniques used to recognize and upgrade annual donors. Most gift clubs offer progressive recognition and benefits to donors at various dollar levels, for example, $100, $500, and $1,000. (See Chapter Eleven.)

Conclusion

The ultimate aim of all segmentation is to group prospects and donors with their peers and colleagues, those with whom they most closely identify, and those with whom they are most interested in being associated.

CHAPTER THREE

TESTING AND STATISTICAL ANALYSIS

No one fundraising strategy or specific application works every time for everyone. Testing is the method employed to determine what specific approach is the best option for a given organization. There are some who will try to convince you that you can apply a cookie-cutter approach to fundraising. For example, in direct mail, many conflicting theories have been put forth:

- Letters should not be more than one page. *Or* the length of a letter does not matter; far more important is the quality of the letter's content (see Chapters Four and Ten).
- Always use a postscript. *Or* postscripts are distracting and overused.
- Use brightly colored or odd-sized mailings to draw attention to your piece. *Or* bright colors and odd sizes detract from the mailing and lessen its dignity
- Personalize everything, and always use first-class postage. *Or* personalization and sending the mailing first class may not be cost-effective, efficient, or even necessary
- It is important to provide postage on return mail envelopes. *Or* it is unnecessary to provide postage on return mail envelopes
- Always add an insert to make the mailing different (as one person puts it, "I like 'lumpy' mailings"). *Or* do not clutter the mailing with inserts.

The list goes on. But the point is this: in fundraising, be it direct mail, special events, telemarketing, or personal solicitation, one size does not fit all. Each nonprofit has an individual message and a distinctive audience. It is only through testing that any nonprofit will finally know what works for it—and what works today may or may not work tomorrow. The one absolute that can be offered is this: each nonprofit has a distinctive mission, and the message that conveys that mission needs to be clear, concise, convincing, compelling, and compassionate. Giving is often based on emotion. Even those who claim to make philanthropic decisions based on the rationale of the case for support are more likely to give, and to give generously, if they are moved by the message. Testing and analysis can work hand in hand with emotion to help determine which approach best appeals to the prospect pool in question.

With each program comes costs and benefits. A successful annual giving program continuously evaluates its programs and looks for ways to maximize the bottom line for the organization. The key is to make informed decisions. In the rush to generate revenue, however, this step is often overlooked.

Annual giving programs must regularly take stock of where they are in order to get to where they want to be. Tracking results, measuring performance, and conducting test programs help the annual giving program refine and improve year after year. Although an annual giving program by definition is a yearly process, it is also a long-term proposition; sustained growth year after year will benefit the organization more than a single year of great success.

Careful study will reveal the overall strength of the program, identify specific strengths and weaknesses, and offer insight into the areas that can be most improved. Testing each individual direct mail piece, telemarketing campaign, brochure, and other components will help identify what is working and what is not in an effort to maximize returns.

In the following example, assume two identical prospect pools of 10,000. The two mailings are different enough to create a pricing difference of almost 40 cents per piece mailed:

	Mailing 1	*Mailing 2*
Prospects	10,000	10,000
Cost of mailing	$0.96	$1.35
Total expenses	$9,600	$13,500
Number of donors returned	150	200
Average gift	$50	$50
Total $	$7,500	$10,000
Net income	($2,100)	($3,500)

Which of these mailings, if either, is successful? Note that both lost money ($2,100 for Mailing 1 and $3,500 for Mailing 2). Is it is possible that both are successful? Neither? One more than another?

If with this organization, an average of 85 percent of donors renew their support in the second year with an equal or greater gift, these programs are both successful:

Renewal	Mailing 1 (Year 2)	Mailing 2 (Year 2)
Prospects	150	200
Cost of mailing	$0.96	$.1.35
Total expenses	$144	$270
Number of donors returned	127	170
Average gift	$50	$50
Total $	$6,350	$8,500
Net income	$6,206	$8,230

At the end of Year 2, the total net income for Mailing 1 is $4,106 ($6,206–$2,100). The total net income for Mailing 2 is $4,730 ($8,230–$3,500). The mailing that lost more money in the first year was actually more successful than the other in the long term. Although an organization would much rather make money in the first year, taking a long-term approach may be better. As the renewal rate decreases, so does the probability that one or either of the mailings is a success. Additional data, such as the renewal rate for the third year and on, would be needed to complete the analysis. This is just one example of the need to analyze results carefully and value the long-term impact of programs and decisions.

Throughout this book, you will be given an overview of many tools, ideas, and techniques that you can use in annual giving programs of all types. No matter whether you are in higher education, hospitals, social service, or some other nonprofit organization, you can add these tools to your repertoire of ideas. In many cases, however, you will not see a definitive answer as to which tool or which techniques are best. This is because it depends on your audience, your organization, your budget, and your own personal preferences. The key to finding out what works best is to test and analyze data. Through careful testing, you can determine which methods work best for you.

Tracking Code Systems

The first step to testing various projects is setting up a tracking code system. Each campaign should be assigned a unique identification code. If multiple solicitations of a similar nature take place during a given period, the codes may follow a consistent pattern—for instance:

DMDR100	Direct Mail Donor Renewal January 2000
DMDR500	Direct Mail Donor Renewal May 2000
DMDR1100	Direct Mail Donor Renewal November 2000

In this example, DM = direct mail, DR = donor renewal, 1 = January, 5 = May, 11 = November, and 00 = 2000. This coding system allows those conducting an analysis to identify quickly the type of solicitation, the prospect pool, and the month and year of the solicitation. Similar codes can be set up for telemarketing, personal visits, and special events.

Those conducting a campaign must keep accurate records of the code, number of prospects, costs associated with the campaign, and other pertinent information in order to create valid comparisons and analysis. A mailing sent to 2,000 people that yields 101 responses may not be as successful as a mailing sent to 1,500 that yields only 99, so having that information readily available is crucial.

When all gifts or pledge payments are entered, the associated code must be entered. Whether using a custom database for fundraising or a simple database or spreadsheet package, access to reports from these codes becomes important as testing is undertaken.

When conducting any direct mail solicitation, telemarketing program, or other event, the first attempt at putting together an appeal is often undertaken with the help of guesswork, peer input, and a generally unscientific approach. As time progresses, careful testing will yield important data to help refine and improve the success rate of solicitations. For a direct mail solicitation, one might choose to test the length of a letter or the type of postage to determine success. For telemarketing programs, one might test the way the script reads, the type of reminder system in place, the number of asks, and the dollar amounts asked for. For special events, perhaps a dinner dance will produce a greater response than a golf outing. Any solicitation method has an infinite number of permutations.

The first year of any effort provides an important baseline on which to base future testing. When initiating a new direct mail solicitation, for example, it is advisable to design a relatively simple mailing, with perhaps only two or three variations. In the two examples in Exhibit 3.1, both for the same organization, one solicitation uses a very personalized approach and the other is less so. All other variables, such as paper type, letter content, and postage, are the same so as not to skew the test.

EXHIBIT 3.1. TWO LETTERS: PERSONALIZATION VERSUS NONPERSONALIZATION.

SCHOOL OF EDUCATION

June 12, 2000

Dear Friend:

I'm writing you today to ask for your help in supporting the Indiana University School of Education. As an alumnus, you know first-hand the opportunities that a doctorate from our institution affords you. Whether you now work in academia or the private sector, your degree undoubtedly opened doors that otherwise might have stayed shut.

The IU School of Education enjoys a strong reputation among scholars and the general public as a world-class institution. In its 2001 guide to the nation's best education graduate schools, *U.S. News & World Report* ranked the IU School of Education 16th overall, with 7 specialty programs in the top 10: administration/supervision, social/philosophical foundations, elementary teacher education, secondary teacher education, higher education administration, counseling/personnel services, and curriculum/instruction.

That's impressive! I for one believe the School of Education can only go in one direction from here — and that's up. Our school can't improve on its own, however. That's why I'm asking you to contribute to the IU School of Education Annual Fund. There is no limit to the benefits provided to the school through this type of giving. Whether funding technology to deliver classes to life-long learners or helping a graduate student attend a professional meeting, your support will have a positive impact.

The support the school receives through Annual Fund gifts helps assure that our school continues its mission of excellence. I urge you to contribute generously to your alma mater to benefit the many students and programs yet to come.

Sincerely,

Peter Magolda

Peter M. Magolda
Class of '94
Ph.D. Higher Education

P. S. Clearly, the more alumni who give to the Annual Fund, the better. Won't you join your fellow alumni in supporting the IU School of Education?

EXHIBIT 3.1. TWO LETTERS: PERSONALIZATION
VERSUS NONPERSONALIZATION, Cont'd.

SCHOOL OF EDUCATION

June 12, 2000

«FULLNAME»
«ADD1»
«ADD2»
«ADD3»
«CITY», «STATE» «ZIP»
«COUNTRY»

Dear «SALUTATION»:

I'm writing you today to ask for your help in supporting the Indiana University School of Education. As an alumnus, you know first-hand the opportunities that a doctorate from our institution affords you. Whether you now work in academia or the private sector, your degree undoubtedly opened doors that otherwise might have stayed shut.

The IU School of Education enjoys a strong reputation among scholars and the general public as a world-class institution. In its 2001 guide to the nation's best education graduate schools, *U.S. News & World Report* ranked the IU School of Education 16th overall, with 7 specialty programs in the top 10: administration/supervision, social/philosophical foundations, elementary teacher education, secondary teacher education, higher education administration, counseling/personnel services, and curriculum/instruction.

That's impressive! I for one believe the School of Education can only go in one direction from here – and that's up. Our school can't improve on its own, however. That's why I'm asking you to contribute to the IU School of Education Annual Fund. There is no limit to the benefits provided to the school through this type of giving. Whether funding technology to deliver classes to life-long learners or helping a graduate student attend a professional meeting, your support will have a positive impact.

The support the school receives through Annual Fund gifts helps assure that our school continues its mission of excellence. I urge you to contribute generously to your alma mater to benefit the many students and programs yet to come.

Sincerely,

Peter Magolda

Peter M. Magolda
Class of '94
Ph.D. Higher Education

P. S. Clearly, the more alumni who give to the Annual Fund, the better. Won't you join your fellow alumni in supporting the IU School of Education?

Following are the results for the test:

	Test 1 (Personalized)	*Test 2 (Not Personalized)*
Prospects	1,000	1,000
Number returned	50	45
Amount	$5,000	$4,500

In this test, the average gift, $100, was the same for both the personalized and the nonpersonalized mailing, but the personalized version yielded a 5 percent response, while the nonpersonalized version yielded only 4.5 percent. In this example, the personalized letter produced a better return overall, though not by a large statistical margin. If acquiring donors is the paramount mission of this piece, personalization may be the better choice. If personalization is much more expensive, the additional expense may outweigh the increased net income. The organization must balance its goals and determine which choice better meets those goals.

Further testing might be conducted in future mailings with personalization in all mailings, but with a one-page letter competing against a two-page letter. Again, these results can be built on through several mailings as the program continues to grow and mature.

It is important to the testing process that the populations be as similar as possible. A list of 2,000 donor-renewal prospects, for instance, might be sorted alphabetically by first name, with the first 1,000 receiving one solicitation and the rest another. It is highly unlikely that prospects named "Alex" will give more often than those named "Zach." Sorting by ZIP code, however, might be less reliable because ZIP codes are determined by geographic location, and this could have an impact on the mailing statistically and thus the test results.

Understanding Trends

Analysis of annual fund data will not only help refine specific programs but will help find strengths and weaknesses in the overall annual giving program. Careful study of annual fund trends, both short term and long term, will help identify areas that need additional emphasis (see Resource 9). Among the many areas to watch are these:

- Total number of donors annually
- Average gift and pledge size
- Tendency of donors to renew in subsequent years
- Percentage of donors who increase gifts annually
- Source of new donors (telemarketing, direct mail, personal solicitation, events)

An annual fund should be able to maintain growth on an annual basis. This growth may be erratic, with large gains followed by more moderate success, but it should nevertheless maintain growth using a three- or five-year moving average. Often significant growth is followed by a short period of flat or even negative growth, the result of growing pains and a large number of first-time donors who are more difficult to renew than those who give each and every year. A plateau may also be reached as a program matures, and organizations that have seen incredible growth for a period of time may flatten out, regroup, and then make significant steps forward. The annual fund tracked in Figure 3.1 had significant growth in four of five years, with an overall positive trend.

In the example in Table 3.1, the organization has done a terrific job of acquiring new donors, but the new donors simply replace those who are no longer supporting the organization. Resources may need to be dedicated to recoup the current donors, while maintaining a respectable level of acquisition of new donors. This may result in fewer new donors but greater growth overall.

FIGURE 3.1. ANNUAL FUND GROWTH.

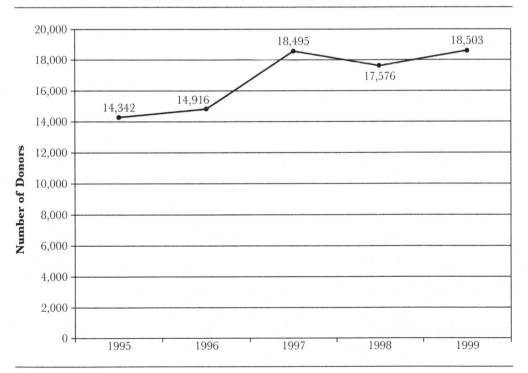

TABLE 3.1. SAMPLE DONOR UPGRADE REPORT.

Year	Renewal Rate of Prior-Year Donors	Amount Given Prior Year	Amount Given Current Year	Amount of Increase	Upgrade Percentage
1996	52.3%	$432,315	$465,664	$33,349	7.7%
1997	52.0%	$425,049	$469,791	$44,742	10.5%
1998	54.0%	$483,300	$516,776	$33,476	6.9%
1999	53.0%	$558,714	$598,134	$39,420	7.1%
2000	53.0%	$567,132	$615,438	$48,306	8.5%

In the example in Table 3.1, donors who renew in subsequent years are increasing their gifts by an average of 8.5 percent. Although only 53 percent of donors are renewing, the overall amount raised is greater than in past years. Addressing the retention issue, while maintaining a strong number of increased gifts, will result in an even more successful program.

Other Forms of Analysis

For individual campaigns, as well as the overall annual fund, it is helpful to network with peers in order to determine industry standards such as typical pledge or response rates from telephone and direct mail efforts, as well as overall productivity for the annual fund. Another effective measurement is to determine the cost per dollar raised: how much money was spent on the effort, including staff costs, compared to the money raised.

Another strategy is to ask donors and prospects to evaluate the solicitation. Donors or prospects may be asked to comment on the overall solicitation, the persuasiveness of the appeal, the case for support, the usability of the response vehicle, or any other areas that may have affected the decision-making process. While numbers provide quantitative advice, hearing from donors can provide a unique analysis of the program. Inevitably you will receive unsolicited advice, through complaint calls and other avenues. Unfortunately, it is human nature to comment only if upset, so it may be prudent to solicit opinions to balance the responses.

Soliciting feedback from donors can be as simple as picking up the telephone to say thank-you and solicit feedback about the organization. At the same time, it may help to contact those who have said no in order to ask them to evaluate the solicitation they received, the telephone call, or the special event.

TABLE 3.2. SAMPLE DONOR RETENTION REPORT.

Year	Number of Donors	Source: Donor Acquisition	Source: Lapsed Donor Retrieval	Source: Donor Renewal	Renewal Rate of Prior Year Donors
1996	14,342	3,435	2,589	8,318	
		24.0%	18.1%	58.0%	52.3%
1997	14,916	4,814	2,645	7,457	
		32.3%	17.7%	50.0%	52.0%
1998	18,495	6,424	4,016	8,055	
		34.7%	21.7%	43.6%	54.0%
1999	17,576	4,656	3,118	9,802	
		26.5%	17.7%	55.8%	53.0%
2000	18,503	5,184	4,004	9,315	
		28/0%	21.6%	50.3%	53.0%

Mailing surveys may also provide useful information. The survey should consist of a series of questions to which the prospect or donor can provide adequate feedback (see Resource 10). This feedback can be helpful in planning for future campaigns. Surveys can be sent to any population: donors, to ask what helped them decide to make a gift; lapsed donors, to ask why they have stopped giving; and nondonors, to ask why they have never given or what the organization can do to garner their support.

Conclusion

Whatever the method, continuous evaluation and reassessment of the annual fund is important. Through this process, the organization can continue to refine its programs.

CHAPTER FOUR

IMPLEMENTING A DIRECT MAIL CAMPAIGN

Direct mail, the most widely used technique in fundraising today, can be both an effective solicitation method and an exceptional educational tool. It allows the sender an opportunity to express the precise needs and accomplishments of the organization while giving prospects an easy way to respond with a gift or pledge. It is also a less expensive option over time than a personal face-to-face visit or telemarketing call. Nevertheless, direct mail start-up costs, especially for large-scale efforts, can be extremely expensive, and it may take as long as two to three years to reach the break-even point. Unfortunately, the passive nature of direct mail (it just sits there, waiting to be read) often results in fewer gifts, and some cases for support do not lend themselves well to interpretation through a written presentation. Still, direct mail continues to enjoy its place as a cornerstone of any annual fund, for the following reasons:

- Direct mail does not require a volunteer network and can be produced by one individual or outsourced to a vendor.
- Direct mail is gift oriented rather than pledge oriented, eliminating the need for pledge reminders, follow-up systems, and billing procedures, which can be taxing on smaller nonprofits.
- Direct mail provides instant cash flow from gifts rather than delays for pledge payments or even possible nonpayment of pledges.

Direct mail may fill other needs for an organization too, such as inviting individuals to participate in special events, attend special gatherings or parties, and fulfill pledges made through telemarketing or face-to-face visits. Although this chapter emphasizes solicitation pieces, the basic components of direct mail carry over into many other facets of the annual giving and development program.

Direct mail solicitation appeals can be an effective method to acquire first-time donors, renew and increase the gifts of past donors, or act as an impetus to retrieve donors who have lapsed for several years. In each case, a different approach is needed, based on the population. Determining appropriate prospect pools, as with any other annual fund program, is an important step in the direct mail process. Once the pool has been selected, a direct mail piece can be designed to approach the prospects being solicited.

Essential Elements of Direct Mail

There are many schools of thought about the most productive direct mail pieces. Some feel color is most important. Others assert that the size of the envelope is key. If you speak with ten direct mail experts, odds are you will hear ten different opinions. The key to success with direct mail is to test various methods until you know which ones work best for your organization and your prospects. What works for others may or may not work best for your organization. Regardless, there are basic elements that must be considered for any direct mail solicitation:

- The solicitation piece
- Outer envelope or other mailing vehicle
- The response device
- The reply envelope
- Enclosures, if any

Once a prospect pool has been selected, determining the purpose and theme as well as a mailing date are the first steps of creating a direct mail piece. Different prospect pools lend themselves to different appeals. Male or female? Young or old? Donors or nondonors? These are the types of questions that should be addressed prior to designing a theme or writing a letter or brochure. In many cases, different groups can receive the same basic information. In others, the appeal may be varied based on demographics. For example, an appeal to those who have not made a gift in the past or are not familiar with the soliciting organization may need to include basic information to educate the prospect. An educational brochure, in addition to a solicitation letter, may be helpful for this group. A renewal appeal may rely less on information and more on results produced through past giving. Experience and testing will help to determine the most successful and cost-effective solicitation method for various prospects.

Determining a time line for the mailing process is significant. Writing, designing, and producing a direct mail piece is more difficult and time-consuming than most people realize. Starting with the date you wish to mail the piece, set a time line that will allow each step to be completed in time to meet that date. For a mailing done in-house on organizational letterhead, this may simply mean the time needed to write a letter, print letterhead and pledge cards, print the letters using a mail merge, and time for stuffing envelopes. More sophisticated mailings may require the additional time needed to work with a designer; produce specialized brochures, envelopes, and materials; work with a printer; edit; approve; proof; and have the outside vendor produce the product. Large mailings can take weeks or even months to prepare.

A reputable direct mail vendor may provide assistance and counsel on all areas of production, from design to mailing. When searching for a direct mail vendor, speak with peers and other development organizations in your area for recommendations.

The Solicitation Piece: The Case for Support

Once a general outline of the piece and a time line are determined, the most important element is created: the case for support. Whether a brochure, letter, or other device, the case for support must be a clear and concise call for action supported by a reason to act. Always remember that you are not your donor, and write accordingly. It is also helpful to remember that a reader may have a mailbox full of bills, solicitations, magazines, and advertisements. The case for support must hook a reader quickly, preferably in the first sentence or paragraph of a letter or in the front panel or page of a brochure. Answer the questions your prospects have:

- Why is your organization important?
- What is your mission?
- What are you doing to make a difference?
- How will their gift help?

The case for support should paint a picture or tell a story about the organization. Specific examples, such as people who have been helped or particular projects that have been funded, should be used throughout the piece. This approach will help keep readers interested in the piece and give the organization a chance to tell a story about how it makes a difference. (See Resource 11.)

If the mailing is to a large prospect pool, it may also help to segment the pool and design different pieces for different audiences. A donor renewal letter, for instance, should include ample thanks for prior support. It should give the reader not only a sense of appreciation but also a sense that his or her gift has made a difference. Share stories or examples that explain how prior giving has affected the organization. It is also an opportune time to ask the donor to increase his or her gift with a specific request for additional funds. The mailing may be tailored in other ways too based on demographics. Testing will help determine the practicality and effectiveness of each approach. (See Exhibits 4.1 and 4.2.)

The case for support should also include a direct call to action, preferably near the beginning of the piece. The reader who gives only brief attention to the piece might not understand, or even get to, the request unless it is made early, clearly, and in a concise manner. Specificity can come later in the appeal. It is important to indicate both how much the organization wants the prospect to give, as well as when he or she should give. A specific request for funds, such as an amount and how it will help, will maximize revenue. A deadline will both urge the prospect to respond quickly and convey a distinct and immediate need. Another option available to the writer is to use a postscript to reiterate the call to action. Readers often turn to the postscript first, so it is a valuable tool.

The Fund Raising School (1995) has identified a few guidelines that typically lend themselves to writing better letters:

- Grab attention; hook your reader in the first sentence. It is often your last chance.
    "At first, I didn't believe what the nurse told me. We found the baby in a shoe box. She weighed less than five pounds."
- State the problem. Tell a story.
    "Marie—that's what the nurses named her—was the first abandoned baby I treated at Memorial . . . but she wasn't the last. I want to tell you about . . ."
- Pose a solution. Tell how your organization's program or cause is attacking the problem.
    "With proper medical attention and love and care, babies like Marie still have a chance."
- Tell how the reader can help (in this case, participate by making a gift).
    "This vital, life saving work at Memorial is only possible because of the gifts we receive from . . ."
- Tell the reader the benefits of becoming involved.
    "By making a gift, you will be paid back one hundred times over with feelings of joy and the knowledge. . ."
    "Your gift to Memorial will ensure that. . ."

EXHIBIT 4.1. SAMPLE SEGMENTATION LETTER: GVHF.

GREATER
VICTORIA
HOSPITALS
FOUNDATION

May 25, 1999

Mr. & Mrs. John Q. Sample
12345-67 Street
Victoria, BC   V0V 0V0

**We need your help to purchase vital new cardiac
equipment for patients in Victoria's hospitals.**

Dear Mr. and Mrs. Sample,

This letter is about a matter of great concern to you and our entire community. I am writing to you because your past support of the Greater Victoria Hospitals Foundation has been very generous.

I am the Chief of Cardiac Services for the Capital Health Region and I am seeking your help in purchasing new equipment for our hospitals. **Your donation can assist us in maintaining the high level of care we have always offered residents of Greater Victoria.**

The support you and other generous individuals have given us in the recent past has made a difference. It has allowed the Royal Jubilee, Victoria General and Gorge Road Hospitals to purchase urgently needed new equipment. These purchases included a perinatal ultrasound and special high-tech incubators for newborn babies. It's wonderful to be able to give tiny babies a better start towards healthier lives.

As a doctor in the Capital Health Region, I want to thank you profoundly for your contribution. It has touched many lives in a positive way.

This year, one of our priorities is in the cardiac services area. Heart and blood vessel disease is the number one health risk in Canada today.

We are proud that **our cardiac program is rated by the American Cardiac Association as one of the top heart programs in North America.** Our medical teams are committed to excellence in patient care. And with leading edge technological advances, we are able to perform over 700 open heart surgeries and 1,100 angioplasties each year.

please see over…

Greater Victoria Hospitals Foundation · Nootka Court Suite H304 - 633 Courtney St. V8W 1B9 · Tel: (250) 414-6688 · Fax: (250) 414-6687

YES Please use my donation to
purchase medical equipment
to ensure the high level of health care all of us in Victoria rely on.

Mr. & Mrs. John Q. Sample
12345-67 Street
Victoria, BC   V0V 0V0

9905C   12345
Please update information if necessary:

_____
_____
_____
_____

Please find enclosed my gift of:

☐$25   ☐$50   ☐$75   ☐$100   ☐$125   ☐Other $ _____

☐ Enclosed is my cheque/money order payable to Greater Victoria Hospitals Foundation
☐ I prefer to use my credit card. Please charge my ☐ VISA , ☐ MasterCard
  Card Number: _____ Expiry date: _____
  Signature: _____

**THANK YOU FOR SUPPORTING
HEALTH CARE IN GREATER VICTORIA.**

☐ I would like some information about planning a gift to Greater Victoria Hospitals Foundation
  through my will.
A tax receipt will be issued for donations. Charitable registration no. 0134395-19-28
Please mail to Greater Victoria Hospitals Foundation, Nootka Court Suite H304 - 633 Courtney St. V8W 1B9

EXHIBIT 4.1. SAMPLE SEGMENTATION LETTER: GVHF, Cont'd.

To continue offering you that high standard of care, we need to purchase new technology and replace aging medical equipment. **Your support will help both men and women with cardiac illness to receive the best diagnosis and treatment available.**

At the top of our list is a new heart and lung machine. During open heart surgery, the heart is not able to circulate blood in the body. A heart and lung machine takes over this vital function to allow our surgical teams to replace and repair damaged or diseased tissue. **This machine costs $130,000.**

Our medical teams also need new patient monitors for our Coronary Care Unit, Intensive Care Unit and Emergency Wards. These monitors will help our medical teams evaluate and stabilize patients with life threatening heart conditions, and alert them when a patient is experiencing acute cardiac distress.

These are only two of the reasons I am writing you today. The fact is, we need your help. Your gift can be sent to us in the enclosed postage-paid envelope. Or you can charge your donation on your credit card simply by calling (250) 414-6688.

If it's more convenient to you, you can even make your gift by installments throughout the year. **And, of course, your gift is entirely tax deductible.**

In the past, your gift has helped thousands of people in Greater Victoria. **Please renew your commitment to our hospitals again now.**

Yours truly,

Dr. Jim Dutton
Chief of Cardiac Services

P.S. **Vital new equipment is needed for our Cardiac patients. We must purchase a new heart and lung machine and patient monitors for our Coronary Care and Intensive Care Units and our Emergency Wards. Your generous donation is a gift that will help many lives.**

INFORMATION FROM YOU WILL HELP US SERVE YOU BETTER

Even if you are unable to give at this time, we value your input. Please fill out this form and return it in the envelope provided.

1. The Greater Victoria Hospitals Foundation will be hosting several information evenings throughout 1999 on new developments in patient care. Would you be interested in attending a session on:

   ☐ cardiac care   ☐ diabetes care   ☐ surgical care   ☐ cancer care

   other _____

2. What would you consider your primary health concern?

   _____

   _____

   _____

Thank you for taking the time to reply!

EXHIBIT 4.2. SAMPLE SEGMENTATION LETTER: PENN STATE.

The Penn State Annual Fund
1 9 9 9 – 2 0 0 0

Penn State Abington

College of
Agricultural Sciences

Penn State Altoona

College of Arts
and Architecture

Penn State Beaver

Penn State Berks

College of Communications

Penn State Delaware County

The Dickinson School of Law

Penn State DuBois

College of Earth and
Mineral Sciences

Eberly College of Science

College of Education

College of Engineering

Penn State Erie,
The Behrend College

Penn State Fayette

Penn State Great Valley

Penn State Harrisburg

Penn State Hazleton

College of Health and
Human Development

School of Information
Sciences and Technology

Penn State Lehigh Valley

College of the Liberal Arts

Penn State McKeesport

College of Medicine

Penn State Mont Alto

Penn State New Kensington

Schreyer Honors College

Penn State Schuylkill

Penn State Shenango

The Smeal College
of Business Administration

Penn State Wilkes-Barre

Penn State
Worthington Scranton

Penn State York

University Libraries

September 7, 1999

> *You asked to be reminded at this time to make
> your annual gift.*

XXXXXXXXXX
XXXXXX
XXXXXXXXX

XXXXXXXX

**An investment that pays ongoing dividends—that's what you get when you
contribute to the Penn State Annual Fund.**

Whether you choose to support your college, a campus, the Libraries, or another
program of your choice, your investment goes to work immediately and has a
lasting impact.

Last year, a record 72,208 alumni contributed more than $47 million to provide
scholarships, equip state-of-the-art laboratories, purchase software and upgrade
technology, create and support internships, add critical books and periodicals to
the Libraries' collections, and provide many more resources that impact the quality
of the student experience.

And, your gifts do double duty. They not only address pressing academic needs,
but they also influence additional gifts. Your philanthropy sets an example for
alumni, friends, parents, corporations, and foundations.

This is especially important now that Penn State has embarked on A Grand
Destiny: The Penn State Campaign. This ambitious fund-raising initiative aims
to raise $1 billion by June 30, 2003 to strengthen the missions of teaching,
research, and service to the nation and the world.

**I'm writing today to thank you for your support last year and to ask you
to consider your 1999-2000 annual gift.** Regardless of the level of your gift,
your participation is important, and we want to make it convenient for you.
Simply choose the way to give that is best for you.

PENNSTATE

17 Old Main   Toll-free: (888) 800-9161
University Park, PA   E-mail: Annual-Fund@psu.edu
16802-1500   Web: www.psu.edu

EXHIBIT 4.2. SAMPLE SEGMENTATION LETTER: PENN STATE, Cont'd.

- You can write a check and return it in the enclosed envelope.
- To pay by credit card, complete the information on the response card and return it.
- Or, you can visit the Annual Fund on the web at www.development.psu.edu and make your gift on-line.

But that's not all. If you would like to break your annual gift into smaller, more manageable payments, you can sign up for the convenience of Electronic Funds Transfer (EFT). Just follow the instructions on the response card, and the amount you choose will be deducted automatically from your checking account each month.

An investment in your University pays off by maintaining the quality of a Penn State degree. Students at Penn State are counting on your annual gift—this and every year.

Please give generously. It not only helps the University that provided you with a great start, but it is also a very special way to say "Thank you, Penn State" and to help students today. I'm counting on you to join the growing throngs who are truly "Penn State Proud" and show it in tangible ways.

For the glory,

Mimi U. Coppersmith Fredman

Mimi U. Coppersmith Fredman
Chair
The Annual Fund

You are an important part of the Grand Destiny campaign, and your annual participation is critical. With your gift this year, you will help move Penn State toward its goal while providing key dollars for academics.

Your response by October 15 will allow your gift to be put to work early in the academic year, and it will save the cost of additional letters and phone calls.

- Ask for a gift today. Be specific about dollars.
  "Your gift of $25 or $40 or as large as you can possibly afford is urgently needed. Please respond today."
- Say thank-you.
- Add a postscript that urges action or has strong emotional appeal. Readers commonly look first at the opening sentence or two and then turn to the end of the letter.
  "Because of gifts from donors like you, today Marie is a happy, healthy eight-year-old. Please give others like her a chance for a normal life by making your gift today."

Many factors influence the budget of the piece. Finding a happy medium will help increase productivity while keeping costs down. A personalized letter will cost more than "Dear Friend," but personalization may produce better results. Then again, it might not. A color brochure, which will cost more than black and white, may produce better results. Then again, it might not. In every case, only experience with your organization and testing will help determine the costs and benefits of various types of mailings.

The Outer Envelope

Once the appropriate case for the support vehicle has been determined, attention must be paid to the outer envelope, the first item a prospective donor will see. This particular letter may well be surrounded by personal correspondence, bills, advertisements, catalogues, and other solicitations. The outer envelope may determine if a prospect will or will not open the piece and read it (see Exhibit 4.3.).

In some cases, the outer envelope will be the same one that the organization uses for regular correspondence—letter-sized (number 10), with a logo or return address. For some direct mail packages, the envelope may be smaller (to attract attention as an invitation might), larger (to attract attention as a sweepstakes entry or package might), or even quirky, such as a cardboard cylinder or address labels.

Addressing may be done with a traditional font using a basic laser printer, a specialized font that looks almost as if it was handwritten, in black or in color, on labels, or printed directly onto the envelope. Budget implications and testing will determine which to choose. Some organizations believe the additional expense of personalized laser printing on an envelope is justified, while others rely on less expensive labels. There are also vendors that hire people with clear handwriting to hand-address each envelope. This approach can be quite expensive, but if testing proves that it greatly improves results, the additional expense might be justified.

Printing a teaser on the envelope may also be effective. It is common to see "OPEN ME!" or "Important Information Enclosed" on the front of the envelope or the back flap. This may (or may not) increase the productivity of a mailing.

EXHIBIT 4.3. DIRECT MAIL ENVELOPE.

Postage may be the most expensive part of any direct mail solicitation. Actual stamps, postage meters, bulk mail, and first-class mail are all options. Some organizations use only stamps to make a mailing look as if it is sent only to the prospect. Others rely on the postage savings from bulk mail to help minimize expenses.

To help maintain your mailing list, the postal service offers several variations of returned-mail service. Each service varies according to the type of postage used and the service requested.

When you are determining the size or type of a mailing device, deciding if and where to place a teaser, and considering the postage and address correction options, be sure to consult with the post office on postal regulations and prices. This important design consideration is often overlooked. Deciding on a paper weight, what to include in a mailing, the size of the package, and the dimensions all affect postage. Regulations and postal rates change often, and it is better to consult with the postmaster prior to spending money to complete a mailing that does not conform to requirements and, hence, may never be mailed.

The Response Device

The response or reply device is an integral part of the direct mail package, and the one you want to see again—accompanied by a check! The reply vehicle must include all the elements needed for your organization to record the gift properly (see Chapter Eleven) yet remain simple enough that the donor does not become too overwhelmed to make a gift (see the samples in Exhibit 4.4).

The reply device may be personalized or a simple form the donor fills out. A personalized device preprints the donor's name, address, identification number, and other information needed to make a gift. Then the prospect simply indicates the amount of the gift and payment mode and returns it in the enclosed reply envelope. The device may also be personalized, with giving options based on the size of prior gifts if the solicitation is to a previous donor. A form alleviates the expenses incurred by printing separate reply devices for each donor and includes blanks for the prospect to indicate his or her name and address information. While this alternative is less expensive, it may be difficult to read handwriting, and for organizations with multiple donors with the same name, it may be difficult to determine who exactly is making the gift.

Preprinted reply devices or blank forms may be separate items or detachable from a letter or brochure. With a personalized letter, a detachable reply device may be less expensive than an additional preprinted form. Again, budgetary constraints and testing will lead the organization to choose the most efficient and effective method.

Donors may be able to make gifts using many different payment methods. If credit cards are accepted, the reply device must indicate clearly the information needed to process the gift. Telephone numbers may be included if a prospect wishes to call in a gift, and if on-line giving is an option, the Web address should be clearly indicated.

EXHIBIT 4.4. RESPONSE DEVICES.

[Front]

PENNSTATE

My Gift to THE ANNUAL FUND
for Academic Excellence 1998-99

☐ College of Education   ACEAF
☐ University Libraries   ILXLI
☐ Where the need is greatest   ☐ Other _____

1998-99 Suggested Gift Amount   ☐ $110   ☐ $125   ☐ $150 $_____ Other

☐ Check enclosed (payable to Penn State)

☐ Electronic Funds Transfer (EFT)—easy, efficient, monthly contribution (see reverse side)

☐ Bill my VISA, MasterCard, Discover or American Express (see reverse side)

☐ My company will match my gift. I have arranged to have my gift matched.

Mr. John Keats
777 Poets' Row
Elysium PA 00000

080-5279-010   AA9BTB

080-5279-010

John Keats
Name
Instructor
Job Title and Occupation
Green University
Company
Shelley Hall
Number, Building, Street
Elysium PA
City, State, Zip Code

Business Phone Number
808-000-7777
Home Phone Number
jkeats@grecianurn.edu
E-mail Address

Please correct your record as necessary.

[Back]

Spouse Information

Spouse's Name

Job Title and Occupation

Company

Number, Building, Street

City, State, Zip Code

Business Phone Number

Home Phone Number

E-mail Address

FOR CREDIT CARD PAYMENT: Visa   MasterCard   Expiration date |__|__/__|__|
Discover   American Express

|__|__|__|__|__|__|__|__|__|__|__|__|__|__|__|__|__| $ _____

X
Signature (Credit Card authorization)

ELECTRONIC FUNDS TRANSFER (EFT): Yes! I want my annual gift to Penn State to be easy and efficient, and to make my annual gift every month. Please deduct $_____ ($10 minimum) each month from my account. I have attached a voided check that provides my account number.

X
Signature (Electronic Funds Transfer authorization)

The authorization to transfer the amount indicated shall remain in effect until I notify the bank or Penn State. A record of the deduction will be made on the regular bank statement. A receipt for the total amount will be sent at the end of each calendar year. In the event of an error, I have the right to reverse the gift with a written notice.

EXHIBIT 4.4. RESPONSE DEVICES, Cont'd.

THE ANNUAL FUND
for Academic Excellence

Dear John,

Thank you for your pledge to the Penn State program listed below. I am grateful that you — and thousands of Penn Staters like you — are helping to make this University better through your support of academic programs.

To fulfill your pledge, please complete the pledge confirmation card below and return it with your check or credit card information. If your employer matches contributions to higher education, you can further help Penn State by arranging to have your gift matched.

Thanks again for your support. I enjoyed talking with you!

Sincerely,

Sam '02 Business Administration

PLEASE DETACH HERE AND RETURN THIS PORTION WITH YOUR PAYMENT.

I have pledged:
$25 Agricultural Sciences (ACAGE)

PAYMENT METHOD:

☐ Check enclosed (payable to Penn State)

☐ Please bill my credit card
  (see reverse)

☐ My company will match my gift.
  I have arranged to have my gift matched.

Pledge Date:	12/4/98
Total Pledge:	$25
AMOUNT DUE:	$25

I HAVE ENCLOSED: $

Mr. John Keats
777 Poets' Row
Elysium PA 00000

92-0019-900/ AT9ARE/P

12/10/98 /

Please update the following information.

Mr. John Keats

Name	Spouse Name
Job Title	Spouse Job Title
Company	Spouse Company
Business Address	Spouse Business Address
City, State, Zip Code	Spouse City, State, Zip Code
Business Phone Number	Spouse Business Phone Number
E-Mail Address	Spouse E-Mail Address

PENNSTATE

92-0019-900

ANF

THE PENNSYLVANIA STATE UNIVERSITY, 17 OLD MAIN, UNIVERSITY PARK PA 16802-1500 (888) 800-9163 E-MAIL: Annual-Fund@psu.edu

Note: Used with permission from Penn State University.

EXHIBIT 4.4. RESPONSE DEVICES, Cont'd.

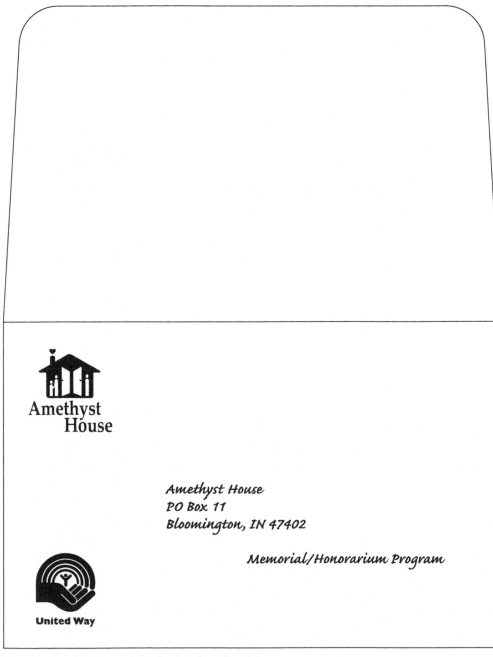

Note: Reprinted with permission by Amethyst House, Inc.

EXHIBIT 4.4. RESPONSE DEVICES, Cont'd.

Amethyst House

     Amethyst House provides transitional housing and supportive services to families recovering from alcoholism and drug addiction. Amethyst House attempts to help addicts and alcoholics rebuild their lives on a sober foundation. In 1998…

- **90 percent of our graduates were employed at time of discharge.**
- **More than 70 percent of our clients received successful discharges.**
- **By helping their parents, we improved the lives of more than 40 children.**

Each Memorial/Honorarium Gift is acknowledged with a letter sent according to your wishes.

Call 000-0000 for more information.

Amethyst House

Foundations for Sober Living

- -

Your Name: _____

Address: _____

Home Phone: _____

City: _____ State: _____ Zip: _____

In Memory/Honor of _____

Send card to:

Name: _____

Address: _____

Home Phone: _____

City: _____ State: _____ Zip: _____

How do you wish letter to be signed?

_____

Enclosed is my gift of $_____ made payable to Amethyst House. Gift amounts are confidential.

We thank you! Your contribution is tax-deductible.

Note: Reprinted with permission by Amethyst House, Inc.

The Reply Envelope

The reply envelope is important because it allows a donor to use the enclosed envelope to return the gift. The reply envelope may be postage paid or require a stamp supplied by the donor. In some cases, the stamp area might say, "Your gift starts here" or other wording to remind donors to include postage and let them know that the savings is passed on to the organization. Again, there are many schools of thought about prepaying for postage on a return envelope, and each organization must determine its requirements based on experience and testing.

Enclosures

Whether or not the organization chooses to include an enclosure in the mailing depends on two primary issues: whether or not there is sufficient budget to accommodate the added cost of printing and postage and whether or not the audience proposed to receive the mailing is already familiar with the organization. If you have the budget and the audience is not familiar with the organization, an enclosure such as a brochure that provides additional detail as to the goals of the nonprofit can be quite helpful.

Direct Marketing and the Internet

The number of individuals with access to the Internet continues to grow exponentially. With more and more organizations capturing e-mail addresses, this medium offers nonprofits an opportunity to produce direct mail without postage costs.

E-mail and on-line giving are a viable option for many prospects. The basic principles for all direct mail remain the same: a strong case for support, a clear message, and a way for the prospect to make a gift easily. The solicitation may include a telephone number to call to make a gift or an address to which payment can be made.

More sophisticated solicitations contain an embedded link that, when clicked, directs the prospect to the appropriate on-line giving form and also populates the form with the prospect's name, address, identification number, and other necessary items to complete the transaction. At that point, the prospect can enter his or her credit card number and complete the transaction. A prospect who does not feel comfortable giving a credit card number can print and mail the form with a check.

On-line giving is developing rapidly. Concerns over security issues such as storage of credit card numbers for billing purposes must be addressed carefully and comprehensively by the nonprofit sector. Currently many organizations are offering "on-line giving" that is nothing more than a form to be filled out on the Web and mailed in with a check or credit card information. This type of giving helps circumvent many security issues. For those interested in electronic processing, the need for a secure server, encrypted e-mail, and other security functions is imperative. In some cases, outside vendors may offer solutions to these issues. In other cases, the organization may wish to invest in a secure server and applicable software and enter into agreements with banks and other companies to facilitate secure on-line giving processes.

Avoiding Errors

Almost all annual giving professionals have experienced the dread of finding a mistake in a direct mail piece after it has been sent. Misspelled words, grammatical errors, and problems with punctuation are just a few examples. Others include larger problems, such as outsourcing a project, only to realize that the vendor forgot to include the reply envelope, or forgetting to include the street address on envelopes and having the entire mailing returned for bad addresses. Mistakes happen, but taking every opportunity to find them in advance is important.

First and foremost, PROOFREAD EVERYTHING! And then do it again. And again. It is also helpful to have a second or third set of eyes read everything. A spell-check program works well, but it is not perfect. Remember that words with multiple spellings and meanings get through too. Sea, it happened in this sentence!

If an outside vendor is used for production, always require a chance to view the completed package before mailing. After a sample few have been produced, take a look and approve everything before mass production. Examine each piece for errors, check the way the items are inserted into the envelope, and confirm that everything is included.

Once a mailing has been sent, it cannot be retrieved. Make sure the best has been done to find errors, because the piece is a direct reflection on the organization itself.

Whatever the mailing or the form it takes, the basic goals of any direct mail solicitation are to persuade the prospect to make a gift and to make it easy for him or her to do so. By writing a persuasive letter or sending a brochure (or both), designing a package that gains the reader's attention and providing a reply device that makes it simple to make a gift, the creator of a direct mail package can help dramatically increase the chances of a solicitation's success. (See Exhibits 4.5 and 4.6.)

EXHIBIT 4.5. SOLICITATION PACKAGE FOR
FAIRFIELD COUNTRY DAY SCHOOL ANNUAL FUND.

1998 -99 FCDS Annual Fund

FAIRFIELD COUNTRY DAY SCHOOL
2970 Bronson Road
Fairfield, Connecticut 06430-2097

A Commitment to Excellence

Note: FCDS uses a nice teaser, "A Commitment to Excellence," to attract attention and urge prospects to open the envelope. This is its theme throughout the annual fund. The envelope is attractive and professional. In this case, the name and address information is personalized and laser-printed directly onto the envelope.

Note: The front of the brochure features an actual student at FCDS. Who can resist this little guy?

EXHIBIT 4.5. SOLICITATION PACKAGE FOR
FAIRFIELD COUNTRY DAY SCHOOL ANNUAL FUND, Cont'd.

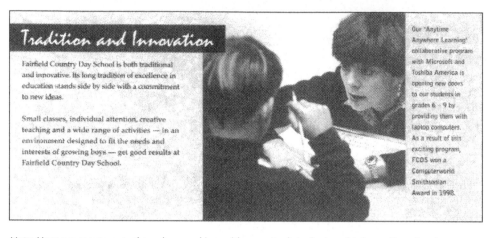

Note: Here we see an actual teacher working with an actual student and information about an innovative program. Indirectly, this leads the donor to realize that his or her gift would help this or similar programs, and the Computerworld Smithsonian Award is mentioned to indicate the success of the program.

Note: Not only are gifts important, but they provide 6 percent of the school's budget. This helps the school maintain its level of excellence, and examples are given that appeal to all.

EXHIBIT 4.5. SOLICITATION PACKAGE FOR
FAIRFIELD COUNTRY DAY SCHOOL ANNUAL FUND, Cont'd.

Note: See how easy it is? The option to designate a gift to a particular interest or area is also given here. If a donor doesn't want to support FCDS in general, there may well be a specific area of interest. Again, the prospect sees a student having fun.

Note: The ongoing theme, excellence, is again reiterated. Donors and prospects want to help a program that is already successful, so this program's success is pointed out repeatedly. Participation is stressed, again giving a reason to make a gift, whatever its size.

EXHIBIT 4.5. SOLICITATION PACKAGE FOR
FAIRFIELD COUNTRY DAY SCHOOL ANNUAL FUND, Cont'd.

Fairfield Country Day School

2970 Bronson Road

Fairfield, Connecticut 06430-2098

Phone: (203) 259-2723

Fax: (203) 259-3249

What Your Gift Can Purchase

$15,000 underwrites the cost of a new mail server for our computer lab

$3,000 purchases foreign language software for our language lab

$1,500 buys a piece of software to be networked on our system

$1,000 pays tuition for a graduate course for a faculty member

$500 buys new uniforms for a sports team

$350 sponsors a teacher's attendance at a math workshop

$250 funds additional bells for our handbell choir

Note: With specific examples matched to giving amounts, donors realize not only why their gifts are important, but also the impact their gifts will make.

PLACE
STAMP
HERE

1998 -99 FCDS Annual Fund

FAIRFIELD COUNTRY DAY SCHOOL
2970 Bronson Road
Fairfield, Connecticut 06430-2098

A Commitment to Excellence

Note: The reply envelope once again captures the "A Commitment to Excellence" theme, allowing it to compliment the overall look of the package and act as a reminder both for this year and the future. FCDS uses envelopes that require the donor to provide a stamp.

EXHIBIT 4.5. SOLICITATION PACKAGE FOR
FAIRFIELD COUNTRY DAY SCHOOL ANNUAL FUND, Cont'd.

1998-99 Annual Fund

Name .... (as you wish it to appear in the Annual Report).
Address .... State .... Zip ....
Telephone: Day ( )................................... Evening ( ).....................................
____ Alumnus, Class of .... ____ Parent of current student ____ Parent of Alumnus ____ Grandparent ____ Friend ....
My gift is $.......................... of which $.............. is enclosed (to be paid in full by June 30, 1999).
____ My check is enclosed (made payable to the Fairfield Country Day School)
____ Charge my: Visa ____ Mastercard ____
Account # .... Expiration date: .... Amount: $............
Signature..
____ My gift will be matched by : .... Form enclosed ....
____ Please send me information about making a gift of securities.
____ Please send me information about including FCDS in my estate plans.

Please see other side for more information

Note: FCDS chooses to use a form for a reply device. It is simple, allowing the donor to record personal information, amount of the gift, and make a gift via check or credit card. In addition, the possibility of a matching gift is explored, as is making a gift via securities (stock) and planned giving.

EXHIBIT 4.5. SOLICITATION PACKAGE FOR
FAIRFIELD COUNTRY DAY SCHOOL ANNUAL FUND, Cont'd.

Alumni Note:

Please use this space to let us know where you are and what you are doing.
We will publish this information in our next alumni newsletter Class Notes.

1998-99 Annual Fund

Last year you gave _____ to the Annual Fund.

Please consider a gift of _____ .

GIFT CLUBS:

Bronson Society: _____ Gold ($5,000 and above)

                        _____ Silver ($2,000 - $4,999)

                        _____ Leadership Gifts ($750 - $1,999)

                        _____ Crusader's Club ($250 - $749)

Please see inside for more information.

Note: For prior-year donors, the back of the device shows not only what the donor gave in the past, but also makes a suggested ask amount based on that level of giving. It also includes ample space for commentary to be placed in the alumni newsletter.

EXHIBIT 4.6. SOLICITATION PACKAGE FOR PENN STATE LIBRARY.

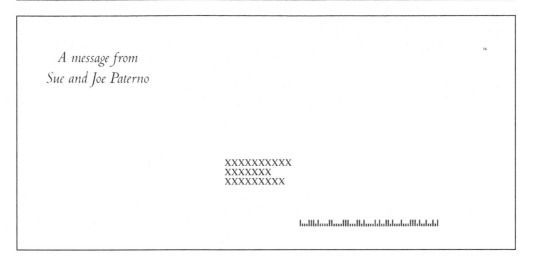

Note: The outer envelope uses the return address of Sue and Joe Paterno. Paterno is the longtime football coach for Penn State University, and almost everyone loves him and would surely open anything he and his wife might send. The envelope is laser-printed with automatic bar coding using a software program. Doing this can qualify you for a reduced postage rate.

EXHIBIT 4.6. SOLICITATION PACKAGE FOR PENN STATE LIBRARY, Cont'd.

May 9, 2000

THE UNIVERSITY LIBRARIES
The Pennsylvania State University
E510 Paterno Library
University Park, PA 16802-1805

XXXXXXXXXX
XXXXXXX
XXXXXXXXX

XXXXXXXXX

We are pleased to announce that after years of generous support from alumni and friends, the construction of the Paterno Library and renovation of Pattee Library are nearly complete. This September, we will celebrate the dedication of the Paterno Library and rejoice in the University Libraries' new and revitalized buildings that house the heart of Penn State scholarship.

The new facilities are beautiful. But they are not enough by themselves!

Inside the buildings are resources vital to Penn State's continuing academic leadership. To remain a leader, Penn State must also continue to improve the Libraries' *collections and services.* That means updating the technology and training staff members in its use, so they can help others. It also means providing the journals, periodicals, books, and reference materials that are indispensable but expensive tools for successful research. For example, more than 140,000 new volumes need to be cataloged, maintained, restored, tracked, and sorted each year. More than 700,000 books circulate each year.

We are proud of the new facility, and we ask for your help to keep pace with the day-to-day needs of a modern university library. Your support in any amount is appreciated. With your gift of $50, $100, $250, or more, a University Libraries bookplate with your name on it will be affixed to one of our volumes. As a thank you in advance, a personal bookplate is attached on the response card for your use.

Return the card with your gift in the enclosed envelope by June 15 so that your gift can be counted in this fiscal year. If you have questions, please call Selden W. Smith, director of development, at (814) 865-2258.

A great university needs a great library. *When you give to the University Libraries, you are supporting educational excellence at Penn State. We are grateful for your support.*

Sincerely,

Sue Paterno   *Joe Paterno*

Note: The letterhead was designed specifically by the Penn State Campaign for the university libraries. The letter is personalized and signed by the Paternos. The first paragraph gives specific and intriguing examples about why the library needs funding. Paragraphs 2 and 3 explain the campaign and how it helps the library. Also included is information about how donors' gift will help and suggestions for giving amounts.

Paragraph 4 explains the enclosed bookplate. In this case, preprinted personalized bookplates were enclosed with each direct mail solicitation with the donors' names on them. If the donor makes a gift by June 15, a similar bookplate with his or her name on it will be placed in a book in the Penn State library—a nice incentive to help motivate the prospect to act soon.

EXHIBIT 4.6. SOLICITATION PACKAGE FOR PENN STATE LIBRARY, Cont'd.

THE UNIVERSITY LIBRARIES
The Pennsylvania State University
E510 Paterno Library
University Park, PA 16802-1805

THE PENN STATE CAMPAIGN

Gift Amount: ❏ $250 ❏ $100 ❏ $50 ❏ other $
Payment: ❏ Check enclosed (payable to Penn State)
❏ Please bill my credit card (see reverse)
Gift Benefit: ❏ Libraries General Fund (ILXLI)
❏ Other (please indicate branch, campus, subject or endowment)

XXXXXXXXXX
XXXXXXX
XXXXXXXXXX

AAJELA
0352294010

A gift for you. Detach here and apply bookplate.

THE UNIVERSITY LIBRARIES

This text belongs to:

XXXXXXXXXXXXX

PENNSTATE

Credit Card Payment: ❏ MasterCard ❏ Visa ❏ Discover ❏ American Express

Account #_____

Amount $ _____ Expiration Date: _____

Signature: _____

Matching: ❏ My company will match my gift. I have enclosed my matching gift form or arranged to have my gift matched.

Bookplate at Penn State: When you send your gift of $50 or more, you may take this opportunity to honor or memorialize someone special. To create a personalized bookplate in a new library volume at Penn State, please print clearly or type:

This gift is in ❏ honor or ❏ memory of _____
Please notify the person below that this gift has been made:
Name: _____
Address: _____

Questions can be directed to Selden Smith, Office of the Dean, University Libraries, The Pennsylvania State University, E510 Paterno Library, University Park, PA 16802-1805; (814) 863-2258.

Note: The response device is preprinted and personalized, including suggested amounts, an option to pay by check or credit card, and the donor's name and address information. The codes at the bottom are the donor's identification number on the Penn State database along with a tracking code to analyze results of this mailing. We also see the bookplate, strategically placed on the response device in an effort to encourage the prospect to detach the bookplate and return the card with a gift.

EXHIBIT 4.6. SOLICITATION PACKAGE FOR PENN STATE LIBRARY, Cont'd.

THE UNIVERSITY LIBRARIES
The Pennsylvania State University
E510 Paterno Library
University Park, PA 16802-1805

Note: The reply envelope is unembellished and requires that the donor provide the stamp.

Note: Used with permission from Penn State University.

CHAPTER FIVE

SPONSORING SPECIAL EVENTS

The most versatile technique available to development programs is the special event. Special events are used to raise money, create awareness, attract new potential donors, and provide recognition and show appreciation. By definition, special events raise money because of a specific activity. Funds may be raised prior to the event, as well as during the event, but the event itself is the focus of the fundraising activity. Often special events are not particularly efficient or effective ways to raise money. The amount of time, energy, and resources needed to plan and execute an event can be costly, and the net income from the event may constitute a very small return. This is not to say, however, that some events are not highly successful fundraisers. Some are. Indeed, for some organizations, their primary special event each year is a signature event that defines the organization in the public's eye and raises a significant portion of its annual gift income. In some cases, it is the largest single funding source during the year.

Budget

Nonprofits using the special event primarily to raise funds need to be especially mindful of the costs. A liberal budget needs to be developed and conservative estimates of income projected to determine if the investment of time, energy, and effort will net an appropriate return. Why should the budget projection be liberal, and the income projection be conservative, particularly for first-time or relatively new events? Inevitably there will be hidden costs and additional costs not projected. Too, most event planners, particularly volunteers, believe in their enthusiasm that others will find the event as persuasive and captivating as they do. This is seldom the case. And even great event ideas sometimes take a year or two to gain notice and attract a crowd. Projecting the break-even point and potential income is easier when there is a track record to serve as a reference point.

Sponsors

Special events are no different from other fundraising techniques in that their success is often determined by their ability to attract key gifts. In the world of special events, the magic word is *sponsorships*. The basic idea here is to secure a name sponsor to underwrite the event fully or substantially, thus ensuring its financial viability. Corporate sponsorships come first to mind, but individuals, families, organizations, and even foundations are possible sources. Recognition for the sponsor is an important element of sponsorships. Almost always, the sponsor wants some benefit, even if its support is done anonymously. How often do you see corporate logos on banners at events or sponsors' names listed in a program? How about complementary seating and special tables at sit-down events?

But sponsorship has a broader application as well. Often runs, walks, dances, and other events have participants gather sponsors to give so much per mile walked or pins scored in bowling. Energetic, enterprising volunteers can generate large sums through sponsorships in this fashion too. The truth is that most special events that are truly successful fundraising occasions enjoy underwriting or sponsorships or have tiered levels of pricing (for example, higher-priced tables strategically located at dinner events).

Be especially cautious about planning events that are dependent on registration fees or sales on the day of the event, particularly if weather can be a factor. Nothing dampens attendance like bad weather. A contingency plan (an alternate site or rain date) should always be a part of the planning for this type of event.

Criteria for Selecting an Event

The Fund Raising School (1995) lists the following criteria in considering and choosing an appropriate special event:

- Who is the audience?
- What is it you want from them?

- Could you reach the audience through a less labor-intensive strategy?
- What type of event will attract the audience you want?
- What prices to or for the event will this market pay?

The Fund Raising School also raises the following questions to consider prior to beginning the actual planning:

- Is the event you have chosen appropriate? For example, a beer bash may attract a new audience, get publicity, and make money, but it is inappropriate for an alcohol recovery program. Dances are neutral in many places but offensive in some communities. A dessert tasting or ice cream social is not appropriate in support of the local diabetes association or a program addressing obesity research.
- Does the event promote your organization's image? You need to find an audience sympathetic to your cause, as well as interested in attending the event.
- Can you afford the front money for this event? You need to have a budget to pay for all the up-front costs before making any money from the event.

The Fund Raising School also advises the establishment of an events committee, a primary leadership committee made up of a small group of five to seven people whose main job is to plan the event and organize other people to do the tasks. If the committee is too large, meetings become events in themselves. The committee should also put together a list of tasks, with deadlines attached. These tasks should include what, when, and who, as well as developing the expense budget.

The list of types of events possible is virtually limitless, bounded only by an organization's ability to consider the appropriate possibilities. Among the most commonly used events are these:

- Lunches, dinners, and galas (see Resource 12)
- Sales and raffles (book, bake, garage) (see Resource 13)
- Auctions (see Resource 12)
- "A-thons" (runathon, walkathon, rockathon, telethon; see Resources 14 and 15)
- Entertainment, fashion, and antique shows (see Resource 16)
- Outings (golf, tennis) (see Resource 17)

Keys to Success

"The key to any great special event is in the details," says nationally known events planner Anne Coulter (1999), "so walking through an event fills in a lot of the detail questions; so does visiting a similar event to see what you like or don't like." Following on Coulter's advice, Harris (1998) details the following planning time line:

Six to Twelve Months in Advance

- Select a theme.
- Select the date, but before confirming it, clear the date with important participants; double-check for conflicts with major institutional, charity, or city functions; and consider whether weather conditions or other demands on people's time (holidays, summer vacation, the start of school) might make that date inconvenient.
- Plan and get approval of a budget.
- Draw up a preliminary guest list.
- Select and reserve a facility.
- Develop a rain plan if the event is to be held outdoors.
- Reserve a block of hotel rooms, if necessary.
- Select and order recognition items (plaques, certificates, awards), and have them engraved immediately.
- Order favors, souvenirs, printed folders, and other giveaway items.
- Reserve special equipment such as vans, buses, tables, chairs, tents, and podiums.
- Audition entertainers.
- Plan audiovisual presentations, and begin taking pictures to build a photo file for use in publications.
- Make preliminary security arrangements.
- Contact the organization's risk manager to discuss insurance coverage.
- Get all necessary administrative approvals.
- Plan promotion and publicity.

Three to Six Months in Advance

- Plan and get approval of printed invitations and all other printed materials.
- Finalize and get approval of the guest list.
- Select the menu, and submit it for approval.
- Print tickets and parking permits.
- Make contact with speakers, and supply suggestions for their remarks.
- Gather biographical information on the speakers, and request a professional photo of each for publicity and programs.
- Keep organization officials, staff, and volunteers informed of all plans, and ask for their support.
- Confirm entertainment bookings.
- Plan the decorations and color scheme. Order props, special napkins, foods, or other unusual needs.
- Finalize the audiovisual presentations.
- Meet with the florist.

- Update security on the plans.
- Begin publicity, if appropriate.
- Send advance announcements to the guest list, if appropriate.

Two Months in Advance

- Address invitations, and set a mailing date.
- Finalize decorations and facility arrangements.
- Make hotel and transportation arrangements for out-of-town speakers. Mail an itinerary to them.
- Secure hosts and hostesses and other staff to assist.
- Double-check the extra help that will be needed, including valets, checkroom attendants, and greeters.
- Make direction and welcome signs.
- Write and print the program and menu cards (if needed).
- Get place cards lettered for everyone on the guest list.
- Check that any ceremonial items needed are clean and in good repair.
- Check that flagpoles and stands are in working condition, and easels for displaying awards and seating charts are available, in working condition, and reserved.
- Inspect the facility, and request repairs to hazards that could cause an accident, such as loose edges on stairs and upturned edges on carpeting.
- Continue publicity on schedule.

Two to Four Weeks in Advance

- Record and acknowledge RSVPs as they are received; send tickets, parking permits, and maps by return mail.
- Ask the grounds department to schedule a crew to mow and trim the grounds of the facility the day before the event. If the event will be held outdoors, request that the area be sprayed with insect killer.
- Take delivery on all printed materials.
- Stuff registration packets (if needed).
- If the event is taking place in another city, ship printed materials and other items to the site. Call the contact person, and ask how to label the shipment so that it will be accepted and not be misplaced on arrival.
- Double-check publicity progress. Revise and update plans if necessary.
- Send detailed final instructions to all speakers with tickets, parking permits, and maps. Supply them with the names of VIPs who will be attending. Remember to include the full name of each VIP's spouse if applicable.
- Notify the caterer if the count seems to be significantly higher or lower than previously discussed.

- Write speeches and introductions, and get them approved.
- Take delivery on favors or mementos. Double-check for the correct amount.
- Get table numbers made.
- Enlarge a diagram of the room to be used as a seating chart.

One Week in Advance

- Ascertain the intentions of anyone who has not sent an RSVP.
- Print out the guest list in alphabetical order.
- Finish place cards.
- Make the seating chart.
- Brief the hosts and hostesses, greeters, and VIP escorts.
- Gather all presentation items, such as gifts, plaques, and trophies. Collect any ceremonial items needed.
- Put everything in a convenient, secure place, and designate one person to be in charge of transporting it all to the event site.
- Plan an arrival briefing for VIPs if necessary.
- Call security, and double-check all arrangements. Provide security with final itineraries and VIP information.
- Send the guest list (with full names, titles, business and professional affiliations, and other specific interests), along with a final schedule of events, to volunteers and staff.
- Deliver prepared introductions, citations, and speeches to those who will read them. Make extra copies just in case.
- Make catering guarantees.
- Have a car filled with gas, cleaned, and placed on standby in case an emergency trip must be made to pick up a VIP or a forgotten item. Be certain the car has the appropriate parking permits for admission to all necessary lots.

On the Big Day

- Arrive early.
- Have all the clothing and accessories with you that you will need for the entire day in case there is not time to go home to change.
- Have all instructions, directions, telephone numbers, keys, extra parking permits, seating charts, and guest lists with you as part of an "emergency kit."
- Check all facilities and grounds. Pick up litter and spray for bugs if necessary.
- Assign one worker to be your assistant to stick close to you to run errands, send messages, and be on call for whatever need may arise.
- Relax and smile. Never tell war stories to your guests or intimate that things might be less than perfect. Chances are that no one but you will notice minor mistakes.

April Harris (1998) has developed a series of checklists that address room setup, equipment, audiovisuals, catering, the bar, the florist and decor, the program, and program participants and VIPs (see Resource 18). Any organization can use these simple but comprehensive forms as a basis for developing its own checklists.

Does it take six to twelve months or more to plan all fundraising special events? Not always. Some are done within six to eight weeks, in rare instances even less. The key to the planning time line is to provide enough time to plan and execute the event properly.

Following are some guidelines for determining the length of time needed to prepare for and properly conduct a fundraising event:

Large events (galas), first-time events, and one-time events require the most time.

Whether the event is done by volunteers alone, by staff alone, or by a combination of both is an important consideration. Volunteer-driven events need more lead time. Volunteers lead busy lives with a multitude of things to do every day. Staff lead busy lives, too, but it is easier to expect them to concentrate the time, energy, and effort at the times it is required. It is, after all, their job. The combination of staff working with volunteers works best. This approach provides more hands with the virtue of having staff to fall back on if something slips between the cracks.

Whether this is the first time or the umpteenth time for the event is another important consideration. Experience is a great teacher. It eliminates oversights and illuminates short-cuts.

Coulter notes that follow-up after the event is also vital:

Review the event. What are you most pleased with? What could you have done better? What do you never want to do again?

Get comments from volunteers and committee members. They will have noticed details you did not.

Remember to thank attendees and volunteers. Send gift receipts when appropriate.

A memorable event takes at least a year to plan well. You should constantly be looking ahead. If you start late, you will end up paying for things you might have received as donations or simply not have a good event. Your guests will remember shortcomings for a long time.

It is important not to overuse the technique for fundraising purposes. For most small to midsized organizations, and especially for those that do not have paid staff to coordinate events and rely on volunteers to assume the responsibility, one major event in a year is probably enough. Only in rare cases should such organizations do more than two to four major events in a year. Events are labor intensive, require the ability to draw a crowd, and usually do not produce large financial returns. Organizations conducting six to twelve or more fundraising events a year as primary fundraisers are too event dependent.

Use special events strategically, and not only as fundraisers but also in support of the overall development effort. Whether the primary purpose is fundraising, friend raising, or expressing appreciation, plan to make every event individual, personal, and distinctive.

CHAPTER SIX

TELEMARKETING YOUR CAUSE

Responsible telemarketing programs, conducted as part of a nonprofit organization's annual giving program, remain a reliable, stable source of gift revenue. Telemarketing programs in a variety of forms designed to benefit both for-profits and nonprofits reached an apparent saturation point in the mid-1990s with individuals receiving calls during the dinner hour or early in the morning and sometimes multiple calls throughout the day. This caused a backlash among consumers and a proliferation of legislation addressing the perceived abuses associated with telemarketing. Nonprofits, although less a target of public complaint, were nonetheless affected by this legislation in a number of states that created standards to tighten loose practices. Another outcome of this public reaction was the various screening devices now available to telephone subscribers; these devices can make completing calls to and reaching the prospect challenging. Nevertheless, well-designed telemarketing efforts continue to produce growing levels of funding for nonprofits.

Telemarketing continues to be a vital part of many annual fund programs. Although it is perhaps not as successful as it was before the proliferation of other telemarketing programs, it offers some advantages that direct mail and personal visits cannot.

It may be impossible for many organizations to visit every prospect regularly due to time, personnel, and budget constraints. Telemarketing offers many of the opportunities of a face-to-face visit without the additional time and travel required.

In addition, although it is more expensive than direct mail, it is less passive because the telemarketer can respond to questions, explain the program more fully than a letter can, and make a direct and passionate request for funds. But like any other program, telemarketing has costs that need to be considered when determining a particular project's success.

Telemarketing is more expensive than direct mail because it requires not only what is sometimes a long-distance telephone call but also the equipment needed to make such calls (a bank of telephones large enough for volunteers or a paid staff), managerial and clerical staffing, pledge forms, postage for pledge forms and follow-up reminders, and more. As a result, telemarketing efforts can cost much more than a standard direct mail piece. In return, however, it often yields much greater results than direct mail. Careful cost-benefit analysis must be done to determine the feasibility of a telemarketing effort.

As with any other element of an annual fund program, telemarketing must be conducted in concert with direct mail, personal solicitation, special events, and other methods. Careful attention must be made so as not to overlap other solicitations, which can negatively affect the overall success of the annual fund. For instance, any solicitation mailings should be sent well in advance of a telemarketing effort to the same prospects to allow ample time for prospects to make a gift as a result of the mailing and be excluded from telemarketing.

Planning a Telemarketing Program

Proper planning is essential for any telephone program, because many decisions must be made in advance of calling. In addition to coordination with other solicitations, it is important to decide whether to conduct the campaign using volunteers or paid callers or to hire an outside vendor. Also, script preparation and information packets, pre–call notification mailings, follow-up mailings for pledge fulfillment, and goal setting must be done in advance.

Planning also includes determining if this particular annual fund project or prospect pool is appropriate for telemarketing. Programs that cannot be easily explained over the telephone lend themselves more to personal solicitation or direct mail. Prospect lists with few accurate telephone numbers or otherwise questionable data need to be closely examined prior to conducting a telemarketing campaign.

Many organizations choose to conduct in-house phonathons using either hired or volunteer callers, while others choose to hire outside vendors to conduct the calling campaign. Both methods can reward an annual fund program, but in each specific case one of the two methods will be more rewarding to the nonprofit, so this is an important choice that will affect the entire campaign.

In-house phonathons offer more direct control over day-to-day operations but can be very time-consuming. Recruitment of callers, training, on-site supervision, and reminder mailings can consume large blocks of time for one or more members of the staff. In-house telephone programs should be conducted only by those willing to invest the time and effort needed to ensure a quality experience for all.

Hiring an outside vendor is often an appropriate decision. For organizations with few employees or the inability to dedicate human resources to a telephone program for any other reason, there are many excellent telemarketing vendors from which to choose. There are, however, several less reputable vendors as well. Choosing a vendor is as important a decision as choosing to use a vendor and should be done with care. Consult with peer nonprofits that outsource their telemarketing programs. Ask about pricing, success, reliability, and quality control measures. Choose a vendor you are comfortable with, because telemarketing may well be the only human link that prospects have to your organization. If an outside vendor is chosen to conduct the calling campaign, it will hire callers, train them, and generally walk the nonprofit through the process. It may also coordinate all back-end activities, such as recording the pledges, sending thank-you mailings, and coordinating fulfillment measures such as reminders and follow-up telephone calls. Pricing will be determined based on all of these separate options. Some telemarketing vendors charge hourly or on a per-call basis. Others take a percentage of the dollars raised.

Conducting your own campaign is both a challenging and rewarding experience. For organizations that conduct lengthy calling programs over a period of months or year round, having a dedicated telephone center is invaluable. Although it is expensive, it avoids the problems of coordination with other organizational operations and allows callers and staff a sense of having a home. A telephone room should provide adequate light and space and be equipped with desks, telephones, chairs, and an area to do the clerical functions required of a telephone program. Organizations that do not need a full-scale telemarketing program or room sometimes use the offices of local businesses—in the evenings and for short periods of time.

Choosing Callers

Smaller campaigns or organizations that have an ample supply of volunteers may be able to conduct a calling program without hiring telemarketers. Individuals who have shown an interest in the organization are often best suited to speak with prospects, sharing personal stories about the reason they support the cause, and they can be valuable representatives of an organization. They can speak from the heart and may require less training about the goals and mission of the organization than an outside vendor. It is also a terrific way to involve those who wish to help. These same volunteers can also be difficult to recruit, hard to train, and may not always feel comfortable asking for money. There may be nothing worse than enlisting a volunteer into an activity that makes him or her uncomfortable.

If volunteers are not an option, many individuals are interested in working full- or part-time making calls on behalf of organizations. In many markets, telemarketers command salaries well above minimum wage because of competition with other telemarketing programs and the difficult job before them. Telemarketing is neither easy nor particularly satisfying for many people. Those who do it well are worth the money because they produce results that are well above average.

Hiring callers allows more control over the script of how to conduct the call, as callers can be told exactly what to say and how to say it. Supervising a paid caller is easier than one who is a favored donor who volunteers for the telephone program. If the choice is to hire callers, it is wise to check local newspaper and other advertisements to see what hourly wages the market offers and then draw up an advertisement (see Exhibit 6.1) . In addition, many telemarketers expect bonuses and other incentives for a job well done.

The ideal telemarketing representative for any organization is enthusiastic and articulate, and understands the mission and goals of the organization. Keep in mind that each of your prospects is being bombarded by telemarketing calls every day. Callers who represent your organization must be good enough to make your call stand out among the others.

During interviews and other conversations with prospective telemarketers, it is important to be very clear about the expectations of your organization. Help them realize that the credibility of the organization is on the line with every prospect they contact. They must be honest, polite, and responsive to even the rudest of prospects. At least one part of the selection process for prospective telemarketers should be an interview by telephone. Ideally, the candidate can be asked to read a script to the interviewer and answer several questions that require quick thinking. This exercise gives the candidate a sense of what the position entails and the interviewer some insight into how the candidate will come across to prospects. The best candidates will read a script yet not sound as if they are reading. They will be easily understandable and enthusiastic during the interview.

For volunteer applicants who are not suited for calling, there are plenty of other responsibilities that require staffing. Stuffing envelopes, answering questions, and providing other support duties to the calling program are all important and may be perfect for those who are not comfortable making telephone calls. The same may be true of hired callers who are not working out on the telephones but whom you do not want to fire; they typically serve as excellent clerical support for the telephone program. In any case, it is important to have only the best possible callers speaking with donors and prospects.

EXHIBIT 6.1. SAMPLE RECRUITMENT ADS.

Training Callers

Both volunteers and paid callers should receive ample training. Training is an investment of time and resources that will provide great benefits. Not only will a well-trained caller make better calls and, in turn, produce better results; a well-trained caller will feel more comfortable in his or her role and be less likely to shy away from asking for a gift and even quitting prematurely.

Facts and information about the organization are important tools for telemarketers. This knowledge can be powerful as the caller persuades prospects to make a gift. Basic information, such as the organization's mission, goals, and successes, is obvious, but the caller should also have ready access to the information that might be needed if more detailed questions are asked. While a telemarketer might not be required to memorize reams of information, it should be available for reference. Exhibit 6.2 shows a fact sheet that sums up the important information for telemarketers who are raising funds for the Kelley School of Business at Indiana University. Any recent news stories or controversial issues that might be discussed should also be brought to the telemarketer's attention. They need to be prepared for the tough questions rather than sound uninformed. Yet even the most prepared callers will be asked some questions that they either cannot handle or to which they do not know the answer. In this case, either have a supervisor present to answer these questions or institute a procedure to have the proper person call the prospect back within a day or two with the answer. It is important to follow up on these requests for information because many individuals who ask the tough questions have enough of an interest in the organization to make a gift as well.

EXHIBIT 6.2. FACT SHEET FOR TELEMARKETERS, KELLEY SCHOOL OF BUSINESS, INDIANA UNIVERSITY.

HISTORY

The Kelley School of Business established its reputation early. Even as the country began to emerge from the Great Depression, business leaders looked to the young school with confidence. Chancellor Herman B. Wells recalled in his book *Being Lucky* that the business community of the 1930s developed a growing appreciation of specialized business training. Indiana University, along with other pioneers such as Wharton and the University of Illinois, offered exactly that.

The school's influence boomed following World War II. Hundreds of GIs returned to campus eager to enter the world of commerce. In 1947, IU added the Graduate School of Business. The school soon became known as a center for business research, a proving ground for technologies, and an innovator of global applications of business theory. In 1997, the school was renamed the Kelley School of Business in honor of Mr. W. E. "Ed" Kelley (B.S., Business, '39), founder and managing general partner of Kelley & Partners, Ltd., and chairman of Consolidated Products, Inc. He and his family contributed gifts and commitments in excess of $23 million to the School of Business and Indiana University.

Today, the Kelley School of Business is consistently ranked among the nation's top echelon of undergraduate and graduate business programs in the country. More than 650 corporations visit the school each year to provide internships and employment opportunities for current and graduating students. Nearly 72,000 graduates of the Kelley School of Business can be found in almost every business industry and sector throughout the world.

GENERAL INFORMATION

Dean:	Dr. Dan R. Dalton, Professor of Management and Dean of the Kelley School of Business
Alumni:	72,000 living alumni
Enrollment:	Undergrad: 3,335 M.B.A.: 580
Faculty:	114 full-time, 39 part-time

EXHIBIT 6.2. FACT SHEET FOR TELEMARKETERS, KELLEY SCHOOL OF BUSINESS, INDIANA UNIVERSITY, Cont'd.

DEAN'S ASSOCIATES

Annual Giving levels at the Kelley School of Business fall into several categories of the "Dean's Associates." This program enjoys terrific name recognition.

$10,000+	Kelley Partner
$5,000–$9,999	Kelley Associate
$2,500–$4,999	Distinguished Associate
$1,000–$2,499	Executive Associate
$500–$999	Senior Associate
$250–$499	Managing Associate
$100–$249	Business Associate

UNDERGRADUATE CONCENTRATIONS

The following business concentrations are part of the Kelley School curriculum:

Accounting
Business Economics and Public Policy
Business Process Management
Computer Information Systems
Entrepreneurship
Finance
Finance—Real Estate
International Studies
Legal Studies
Management
Management for Not-for-Profit Organizations
Marketing
Marketing—Distribution Management
Operations and Decision Technologies

M.B.A. PROGRAM

The following major fields are offered in the Kelley School M.B.A. program:

Entrepreneurship
Finance
Human resources management
Information systems
International business
Management
Marketing
Operations leaders program
Production and operations management
Individually designed major

EXHIBIT 6.2. FACT SHEET FOR TELEMARKETERS, KELLEY SCHOOL OF BUSINESS, INDIANA UNIVERSITY, Cont'd.

ANNUAL FUND SUPPORT

- In addition to alleviating some of the financial burden of higher education, scholarships help attract the best and the brightest. The school awarded $290,330 in support to worthy business students last year.
- Student clubs and organizations were the beneficiaries of annual gifts last year. This assistance encourages planning and scheduling of professional activities, as well as an increased level of involvement among students.
- To remain competitive in attractive world-class faculty, annual gifts helped provide summer research grants to faculty members.
- Classroom technologies have been updated and increased through both gifts-in-kind and annual fund support. This helps keep the Kelley School of Business on the cutting edge of technology for business education.

NO BETTER TIME TO SUPPORT

- To be completed in 2001, the new Corporate and Graduate Center will be situated directly across from the existing Kelley School of Business. At 112,000 square feet, this public-private partnership will be among the most technologically advanced business education facilities in the world.
- Phase II, renovation of the existing business school building, constructing of a new auditorium complex, and a transverse connecting the two facilities across Fee Lane will begin at completion of the new Corporate and Graduate Center. Both undergraduates and graduate students will soon enjoy the best facilities available.
- According to a study by Cornell University, the Kelley School of Business has the top-ranked business library in the nation. With the cost of library materials nearly doubling in the last five years, private support is needed to preserve this top-notch library facility.
- Each year, the Kelley School of Business awards more scholarships than any other department on campus. Each year, nearly 300 scholarships are distributed, and there is a need for more! Private support helps fill this critical need.

Callers should also be offered plenty of reasons to give. Why is funding needed? How will these gifts help? Although these reasons may be embedded in the script, there should be others available for when a call gets off-track and does not follow the script. Exhibit 6.3 contains a list of reasons for prospects to give to Indiana University. The telemarketer should preface each ask with a persuasive reason to give. If there is a specific story or example that can summarize the importance of the cause, this is an excellent resource for the caller. In many cases, it is possible to word the reasons so that a caller can simply pick one, read it, and then ask for a gift.

EXHIBIT 6.3. SAMPLE REASONS FOR PROSPECTS TO GIVE.

REASONS TO GIVE TO INDIANA UNIVERSITY

- Indiana University is a state-*assisted* school, not a state-supported school. Less than 25% of IU's budget comes from the State of Indiana. Alumni support helps IU maintain its reputation as a leader in higher education.
- The costs of higher education continue to rise. Alumni support helps many students attend IU whom otherwise could not afford to do so. These students rely on scholarship support and other types of financial aid that can come from Annual Fund contributions.
- IU continues to invest in new technologies, such as new computers, software, lab equipment, etc. This is important so our graduates will know how to use the latest technologies in their chosen careers. Alumni support helps us keep up-to-date in these areas.
- Competition for the best faculty is fierce. IU professor salaries rank 9th in the Big Ten, and alumni support helps attract and retain the best professors.
- Participation is key to our programs; gifts need not be large, but we want as many people to help as possible. For every 10 people that give $100, we have an additional $1,000 for scholarship support or new equipment.
- The Main Library, unit libraries, and residence hall libraries all rely on private support to help maintain the most recent texts, journals, and information technologies. Costs associated with these items have increased significantly over the past few years and alumni support helps us maintain this nationally ranked library system.
- IU has many undergraduate and graduate programs that are ranked in the top twenty nationally. This quality is a direct result of alumni support. Contributions help make a *good* university a *great* university!
- Organizations require flexibility to react to unforeseen needs and opportunities. Private support allows IU to react to these situations and take advantage of last-minute opportunities.
- IU is an organization larger in scope than just a few buildings and students. It includes faculty, staff, students, and *alumni*. As when you were a student, we have always relied on the support of former students to help current students. We want to continue this tradition so today's students receive the best education possible.

Callers should be provided with a detailed script or outline of the call that contains all basic elements: an introduction, the case for support, reasons to give, specific asks for money, and appropriate closings. Outlines, which may be less detailed than scripts, also highlight these basic elements. For some organizations, reading the script will be extremely important. With specific facts and figures, details, and ideas they wish to share with prospects, a script may need to be read word for word, from start to finish. For others, it may be appropriate for the caller to change his or her approach based on the individual on the line. For these organizations, using fact sheets and talking points as an outline may be better. Talking points would incorporate facts, reasons to give, and the organization's priorities into a series of one- or two-line statements that should be included in every call. This helps ensure that the most important information is shared without the need to read an entire script verbatim.

Whether using an outline or script, a caller should have a clear understanding of guidelines and goals for each call. An ask is often more successful if the caller asks for specific dollar amounts, linked to specific giving groups or clubs or simple arbitrary round numbers. Either way, a prospect is much more likely to give when asked for a specific amount than when simply asked, "Would you like to support the organization?" In addition, it is often more successful to ask for a gift multiple times even if the prospect initially says no emphatically. If this policy is in effect, callers must know in advance what guidelines are in place to avoid problems between callers and the staff managing the calling room. (Determining a proper level of persistence is covered later in this chapter.) Another example might be particular facts and figures that must be used in every call. In many cases, in addition to requesting a gift, the telephone call can be used as a marketing tool. If you desire each telephone conversation to include specific information about your organization, this must be relayed in advance, especially if callers are permitted to deviate from a provided script.

When preparing a script, keep in mind the limited time a telemarketer has with a prospect. Although scripts vary according to the organization and type of prospect being called (see Resource 19), they should be concise and contain the following elements:

1. An introduction that clearly indicates both who is calling and the reason for the call
2. A brief case for support
3. Reasons to give
4. A request (or requests) for funds
5. A conclusion that is based on the result of the call

In any call, the most common response is no, so callers must be skilled in ways to overcome objections. Lack of money, no interest in the organization, and refusal to make pledges over the telephone are common objections, though each organization will also have objections specific to its program. Callers should always be trained to deal with these objections tactfully while continuing to ask for the prospect's support. In order for telemarketing to be successful, an organization must determine the level of persistence it will tolerate. Persistence determines success—but there can be too much of a good thing. Good telemarketers can overcome multiple objections while attempting not to offend the prospect. It is not uncommon to hear two, three, four, or more negative responses and then convince a prospect to make a gift. The difference between persistence and badgering may become a thin line, one that each organization must determine through careful introspection and testing. Regardless of the number of times a prospect should be asked after saying no, callers must be prepared to deal with the typical objections they hear. In general, a caller should understand the objection and not interrupt the prospect. Each prospect has circumstances that the caller may or may not understand. The caller's job is to empathize with the prospect but not judge the situation. Instead, the caller can share that the prospect is not alone and that others are in the same situation (or a similar situation) and are still able to help. It is helpful to provide a list of the most common objections the telemarketer will hear and a corresponding list of suggested responses (see Resource 20). This list will help the callers and help to ensure that the callers are responding as you want them to when dealing with objections.

If the organization is providing donors or prospects with additional materials, such as solicitations or newsletters, copies should be made available for the telemarketers to peruse. This information helps prepare them for any questions or comments they might receive, and it helps coordinate appeals and marketing efforts. In some cases, an organization may wish to send a pre–call notification piece, perhaps a letter or postcard, to inform the prospect that he or she is going to be called for a worthy cause (see Exhibit 6.4). The benefit of this advance notice is that it may help the prospect decide to make a gift. In turn, it may also warn the prospect not to answer the telephone. Again, experience and testing will help determine the need for a pre–call notification piece.

Perhaps the most important element of a call is the introduction. First impressions count. Often the first five to ten seconds of a conversation determine if a prospect is willing to listen or will hang up quickly. Above all, callers must be enthusiastic and have plenty of inflection in their voice. (If a telemarketer thinks he or she is being enthusiastic, more often than not he or she can still be more so.) With millions of telemarketing calls being made daily, prospects need a reason to listen. Callers must not sound as if they are reading a script, even if they are. They must sound interested in what they are doing and share their enthusiasm. Above all, they should get to the point quickly and let the prospect know the purpose of the call.

Making the ask is often the most difficult part of a telephone call. Telemarketers who may be terrific otherwise often find that when it comes to asking for money, they have a hard time. They should be reminded that this is the primary reason for the call, and the prospect also understands this. Making an ask must be a requirement of each call, often more than once and certainly with specific amounts throughout the call.

EXHIBIT 6.4. PRE–CALL NOTIFICATION MAILING.

Give them something to write home about.

Dear Fellow IU Parents and Families,

For a student, choosing a college is one of life's biggest decisions. For our youngest daughter, Sarah, going to IU was a conscious decision; and she knew from day one that she made the right choice. Sarah was so happy academically and socially at IU that her sister, Beth, chose IU for her graduate degree. With both daughters at IU, we couldn't be happier. Beth and Sarah feel IU is providing them with a great college education in a very supportive environment.

What we appreciate about IU is the number of support services that are offered to students. With programs such as campus safety, career counseling, library resources, student scholarships, and disabled student services, Beth and Sarah and their friends have the resources they need to learn on their own or with the assistance from the right source.

In turn, programs like these are supported by thousands of generous parents through the Parents Fund. In a few weeks, an IU student will contact you to discuss your participation in this year's Parents Fund. We have witnessed first hand how the Parents Fund has positively affected Beth and Sarah's IU experiences, and we continue to give every year. Your participation and support are just as important. Please join us this year by supporting the Parents Fund. Be the right source of help for your son or daughter.

Thank you for your support.

Don Bauer   Mary Jane Bauer
Co-Chairs, 1999-2000 IU Parents Annual Fund

 Indiana University Foundation
P.O. Box 500
Bloomington, IN 47402

Nonprofit Organization
U.S. Postage
PAID
Permit No. 103
Bloomington, Indiana

Asking for a specific amount can be much more successful than simply asking, "Could you make a gift?" Requiring callers to ask for a specific amount or amounts can help generate more significant gifts or pledges from those who would otherwise simply offer five or ten dollars.

An organization will not know in advance the capabilities of each prospect it calls. But it can maximize its revenue by using a negotiated ask or starting high and working down through a systematic approach. If specific giving recognition levels are in place, the organization may already have a good idea of the amounts that should be solicited. Callers can start by asking for the most prestigious gift, using installments if appropriate. If the prospect says no or indicates that the amount is too high, the caller can proceed to the next appropriate level. This can continue throughout the call. Often prospects say no to the first ask, regardless of the size. Thus, starting with a larger gift provides a much better chance of realizing a gift or pledge when subsequent lower amounts are suggested. This also gives the telemarketer a chance to continue the conversation, share additional reasons to give, and be persuasive in general.

Telemarketers should also be encouraged or, in the case of paid callers, required not to change the asks based on what they feel a prospect is capable of giving. A prospect who is asked for $1,000 may say, "Oh, no, that's way too much." But a telemarketer who immediately responds with an ask for $25 may miss an opportunity. Instead, a $500 ask may be more appropriate. Eventually, with proper handling of the call, a gift can result that is not only comfortable for the prospect but also may be a larger amount for the organization than might otherwise occur. It is common for a telemarketer to make a quick assumption on how much a prospect is able to give based on location, age, gender, profession, or other demographic information. This type of conclusion must be discouraged, because only the donor truly knows what he or she is capable of giving.

Similarly, when a prospect offers an unsolicited amount, which may be well below the amount being requested, a telemarketer may be able to increase the amount in a tactful way. Of course, any amount should be accepted and appreciated. A strong thank-you is important, but it is not unheard of to request a slight increase. For instance, if a telemarketer has asked for $1,000 and the prospect offers $25, the telemarketer may be able to ask the prospect to upgrade to $50 or $100 using installments or other incentives. The same is true when calling past donors. Those who have been giving $100 each year may be asked to increase their gift using these same tactics.

When asking for a gift, whether an increase or a standard level of giving, the caller must ask in a positive manner (see Exhibit 6.5). There is a big difference between, "Do you think you might be able to give $500?" and "It would be terrific if you could support us this year with $500!" Often the difference between a yes and a no is simply how the question is asked.

EXHIBIT 6.5. POSITIVE DOLLAR ASKS.

Just asking for a pledge is important, but it is the way you ask that makes the difference. You need to bring enthusiasm about IU into your asks and believe that the prospect can make a pledge. If you don't sound like you believe in the program or the prospects' ability to pledge, you won't get the gift. If you are excited about the program and believe prospects will make a pledge, they will.

Following are some ideas you can use for positive dollar asks:

- The first gift I want to mention is our most prestigious gift of $500, which can be given in two installments of $250. It would be terrific if you would be the next to pledge such a generous gift.
- Many others have been able to give a gift of $250. Again, this can be done in installments to make it a little easier. I'd love to put you down for that.
- Our most popular pledge for this program has been $50 this month and $50 next month for a total of $100. It would be just great if you could give $100 this year.
- I want to include you in our efforts because participation is the most important aspect of our program. If every single person can contribute just $50, we'll be able to meet and even exceed our goals. Can we count on you for a pledge of $50?

When the calling organization has a clear affinity with the prospect, the caller may be able to establish a closer relationship in the conversation. For instance, when calling former patients from a heart transplant unit, a caller might want to inquire about how things are going. Not only will this help establish a rapport with the prospect, but good news may well translate into a larger gift. When calling on behalf of a school, college, or university, the caller may want to ask about the prospect's feelings about campus, what it was like when he or she was there, and how the person's degree has helped him or her. Fond memories can be a powerful persuasive element in any telephone call. Rapport also helps differentiate this telemarketer from the other telemarketers who probably called earlier in the day. Prospects are much more likely to make a gift when the telemarketer becomes more than just a voice on the telephone, and establishing a conversation can help accomplish that.

If a call does not result in a pledge, the telemarketer can still take the opportunity to update any pertinent information, such as the prospect's address. The caller should remain polite, thank the prospect for his or her time, and remind the person to support the organization in the future. When a call results in a pledge or gift, the caller should be prepared to handle the corresponding paperwork to confirm the pledge (see Exhibit 6.6).

EXHIBIT 6.6. PLEDGE CONFIRMATION SCRIPT.

1. Thank you so much for your pledge of $_____!

2. I'm going to send you a pledge card in the morning with your pledge of $_____ noted on it. Will you be able to complete that pledge within 30 days?

   <<<If not, schedule payment plan and/or installments.>>>

3. Terrific. Let me make sure I have your correct address listed here. I have you down as:

   <<<Read home address, including city, state, and ZIP.>>>

   <<<If address is incorrect, get new address and update records.>>>

4. While I have you on the phone, let me update your business information as well. I have you listed as:

   <<<Read title, company, and address. If none, explain and ask.>>>

   <<<If new information, update appropriately.>>>

5. Do you or does anyone in your household work for a company that has a matching gift program?

   <<<If no, proceed. If yes, ask the person to obtain forms from the human resource department.>>>

6. Thank you again so much for your time tonight. Let me just verify one last time that I have everything correct. That's a gift of $_____ designated to (*name of program*) and it will be paid in (*installments/time frame*). Do I have it correct?

7. Great! Thanks again, and have a great night!

Callers must be trained to remain polite under all circumstances. They will be insulted, and they will encounter extremely rude people when calling. Regardless, they must maintain their composure and be polite and respectful representatives of an organization, whatever the outcome of the call.

Role Playing

Prior to making calls to prospects, new callers will find role playing helpful in the training process. This gives them a realistic sense of what a call will be like and a chance to work on their skills. Role-play calls can be conducted by the organization's telephone supervisor, more advanced callers, or even other new telemarketers. In all cases, constructive feedback should be given. If possible, the ability to play a recording of actual calls is most helpful to neophytes. If recordings of actual calls are used, it can help to play both a terrific and a dismal one. Let the trainees tell you what they like and dislike about each, and provide your own thoughts as well. Throughout role playing, the calls should become progressively more challenging (while not scaring new callers off). Attempt to give a caller several objections, ranging from "I don't have any money" to "I don't pledge over the telephone" to any others you know are common for your organization. Role playing will give callers multiple chances to hone their skills in the most realistic way possible without making actual calls.

The Calling Session

Prior to the calling session, everything should be in place and ready to go. The telemarketers should have access to telephones, pens, pencils, and any other necessary materials for the calling program. A work area should be provided that is free from clutter yet offers all the tools needed to succeed.

Each caller should be provided with a substantial number of prospects at the beginning of the session. Names, addresses, telephone numbers, and any other information that might prove helpful should be included. When calling to renew prior donors, an indication of past giving amounts should be provided.

Each prospect should have a form on which callers make notes and record the results of each call (see Exhibit 6.7). Callers must indicate pledges and refusals, as well as calls that result in answering machines, no answers, and other possibilities. The forms should be prepared in advance and cover all eventual conclusions to a call. It is helpful if the same form provides a detachable pledge form to be mailed following the call if needed. If the organization accepts credit cards, there should be space for the proper information to be recorded in order to charge the gift to the credit card. When a calling program crosses multiple time zones, care should be taken to separate the cards accordingly so that calls can be made during optimum hours—not too early or too late.

Accurate record keeping is essential. Each attempt should be recorded, regardless of the result. Calls resulting in busy signals may be dialed again later in the session. No-answers might be separated and called the next day or after going through the session's entire list. Wrong numbers may be researched on the Internet or through directory assistance the next day and prepared for calling in the future. Individuals who say no may be so coded and saved for future phonathons or simply disposed of for that solicitation cycle. Pledge cards should be sent as soon as possible to facilitate fulfillment, and copies of the information should be retained. In the event that pledges are not paid on a timely basis, a system for follow-up reminders should be in place.

EXHIBIT 6.7. PROSPECT DATA FORM.

I.U. Parent Annual Fund　　　Letter Sent: _____　　　Transaction # _____

Prospect Data Form　　　Constituency:

Type: P　　Tender: C
Fund: A　　Solicit: PM

Donor Type:　　　　　I.U. Alum:　　　　Pledge Date _____ Pledge Amount _____

Corrections

Parent Name:

Parent Address:

Home Phone:

Student Name:

Major:

Housing Code:

Sex:　　　　　Other Children:

Name_____
Street_____
City _____
State _____ Zip_____
Phone _____
Company/Title _____
Street_____
City _____
State _____ Zip_____
Phone _____

Telephone Activity

Date	Caller	Refusal	Pledge	Special	NA	NDC	Research	Comments

Pledge Details: Company Match　☐ Yes　☐ No　　Pledge Payment　☐ 3 wk　☐ 6 wk ___

Refusal ☐ Why? _____

- -

Indiana University
Parent Annual Fund
P.O. Box 500, Bloomington, IN 47402

Telephone Pledge Confirmation

Thank you for your pledge of $ _____ to Indiana University. Your support and interest are deeply appreciated. **Please make your check payable to Indiana University Foundation,** and return it with this completed card by _____

Sincerely, _____　_____
　　　　　Caller　　　　　　　Date

_____ **Enclosed is my pledge payment for $** _____ .

_____ I work for a **Matching Gift Company** and have enclosed the proper form.

Note:_____

I.D. #
Type
Initial

Your pledge payment qualifies as a charitable deduction for federal income tax purposes.

Prior to making calls, a short briefing may be in order. This allows the supervisor one last chance to impart any knowledge or to reiterate specific issues that must be addressed. It also allows callers a chance to get settled in and ready to call. Many times, this may also include light-hearted banter to get everyone in a good mood or perhaps an icebreaker to introduce the callers and create a team environment. Anything that creates a positive atmosphere in the calling room enhances productivity.

Motivation is key to caller success. Volunteer callers appreciate dinner, T-shirts, mugs, pens, and other trinkets as thanks for their efforts. Often local businesses can be persuaded to provide gift certificates or other items to raffle during the calling campaign. Paid callers may react well to monetary bonus programs (see Exhibit 6.8). Bonus money that is based on performance will both enhance results and help retain the best callers. It is often less expensive to pay good callers more than to spend money hiring and training replacements.

EXHIBIT 6.8. BONUS SHEET FOR CALLERS.

BONUS! 10-1-99
GET 'YER BONUS!

Business Nondonors	Business Donor Renewal
($75 average pledge required)	(10% overall upgrade required)
12%–14% Pledge Rate = $1.00	72%–74% Pledge Rate = $1.00
15%–17% Pledge Rate = $2.50	75%–78% Pledge Rate = $2.50
18%–22% Pledge Rate = $4.00	79%–83% Pledge Rate = $4.00
23%–26% Pledge Rate = $6.00	84%–88% Pledge Rate = $6.00
27%–32% Pledge Rate = $8.00	89%–93% Pledge Rate = $8.00
33% or more gets $10.00!	94% or more gets $10.00!

Fun Stuff Bonus
- First 5 pledges on Nondonors get CDs from The Record Store!
- First 5 upgrades on Donor Renewal get T-shirts from IU Bookstore!
- Every pledge tonight on Nondonors and every upgrade on Donors: Put your name in the hat for exciting prizes! We'll draw throughout the night. If your name comes out, you win! It's just that simple, so get those pledges!

Drawings and Prizes

5:45 P.M. Drawing: $1.00	8:15 P.M. Drawing: 75 cents!
6:15 P.M. Drawing: IU mug	8:30 P.M. Drawing: Surprise!
6:38 P.M. Drawing: 15 min. free call	8:50 P.M. Drawing: Poster
7:00 P.M. Drawing: $2.00	9:00 P.M. Drawing: T-shirt
7:45 P.M. Drawing: Book	9:15 P.M. Drawing: 15 min. call
8:00 P.M. Drawing: $1.00	9:29 P.M. Drawing: Choice

9:30 END-OF-NIGHT DRAWING IS A WHOPPING $10!

Motivating callers is often difficult. Throughout the session, telemarketers face constant rejection and sometimes outright rudeness. This can be trying, especially after several hours of defeat. It is important to continue to motivate the callers and remind them that a pledge or gift could come from the next call. If a caller becomes upset or disgruntled because of a string of refusals, this emotion can carry over into his or her next call, and the effect will snowball. A supervisor who sees this happening should suggest that the caller take a break or simply empathize with the caller, which can make a big difference.

Coaching callers throughout the session is an effective way to improve both morale and results. Using either a monitoring system set up by the telephone company or by simply listening to the callers by moving around the room, you can often make helpful suggestions as the session progresses. Hearing a caller consistently fail to ask for a gift, for instance, could prompt you to discuss the importance of this element of a call. If you hear a lack of enthusiasm, ask the caller to sound more upbeat. Training does not end when the calls are taking place. Callers are always learning and evolving; the supervisor can ensure that the evolution is a positive one. Exhibit 6.9 shows an example of a caller evaluation form that can be used by the telemarketing management staff during a calling session. This type of immediate feedback allows a caller to identify potential areas for improvement in future calls.

In addition to motivating each caller individually, it is helpful to work on the calling room as a whole. Setting goals for all callers to reach helps facilitate a team atmosphere, and callers will work to improve statistically in order to improve the team's results. Set a room goal based on the number of callers working and the number of pledges expected from each. Perhaps the room should raise $8,000 during the session if everyone does a good job. If so, for $9,000, promise to buy everyone pizza or purchase movie gift certificates for prizes if the room meets goal. There are unlimited ways to play games, set goals, and motivate the callers.

Fulfillment

A pledge is only as good as the paper it is written on. It is not truly worth anything until the organization has received payment. An important, yet sometimes overlooked, part of any telemarketing program is the fulfillment process.

Callers must be very clear about what is taking place when they record pledges. They should be instructed to read a specific confirmation that outlines the amount of the pledge, preferably saying the amount at least twice, the agreed-on installments, and the payment method. Also, the prospect should be asked if he or she works for a company that matches gifts if the organization is a qualifying one. The caller should give a set due date to facilitate prompt payment of the

EXHIBIT 6.9. COACHING EVALUATION FORM.

Caller Name: _____   Program: _____

Date: _____   Manager: _____

Introduction/Enthusiasm: _____

_____

Giving Ladder:

$1,000   yes/no _____

$500   yes/no _____

$250   yes/no _____

$100   yes/no _____

$50   yes/no _____

Plus-Ten Program yes/no _____

Rapport _____

_____

_____

Positive Dollar Ask _____

Objection Response

Reflect   yes/no _____

Deflect   yes/no _____

Ask   yes/no _____

Closing/Confirmation

Thanked the alum for the gift? yes/no _____

Explain and ask for matching gift? yes/no _____

Confirm address (including ZIP code)? yes/no _____

Read confirmation verbatim? yes/no _____

Comments: _____

_____

_____

Caller Goals:

_____

_____

_____

_____   _____

Evaluator's Signature   Caller's Signature

pledge. If the organization accepts credit card payment, the caller should note the required information and then repeat it to ensure understanding. It is also important at this time to note any change of address, as there is nothing worse than getting a pledge and having it returned by the post office because of a faulty address. Throughout the process, the caller must continue to be thankful. The time taken to confirm a pledge is necessary to avoid any miscommunication and increase the odds of the prospect's paying the pledge. Exhibit 6.10 demonstrates one tool available to assist in determining if overall telemarketing efforts are on track. This report breaks down the number of pledges, refusals, and contacts (completed calls) by caller and by program.

If the prospect makes a gift by credit card or by direct withdrawal from the donor's bank account via electronic funds transfer during the call, the process is complete. A letter of thanks and receipt, as would be done with any other donor, is all that is left. But if the prospect simply makes a pledge, it is important to continue the process until the pledge has been paid or you are confident it will not be paid at all. A pledge that is more than six months overdue will probably never be paid.

Pledge forms should be mailed to the prospect within twenty-four hours after the telephone call. The prospect thus receives the information while the pledge is still fresh in his or her mind. Ideally the telemarketer will jot a personal note of thanks directly on the card, again reminding the donor prospect of the call and his or her personal commitment to the organization. The information being sent to the prospect should also include an envelope in which to place and return the pledge card and check. A system should be in place to track pledges and pledge payments, as well as generate follow-up mailings at later dates.

Both pledge card and tracking system should clearly specify the personal data of the prospect, the amount of the pledge, the agreed-on installments and dates of payment, and any other important data. This information will help alleviate any future misunderstandings.

If payment is not received within a certain time, usually thirty days, a second pledge form may be sent with a reminder letter. This may be continued at any interval and for any length of time; thirty, sixty, and ninety days are common. In some cases, a follow-up telephone call is a gentle reminder to the prospect that he or she made a pledge and this is a courtesy call to ensure that everything is okay and to facilitate payment. The follow-up call is an opportune time to ask about credit card payment as well; it not only guarantees fulfillment, but it may be easier for the donor to simply pay at that time if he or she has been putting off sending a check. Sometimes the prospect will want to reschedule, decrease, or cancel the pledge. The individuals making the fulfillment calls will need to have available the appropriate forms to complete these actions. When payment is received, the payment should be recorded to avoid any further reminder mailings.

EXHIBIT 6.10. CALLER STATISTICS, INDIANA UNIVERSITY TELEFUND (2/1/2000–2/10/2000).

Caller	Program	Pledges	Refusals	Contacts	Total $	Avg. Pledge	Pledge %	DPC[a]	$100 to $249	$250 to $499	$50 to $999	$1,000+	Cumulative
newmarks													
	American Studies												
	Lapsed Donors	1	0	1	$10.00	$10.00	100.0%	$10.00	0	0	0	0	$10.00
	Arts & Sciences												
	Lapsed Donors	1	0	1	$50.00	$50.00	100.0%	$50.00	0	0	0	0	$1,195.00
	Education –												
	IUB Lapsed Donors	2	4	6	$200.00	$100.00	33.3%	$33.33	2	0	0	0	$645.00
	Geological Studies												
	Lapsed Donors	1	1	2	$50.00	$50.00	50.0%	$25.00	0	0	0	0	$60.00
	HPER Lapsed Donors	1	2	3	$35.00	$35.00	33.3%	$11.67	0	0	0	0	$35.00
	Journalism												
	Lapsed Donors	2	0	2	$60.00	$30.00	100.0%	$30.00	0	0	0	0	$60.00
	Kelley School of Business												
	Lapsed Donors	1	6	7	$250.00	$250.00	14.3%	$35.71	0	1	0	0	$325.00
	Music Lapsed Donors	2	2	4	$50.00	$25.00	50.0%	$12.50	0	0	0	0	$90.00
	SLIS Lapsed Donors	1	2	3	$35.00	$35.00	33.3%	$11.67	0	0	0	0	$40.00
	SPEA (UB)												
	Lapsed Donors	0	1	1		$0.00	0.0%		0	0	0	0	
	University Libraries												
	Lapsed Donors	1	0	1	$50.00	$50.00	100.0%	$50.00	0	0	0	0	$75.00
	Unrestricted												
	Lapsed Donors	10	9	19	$940.00	$94.00	52.6%	$49.47	3	2	0	0	$1,480.00
	Total for newmarks (nights worked: 1)	23	27	50	$1,730.00	$75.22	46.0%	$34.60	5	3	0	0	$4,015.00

provos

Arts & Sciences Lapsed Donors	1	1	2	$50.00	$50.00	50.0%	$25.00	0	0	0	$150.00
Education – IUB Lapsed Donors	4	6	10	$220.00	$55.00	40.0%	$22.00	1	0	0	$535.00
Fine Arts Lapsed Donors	1	0	1	$25.00	$25.00	100.0%	$25.00	0	0	0	$25.00
Geological Studies Lapsed Donors	0	1	1	$0.00	$0.00	0.0%	$0.00	0	0	0	
HPER Lapsed Donors	1	4	5	$20.00	$20.00	20.0%	$4.00	0	0	0	$95.00
Journalism Lapsed Donors	0	1	1	$0.00	$0.00	0.0%	$0.00	0	0	0	
Kelley School of Business Lapsed Donors	4	5	9	$210.00	$52.50	44.4%	$23.33	1	0	0	$210.00
Optometry Lapsed Donors	0	1	1	$0.00	$0.00	0.0%	$0.00	0	0	0	$25.00
SPEA (IUB) Lapsed Donors	0	1	1		$0.00	0.0%	$0.00	0	0	0	
University Libraries Lapsed Donors	2	3	5	$150.00	$75.00	40.0%	$30.00	1	0	0	$580.00
Unrestricted Lapsed Donors	5	11	16	$150.00	$30.00	31.3%	$9.38	0	0	0	$340.00
Total for provos (nights worked: 1)	18	34	52	$825.00	$45.83	34.6%	$15.87	3	0	0	$1,960.00

ridgewayk

Parents Fund Junior Nondonors	1	25	26	$25.00	$25.00	3.8%	$0.96	0	0	0	$3,075.00
Total for ridgewayk (nights worked: 1)	1	25	26	$25.00	$25.00	3.8%	$0.96	0	0	0	$3,075.00

Note: [a]Dollars per contact, computed by dividing the total amount pledged by the number of calls made. This is an indication of overall performance that measures the average pledge revenue per phone call.

Particularly large pledges or gifts may require additional attention. If most pledges for your organization are $100 or less, for example, all pledges or gifts above that amount may deserve a special telephone call from a well-placed individual in the organization. Not only will this result in better fulfillment of the larger pledges, it will generate goodwill that will carry over into future years and telephone calls.

Tracking Results

It is important to monitor statistical information in the calling room (see Exhibit 6.11). Individual caller statistics, room performance, particular prospect pools and programs, and any other ways the calls are organized can help identify problems and increase productivity. Keeping track of statistical performance can be as simple as recording the amount each caller raises on a daily basis to a more complicated system that tracks each caller by session, program, total pledges, total payments, refusals, dollars, and other factors. This also allows tracking by program, day, date range, and so forth. Use of a database package such as MS Access or a spreadsheet such as MS Excel is helpful for programs that call for significant periods of time.

Tracking caller performance is especially important when callers are paid. Paid callers must at the very least earn enough to justify their employment. Callers who make $10 per hour and generate less than that in fulfilled pledges are costing the organization money. Callers who are consistently below the average can be retrained, receive additional coaching, or, when appropriate, be relieved of their position as telemarketer. Each refusal is an opportunity missed, and callers who receive an abnormally high number of refusals each session are using up those opportune prospects.

The same can be said for the overall program or particular prospect pools. In some cases, such as donor acquisition, slight losses may be justified for the long-term gain to the organization when they are renewed. Significant losses, however, may indicate that a different prospect pool may be needed or that the program is not appropriate for telemarketing. Careful analysis may help pinpoint the prospect pools that are performing well, and further calling on those pools will yield better results than calling those that do not reap rewards. Both you and your callers' time may be better spent elsewhere.

It is important to keep the callers, paid and volunteer, well informed of the calling program's progress. Callers respond well and tend to understand the impact of their statistics when presented with them regularly. In many instances, a caller may not realize that he or she is performing sub-par. Showing a particular caller the program's overall results and then indicating that his or her performance is

EXHIBIT 6.11. PROGRAM STATISTICS, INDIANA UNIVERSITY TELEFUND (2/15/2000–2/15/2000).

Program	Pledges	Refusals	Contacts	Total $	Avg. Pledge	Pledge %	DPC[a]	$100 to $249	$250 to $499	$500 to $999	$1,000+	Cumulative
IU Northwest Nondonors	46	398	444	$2,550.00	$55.43	10.4%	$5.74	11	1	0	0	$12,940.00
Parents Fund Freshman Nondonors	18	10	28	$2,075.00	$115.28	64.3%	$74.11	9	2	1	0	$153,644.00
Parents Fund Junior Donors	21	3	24	$1,165.00	$55.48	87.5%	$48.54	4	1	0	0	$33,380.00
Parents Fund Lapsed Donors	45	90	135	$2,240.00	$49.78	33.3%	$16.59	8	1	0	0	$11,696.00
Parents Fund Recent Grads	2	0	2	$60.00	$30.00	100.0%	$30.00	0	0	0	0	$3,445.00
Parents Fund Senior Donors	21	11	32	$2,375.00	$113.10	65.6%	$74.22	5	0	3	0	$24,191.00
Parents Fund Soph Donors	18	8	26	$1,130.00	$62.78	69.2%	$43.46	6	1	0	0	$32,690.00
Varsity Club Former Donors	3	11	14	$200.00	$66.67	21.4%	$14.29	1	0	0	0	$43,590.00
Grand Total:	174	531	705	$11,795.00	$67.79	24.7%	$16.73	44	6	4	0	$315,576.00

Note: [a]Dollars per contact, computed by dividing the total amount pledged by the number of calls made. This is an indication of overall performance that measures the average pledge revenue per phone call.

below average may help motivate the caller to try harder. The same is true for the entire team of callers. When they realize that as a group they are below goal, they may work together to accomplish better results.

Advanced Caller Training

Organizations that conduct year-round or lengthy calling programs may retrain callers throughout the year. In addition to regular caller coaching, it may make sense to conduct advanced or additional caller training sessions, which can help both the best callers and the weaker callers. For the best callers, it helps to get them together and discuss the reasons that they are successful. Perhaps they are using different techniques. By sharing these in a group environment, they both reinforce their techniques and impart them to others. At the same time, callers who are not as successful can use this opportunity to learn from the best. Often callers may listen to and accept advice from peers more willingly than from supervisors or others who are not routinely on the telephone dealing with similar situations.

Cleaning Up Lists

Keeping telephone numbers current often seems to be an impossible task. People move more now than ever before, and area codes seem to be constantly changing. A surefire way to conduct an unsuccessful calling program is to make calls to the wrong numbers. In many cases, lapsed donors lapse only because they move and, intentionally or unintentionally, forget to update their information with charitable organizations to which they have given in the past. Having an accurate telephone number is an important goal for any telemarketing program.

Researching small prospect pools can be done in-house relatively easily. Calls can be made to directory assistance to search for updated telephone numbers. The Internet has several search engines dedicated to finding telephone and address information. Several companies sell CD-ROMs with relatively current telephone numbers. Using any or all of these technologies can help find many new and correct telephone numbers.

For large lists, several outside vendors provide telephone look-up services. These services vary dramatically in both price and service. Some hire telemarketers to call directory assistance on your behalf. Others maintain enormous databases and contract with major telephone companies to use their databases, which then run your list against theirs to locate new numbers. If you have social security numbers for your prospects, some vendors offer a cross-reference with major credit bureaus that will search for up-to-date telephone and address information based on the social security number.

In all cases, the data will be helpful but not 100 percent accurate. Even the largest credit bureaus have faulty data. But if you do not have a number, 95 percent accuracy may be close enough. Major telemarketing trade publications and peer groups can provide a current list of the vendors that provide these services.

Legislation

Due to the proliferation of telemarketing, new laws are being introduced regularly that address telemarketing issues. Some states require that some types of telemarketers register with them before making calls. Some require separate do-not-call lists that telemarketers must adhere to or face stiff penalties. Others allow calling at only certain times of the day. These laws change regularly and vary depending on the type of organization making the telemarketing calls. Check with your state's attorney general or an attorney for details. Even if your state, or those that you are calling, do not legislate telemarketing, it will benefit both the organization and other telemarketing organizations to avoid early-morning or late-night calls and to honor a prospect's request not to be called in the future.

Automated Telemarketing

For organizations conducting particularly large in-house telemarketing programs, automating the telephone center may well prove a sound investment. Automated telemarketing systems offer a technological leap over paper-based telemarketing. Systems come in all formats, with prices that vary accordingly. The cost depends on the system selected, the functionality it provides, and the number of calling stations required. An automated telemarketing system, when implemented correctly, can yield a significant increase in calls with fewer callers. In addition, it helps reduce the amount of paper and data entry needed for the telemarketing program. Callers receive prospect information on a computer screen, see the script on the screen, and enter pledges, refusals, address corrections, and other comments on-line. The computer dials the telephone, prints pledge forms, generates reports, and generally takes care of the telephone room. Of course, callers are still the most important element of this system.

The more advanced systems generate a different script based on the prospect, adjust the ask levels based on a person's prior giving record, and help handle objections a caller receives with a click of a button. They also track the results of each call, return calls to busy signals and answering machines, schedule call-backs when the prospect requests it, and ensure that prospects are called at the appropriate time in their time zone.

At the end of each day's calling, the system can produce unlimited reports, including caller productivity, prospect productivity, the most common objections, percentage of answering machines reached, and other information. Any data element that is recorded can be reported.

Choosing and installing an automated telemarketing system is a significant investment for any organization. Many vendors offer systems to fit any organization. As in choosing an outside vendor to outsource telemarketing, it is wise to discuss automated telemarketing systems with others in peer organizations. Automating a telephone room is no easy task and should be attempted only after experiencing a manual telephone room for some time. The experiences gained in a manual environment will help pinpoint the functionality that is needed in an automated system. Supervisors of a telemarketing program that chooses to upgrade to an automated system should be ready to learn more than just the basics relating to computers. They should become knowledgeable about multiple file types and operating systems, networking, database theory, and various types of dialers and telephony devices.

Conclusion

Proper planning and preparation can make telemarketing an important part of the annual fund for all sizes and types of organizations. As with any other annual fund program, peer input is invaluable in the planning stages. Consult with others, borrow ideas and scripts, and enjoy the benefits of this important annual fund component.

CHAPTER SEVEN

SOLICITING FUNDS IN PERSON

Personal solicitation remains the most effective way to solicit gifts for the annual fund as well as for major gifts. It is an excellent way to generate larger gifts and higher percentages of participation than other solicitation methods. Whereas a direct mail piece may garner up to 15 percent participation and a telephone call as much as 50 percent, a personal solicitation, done well, can have a 75 to 80 percent success rate.

There are relatively few limitations to this method of solicitation, although some nonprofits cannot mobilize, organize, and energize enough volunteers to call one-on-one on a significant portion of the prospect pool. In addition, because of the research and cultivation typically necessary prior to a one-on-one ask, the cost of personal solicitation is sometimes prohibitive for some organizations. Nevertheless, even in the smallest nonprofits and grassroots organizations, it is easy to imagine a passionate chief executive officer or committed board member making personal contacts with a few carefully selected prospective major donors. In such cases, all that is needed is an attractively prepared case for support, a bit of training, and courage. Here, the costs can be very low and the returns extremely high.

Determining the Prospect Pool

There are three levels of prospects:

Expect—A donor who has already given to the organization at the key gift level before to the organization can be expected to do so again if properly stewarded, cultivated, and solicited.

Prospect—A donor who has given to the organization before is now being cultivated at a higher level. For example, someone who has been giving at the $100 level annually is a legitimate prospect for consideration as a $500.

Suspect—Just because potential donors have the means to contribute does not mean they are prospects. To be a legitimate prospect requires more—interest in the organization, involvement with the organization, and, generally where the focus is on lead or major gifts, a prior history of giving at a significant level. Pursuing potential donors who are suspects in the hope of moving them up to prospects is a generally futile chase that all too many organizations engage in. This is done at the expense of time, energy, and resources that could have been spent with those who do care and will, when properly motivated and asked, give.

When donor potential exists but probability does not, it is mandatory for the institution to move these prospects through the cultivation cycle. The cultivation of potentially key donors is a systematic and continuing effort to develop a power structure, either actual or potential, for an institution. It has four steps:

1. Identify
2. Inform
3. Involve
4. Invest

In nearly every instance, the final three steps constitute a continuing cycle of learning additional information about potential donors, heightening their interest through the dissemination of information (personal contact and mailings), encouraging meaningful involvement (such as volunteer service or active participation), and, ultimately, receiving significant financial investment. Involvement is the highest level of cultivation in that it requires that the prospect be brought into active contact with the organization through service on a committee, membership on the board, or some other equally important way.

Facilitating the Process

How does a nonprofit know who its best prospects are? There are a myriad of ways in which that question can be answered, the most productive of which is through conducting research. The nature of the work involved in the field of fundraising in general, and prospect research in particular, requires gathering and analyzing vast amounts of information.

There are different levels of information gathering. Journalists, for example, talk with associates and acquaintances about a story subject and research newspaper articles and the like to find the information they need to make their story interesting. Private investigators track down credit histories, telephone records, driving records, and other items to find what their clients want to know. The role of a prospect researcher is different yet in many ways similar to those of journalists and private investigators, and it is vital that the differentiation be clear. This not only protects the integrity of the researcher and the institution; knowing that it is not the intent of development offices to intrude into their private matters provides a degree of comfort to donors and prospective donors.

For fundraisers in general, the Association of Fundraising Professionals (AFP) has a Code of Ethical Principles and Standards of Professional Practice that is subscribed to by the fundraising community. The Council for Advancement and Support of Education (CASE) provides a statement of ethics for advancement professionals in the world of higher education. The community of prospect researchers also adheres to ethical guidelines: those adopted by the Association of Professional Researchers for Advancement (APRA). These guidelines generally state that APRA members will support and further the individual's fundamental right to privacy and protect the confidential information of their institutions. APRA members are committed to the ethical collection and use of information. Members are to follow all applicable federal, state, and local laws, as well as institutional policies, governing the collection, use, maintenance, and dissemination of information in the pursuit of the missions of their institutions. APRA encourages its members to respect all people and organizations. (See Resource 21 for these code of ethics samples.)

It is highly recommended that individual nonprofits, regardless of size, develop an internal ethics policy. The ethics statement issued by APRA is a general, one-size-fits-all policy, but each nonprofit is different, and the expectations of boards, volunteers, and fundraisers are different. It is up to individual nonprofits to establish ethical guidelines that generally follow those set out by APRA, CASE, and AFP but are fine-tuned to the needs and expectations of their own institution and then to communicate those standards.

Prospect research can be provided by staff members, volunteers, or demographic services. Regardless of the method used, however, the basic principles of research include the following:

- It is ongoing and cumulative. One piece of information leads to the next.
- It is selective. Those conducting the research should be selective about whom they research and what information they gather.
- It is confidential. All information obtained by research must be held in the strictest confidence. This is vital.
- It is accurate. All information should be accurate and verified or attributable to a source.
- It is tied to funding needs. Researchers need to know the priorities set by the administrators of their institution and work within those guidelines.

As information is gathered about ownership, control, influence, and the wealth of individuals, corporations, and foundations, the larger task becomes how to reduce great quantities of information to readable, understandable, concise reports pertinent to the current goal. To meet these objectives, volunteers and staff must correlate, control, and interpret data in order to carry out the following five tasks:

1. Develop a strategy for action.
2. Determine appropriate projects to which the prospect can be assigned.
3. Identify the prospect with the right groups.
4. Assign the right people to cultivate the prospect.
5. Establish a time schedule for implementation of the cultivation and solicitation program.

The best prospects for personal solicitation to any organization are those who are committed to the organization and have already given. Many will already have accepted leadership positions in the organization. These same volunteers may be able to help identify other potential prospects, reaffirming that the best research is done in the field, not in the office. A twenty-minute face-to-face conversation with a prospect or donor often yields more information and gives more insights than hours of in-house or on-line research. People will say amazing things about themselves to those who show genuine interest and listen to them. There is no substitute for being with prospects.

Therefore, it is vital to keep a record of the prospect's contacts with the organization. A contact report needs to be clear and concise with a meaningful summary—something that quickly tells the reader if this is relevant to his or her specific fundraising activities. Details of a contact report may include the following information:

- Date of contact
- Place and purpose of previous contact
- Results of the contact
- Next steps to be taken
- Staff assigned
- Volunteer assigned

Another way in which prospects can be identified is by making use of the explosion of information that has become available on the Internet. Many sites offer fee-based or free information, so an organization with even the smallest of budgets can do effective research over the Internet. Vicky Martin, IU Foundation's director of research management and information services, has prepared a list of Web sites that have been helpful to the IU Foundation research office (see Exhibit 7.1).

Another tool for identifying prospects is the demographic screening service. Although screening is not new, such services have become more sophisticated with the use of computer-based methods. According to Barth (1998), screening companies often use a combination of tools to provide data. One such tool is geodemographic screening, or matching constituents against the characteristics of their neighborhoods and against models of consumer behavior in order to rate their probable interests, lifestyles, and philanthropic giving trends. Companies that provide geodemographic screening include Grenzebach Glier & Associates, Bentz Whaley & Flessner, Marts & Lundy, and Econometrics. Regardless of the type of demographic service used, these data should enhance, not replace, your own. Because these kinds of screenings often increase the workloads of research staff by asking them to validate or negate the ratings for particular prospects, it is a good idea, before contracting with a screening vendor, to answer some questions:

- What would be the purpose of our using this service?
- What do we want to achieve?
- How will the results be processed?
- How many data can we process internally?

With all of these tools available, there can be a temptation to overresearch. Avoid it. Quality is much more important than quantity, and the most useful information is that which is pertinent at the moment.

Once research is completed, the development team—fundraisers, volunteers, researchers, and others—should review the results to determine whether all the needed information is there and whether the prospect belongs in the prospect pool. Prospects who do not belong should be deleted from the list early in the review process.

EXHIBIT 7.1. VICKY'S BOOKMARKS.

Address/Phone/ZIP Sites

AmeriCom Area Decoder,   http://decoder.americom.com

AnyWho: Telephone number, e-mail,
home page URL, fax, toll-free number,
and address   http://www.anywho.com

Directory Assistance   http://www.555-1212.com

ZIP Code Lookup and Address Information   http://www.usps.gov/ncsc

News Sites

American Journalism Review News Link   http://www.ajr.org

@BRINT: The Premier Network for
Business, Technology, and Knowledge
Management: Forums, articles, magazines,
events, resources, analyses, and news   http://www.brint.com

Business Wire 1999   http://www.businesswire.com

CFO Magazine and Treasury and
Risk Management   http://www.cfonet.com

Dow Jones Reuters Business
Interactive LLC   http://www.bestofboth.com/index.html

Folio: The Magazine for
Magazine Management   http://www.foliomag.com

Gebbie Press: PR Media Directory:
Newspapers, radio, TV, magazines, press
releases, faxes, e-mail, publicity, freelance,
journalism, marketing   http://www.gebbieinc.com/index1.htm

Minority Business Entrepreneur Magazine   http://www.mbemag.com

NewsDirectory: Newspapers and media   http://newsdirectory.com

News Headlines from Interlope News   http://www.interlope.com

NewsHub—Headline news every
15 minutes   http://newshub.com

PointCast download page   http://www.pointcast.com

Wall Street Reporter.com   http://www.wallstreetreporter.com

Corporate Information Sites

CEO Express   http://www.ceoexpress.com

CommerceInc   http://www.commerceinc.com/index.shtml

Company Sleuth   http://www.companysleuth.com

Corporate Information   http://www.corporateinformation.com

CorpTech Database of 50,000
U.S. Technology Companies   http://www.corptech.com

EXHIBIT 7.1. VICKY'S BOOKMARKS, Cont'd.

Dun & Bradstreet	http://www.dnb.com/dnb/dnbhome.htm
Financials.com: Annual reports, stock quotes, and more	http://www.financials.com
FirmFind	http://udese.state.ut.us/cgi/foxweb.exe/firmfind
Global Corporate Information Services	http://www.gcis.com
Hoover's Online	http://www.hoovers.com
Industry.net	http://www.industry.net
InvestorGuide: The Leading Guide to Investing on the Web	http://investorguide.com
Online Investor	http://192.41.31.102/onlineinvestor.index.html
Search SEC EDGAR Archives	http://www.sec.gov/cgi-bin/srch-edgar
10K Wizard Quick Search Menu	http://www.tenkwizard.com
Thomas Register of American Manufacturers: Industrial manufacturing supplies, equipment, plastics, valves, fasteners, motors, compressors, engineering, CAD/CAM, sheet metal fabricating	http://www.thomasregister.com
WSRN.com: Financial research	http://www.wsrn.com

Investor and Insider Information Sites

Quicken.com—Insider Trading	http://quicken.com/investments/insider
Stock Quotes	http://www.streetnet.com/quote.html
Stock Splits	http://www.stocksplits.net
Thomson Financial Wealth Identification	http://www.wealthid.com
Yahoo! Finance	http://quote.yahoo.com/?u

Foundation Information Sites

The Foundation Center	http://fdncenter.org
GuideStar: The Donor's Guide to Nonprofits and Charities	http://www.guidestar.org
Quality 990: Improve IRS Form 990 Reporting	http://www.qual990.org

Biographical Information Sites

American Medical Association Doctor Finder	http://www.ama-assn.org
Ancestry.com: Online Genealogy	http://www.ancestry.com

EXHIBIT 7.1. VICKY'S BOOKMARKS, Cont'd.

Indiana Biography Index Overview	http://199.8.200.90:591/ibioverview. htm
International Directory of Finance and Economics Professionals	http://linux.agsm.ucla.edu/dir
Lawoffice.com: Lawyers and information about the law	http://www.lawoffice.com
Martindale-Hubbell Lawyer Locator	http://www.martindale.com
Outstanding Americans	http://oyaawards.com

General Information Sites

The Careful Donor	http://donors.philanthropy.com
Chambers of Commerce and Other Related Associations on the Internet	http://www.indychamber.com/chambers.htm
Council for Advancement and Support of Education (CASE)	http://www.case.org
Guide to Understanding Financials	http://www.ibm.com/FinancialGuide
Indiana University Libraries Online Resources	http://www.indiana.edu/~libfind
KPMG Knowledge Management	http://kpmg.interact.nl/publication/survey.html
Lexis-Nexis Academic Universe	http://web.lexis-nexis.com/universe
Librarians' Index to the Internet	http://sunsite.berkeley.edu/InternetIndex
Price's List of Lists	http://gwis2.circ.gwu.edu/~gprice/listof.htm
Primary Source Media: City Directories Online	http://citydirectories.psmedia.com/index.html
Prospect Research Online	http://www.rpbooks.com
Travelocity: Online airfares, hotel, and car reservations	http://www.travelocity.com
Travelweb: Hotel Reservations and Flight Reservations	http://www.travelweb.com
University of Virginia Prospect Research	http://www.people.virginia.edu/~dev-pros/index.html
Yahoo! Real Estate: Home Values	http://realestate.yahoo.com/realestate/homevalues

Search Engines

Alta Vista	http://altavista.digital.com
Dogpile	http://www.dogpile.com
Google	http://www.google.com

Rating Prospects

The next step is an in-house financial rating of the prospects. This rating includes prospects' *potential* to give (what they would give if the institution were their number one philanthropic cause and they wanted to make a big gift) and a *probable* gift size (the gifts they could pledge over the next twelve to eighteen months). To determine the probable gift, look at the prospect's giving history (including the largest previous gift), other obligations, financial health, type of investments and rate of return, family obligations (parents, children), attitude toward giving, ties (if any) to the institution, and conspicuous consumption (the visible signs of wealth—private schools, estates, vacation homes, and so forth).

This prospect rating is often done by staff, but it also must be done by volunteers in order to validate the staff effort. During any rating session conducted by or with volunteer evaluators, the sole criterion should be what a donor *can* do, given his or her personal circumstances. Staff members should not participate in this evaluation other than to explain the purpose of the session, keep the session moving, and clarify and answer questions about form and procedure. Four rating session procedures are commonly used.

In *group discussion*, evaluators engage in roundtable discussion until they agree on a rating. A group leader should conduct this session. A professional staff member should be present to record observations but should not make any comments that could influence the ratings. This is the best method of evaluation, but its success depends on the group leader's ability to initiate discussion and the group's willingness to participate openly and forthrightly, as well as on the evaluators' ability to make informed ratings.

In *group/individual ratings*, each member of the group is given a rating book and works individually, without discussion, to rate the prospects and offer appropriate written comments. A professional staff member collects the evaluations at the end of the rating session and tabulates the information after the meeting. The major disadvantage here is lack of exchange of ideas or information within the group. The advantage is that the confidentiality of this method may lead the evaluators to provide higher evaluations as well as more pointed and more useful comments. The success of this kind of session often depends on getting someone who is well known and well connected to serve as host or hostess.

In the *individual/one-to-one* approach, a professional staff member meets individually with volunteer evaluators and verbally goes through the prospect list, recording pertinent comments on the evaluation form. The advantage of this process is that the evaluator can feel complete assurance of confidentiality: no one else will hear the comments or know the evaluator's personal feelings about the prospect. The disadvantage is that the validity of the evaluation is limited to the extent of the evaluator's knowledge: there are no second or third opinions. Moreover, the evaluator may not know a number of the prospects well enough to rate them, and so it will be necessary to hold additional rating sessions with other evaluators.

In the *individual/solitary* approach, evaluators are given a list of prospects and rating instructions and are left on their own. The evaluation book is either picked up or mailed back by a mutually agreed-on date. This procedure should be used only in special circumstances. Its advantage is that it gives the evaluator time to reflect on and consider the ratings and comments; properly used, this procedure generally leads to thoughtful, thorough evaluations. Its disadvantage is that individuals often put off doing the evaluations and thereby stall the process.

No matter which procedure is used, the evaluations should be done by knowledgeable individuals. Second-hand and hearsay information is of little or no value—and speculation is just that. The best evaluators tend to be bankers, lawyers, investment counselors, financial planners, insurance executives, the socially prominent, and those actively involved in organized philanthropy in communities with organized efforts.

This entire process must be conducted with an appropriate or even high level of sensitivity for individual confidentiality. Many times those who make the best raters will find themselves evaluating names that present potential or real conflicts of interest. In all such cases, the rater must excuse himself or herself from that particular rating.

Estimating an Individual's Giving Potential

Armed with a prospect list that is as accurate and complete as possible and segmented for maximum effectiveness, the next step is to determine how much of an ask to make. When giving potential is being considered, any information known to the organization about an individual's financial circumstances should play a part. Factors to be considered in assessing potential include accumulated or inherited wealth, stocks and bonds, real and personal property, full or part ownership in business enterprises, access to family or other corporations, foundations or trusts, and annual income level. In fact, making an appropriate ask is vital to accomplishing maximum support.

Almost always, making the ask too small means that the prospect will give at a lower level than is appropriate for his or her capability, and you will only get what you seek. (When was the last time a donor gave more than you requested, and how often does that happen?) In addition, the prospect is probably not going to be made aware of options for future giving if the aim is too low. Even if the donor cannot make a large gift today, set out the options for the future—options that other donors are currently exercising.

Aiming too high can also be a problem, however. A donor can immediately be turned off by feeling as if the solicitor is interested only in major gifts and that his or her gifts either are not enough to make a difference or that smaller gifts are not appreciated. It is important to remind annual fund donors that the power of their gifts cannot be minimized. Added together with gifts from other donors, their gifts can truly accomplish great things. Forced to make a decision, however, always aim high. Unless the ask is so far out of line as to be embarrassing to the prospect, most people are flattered that the organization suspects that they are so successful.

One of the most able volunteers who ever served philanthropy always asked for twice as much as the rating said the prospect could give. He usually got more than the rating predicted. Even when he got only half of what he asked, he knew he had done well. And sometimes the donor was relieved he or she got off so easily, never realizing the volunteer had accomplished his mission. The only time the volunteer ever came away disappointed was when he got exactly what he asked for. When that happened, he was sure he had not asked for enough.

Another common challenge related to requests for contributions is how much to ask repeat donors to give. The hope is that relationships with these donors will be long and fulfilling for both parties. The most common error made with current donors, then, is not making a serious and genuine effort to upgrade their gifts from year to year. Donors who make gifts year after year are becoming insiders, thanks to the newsletters, visits, and personal contacts they have received. As donors age and their relationship with the organization matures, the gift itself should increase along with the donor's capacity to give. As donors move along the continuum, it is not unusual to target repeat donors for gifts that reach as high as $10,000 to $25,000 and even higher on an annual basis.

Making the Ask

Follow-through is essential in making contacts with key gift prospects. There is no substitute for persistence and patience. In small to midsized organizations, it is possible, and where it is possible it is preferable, for the staff to meet together, often with volunteers present, to review the status of prospects and their ongoing management. In larger, more complex organizations, it is a necessity to cover this process with an umbrella prospect management program or system.

Each negotiation is a campaign in itself (Campbell, 1985). Do the necessary homework. Know the prospect—his or her needs, wants, hopes, and ambitions. Identify at least two possible projects that correspond to the prospect's interests. Document the need for each project and the benefits that will accrue if it is funded. Prepare a presentation—from a formal proposal to a simple letter—to take to the meeting with a prospect, and perhaps leave it with the person. The written proposal should cover at least these four items:

- Statement of the opportunity or need.
- Proposed action for meeting the need or fulfilling the opportunity.
- Financial data, including information about costs, other funds available, and the amount being requested.
- A summary statement of the benefits that the donor will derive from the gift. Candidly discuss opportunities, issues, and problems. Ask for the person's counsel and advice. Follow up, report back, and show appreciation at every possible opportunity.

When the time for the call arrives, select solicitors who have made key gifts themselves. Teams of solicitors, most commonly two or three people, usually work better on these calls. If a volunteer is uncomfortable asking for the gift or is nervous or shy, a staff member can go along to the meeting. Another option is to give the volunteer a script, and rehearse it thoroughly with him or her. Training of volunteers is vital in order to achieve maximum success. (See Chapter Nine.)

The first step is to make an appointment with the prospect on his or her own turf; the solicitor needs to go to the prospect. When making the appointment, be up-front about the reason for the visit. Say that you are seeking feedback about the program, as well as looking to gain the prospect's financial support for the organization's objectives. It is better to be honest from the outset, so that the donor does not feel sandbagged in the actual meeting.

During the visit, allow an initial period for conversation on topics of mutual interest, and then introduce the business portion of the visit. Present the background that has led to the occasion of this presentation. Do not let the conversation become a monologue; allow ample opportunity for the prospective donor to participate. Ask questions, and listen carefully to everything that is said. Finally, ask for the prospect's participation, and be clear about how much the institution is hoping to receive.

Be aware of body language—dress, actions, eye contact. First impressions are important. Consider objections and criticisms as opportunities for discussion and indications of interest. Deal with them as such, but never enter into an argument or debate with a prospect.

Take ample time in a solicitation. Arouse interest to the point where the prospect asks, "How much do you want?" Remember that people give to help people. Sell the institution's programs and concepts, not the costs. Logic, emotion, and enthusiasm are the best motivators. Tax advantages seldom play a part in large gift decisions. They are most often a secondary benefit.

Ask for the gift! Keep the sights up, and be specific about the amount. If you can, cite some other lead gifts in the major gifts range. It is not uncommon to ask for two to four times what it is thought a prospect will give, and there is no known case of a volunteer or a staff member being shot for asking for too much. A large request, if it is within the giving ability of the prospective donor, is usually flattering.

Should a negative response become evident, listen carefully to the reasons. Find out what must be done before a gift can be secured. Then leave the meeting without closing, and plan a strategy for the next visit. Gifts that are made in haste or are made by an unconvinced donor tend to be minimal. Clearly establish the next move, including a date for a possible follow-up meeting. It is better not to leave the pledge card with the prospect, although some solicitors do this and some prospects insist on it. If the pledge card is left with the prospect, the solicitor loses a primary reason to follow up, and it is possible that the prospect will either file it or make a minimal gift.

During many solicitations, the prospect will raise objections. Some objections are subliminal. For instance, some elderly donors who are alone or lonely will object to closing, not because they have an objection to the case or reservations about investing, but because they fear that after a gift decision is announced, the institution will cease giving them the attention that comes with cultivation and solicitation. Most objections are more straightforward, however: "This is a bad time for us financially. All our assets are currently illiquid" or "I do not agree with your chief executive officer's priorities."

Whatever the objection, hear it out completely. In discussing the objection with the prospect, restate it, and make sure it is understood in context. Explore ways that the objection could be overcome. Never let the objection lead into an argument, however, and do not make the objection bigger than it is. Respond to it with facts, and never make excuses. If the objection is weak, deal with it as quickly as possible and move on. It is perfectly legitimate to compromise on objections if they will not be a hindrance to reaching the key gift.

Determine whether the prospect will donate if the objection can be overcome. If so, do what reasonably can be done to remove it. Always remember that objections are really questions and that the prospect's investment in the project will help overcome the objections. Remembering this fact will help in converting objections into reasons for giving. If an objection cannot be overcome, then move along to another prospect; do not waste time on prospects who for whatever reason are absolutely not going to give.

After the visit, write a short note of thanks for the prospect's time and interest. As appropriate, the staff should then draft a further note of thanks from the chief executive officer and perhaps from the board chair. Prepare a complete summary report on the visit, with particular attention to new information on the potential donor's special interests, background, and idiosyncrasies. Be sure to include at least the following information:

- Name of company, foundation, or individual visited, date visited, and place of meeting
- If a foundation or corporation, names and positions of people visited
- Who went on the visit
- The purpose of the visit
- What points were highlighted or conveyed during the visit, and whether this was done successfully
- As much detail as possible about what happened at the meeting (what comments were made by whom and responses to those comments)
- Whether any materials were distributed during the meeting and, if so, what they were
- What concerns (if any) were voiced by the prospect and what positive comments he or she made
- Whether a request for funding or assistance was made and, if so, specific details
- Whether additional action or follow-up is needed and, if so, what types, by when, and by whom
- Whether other people should be alerted to the fact that this visit was made and, if so, whom they are
- As appropriate, thoughts and recommendations on the best strategies or approaches for cultivating and soliciting the prospect

Errors to Avoid in Solicitation

The Public Management Institute (Conrad, 1978) has identified the fourteen most common major errors that are made in soliciting gifts:

1. Not asking for the gift
2. Not asking for a large enough gift

3. Not listening—talking too much
4. Not asking questions
5. Talking about the organization and its approach rather than about the benefits to its clients
6. Not being flexible, and not having alternatives to offer the prospect
7. Not knowing enough about the prospect before the solicitation
8. Forgetting to summarize before moving on
9. Not having prearranged signals between solicitation team members
10. Asking for the gift too soon
11. Speaking rather than remaining silent after asking for the gift
12. Settling on the first offer that a prospect suggests, even if it is lower than expected
13. Not cultivating the donor before soliciting
14. Not sending out trained solicitors

These mistakes are all avoidable with the right preparation, approach, and presentation to the prospect.

Conclusion

With these methods for solicitation and follow-up in hand, personal solicitation can be a tremendously effective addition to any organization's annual fund efforts. In all of this, remember that donors have rights that must be respected. The issues of privacy and confidentiality and the matters of appropriateness and sensitivity should always be considered. The thoughtful professional will be guided by the Donors' Bill of Rights (see Exhibit 7.2).

EXHIBIT 7.2. DONORS' BILL OF RIGHTS.

Philanthropy is based on voluntary action for the common good. It is a tradition of giving and sharing that is primary to the quality of life. To assure that philanthropy merits the respect and trust of the general public, and that donors and prospective donors can have full confidence in the not-for-profit organizations and causes they are asked to support, we declare that all donors have these rights:

I.
To be informed of the organization's mission, of the way the organization intends to use donated resources, and of its capacity to use donations effectively for their intended purposes.

II.
To be informed of the identity of those serving on the organization's governing board, and to expect the board to exercise prudent judgment in its stewardship responsibilities.

III.
To have access to the organization's most recent financial statements.

IV.
To be assured their gifts will be used for the purposes for which they were given.

V.
To receive appropriate acknowledgment and recognition.

VI.
To be assured that information about their donations is handled with respect and with confidentiality to the extent provided by law.

VII.
To expect that all relationships with individuals representing organizations of interest to the donor will be professional in nature.

VIII.
To be informed whether those seeking donations are volunteers, employees of the organization or hired solicitors.

IX.
To have the opportunity for their names to be deleted from mailing lists that an organization may intend to share.

X.
To feel free to ask questions when making a donation and to receive prompt, truthful and forthright answers.

DEVELOPED BY
American Association of Fundraising Counsel (AAFRC)
Association for Healthcare Philanthropy (AHP)
Association of Fundraising Professionals (AFP)
Council for Advancement and Support of Education (CASE)

ENDORSED BY
(Information)
INDEPENDENT SECTOR
National Catholic Development Conference (NCDC)
National Committee on Planned Giving (NCPG)
Council for Resource Development (CRD)
United Way of America

Source: Courtesy of the American Association of Fundraising Counsel, Inc. Reprinted with permission.

CHAPTER EIGHT

KEY PROGRAM ROLES AND RESPONSIBILITIES

People give to people. The importance of the human dynamic in the fundraising process cannot be overstated. This chapter addresses the roles and responsibilities of key volunteer campaign leaders, board members, and the annual fund chair.

Key Volunteer Campaign Leaders

Volunteers are key to the success of annual giving programs, particularly in small organizations with little or no staff and limited or restricted budgets. They are important because peer-to-peer solicitation works best, but also because annual giving programs are extremely labor intensive. Three of the four fundraising techniques most commonly used in annual giving programs—special events, telemarketing, and face-to-face solicitation—are well served by the application of many hands.

The Importance of Volunteers

The trend, some suggest, is away from using volunteers and toward having staff-driven campaigns because volunteers ask too many questions and express too many opinions. There is also an obvious and growing problem of supply and demand: good volunteers are in short supply and in great demand. But do not be seduced by the short-term simplicity of believing, or especially of trying to convince others in your organization, that identifying, training, and staffing volunteers is more trouble than it is worth.

Nothing could be further from the truth. Research on this point stretches over time and is abundant, and the results are absolutely clear. Included among the most recent research in this area are data collected by the Gallup Organization (INDEPENDENT SECTOR, 1996; American Association of Fundraising Counsel Trust for Philanthropy, 1997). Gallup's fifth biennial household survey of giving and volunteering highlights two findings. First, among individuals who volunteer for nonprofit organizations, 90 percent also make financial contributions to charities; among those who do not volunteer, 59 percent contribute. These percentages have been relatively stable over time. The results indicate that nonprofits able to increase volunteers' participation can boost giving levels—moderately during recessions and measurably when the economy improves. Second, in 1993, the average gift among households with volunteers was 55 percent higher than among households with no volunteers. Among volunteers, the average contribution represented 2.6 percent of household income, whereas in households without volunteers, the average was 1.1 percent of income.

Key volunteers are at least as valuable as key prospects. Good ones are fewer in number and will have multiple impacts that go beyond making gifts. Organizations that incorporate volunteers meaningfully into the fundraising structure will make the giving environment immeasurably more conducive to the acquisition of large gifts. Genuine involvement of volunteers includes their proper orientation, personalized professional staffing, shared planning and decision making, and allowance for honest differences of opinion. It means making a conscious decision about the selection of each volunteer for every role that the institution envisions. It requires the same thoughtful commitment to peer-to-peer personal recruitment as used in the solicitation of key donors, and it takes account of the fact that volunteers' time is often more valuable to them than money.

Volunteers' active participation in guiding the development of the case statement, creating strategies for others' involvement, and providing peer influence and leverage on solicitation calls all lead effectively to receiving large gifts. Use your volunteers or risk losing them—and if they go, realize that your donors, who are also volunteers, are also being lost.

Staff must always remember that most volunteers agree to serve on boards or committees in the hope that they can be of constructive help. Typically volunteers look to the institution and ask it to show them how they can best serve. They assume that the institution will be wise enough to give them tasks that are within their experience and capabilities and that are important to the institution's goal. They expect to be used wisely and successfully.

Linda and Jack Gill reside in Houston, Texas, but have business interests that take them around the world. Both serve on local, regional, and national boards, and they have established the Gill Foundation. Say the Gills (personal communication, April 2000), "Sure, we give as donors, but our time, contacts, and relationships are more valuable than our money. That's why we are dedicated volunteers, serving on boards of foundations, hospitals, and symphonies. 'To those to whom a lot has been given, a lot is expected.' We feel privileged and obligated to support education needs in every way we can."

It is not the number of meetings attended that determines a volunteer's power. Some volunteers are of great importance because of the one principal contact they can make with the top-flight prospect. It is the responsibility of the staff to be certain that the best assignments go to volunteers who have demonstrated records of performance or the best credentials and that other volunteers are brought along through training to higher levels of performance. Always make assignments on a peer-to-peer basis (for example, corporate chief executive officer to corporate chief executive officer) or on a peer-down basis (for example, corporate chief executive officer to corporate vice president), and always be certain that the top volunteers are assigned to the top potential donors.

Choosing Volunteer Leadership

The selection of volunteer leaders is perhaps the most crucial of the decisions to be made in fundraising. The chair of the governing board, the general chair of the campaign, and the chief executive officer of the institution have the principal roles in any annual fund, especially in the early phases. They are responsible for setting the pace and establishing the right atmosphere for fundraising. They also have to be confident that the planning stage is completed correctly and precisely, and that all the tools necessary for a successful annual fund are present. The success or failure of most fundraising efforts is ultimately attributable to these individuals.

There is no substitute for the influence that a volunteer leader can have on certain prospective donors. In many cases, the influence of the institution's staff is negligible compared to that of the right volunteer. Always remember, however, that all volunteers can do something, but only a few can do a lot. And since the success of any annual fund depends on what the top 20 percent of donors do, it becomes critically important to the success of the campaign that the right volunteer leaders be enlisted, the term *right* meaning that they have the ability to influence others to contribute.

"A good fundraising program has two kinds of leadership—the layman who leads and the staff member who manages and serves. The better each is and the better they work together, the better the results will be. Leadership in itself, let it never be forgotten, is always the key factor in successful fundraising, whatever the cause, whatever the goal, and whatever the scope of the campaign" (Seymour, 1966, p. 179).

In seeking volunteers who are willing to work for the institution, first look to the organization's own family of constituents. If it is a college or a university, then its alumni, the parents of its alumni or current students, and its friends constitute the closest family members. For many community service organizations, those closest include the individuals who use the services of the organization and their families. Other places to find volunteers include the corporate community, churches (if the institution is a church-related organization), other volunteer organizations, and groups of local citizens.

The power structure of a community may be a supplemental source of leadership. Community leaders fall into four main groups:

• Those who have inherited both wealth and its tradition of public service
• The newly rich and newly powerful (the Horatio Algers of the modern world)
• The top professional managers of key corporations
• Respected and admired men and women of the community

For an annual fund to be successful, its top leaders, whether they come from within the institution or the community at large, must make a commitment of time, effort, and dollars. The top leadership group should consist of respected individuals who have the following characteristics:

• Immediate name recognition with the groups served by the institution
• A strong identification with the institution
• A history of association and active involvement with the institution
• A substantial record of giving to the institution
• The ability and willingness to be forceful, dynamic leaders
• Connections with colleagues and friends who are also leaders and who represent the institution's various constituencies

An organization chart and job descriptions should be prepared for the leadership group and should clearly describe specific responsibilities, as well as the amounts of time that will be required (this figure will include time spent in meetings) (see Exhibits 8.1 and 8.2). Recruitment should begin at the top and work down, so that these volunteers recruit the people who will be working for them. Volunteer leaders can accomplish everything from providing additional publicity of your program through positive word-of-mouth to actually soliciting friends and associates on behalf of the program.

EXHIBIT 8.1. VOLUNTEER JOB DESCRIPTION FOR TEAM CHAIR.

Solutions For People
UNITED WAY OF CENTRAL INDIANA

United Way of Central Indiana
Resource Development Division
Volunteer Job Description

Position: Team Chair

Reports To: General Campaign Chair

Summary: The team chair oversees the UWCI campaign in companies in a specific
geographical area of Marion county. Utilizing a team of key volunteers, the chair
analyzes potential for campaign growth and ensures that the maximum number
of companies are personally contacted and engaged with corporate giving and
employee campaigns.

Specific Responsibilities:

- Attend scheduled campaign cabinet meetings and report progress of team activities
- Analyze team's past performance and identify opportunities for improvement and growth
- Schedule and convene regular team meetings
- Recruit and manage at least 6 volunteers to call upon designated companies
- Personally call upon five (5) companies to secure campaign commitments and ensure that all
  strategic accounts (1999 contributions of $5,000+) have been contacted
- Determine team goal and strategies needed to be successful
- Track account progress to ensure campaigns are completed in a timely manner
- Report projected final team goal at end of campaign
- Assist in problem solving on targeted accounts

Time Commitment: Attend seven (7) cabinet meetings, Feb. - Nov., 1 hour each
Attend monthly team meetings, Feb. - Nov., 1 hour each

Key Staff:

Team A	Team B	Team C
XXXXXXXXX	XXXXXXXXXX	XXXXXXXXXX
XXX-XXXX	XXX-XXXX	XXX-XXXX
XXXX@uwci.org	XXXX@uwci.org	XXXX@uwci.org

EXHIBIT 8.2. VOLUNTEER JOB DESCRIPTION FOR LEADERSHIP GIVING CHAIR.

Solutions For People
UNITED WAY OF CENTRAL INDIANA

United Way of Central Indiana
Resource Development Division
Volunteer Job Description

Position: Leadership Giving Chair

Reports To: General Campaign Chair

Summary: United Way is implementing a strategy to diversify and strengthen its fund raising capabilities, with an overall plan of achieving a goal of $40 million in the year 2001. A critical objective to this plan is to increase the number of donors giving at least $1000 annually and, among current leadership contributors, to increase the amount given.

Specific Responsibilities:

- To lead by example in making a leadership commitment.

- Recruit two councils of ten to fifteen members willing to solicit gifts from their peers.

- Secure gifts from council members prior to their own solicitation of gifts.

- Host an organizational meeting to review a list of prospective and current leadership donors to be solicited.

- Commit to soliciting at least five donors or prospects for each council.

- Host team meetings and briefings.

- Attend all scheduled campaign cabinet meetings and report on the progress of the Leadership Giving Council.

Time Commitment:

LGC I April - July, 2000
LGCII September - November, 2000

Key Staff:

XXXXXXXXX
XXX-XXXX
XXXX@uwci.org

The dramatic increase in fundraising competition has had a significant impact on the ability to enlist top volunteers. The percentage of nonprofits increased more than 60 percent between 1988 and 1998. As a result, there are relatively fewer qualified, interested individuals to fill key leadership roles. Experienced volunteers now ask tough questions before they commit themselves to a project, including such things as these:

- How will my role be supported by staff?
- How much time will it take?
- What resources will I be provided?
- Is the board behind this project 100 percent?

Responsibility for enlisting and motivating these top volunteers falls to the chief executive officer, the professional staff, and key members of the board. They must be prepared to win the commitment of top volunteer leaders.

The Annual Fund Chair

The primary leadership role related to the annual fund is typically that of the annual fund chair. This individual generally has the following duties:

- Serves as the annual fund's chief executive officer
- Enlists chairs for any principal functioning units of the annual fund organization
- Cultivates and solicits a limited number of appropriate prospects
- Assumes specific responsibility for personal and corporate commitments from members of the annual fund steering committee and all the principal operating chairs
- Serves as chair of the annual fund steering committee and presides over its meetings
- Makes day-to-day decisions regarding the problems of the campaign, in consultation with the chief executive officer, the chief development officer, and others at the institution when important considerations arise
- Acts as the annual fund spokesperson for all news stories, institutional publications, special events, and other functions

The person who accepts this role will be the key to the campaign and, more often than not, the measure of its success. The annual fund chair should have the following characteristics:

- Demonstrated capabilities
- Influence, affluence, and the willingness to use them on behalf of the institution
- Dedication to seeing that the job is done on schedule
- Ability to command respect without demanding it
- A personality and character to which others will readily respond (people give to and work for people, not only causes)
- Intimate knowledge of the institution and the full scope of its program
- Persistence that compels others to follow suit
- Accessibility
- Willingness to follow the campaign plan and procedures and to accept direction
- Willingness to devote sufficient time to leadership
- Awareness that the early phases of planning and recruiting may require a considerable amount of his or her time
- Determination to overcome obstacles and invalid excuses
- Willingness and ability, at the start of the campaign, to make a personal pledge that is generous, thoughtful, and proportionate (in the event that the chair represents a corporation, a significant commitment from the company should set an example of leadership for other business and industry prospects)

Populating Volunteer Boards

Once the critical role of annual fund chair has been filled, the next step is to provide that individual with the necessary support that a volunteer board can provide. Building a governing board is akin to piecing together a puzzle. It is a collection of individual pieces that when put together correctly forms a complete picture. And like puzzles, every governing board will look distinctive even if each has the same number of pieces.

The process of thoughtfully building a board for a small nonprofit is even more important in many ways than for the large, well-financed, fully staffed organization because bigger organizations can employ staff and even specialists, afford vendors and consultants, and pay for specialized services if it so chooses. These options are luxuries beyond the reach of many smaller nonprofits. Instead, these organizations must turn to pro bono sources and board members with professional expertise adequate to meet the organization's needs.

These board members often must be more actively involved in the day-to-day life of their nonprofits. Not all board members will be chosen because of their abilities in fundraising, although all board members have a responsibility to be generous within their own means and to support the annual fund to the best of their ability.

Many nonprofit boards require that certain members be appointed as representational members. Others will be added because of their complementary program or service expertise. Beyond this, other roles should be considered: an attorney who can help with planned giving, a marketer who can assist with marketing, a media person to aid with media relations, an accountant to help with financial matters, or an investment professional if the nonprofit is supported by an endowment.

Each institution must look to its needs and match its board membership to meet those needs. The goal is to pick board members who believe in the cause, will be active in their advocacy, and will give generously of themselves and their talents. Beware of the "professional" board member who agrees to serve to further his or her business or personal agendas as opposed to the organization's. The governing board needs to consist of members who individually and collectively can perform four main functions (Stuhr, 1977, p. 46):

1. Define the concept of the institution, set institutional goals, and approve plans for reaching them.
2. Hire the chief executive officer and evaluate his or her performance (rather than just rubber-stamp administrative recommendations), give affirmative support to administrators, and lend administrative support to board leaders.
3. Audit and assess the performance of the institution in all its parts, as well as the work of its top executives in the pursuit of established goals.
4. Take appropriate action on the board's assessments of what must be done to reach institutional goals and to build a more effective institution.

To carry out these four functions effectively, a board is annually asked to endorse and support the annual campaign by helping in one or more of a number of areas:

- Setting goals
- Encouraging the staff
- Formulating plans
- Identifying, cultivating, and soliciting key gift prospects
- Readily accepting major posts in the campaign (the community expects the institution's lay leaders to accept the key jobs)
- Taking on sufficient dollar goals for themselves to launch the campaign

Leadership from the governing board is the single most critical factor in the success of any fundraising effort (Broce, 1979). Without board members' visible and unanimous commitment, it will be difficult, if not impossible, to motivate others to participate. It is the governing board members, independent of others, who eventually must commit themselves to seeing that a stated goal is reached because they themselves have unanimously determined that it will be reached.

Leadership from the top—in recruiting workers, cultivating prospects, soliciting support, and giving—is absolutely crucial to any successful annual giving program (Gerber, cited in Stuhr, 1977). Additional people will be needed as volunteer leaders, workers, and financial givers, but what governing board leaders give cannot be matched by any other group. More than anything else, the role of the governing board's members is to establish a policy framework within which the institution will operate and to set an example for others. Where the annual giving program is concerned, the board member sets an example for others in the following ways:

- Taking a place in the volunteer organization and becoming a worker
- Early in the campaign, making gifts that are generous and appropriate to his or her means
- Being informed and enthusiastic about the campaign and the institution
- Working to bring other volunteers into the program
- Communicating with others in the constituency about the institution and the campaign

The volunteer board as a whole must be significantly involved in the annual fund from the start (Livingston, 1984). For example, the board's executive committee, its finance committee, and its development committee must be informed about and supportive of the program. Because much of the money to be raised through the annual fund will come through the efforts of board members, it is mandatory to get their approval to raise money, and it is imperative that they be sold not only on the goal but also on the institution. The more enthusiastic they are about the institution and its leaders, the more effective they will be in raising money.

Early Stages of Planning

The plan for the annual giving campaign is ordinarily developed by an institution's administration. Administrators are involved daily and are probably more aware of needs than outside board members are. This is not to say that there will never be occasions when the board suggests a priority; the initial step, however, is usually taken by the chief executive officer of the organization in discussing needs with the chair of the volunteer board.

The board and the development staff then organize the effort. The board's primary role in this area is to ensure that the annual fund is properly planned. It should look at the organization and structure; the people involved; the individuals, corporations, and foundations being solicited and how they will be approached; how much they will be asked for; the timing of efforts; and the marketing aids being used.

Soliciting the Board Members

After approving the annual fund plan, the board members themselves should be asked to give. Their involvement in planning, for both the institution and the annual fund, is extremely important because involvement begets investment: the institution should evaluate both the potential and the probable giving ability of each board member and should also ask key board members to help rate fellow members. As part of the involvement and cultivation process, board members should be shown the first draft of the case for financial support. Their reactions to it should be sought, as should their involvement in formulating the final draft. It is important that the institution not take board members for granted and that they be cultivated at the highest level.

Before board members are solicited, the possibility of a formula for board members' giving should be considered—a certain percentage of net worth or of annual income, for example. The degree to which a board member's giving might be a leverage factor in setting the total goal should be considered as well: "If the board gives $1 million, we would have a chance of raising $4 to $5 million." Most important, a key group of board members should be involved in resolving these matters and establishing the goal for the board's giving. Once this goal has been established and the board has been fully involved and properly cultivated, it is time to solicit gifts from board members.

Remember that the single greatest mistake made in fundraising is *not asking for the gift*. Early in the campaign, the institution must ask its board members to give and thus serve as an example to others (potential donors in the local community, major donor prospects, service users, and friends of the institution). But each solicitation should be carefully planned; no board member should ever give before having been asked to do so, because when board members' gifts (as well as gifts from others) are offered in advance, they are generally much smaller than if they had been properly solicited.

The solicitors should be carefully chosen, and each needs to have made a personal financial commitment first. Members of the board should be solicited by the chief executive officer or other board members. In making a solicitation, it is important to know the board member's areas of interest and relate them to the campaign because the biggest gifts are generated when board members are asked to provide support in their areas of personal interest. Whenever possible, however, volunteer board members should be encouraged to make unrestricted gifts to the annual fund. This flexible money permits nonprofits the greatest latitude in meeting all of their priorities. And board members are those most completely equipped to understand the importance of this type of contribution. If a good job has been done of making them insiders, they will likely join in the support of this important cause.

In the annual fund, 100 percent participation from the board is a powerful signal to other donors that the institution has vitality, vigor, and the confidence and enthusiasm of its governing board, who should know the institution better than anyone else.

Board Members as Solicitors

Once board members have given, their role becomes that of solicitors. Every board member should be responsible for some part of the campaign. It is not necessary that the campaign chair be a board member; ideally, however, all members of the board should be in leadership positions and should have groups of nonboard solicitors working for and with them. This arrangement makes the board's involvement better known and demonstrates the board's backing of the program. It also provides the nonboard solicitors with people who are knowledgeable about the institution and can answer their questions and accompany them on calls.

Board members should be used to identify potential solicitors, such as people with past, present, or future involvement with the institution. Board members presumably have useful contacts in the community, and as solicitors they should use those contacts to bring in people who could be significant givers. They should ensure that enough of the right people are involved to get the job done in an organized manner and that the people brought in also have enough contacts to be useful solicitors or significant contributors themselves.

Several such people should also be numbered among the institution's board. Board members should be asked to make important fundraising calls; their participation will add to the significance of these calls. They need not be involved with all the calls, however. Being a board member is a part-time responsibility, and most board members probably have full-time positions; they cannot afford to spend a great deal of time making calls, and so the calls that board members will make should be carefully selected. Board members are most helpful in calling on people they know or on people of similar standing in the community or the corporate world. If an institution's board includes the chief executive officer of a significant corporation, the institution should use that person to make calls on other chief executive officers.

Legon (1997) concludes that board members who are effective fundraisers share the following characteristics:

- A natural relationship with or commitment to the institution
- Willingness to contribute
- Willingness to use the appropriate method of asking and thus persuade others to give
- Enough interest in the institution to ask tough questions and ensure that staff members carry out their administrative responsibilities
- A passion about the institution and its mission and a willingness to become advocates on its behalf
- Thorough knowledge of the institution, including its past and present, its traditions and values, and the likely direction of its future

Foundation Boards and Development Councils

Today, in both the United States and Canada, there are many public, multicampus universities as well as large national organizations with headquarters at one location and geographically scattered affiliates or branches. A prevalent arrangement in such institutions is to have the fundraising program assisted by a foundation, a development council, or an advisory board that has focused responsibility for fundraising but does not have broader responsibility for governance and oversight. Under this arrangement, the institution's fundraising staff faces a special set of challenges in working with the volunteers provided by such foundations, councils, or advisory boards.

An advisory board or development council of this type is different from an institutional governing board. First, this type of group, because it has focused responsibility for raising money—indeed, that is its primary, if not only, purpose—should consist almost totally of influential, affluent individuals. (A governing board is necessarily attentive to issues of representation and must appoint members who reflect the diversity of the organization; an advisory board or development council need not do so.) Second, because of its highly focused responsibility, this group's members are often not in a position to make institutional policy, set priorities, direct investments, or directly shape the future of the institution. Therefore, the challenge for the institution's development staff and top administrators is to involve this group in a meaningful way so that the members' inability to chart the organization's direction does not defeat their enthusiasm, desire, and singular ability to help.

To further this purpose, it is imperative that the institution's governing board make itself accessible to this group. For example, one or two members of the governing board should serve in the group and ask its members for advice, listening carefully and thoughtfully to what they have to say. The group's members should be substantially and deeply involved in the processes of planning the campaign, setting priorities, and making the case for giving. If they are to seek—and give—substantial investments, they must feel included and important.

CHAPTER NINE

WORKING WITH VOLUNTEERS

Every organization wants the most capable, the most visible, and the most committed people out in front. The people who fill such roles usually are found among the prominent members of the organization's constituency or community. They are immediately recognizable not only for what they do for particular institutions but also for what they do in the professional, civic, or political arenas. Ask busy people to volunteer. The secret in using the time of busy people is to have them do what is crucial to the project but no more; the next level of volunteers can do what is at the next level of critical importance.

Recruitment of volunteers is a shared task and is usually done most successfully from the top down. The annual fund chair should be recruited by the top people in the organization. Before doing the recruiting, the institution should have searched for the right person, figured out what it wants from that person, and, as an enlistment aid, prepared the institution's case statement. Having done all these things, the institution should not send in a low-level manager to ask for the commitment. Sending the chief executive officer and the board chair speaks to the importance of the commitment.

In recruiting the next level of volunteers—any cochairs and volunteer board members—the annual fund chair reviews the pool of potential draftees with the staff and then participates in the recruitment visits. The annual fund chair should do the actual asking but should be accompanied by the chief executive officer and the board chair. Some feel that the chief executive officer and the board chair need not be involved, but that belief is erroneous. The last thing an organization wants to do is convey to its newly committed annual fund chair that he or she must do the job with no help whatsoever. The organization must convey the sense of a well-built, well-staffed, rolling bandwagon. The development staff can assist the division chairs, the cabinet, in the recruiting that they do. This process continues all the way down through the organization until, ultimately, volunteers are recruiting other volunteers without staff assistance.

The recruitment process is also a key part of the training and motivation process. No clear-thinking volunteer will accept a responsible assignment without asking a lot of pertinent questions. The institution must anticipate such questions and organize accordingly. Inform but do not propagandize. Explain problems honestly. The objective is to inform volunteers fully about the project and the annual fund's objectives and to give them confidence that they can do their assigned tasks successfully and with enjoyment. In fact, enjoyment is one of the greatest motivators, and it is the staff's responsibility to make volunteering a satisfying experience. The best way to do this is to choose the right people for the right tasks, thereby ensuring success.

Because the kinds of people sought for the top volunteer jobs are known in the community, it is not difficult to learn a great deal about them, and it behooves the organization to learn as much as it can. The more an institution knows about these top leaders, the better prepared it will be when the time comes to ask them for their help in achieving its goals. Hale (1980) provides a partial checklist for ensuring a successful first encounter in the recruitment of a key leader:

- Relying on the case statement, point out in some detail the importance of the campaign to the institution in general, those who will benefit from the services of the organization, and those who will benefit later. Stress the philosophical side of the case. People respond to ideas first, mechanics second.
- Meet personally with the prospective volunteer leader at a place and time most conducive to an unhurried discussion.
- Make it clear what the job is that is being offered.
- Assure the prospective volunteer that the institution will provide all of the backup needed to conduct a successful campaign.
- Assure the prospective volunteer that the top leadership of the institution on the board and among the institution's friends will be willing to help.
- Clarify the amount of time needed to do the job.
- Describe the goals and how they were set. Let the prospective volunteer see that they are obtainable.
- Answer all questions fully.
- After providing the institutional background, describe aspects of the program that the institution thinks will be most meaningful to the candidate.

• Decide before the meeting who among those calling on the person will actually ask the person to take a volunteer assignment in the campaign. Try to work out ahead of time how the prospective volunteer will be approached.

Communicating with Volunteers

The organization's staff serves behind the scenes in a supporting relationship to the top volunteer leaders. In working with these volunteers, the staff function should be carried out with a passion for anonymity. Staff members should coordinate and stimulate; furnish technical know-how, supply mechanical and clerical support, furnish resource information, and keep records; and help to motivate and energize the volunteers. But at the center of the activity—in the spotlight—are the volunteers themselves. Says Jack Kimberling (personal communication, April 2000), a retired Los Angeles attorney who has served on local, regional, and national boards, served as co-chair of a national capital campaign, and is the largest donor in the history of the Indiana University Bloomington School of Law, "I expect staff to be knowledgeable and up to date using best practices as well as sharing them with me." Adds Kimberling, "Staff should be dedicated to the principles and goals of their institution, to be hard working, and to work for the good of the organization, not personal glory."

Dunlop (1981) recommends that the staff be guided by the following principles:

• Before the first meeting with a volunteer leader, it is good for the staff to find out certain information about the person (birthdate and birthplace, religious affiliation, business background, family status, location of home, directorships, political affiliations, clubs, honors, awards). Some might question the value of taking the time for such details, and some of the benefits are obscure. Attention to these details is nevertheless worthwhile, if only to avoid embarrassment.

• First impressions are important. At the initial meeting with the volunteer leader, the staff member should try to appear presentable, considerate, reliable, well organized, and knowledgeable. To be "presentable" means to avoid appearing too different. People feel more comfortable around people who seem similar to themselves. Individual manner, speech, and dress will affect how volunteers feel about staff.

• To show consideration, begin the first meeting with the volunteer leader by asking how much time he or she has to spend at this meeting. Respect the time limit the volunteer suggests, and use a watch, if necessary. This detail shows that the staff recognizes the demands on the volunteer's time and values the time given.

• To appear well organized, make open use of an agenda. Give the volunteer leader the original, and work from a copy. Let the volunteer see that items are checked off as they are covered to reinforce a sense of accomplishment and refocus attention on the agenda items still to be discussed.

• To build confidence in the staff's reliability, take notes openly. This stresses the significance attached to the thoughts and ideas being discussed.

• To show that the staff is well organized and plans ahead, consult the volunteer leader about the stationery to be used in his or her work for the institution. Some volunteers may permit the use of their own business stationery, but others will not. Some volunteers have several other pieces of stationery from which to choose. The staff should understand the criteria for the use of each piece. Also ask whether the volunteer's secretary can provide samples of the volunteer's writing style, as a guide for drafting letters and other material. If the staff will be preparing printed materials to go out over the volunteer's signature, ask for three or four sample signatures in black ink, and have a pen with black ink and paper ready for the volunteer at the time this favor is asked. Ask whether the staff may consult the volunteer's secretary for the salutation to be used in writing to the key people with whom the volunteer will be dealing on behalf of the campaign. By giving attention to these details, staff members demonstrate to the volunteer the forethought that they have given to all aspects of the volunteer's work.

• An additional show of consideration comes in asking the volunteer leader about the best times for the staff to call and about when he or she would like to avoid being interrupted.

• To give a sense of urgency to the work that the staff plans to complete with the volunteer leader, set the time and place of the next meeting. Doing so suggests a general time frame for the accomplishment of tasks even if specific deadlines have not been set.

• In routine contact with the volunteer leader, be prompt. The emphasis on promptness should go beyond being on time for appointments. It is a matter of faithfully delivering whatever has been promised, when it was promised (whether that means a report, the draft of a letter, an opinion, or a staff member for a meeting). Courtesy also requires that staff members not keep the volunteer waiting on the telephone. If an organizational secretary places calls for staff members, never keep the volunteer leader waiting for the staff member to come on the line. Consider how discourteous it seems when a call interrupts a volunteer's work and then keeps him or her waiting.

• Document the work accomplished at each meeting with the volunteer leader. Put each key decision, strategy, or plan in writing, and then invite the volunteer to make additions or corrections. This practice ensures that there is mutual understanding of decisions and provides a timely reminder and reference for the work being done.

• A volunteer leader's suggestion should never be rejected at the time when it is offered, no matter how unworthy it may seem. If no merit can be found in the volunteer's idea, simply say that it is something the staff would like to consider further or that the idea is new and there is a need to consult others about it. Then hope that at least some worthwhile element can be found in the idea. This delayed response allows the volunteer to save face and gives everyone more time to consider the suggestion.

• Never delegate the proofreading of material that will bear a volunteer leader's signature. It is the staff's responsibility to make sure the copy is perfect. When it is perfect, submit it to the volunteer "for your consideration or approval," not "for your signature." No matter how many drafts have been gone through, always be graceful about giving the volunteer an opportunity to make additional changes. Remember that when a volunteer has been asked to sign something, it becomes his or her work, and he or she has the final word in its preparation.

• Be candid with the volunteer leader. Sometimes staff members are tempted to offer optimistic encouragement rather than candor. It may be acceptable to project optimism in publicly announcing or discussing the campaign's progress, but not in talking with a volunteer campaign leader.

• Staff behavior shows an attitude; keep it on the professional side. The objective of staff relationships with the volunteer leader is not to become his or her bosom buddy. As Seymour (1966) has said, "A party may be a party to a layman, but remember a party is a business meeting to you."

• Do not be an expert. No one likes the person who is right all the time, and a know-it-all attitude defeats the very relationship that the staff is trying to build with the volunteer campaign leader.

Educating Volunteers

The adage "easier said than done" certainly applies to educating volunteers. Orientation is necessary, and so are meetings. The annual fund needs the power and stimulus that result when people come together to consider and attack a problem. In order to have a successful training session or meeting, however, the staff needs to take the following steps:

• Provide plenty of advance notice to the volunteers.
• Draw up a well-planned agenda, with a copy for everyone, and mail it in advance.
• Give the meeting a purpose.
• Envision a result of the meeting (decisions made, actions taken).
• Make sure that the minutes of the meeting summarize what is to be done as a result of the meeting.
• Put someone in charge of the meeting who will start on time, keep the meeting on track, and end on time.

Volunteers expect professionalism from staff members. The staff must provide good training and the tools to complete the annual fund campaign successfully. As professionals, they must do their work in a businesslike manner and in a similar atmosphere, with well-prepared materials and a comprehensive training program. The ultimate objective of the institution is to have the volunteers catch fire with enthusiasm. A carefully planned volunteer training session can help to do this, and well-planned meetings can keep fanning the flame. Among the points to be covered at any orientation session are the following:

- A clear explanation of each person's role in the campaign (a chart will help)
- The points in the case statement that have caused the annual fund to take on philosophical meaning
- Information and effective tools for each person to complete the assignment
- Questions, with complete answers
- Instructions for the volunteers (what they are to do, with whom, when, where, and why)
- Careful selection, rating, and assignment of prospects
- Guidelines on preparing for a successful call
- Clear instructions on what to do and what not to do on a call
- Instructions on what to do after a call
- Whom to telephone if there is a problem
- How to handle objections
- The importance of large gifts

A number of other elements may be included, as appropriate:

- A tour of the institution's facilities
- Role playing of a solicitation call on a prospective major donor
- Presentation of any audiovisual aids that have been prepared to make the case or assist the volunteers
- A time line for making solicitations
- Appropriate remarks from the board chair, the chief executive officer, and the annual fund chair
- Introduction of the staff members and the assignment that each will have during the campaign

The quality of the orientation session depends on the person in charge, those in attendance, expectations before the meeting, the planning that has gone into the meeting, where the meeting is held, how the room is arranged, the program, and the enthusiasm of the leaders.

During the volunteer training session, the explanation of the annual fund plan, the timetable, and objectives should be the shared responsibility of the institution's chief executive officer, the annual fund chair, and the chief development officer. If the chief development officer is also serving as annual fund director, it is especially important that the volunteers recognize this fact so that they will know this person as their contact within the organization.

During the training session, the staff member who will direct the annual fund should be the one to explain the mechanics of the campaign and the materials in the workers' kit. (See Resource 22.) Not only does the professional know the materials best, but having this person provide the overview demonstrates the competence of the director and builds confidence that the program is well conceived and carefully planned.

Volunteers should feel equipped to answer the major questions that prospective donors probably will ask, and the staff must prepare all the explanatory materials that will enable each volunteer to be a complete advocate of the program. These materials will be found in the volunteer worker's kit, a staff responsibility, which contains the following elements:

- The case statement
- Campaign objectives
- A description of the campaign plan
- Information about how to give noncash gifts
- Pledge cards
- Rating instructions
- Information about the range of gifts needed
- Report forms and envelopes

The kit will also include other supporting materials. Chief among them is a volunteers' guide. This type of guide can be prepared in many different forms and formats, but it should always stress the following points to each volunteer:

- Know the case. Be able to present it concisely and with enthusiasm.
- Make your own gift before you solicit anyone. It gives you a psychological boost and helps you ask others.
- Be positive; never be apologetic. Assume that the prospect is going to give. Remember that you are asking not for yourself but for an institution worthy of support.
- Make personal calls only. See prospects on a face-to-face basis; do not use telephone calls or letters except to arrange or confirm meetings. (If volunteers will not do this, the organization will be better served to use their talents in areas other than fundraising.)

- Keep your sights high, and emphasize that this is an important campaign. Ask the prospective donor to consider the amount suggested on the rating card.
- Go back to see the prospect again as necessary. It is best not to leave the pledge card to be returned later. If the prospective donor wants to consider making a gift, tell him or her that you will return at a later specified time. Decisions for larger gifts take time; therefore, be prepared to make a number of visits if you need to.
- Get the job done—do not procrastinate. Take the best prospects first. Success will build your confidence. Report gifts promptly so that others will see your success and so that the institution will be able to announce progress toward its campaign goals.

At this point, it is also necessary to discuss what can be done about hesitant or reluctant solicitors and what staff members can do to help:

- Recommend that volunteers make their own gifts first. It is a fact that the volunteer's commitment is a source of psychological strength in asking another to make a commitment.
- Suggest that volunteers team up to make calls on their prospects, so that one volunteer can bolster another. The team approach should be used anyway for most major prospects; therefore, suggest this approach to unsure or reluctant volunteers.
- For some volunteers, asking for the gift is the most difficult part of the personal call. Give them phrasing that helps take the unease out of the request—for example, "I hope you are in a position to consider a gift for this campaign," followed by silence. Let the prospective supporter speak next. Alternatively, a closing such as this can be used: "For this campaign to succeed and for our organization to serve our community better, we will need gifts at these levels. [Show a gift chart that does not go significantly below the rated amount but does go higher.] Where do you see yourself participating?" This closing assumes that the prospect will find a gift level that he or she is comfortable with, at the range anticipated. And some donors give more than the rating.

Staffing Volunteers

An axiom of any fundraising program is that no institution can hire enough development staff to do the job of fundraising alone. Volunteers are invaluable in research (the basic element of all fundraising), and they are absolutely indispensable in cultivating prospects and selling the program. Therefore, staffing volunteers is vital. It is not often that they provide their own steam; try to solve the problems that crop up or motivate themselves (Kughn, 1982).

The key to effectiveness in using volunteers is to assign them tasks that they can and want to do. Those tasks must also be important. Thus, volunteers should have assignments consistent with their interests, as well as with their abilities. Before giving a volunteer an assignment, it is necessary to ask, "Is success possible for this volunteer?"

The organization has the right to expect certain things from volunteers. In addition to taking specific assignments, volunteers should take responsibility for the following areas of communication:

- Informing the staff if something occurs that has affected their ability or willingness to do the job
- Promptly reporting all progress concerning their prospects
- Never overstepping or exceeding the scope of their assignments without first clearing the changes with the staff
- Letting the staff know if conflicting interests arise that could put the institution at a disadvantage
- Checking with the staff before departing from agreed-on plans

Dealing with Volunteer Challenges

Perhaps the greatest enemy in any campaign is volunteers' procrastination. Maintaining volunteers' efforts can be frustrating, especially during the campaign's dog days—that period after the public announcement, when the initial excitement and enthusiasm of the campaign have long since passed, the arduous, detailed work of concluding the campaign is at hand, and everything seems to have come to a halt. This is a point that most annual fund campaigns reach. Procedures for maintaining momentum should be planned well in advance. The following suggestions should prove helpful (Picton, 1982):

• Use the campaign organizational structure. Require all chairs to keep in touch with the volunteer leaders in their part of the organization and those leaders to keep in touch with their workers by visit or by telephone on a regular basis. Push for the successful completion of each prospective gift. All chairs, cochairs, and workers are responsible for regularly reviewing the assignments of each volunteer under them. Do not push volunteers for gifts per se. Keep volunteers aware that the suggested level of giving or rating of each prospect must be asked for and received if the campaign is to be successful.

• Try to keep everyone aware of deadlines. Whether through a regular, scheduled report meeting or the final report meeting, push constantly so that each person will complete assignments on schedule. Most people need deadlines. Arrange to have each worker called and reminded of report meetings a day or so in advance, and ask if he or she will have a report. If not, when?

• Pay particular attention to uncompleted assignments that are of significant importance to the campaign's success: the top 10 to 20 percent of the prospects expected to give the majority of the campaign objective. Although it is rare that all larger gift assignments are completed by the deadline, every effort should be extended to push for this conclusion. Key annual fund gifts sometimes take a longer time to gel. Nevertheless, careful, thoughtful follow-up is essential. No matter how often they are reminded of the importance of the top few prospects to the success of the annual fund, staff and volunteers are still inclined to spend an undue amount of time and effort on the smaller donors. Do not neglect them, but concentrate efforts where the returns can be greatest.

• A committee composed of the chief executive officer, chief development officer, campaign chair, and selected key volunteers already committed should be established to concentrate on these key problems and other major obstacles that may arise. Having a troubleshooting committee should make it easier to enlist the annual fund chair, since that individual can accept the position knowing there will be someone to turn to if necessary. And this committee is a good vehicle to have available when attempting to enlist a powerful individual who may not want or be able to accept major campaign responsibilities.

• Regular reports indicating the status of the program will be given at report meetings. Be certain the official report is mailed to all volunteers immediately as a follow-up. Showing comparative results by division or teams can be a helpful tool to help overcome procrastination. Keep deadlines before volunteers; most people work better when under pressure. Also send reports to major donors and prospects to keep them attuned to the campaign. And remember that many donors increase an original gift, so continued cultivation of donors as well as prospects is essential during the campaign.

• Having media attend key report meetings will be helpful, especially if there is something eventful to report. If the media will not come, see that a report is filed with them. Widespread word of success adds momentum. Any announcement of a significant gift should be carefully planned so that it is featured properly.

Even the best leaders and volunteers, those well trained and committed to the cause, sometimes find fundraising challenging and difficult. It is the job of the staff to help everyone fight through these periods, maintain momentum, encourage and lift those who are flagging, and express the right mixture of confidence and enthusiasm, tempered by sober reality, to carry the campaign through to victory.

Using Volunteers to Say Thank-You

Peer-to-peer solicitation is an accepted and proven technique in fundraising—and the best way to maximize giving. Therefore, peer-to-peer recognition should follow as naturally as night follows day. But often it does not. Today, there is a growing tendency to overlook volunteers when recognizing and thanking donors.

Kimberly Ruff is a marketing professional, mother, and wife. She is a past president of Amethyst House, which operates two homes in Bloomington, Indiana, that provide housing facilities for recovering alcoholics and addicts and their dependent children. Amethyst House has an office staff of three, along with twelve others who help full or part time in its houses. Its annual budget is $300,000. In the year 1999–2000 it raised $70,000 from a prospect pool of fifteen hundred names. Says Ruff, "A simple thank-you and the appreciation of the executive director and my fellow board members" is all the recognition she desires. Like the vast majority of volunteers, she serves Amethyst House "because I was asked. They needed someone with a marketing expertise and I had an interest in the cause."

Organizational leaders and annual fund chairs, in their eagerness to express appreciation from the top, a perfectly legitimate and appropriate gesture, often fail to share these special moments. These moments of triumph should be treasured and savored with those directly involved in delivering the gift including the volunteers (or lower-level staff members) who closed it, too. Not sharing the glory is a mistake. The next time the opportunity presents itself, ask a volunteer to say thank-you in your behalf to five donors instead of, or in addition to, asking five prospects to give. Watch their reaction, and make note of the results. Never forget that this type of involvement is yet another way of building on your personal relationship with both the donor being thanked and the volunteer doing the thanking.

Conclusion

It has often been said that an institution receives important gifts by having important people ask important prospects for the support of important projects. Giving volunteers the time, attention, and service they require and deserve will pay great dividends. And never forget to say thank-you.

CHAPTER TEN

PROMOTIONS, COMMUNICATIONS, AND MARKETING

Publications and publicity alone do not raise money, but funds cannot be raised without them. It is interesting that they are especially helpful with those who are not institutional insiders by giving confidence and providing support and security to volunteers and staff alike. Therefore, fundraising materials must be planned in the light of their specific purpose and with the belief that they will be read and heeded.

Types of Fundraising Communications

The case statement and its derivatives are clearly the most important pieces of fundraising literature. In the annual fund, the case statement may range from extensive appeals to the more common short-form case (see Resource 23). A short-form case is an abbreviated, focused statement that can generally be read in two to three minutes or less. It is often a four- or six-panel presentation in a format that answers basic questions (Who? What? Where? Why? How?). It also typically includes a gift response form. The format of the case is not as important as the fact that the case is presented. Raising money is much more difficult lacking a rationale for why it is needed and how it will be used.

In addition to the case statement, the annual fund campaign will also need other written pieces:

- Contribution and pledge cards or forms (see Exhibit 4.4)
- Instructions to workers and volunteers (see Resource 22)
- A fact sheet on the institution (see Exhibit 10.1)
- A newsletter (see Resource 24)
- Transcript materials (sample solicitation letters for volunteers) (see Resource 22)

EXHIBIT 10.1. SAMPLE ORGANIZATION FACT SHEETS.

Tulip Trace Council of Girl Scouts, Inc.

It Starts With You...

Committed to girls in Bartholomew, Brown, Decatur, Jackson, Jennings, Johnson (Edinburgh), Lawrence, Monroe, Morgan, Orange, Owen, and Scott counties since 1962

What We Do

The Girl Scout mission is to inspire girls with the highest ideals of character, conduct, patriotism and service that they may become happy and resourceful citizens. The Girl Scout program links girls and adult female role models in a working partnership which stimulates self-discovery, provides fun and friendship, helps develop skills and builds self-confidence.

Who We Are

Tulip Trace Council of Girl Scouts, Inc., is one of more than 319 Girl Scout councils in the nation chartered by Girl Scouts of the U.S.A. - the world's largest organization for girls and young women.

Who We Serve

Girl Scouting is open to all girls ages 5 through 17 (or in grades kindergarten through 12) who accept the ideals as stated in the Girl Scout Promise and Law.

Girl Scout program age levels include:

Daisy Girl Scouts   ages 5-6 or grades K-1
Brownie Girl Scouts   ages 6-8 or grades 1-3
Junior Girl Scouts   ages 8-11 or grades 3-6
Cadette Girl Scouts   ages 11-14 or grades 6-9
Senior Girl Scouts   ages 14-17 or grades 9-12

The Girl Scout Promise

On my honor, I will try:
To serve God and my country,
To help people at all times,
And to live by the Girl Scout Law.

Girl Scouts.
Where Girls Grow Strong™

EXHIBIT 10.1. SAMPLE ORGANIZATION FACT SHEETS, Cont'd.

BHF

BLOOMINGTON HOSPITAL FOUNDATION
FAST FACTS

Purpose: Bloomington Hospital Foundation "…. is organized exclusively to promote, encourage and receive any contribution, gift, bequest, devise, or grant from any source whatsoever for the use and benefit of Bloomington Hospital" from The Code of By-laws of The Bloomington Hospital Foundation, Inc.

Mission: Bloomington Hospital Foundation exists to provide philanthropic support for Bloomington Hospital and Healthcare System in the following ways:

1.   **Community Development**

Promote increased participation, understanding and communication between BH&HS and the community it serves by
- Recruiting and educating volunteers
- Planning, implementing, supporting and providing educational programs

2.   **Fund Development**

Increase philanthropic support
- Matching donor interest with needs of Bloomington Hospital and Healthcare System
- Continuing to expand and offer creative giving opportunities
- Expanding opportunities for planned giving

Bloomington Hospital Foundation was founded in 1965.

- There are 15 members serving two and three year terms. Foundation Board members are: Chair; Patsy Fell-Barker, Vice-chair; John Haury, Recorder; Joan Olcott, Corresponding Recorder; Nancy Bryan and Mary Oliver, Bursar. John Allen, George Allison, Ben Beard, Dr. Mike Bishop, Mark Bradford, Cary Curry, Carolyn Doty, Maria McKinley, Jeanne Speakman and Henry Wahl.

Bloomington Hospital Foundation's Development Council was formed in 1998.

- The Development Council is a volunteer network of community and business leaders working to increase the ongoing community and philanthropic support for Bloomington Hospital and Healthcare System. There are 65 volunteer members. All are key leaders from the community. Development Council Executive Committee: Cary Curry, Chair; Mark Bradford, Cheri and Tim DeBruicker, Margaret Frisbie, Tally Weigand, and Lara Boulton.

P.O. Box 1149 • Bloomington, Indiana 47402 • 812-353-9528 • 800-222-9589 ext 9528 • fax 812-353-9321

EXHIBIT 10.1. SAMPLE ORGANIZATION FACT SHEETS, Cont'd.

Facts about the program

- Number of Foundation donors: 4,053: Jan 1, 1997 - Dec. 31, 1998

- Net assets: $8,691,071

- Total Board approved expenditures fiscal year, 1997 -1998: $950,018

- Expenditures include the purchase of a Healthmobile and equipment, three assisted medical transport vans, Adult Day Services scholarships, BHF education funds, specialized playground equipment: for Michael's House in Bedford and Children's Therapy Clinic in Bloomington.

About BHHS

Bloomington Hospital and Healthcare System is a regional referral center serving a patient base of 310,000 in nine counties in south central Indiana: Monroe, Owen, Brown, Daviess, Greene, Lawrence, Martin, Morgan, and Orange. Forty percent of Bloomington hospital's inpatients live outside of Monroe County.

Bloomington Hospital Foundation Staff

- Susan Lyons, Director; Anne Cady, Coordinator; and Cindy Stanger, Coordinator

- BHF is a 501(c)(3) nonprofit organization.

3/13/2000

A vital piece of campaign literature is an instruction booklet for workers with a step-by-step program designed to educate volunteer solicitors and make them feel at ease. It should also describe the suggested procedure for cultivating prospects and securing gifts. Some annual fund campaign directors also prepare information for volunteers that focuses on how to close the gift and outlines the skills needed to close.

A fact sheet about the institution need not be elaborate. Nevertheless, it should be comprehensive and provide a variety of important general information that will educate volunteers and provide answers to many of the routine questions that prospects may ask, especially if they are not intimately familiar with the nonprofit.

The campaign newsletter is another piece of literature that takes infinite shapes and forms. It is important that the newsletter appear regularly. It should make liberal use of pictures of volunteers, donors, and others participating in the campaign and, within reason, should include the greatest possible number of people's names. The best newsletters have a well-thought-out purpose. They serve not only to provide recognition and reward for volunteers and donors but also to set the tone for the campaign and move the fundraising effort forward in an organized, efficient, effective manner.

Another important component of campaign literature is gift or pledge documentation. The response device (reply form) for annual fund appeals is generically referred to as a pledge card. In fact, *pledge card* is more appropriate to special projects and multiyear campaigns, where a primary emphasis is placed on securing multiple-year pledges to increase the size of the gift by permitting donors to give over time, usually three to five years. What the annual fund seeks is current, even instantaneous, gifts—in other words, cash now. Immediate gifts create positive cash flow quickly and eliminate the need for follow-ups that are time-consuming, labor intensive, and expensive. Too, pledge collection usually carries with it a shrinkage factor that may run 5 to 10 percent or more for many annual giving programs even when a solid pledge reminder system is in place.

Designing Response Devices

Three basic forms of response devices are used commonly in annual giving: a gift form or card, a confirmation form or card, and a reply form or card. The gift card used in personal solicitation provides a space for typing or printing the name and address of the prospect, a statement indicating that the donor's commitment is made "in consideration of the gifts of others and toward the campaign goal," a place to record the amount of the commitment, a statement of the payment schedule if it is a pledge, and a description of the frequency with which payments are to be made. It also includes a place for the donor's signature and a space for indicating both the amount paid, if any, at the time the solicitation is made and the balance remaining. It is important that a statement appear on the face of the pledge card that contributions "are deductible for federal and state income tax purposes as provided by law." There should also be instructions on how to make checks payable.

In addition to the basic pledge card, some commitment forms, specifically those used in face-to-face solicitations, have two perforated, detachable pieces referred to as ears. The first ear contains a confidential statement indicating the gift rating of the prospect, to guide the solicitor in making the call. The information included here is highly confidential, and the volunteer should detach it before seeing the prospect; it should never be shown to a prospect. The other ear is a temporary acknowledgment form. If its use is required, this ear should be separated from the pledge card at the time the commitment is made. These forms usually include places for writing the name of the donor, the total amount of the gift, and the amount paid, if any, at the time of the solicitation. There is also a place for the volunteer to sign and date the temporary acknowledgment. The temporary acknowledgment usually indicates that an official gift receipt will be mailed in the near future.

The reply card is used in direct mail, and the confirmation card is used to follow up telemarketing calls. Both share common characteristics with the gift form, although neither generally contains ears. There are three basic but extremely important concepts to incorporate into any one of these vehicles:

• Suggest a gift amount. Most forms offer a range of giving options, including a space or line for "Other." Do not offer more than five or six options. More is too confusing. When displaying the options on the card, put the high dollar figure first, as in this example:

____$1,000   ____$100
____$500   ____$50
____$250   Other:_____

Putting lower numbers first makes it too easy and convenient for the donor to check the first option and move on. Work the donors down from the top of the ladder, not up from the bottom. Attempt to raise sights and stretch abilities. A family of four stopping for burgers, fries, and soft drinks at a fast food restaurant can usually spend $20.00 or more at the drive-by window. It is trite but true that $25.00 just does not go as far as it once did. So do not show dollar amounts that are too low, say, $5.00 or $10.00. Never present an option that represents an amount less than the out-of-pocket cost of raising the gift—the cost of the solicitation itself and administering the gift once received. If it costs the organization $10.50 to raise and administer a gift in actual costs over and above the normal, fixed, and usually undistributed costs of running the organization (salaries and benefits, operating costs, and overhead), it is hypothetically possible for an organization to raise so many small gifts that it spends more money receiving and administering these gifts than it raises. Accept small gifts graciously, and never refuse them. Just do not seek them.

• If there are multiple possibilities for the donor to check off how his or her gift is to be used, always list the most pressing need first in the series—for example:

_____ *Where the Need Is Greatest*
_____ Summer Camp
_____ Vacation Bible School
_____ Youth Education
Other: _____

Not only list it first, but set it apart typographically by using all capitals, boldface, italics, or some other device that makes it stand out. Among those who exercise an option, generally between 65 and 80 percent check the first choice, so be sure that option represents your greatest need. Even when given options, many donors will fail to exercise them. Given no direction by the donor, the nonprofit may treat these gifts as unrestricted and use them where the need is greatest.

• While an outright cash gift is preferred and should be encouraged, offer an option to select a pledge payment plan too. This opportunity may increase the size of the overall gift or permit a donor who might not be able to write a check today to participate at a more opportune time. The common format here is:

_____ Monthly   _____ Semiannually
_____ Quarterly   _____ Annually
                        Other: _____

Careful incorporation of these three key elements into the response device can make a great difference in the results achieved and in the flexibility afforded to the nonprofit to use annual gifts to meet its most pressing needs. Careful attention to a fourth detail, providing ample space for address corrections and notification of other elementary demographic information, can go a long way toward keeping the database current. No good result ever comes from mailing to a bad address or calling a telephone number no longer in service.

Purpose of Materials

The number and quality of support materials developed in support of any annual fund is going to be influenced by the overall fundraising goal. Although the same aids are needed to support all campaigns, more funds are available to budget on such expenditures when the goal is $600,000 than when the goal is $150,000. Efforts and expenditures made in all campaigns must be to scale. However, just because the fundraising goal may permit larger expenditures, expenditures should always be dictated by common sense, good taste, and prudent judgment. Never skimp on quality, however. In addition to the various printed documents, appropriate audiovisual materials should routinely be prepared—for example, a traditional synchronized sound-slide show, motion pictures, audiocassettes, videocassettes, flip charts, graphs, posters, and Web sites.

It is also important to design the presentation of the case so that it is easy to interpret differently for various market segments. The same information about the organization may be viewed differently from the perspective of a corporate executive, a wealthy philanthropist, a vendor, or a neighborhood group. In designing literature and institutional approaches to various constituencies, it is important to remain flexible so that the approach can be specifically tailored to produce optimal results. With the explosion of technology and the ever-widening possibilities for delivering the message, all materials should be adaptable to distribution via the World Wide Web and through telecommunications media and all the other emerging technologies as well as through more traditional and conventional methods.

No function of the campaign literature and audiovisual material can be more important than supporting and sustaining a mood of importance, relevance, and urgency and an atmosphere of optimism and institutional community. This function becomes more and more important as campaign goals go higher and higher and as schedules have to cover more and more ground. As solicitation moves from the inside out, from one group of potential givers to another, and as the few traveling teams of official advocates go from group to group, the risk of having the campaign die on the vine becomes real indeed.

The key to avoiding this problem is for the annual fund chair, the chief executive officer, and others to keep delivering the message of the campaign, actively and continuously engaging in the case-stating process and never letting up until the job is done. They should never make speeches or write reports without referring to the unfinished task, doing so with all the gravity due its importance and with the confidence of certain and complete success.

What they and the campaign publications say, and keep saying, is important in itself; almost equally important is that everything and everyone say it again and again and carry the same message, even if it is stated with different emphases for different constituencies. Continuity is the business of all institutional communications, whether they are disseminated through magazines, newsletters, or Web sites. Indeed, this is the principal business of campaign bulletins or newsletters, which nevertheless sometimes make the mistake of dealing almost solely with progressive statistics. These bulletins deserve careful planning so that every issue deliberately plays up the attainment of higher standards, the involvement of respected people, praise from outside the institution, significant growth in the campaign, quotations worthy of repetition, and every good thing to be thought of that can make for confidence.

Preparing Fundraising Publications

Jana Wilson, director of development publications at the Indiana University Foundation (personal communication, November 1999), says that fundraising publications should be to the point—brief, simple, and clear. In an environment of twenty-second electronic media sound bites and *USA Today*–style print media reporting, no audience, unless the individual is keenly interested, and most will not be initially, will respond to lengthy pieces that are poorly designed, written, or presented. Hence, the first thing you must know is what the point of a particular publication is. Wilson achieves this by doing a creative strategy for every publication. "No matter what the project is, you need to know what you have to say, who you're saying it to, and how you want to say it," says Wilson.

The basic elements to be considered in formulating a creative strategy are these:

- Objective: What do you want this piece to do?
- Strategy: How are you going to use it?
- Target audience: Who is the publication for?
- Primary message (call to action): A single sentence. If it cannot be said briefly, you may be trying to do too much with one publication.
- Secondary message: Whatever else needs to be said.
- Tone: Is it light and festive? Warm and nostalgic? Edgy and high tech? Everyone needs to be on the same wavelength.
- Deadline: You can work backward to determine when the various parts of the project need to be done.
- Budget: Know what it is, and plan to meet it. The budget will determine a lot about how the publication looks. Usually, you get what you pay for.

If an institution does not have a top-quality publications department, and most small shops do not, it should seriously consider hiring outside help to produce its annual fund materials, especially the major ones. If outside help is used, do not relinquish control over the finished product. Monitor progress, and require periodic checks with the campaign leaders. Do not scrimp on campaign publications. Prestige pieces are a necessity, and they will pay for themselves. In creating the communications package for a campaign, review the proposed strategy, audience message, and goal for each piece. If necessary, restate the message as it should appear in each communication, remembering that different communications are written to address and reach different audiences.

Always develop logic to support the request or message in each communication. Analyze what the audience has indicated it would like to hear; make sure to use the feedback process to secure important information. Write, dictate, or design the first draft of a communication, and then edit to eliminate triteness, fuzziness, and pet phrasing. Then test the communication with a segment of the target audience, and listen for a response. It may be necessary to revise this communication after audience feedback and review.

Writing Style

The principles of clear, concise, idiomatic writing that apply to nonfiction generally can be the guide for brochures as well. To the point of clear, concise, precise writing, Paula La Rocque (1992) offers these guidelines:

1. Keep to one idea per sentence.
2. Keep sentence length low. Vary lengths, but consider a sentence that runs past twenty-three words a long one. If you must use a long sentence, place a short one before and after it.
3. Do not have more than three figures of any kind in one sentence.
4. Do not have more than three prepositional phrases in any sentence. If the phrases run consecutively or have the same preposition, even three are too many.
5. When unraveling an unclear sentence, find the subject-verb-object relationship. Do not fall unnecessarily into the passive voice.
6. Reduce difficult words to single-syllable or simple terms. Recast jargon and journalese, pretentious or repetitive phrasing, into everyday words.
7. Do not back into the sentence with unnecessary clauses or clauses that delay the subject and should come later in the sentence, if at all.
8. Prune all deadwood and redundancy from the sentence (for example, use "now" instead of "at the present time" and "soon" instead of "in the immediate future").

9. Do not pack the lead. Specificity is wonderful, but where we cannot be specific without burdening the beginning, we should choose a general, clear statement and support it with details later.
10. Maintain a graceful, conversational word order. Read the work aloud to yourself to check rhythm and readability.
11. Choose concrete over abstract terms.
12. Use single, strong verbs instead of several weak ones (for example, "They decided" instead of "They made a decision," "They tried" instead of "They made an effort," and "They intend" instead of "They have the intention").

Fundraising literature too often contains a good deal of specialized language—professional jargon that is familiar to educators, medical staff, or seminary scholars but a deep mystery (and an annoyance) to almost everyone else. Try to avoid it. Keep in mind that most donors, and all major ones, will be laypeople who respond best to plain language, short sentences, and familiar usage. One rule of good writing that particularly applies to fundraising brochures is to avoid generalities and look for specifics. Every institution has its own history, achievements, and vital statistics. Know them, and include them in the writing.

David W. Barton Jr., retired president of Barton Gillet, is fond of reminding people that the characters in Mark Twain's *Huckleberry Finn* speak in five distinct dialects. He specifically mentions that Twain pointed to this phenomenon in the book's introduction because he had taken pains to get the dialects right: the characters speak authentically, and Twain wanted readers to appreciate what he had accomplished. Like Twain's characters, every institution speaks in a different voice, with a different tone and a different stylistic emphasis. If an institution can capture its own flavor and essence in its campaign literature, its constituents will respond. The difference between the right word and the nearly right word is the difference between lightning and a lightning bug. In the same way, the right word and the right image aimed at the right person at the right time and in the right way can produce lightning.

Design and Layout

The institution must also be concerned about the layout and design of its publications and on-line presentations. Graphics should be done by a professional designer, but it is the writer's responsibility to gather the necessary material and guide the designer on tone and style. It is helpful to give the designer a few samples of the institution's recent literature as a guide to its style, unless the pieces are particularly poor and the institution wants to start over. Try to give the designer more illustration material than can actually be used so that he or she will have a range of choices. Avoid extremes, being neither too conservative nor too modern. The institution wants to raise money, not win graphics or arts awards. Clean, readable, attractive campaign communications are the goal.

Photographs, because of their immediacy, are generally favored over artwork. They should be informal, candid, and unposed. Use pictures that add warmth to the story and bring the institution to the donors. In today's publications, larger pictures are generally favored over smaller ones, and an uncluttered look is preferred to a cluttered one. Institutions occasionally have orderly, up-to-date picture files and can simply provide a selection for the designer. If that is not the case, hire a professional photographer to take a fresh set of pictures for the publication.

In preparing information for campaign workers, package the materials conveniently and compactly. Summarize key information, and do not overload volunteers with unnecessary facts. Provide sample questions and answers, as well as simple charts and graphs, to aid them in their understanding and acceptance of the campaign.

Developing a Realistic Plan for Marketing and Communications

Effective campaign communications are not enough. For an annual fund campaign to succeed, a comprehensive plan is also required for marketing and communications. The objective of any marketing plan should be to increase awareness, understanding, and appreciation on the part of targeted audiences in selected geographical areas, with the aim of motivating support. Target audiences vary according to the size and kind of institution. The ultimate marketing challenge for an institution seeking to maintain and enhance its reputation is to bring sharp focus to the past achievements that have contributed to its current high stature, current achievements in its area of interest, and its future hopes and aspirations.

Donors at all levels and from all sources are more inclined to contribute to institutions that can make this part of their case. Effective marketing and communications programs produce a climate for fundraising but should not be expected to attract gifts or volunteers directly. As is true in every other phase of fundraising, it is paramount that those involved with developing and implementing a communications plan learn about the organization and its cause very well.

Once the institution has done its homework—defined its mission and priorities—and the fundraising strategy has been established, it becomes a task of the communications program to identify the audiences to be informed and cultivated, state the campaign's message (understanding what response is being sought from each target audience), and identify potential methods for communicating this message to the selected audiences. Among the instruments available for communicating the message are personal visits; open houses; speeches; audiovisual presentations; letters (personal letters or mass mailings); brochures; leaflets; graphs, charts, and other visual displays; special press conferences to announce significant gifts; films; radio and television public service announcements or purchased time; groundbreaking or dedication events; news and feature stories in newspapers or magazines; newsletter, magazine, or newspaper advertisements; and creative use of technology.

The ability to attract media attention will be affected by a number of variables—for example:

- The size of the institution's media market
- The size of the fundraising goal
- The level of community interest in the campaign (newsworthiness)
- Contacts the institution has with the media
- Participation in the campaign as leaders or volunteers by key media executives

The vast majority of nonprofits conducting annual giving campaigns will not have access to media coverage. Nevertheless, they should try to pursue such coverage if possible. In addition to cultivating newspaper and broadcast media coverage, use institutional publications to provide continuing publicity. Printed materials, such as the annual report and other external magazines, bulletins, and announcements for institutional events, should all keep the campaign before the public. When the campaign is completed, a victory celebration could be held and a final report issued.

It is important that community leaders be involved in making decisions about the communications program. To this end, a communications advisory committee should be established. This committee is of great importance in any well-planned and professionally administered campaign. Committee members should be experts—public relations executives, marketing experts, media professionals, Web masters, and senior members of advertising firms. This group should recommend and review program materials, media coverage, and special events. Not only can the members of this committee give professional advice, they can also offer active assistance in working with the media. They can publicize the institution's efforts in areas where it is not known, accompany representatives of the institution on visits to media outlets and representatives, and make telephone calls to say that a story or an idea for one is on the way.

Naming the Campaign

Whatever the campaign is called, its name should have dramatic impact and meaning for the institution as well as its constituents. Symbols, logos, titles, themes, and other identifiable marks should be developed for and used throughout the campaign. This is another area in which a communications advisory committee can often be extremely helpful.

First, determine how you want people to perceive your organization. You want to conjure up a specific message in the minds of individuals who see your logo and communication vehicles. It is important to be sure that the image you come up with is consistent with this perception. Thus, the first step in determining what look to pursue for the organization is identifying with what traits you wish to be associated. Perhaps you are a traditional organization with a long history of service, a fact you wish highlighted in your communications. Your look or logo then would not be unusual or wildly colored.

Once you have identified the type of image you wish to project, begin to incorporate that into all communications, thereby increasing the exposure as well as encouraging familiarity with the style. One institution that has employed this tactic to great advantage is Penn State University. Although there are many contacts sent to a prospect each year, all carry the familiar annual fund logo, thereby removing any doubt as to where the piece originated.

Another item to keep in mind when designing an image is the cost of the pieces produced. You need to walk the fine line between ensuring that your piece is of a good quality—one that is accurate as well as presentable to your donors and prospects—with the idea that too slick or expensive a look can actually be counterproductive. In the latter case, your donors may wonder about the contributions they have made—in other words, if you really need their gift, how can you afford to produce these expensive solicitation and stewardship pieces? The committee can be very helpful in bringing an unbiased, balanced, professional perspective here.

When establishing a committee to review and decide on matters like those noted, the institution should select members for specific purposes—for areas to be reached or for the kinds of stories the institution is likely to produce more abundantly. Bring these committee members to the institution, if at all possible, to orient them to the institution as it is now, not as it was when they last visited. Be professional, and do not ask members of the committee to help sell what is not legitimate news. Keep the committee informed about successes, and give credit to those who helped. Make sure that committee members know they are appreciated.

Send letters from the chief executive officer welcoming them to the committee and, at the end of the first year, thanking them for their time and effort and noting their successes. Give them recognition for their efforts in institutional publications, and invite them to institutional events.

Conclusion

The basic steps in a communications program for a fundraising campaign are as follows:

- Gain support for the campaign from all the organization's constituencies, beginning with members of the institutional family and making sure to keep all constituencies adequately informed about the campaign's progress.
- Secure broad agreement on the plan from all the major parties involved in the campaign.
- Work closely with all elements of the development or advancement structure within the organization to secure their support and cooperation.

Above all, every communications effort connected with the annual fund must be planned and carried out with the dignity and sophistication that the institution merits. A campaign's communications effort, well done, will pay dividends far into the future.

CHAPTER ELEVEN

GIFT ADMINISTRATION AND DONOR APPRECIATION

Once fundraisers receive a gift or pledge, they tend to move along to the next donor and gift. However, it is just as important that gifts and pledges be processed and handled properly as it is to raise them successfully. Days, months, and even years of careful cultivation can be harmed by an organization's failure in these invisible but very important processes.

Budget

Generally, mature nonprofits that hold the cost of fundraising to 15 to 20 cents on the raised dollar (500 to 750 percent return on investment) are considered productive; those that keep costs in the range of 10 to 15 cents per dollar raised (750 to 1,000 per cent return on investment) are viewed as extremely productive; and those that keep costs at or below 10 cents on the raised dollar (more than 1,000 percent return on investment) are deemed highly productive. For growing nonprofits and those whose programs are primarily based on the annual fund, costs of 20 to 50 cents on the dollar raised (500 to 100 percent return on investment) are considered productive and generally represent acceptable returns on investment. Older nonprofits with mature fundraising programs that fall in this range are considered only marginally productive.

Sometimes fundraising costs exceed 50 percent of the total dollars raised. Such a situation can occur in a start-up program or where the fundraising is primarily a lower-dollar, broad-based participation program. It may also occur in a program with such a small or nonexistent staff that the organization must outsource most or all of its program to be served by paid solicitors. Too, a program may be attempting to attract new donors in large numbers, or other special circumstances can be in evidence. All are labor intensive and the costs can be pervasive, at least over the short term.

In the end, it is the responsibility of the governing board, based on recommendations from management and its own careful discernment, to approve the fundraising budget and determine acceptable return on investment guidelines. If the board feels it can comfortably endorse and, if necessary, defend its budget to its donors, friends, and "loving critics," then it has a budget that probably is reasonable, whether it fits within these guidelines or not.

Two fundamental points are of primary importance. First, it takes ample funding to ensure the success of a campaign, and too much attention can be focused on fundraising costs. With so much at stake, it is foolhardy to be too restrictive of campaign expenses; to fixate on costs is to adopt the perspective that the glass is half empty. It does matter how much is spent, but the real issue is how much is realized. No matter how cost-effective an effort is, it is always possible to argue that even more costs could be squeezed out of the budget if only the annual fund managers looked harder. But it is time to change the dialogue, establish a new paradigm, and focus on returns—and an investment in a campaign, wisely made, will yield very high returns. *It costs money to raise money.* Is a 1,000 percent return on investment acceptable? How about 500 percent? That is a 20 percent cost factor.

Second, all of the campaign's needs should be considered and included at the outset. One corollary to this is the establishment of an internal procedure that provides for constant monitoring and scrutiny of budget expenditures (see Exhibit 11.1).

In addition to the costs of conducting the annual fund, there is the little-discussed loss called shrinkage—that is, losses resulting from unpaid pledges. Normal shrinkage is usually at least 1 to 3 percent of the amount raised in an annual campaign; a range of 5 to 10 percent is more typical. The job of the professional staff member is to ensure that it stays as low as possible.

Some losses are uncontrollable, as in the case of a donor's death or the failure of the donor's business. Some, however, are caused by inadequate pledge reminder and billing systems. An organization that does not have a responsive system enabling it to bill accurately and on schedule may be headed for collection difficulty. The institution must check this system and make any necessary corrections before the campaign begins. A status report on the campaign and information about what is being done with the funds can be included with the billing statement. This practice can help payments flow and is sound cultivation for later gifts.

EXHIBIT 11.1. ANNUAL CAMPAIGN BUDGET REPORT.

For the month of

Current Month			Prior Year Actual	Percent Variance	Line No.	Description	Year-to-Date			Annual Budget	Amount Remaining	Prior Year Actual	Percent Variance
Actual	Budget	Percent Variance					Actual	Budget	Percent Variance				
					1	Salaries							
					2	Overtime wages							
					3	Fringe benefits							
					4	Less: Allowance for attrition							
					5	Total personnel							
					6	Training and recruiting							
					7	Travel							
					8	Representation							
					9	Supplies							
					10	Printing							
					11	Postage and shipping							
					12	Telephone							
					13	Copier maintenance and supplies							
					14	Building repair and maintenance							
					15	Vehicle repair and maintenance							
					16	Computer repair and maintenance							
					17	Other equipment and furnishings							
					18	Legal fees							
					19	Professional and other fees							
					20	Insurance							
					21	Miscellaneous							
0	0	0.00%	0	0.00%	22	Total program	0	0	0.00%	0	0	0	0.00%
0					23	Capital expenditures	0						
					24	Total expenditures							

Using Paid Solicitors and Consultants

Employing paid solicitors can eat into an organization's net income, but it can be the right approach for some nonprofits. Many organizations with funding needs and with the desire to launch fundraising programs have very small staffs. One-person offices are common, sometimes fundraising is only one aspect of a staff member's responsibilities, and many grassroots organizations have no professional development staff members at all. A 1999 membership survey by the Association of Fundraising Professionals (AFP) found that 52.5 percent of its members work by themselves or with three or fewer colleagues. Less than 15 percent work in situations with ten or more staff and support persons. It is possible to conduct a successful fundraising program under these conditions, but the organization usually needs to improvise. In many cases, a dedicated volunteer or team of volunteers has conducted a successful program for an organization with no paid development staff. In other instances, a member of the administrative staff has carried out the task. Others turn to paid solicitors or consultants.

Fundraising counsels do not solicit or retain custody of contributions. The American Association of Fundraising Counsel (AAFRC) guidelines prohibit consulting firms from handling funds. Paid solicitors, on the other hand—firms as well as individuals—are employed to solicit contributions. In some cases they also have possession of contributions, a practice to be avoided whenever possible. This is common sense. The handling of money can present temptation. The best way to resist temptation is to avoid it. There are also the matters of institutional accountability to the donors and fiscal integrity. Nonprofits ought to receive and handle contributions made to them. It is far better that the organization receives its own gifts and pays the solicitor than to have the paid solicitor forward the organization's portion of the contributions to it. If the nonprofit is not capable of receiving and properly handling its own funds, a third party—a bank, an attorney, or an accountant—should receive and handle the funds. This is a specific way in which a board member may be of service to the organization. At a minimum, there is a need to establish some kind of reliable verification system if the paid solicitor is to handle the funds.

Increasingly, fundraising consultants or firms are providing services related to annual campaigns, from telemarketing assistance to such areas as grant writing, interim staffing, staff or volunteer training, mail services, publications, and special event planning. In the 1999 profile of AFP members, respondents were asked if their organization retained professional fundraising counsel or service firms in the last two years. Approximately three-quarters reported using one or more services.

Creating and Using Report Forms

Before the campaign begins, the institution should create the printed forms and computer programs needed to record, retain, retrieve, and reproduce the information associated with the wide variety of campaign tasks. There are two types of basic reports for which the professional staff is responsible: financial reports and reports on volunteers and prospects. The number and sophistication of the financial reports will vary according to the size and complexity of the campaign. In an established development office, a great number of operating procedures will probably already be in place, particularly those pertaining to fiduciary matters but also those pertaining to the wider scope of the office's activities. An example of the kinds of forms routinely generated in support of an annual campaign are included here. Exhibits 11.2 and 11.3 show sample monthly campaign progress reports. From these types of forms, information can be maintained and conveyed using hard copy or computerized procedures.

EXHIBIT 11.2. CAMPAIGN PROGRESS REPORT FORM.

Week ending _____

I. Campaign goal $

II. New gifts and pledges

III. Total previous gifts and pledges

              Grand total gifts and pledges

IV. Amount needed to reach goal

V. Recent campaign activities

VI. Appointments scheduled

Donor Category	Campaign Goal	Received to Date	Balance Needed
Board	$	$	$
Individuals			
Corporations			
Foundations			
Other			
TOTALS			

EXHIBIT 11.3. PROSPECT STATUS SUMMARY REPORT FORM.

Major Prospects	Researched	Prospect	Assigned to Staff	Possible Volunteer(s)	Assigned to Volunteer	Meeting Held	Letter and/or Proposal Submitted	Gift/Pledge Made; Seek More	Refused; Try Again	Adequate Gift/Pledge Made	Firm Refusal	Comments

Account and Gift Administration

The organization is responsible for providing, at a minimum:

- Fund and account structure
- Documentation of donor intent—agreements with donors
- Donor reporting
- Change or revision of donor intent
- Gift substantiation and receipting
- Pledge accounting and write-offs
- Gift-in-kind policy
- Matching gift processing
- Pledge reminder system

Gift Receipts

Gift receipts must meet five Internal Revenue Service (IRS) requirements:

1. State the amount of cash contributed.
2. Describe—but not value—any property contributed.
3. If the donor received no goods or services in return for the donation, the acknowledgment must so state.
4. If the donor received goods or services in return for the donation—other than an "intangible religious benefit" or token items of "insubstantial value"—the acknowledgment must describe them and provide a "good-faith estimate" of their value.
5. If the only benefit the donor has received is an "intangible religious benefit," the acknowledgment must so state. (See Exhibit 11.4 and Resource 25.)

Currently the IRS does not require a gift receipt for donations of less than $250, but it is both good business practice and good donor relations for nonprofits to acknowledge and receipt all gifts formally. Gifts of $250 and more must be receipted by the nonprofit to enable the donor to claim a tax deduction.

Where membership dues are involved, the donor may deduct only the amount that is more than the value of the benefits received. Membership benefits may be disregarded if the amount is $75 or less. The nonprofit must give a written statement or a gift receipt if the value is $75 or more. It must indicate that the donor can deduct only the amount paid that exceeds the benefits received and must give a good-faith estimate of the value of those goods and services (benefits).

EXHIBIT 11.4. GIFT RECEIPT.

GREATER VICTORIA HOSPITALS FOUNDATION
H304 – 633 Courtney Street, Victoria, B.C. V8W 1B9

Date: 03/16/2000   **F 065289**
Amount: $100.00
Fund: Foundation

John Doe
123 Park Street
Victoria, BC V8W 1B9

Official Receipt for Income Tax Purposes
Charitable Registration #0134395-19-28

Valuing Noncash Gifts

On the gift receipt, noncash gifts are to be described but not valued. However, for the donors' purposes, values need to be established. In order to do this, Taylor (1998) offers the following advice.

Gifts of Stock and Bonds

A stock or bond gift is not a gift until it's under the control of the donee organization or its legal agent. This means that an organization can't recognize the gift or record it until the stock or bond is registered in the institution's name and under its control. Stocks are valued at the mean between the high and low trading range on the date of legal transfer. Bonds are different. An institution has a little more leeway with bonds since they are not traded on a central exchange. The usual procedure is to gather data from two or three brokerage firms who make markets in the particular bond being given and use this as a basis for determining the amount of the gift.

Gifts-in-Kind: Artwork, Property, etc.

Where there is no established fair market value and the absence of already tested Internal Revenue Service guidelines within which acceptable values can be set, there is a need to get an appraisal. Have the donor provide a copy of an appraisal that was done within 90 days of the gift date. (The donor will need that appraisal to claim a tax deduction anyway.) Use the figure given by the appraiser as the value for gift reporting purposes.

If the donor won't get the appraisal in the time the organization needs it, the organization can use the opinion of a local expert, like a curator, although the organization might want to confirm that estimate with a qualified outside source. On the IRS receipt, just describe the gift—don't mention a value.

For an in-kind gift (goods and property) to be considered a deductible gift, it must further the mission of the donee institution. It can either be something truly needed, or be something that can be sold and the money used to further the organization's mission. The value of donated in-kind services, i.e., a professional person's time, is not tax-deductible, however.

A complete review of the rules regarding income tax charitable deductions can be found in Dove (2001), Resource 20.

Documenting Pledges

When a donor commits to future charitable contributions, a pledge for the commitment can be recorded on the donor record. Having one or more of the following documents in hand indicating the commitment will suffice:

- A signed donor gift or pledge intent memorandum
- Pledge data form
- Solicitation card
- Pledge card
- Contract to make a will
- Donor-signed correspondence
- Payroll deduction form
- Electronic funds transfer (EFT) form
- Correspondence or memo outlining a conversation and the commitment of the donor and signed by the development officer

A gift agreement (see Resource 26) by itself is an acceptable document to record a pledge only if all of the following information is included in the documentation received from the donor or development officer:

- Donor signature (preferred)
- Pledge amount
- Indication of whether the pledge is conditional or unconditional (see below)
- Installment dates (annually, semiannually, quarterly, monthly or date certain)
- Installment amount
- Account name and number
- Indication of whether the donor should receive a reminder

Verbal commitments should not be recorded on the donor record without the accompaniment of additional signed donor correspondence or a signed memo from the development officer outlining the conversation and commitment.

Conditionality

A pledge may be designated as conditional or unconditional. The maker of a *conditional pledge* promises to make a donation only if specified future *and* uncertain events or conditions occur. The pledge should be recorded on the gift system, but it should not be recorded on the audited financial statements until the condition has been met or waived by the donor. This is because the donor is not bound by the promise until the event or condition occurs.

The maker of an *unconditional pledge* promises to make a donation that depends only on the passage of time (such as predefined installment due dates or at death). This sort of pledge should be recorded on the gift system as well as the audited financial statements.

Nonacceptance of a Gift

Occasionally, a donor's intent differs from the contemporary wishes of the nonprofit. Lyon (1998) says that when the basic terms that the donor proposes are unacceptable to the nonprofit (for example, they are too rigid or compromise the integrity of the nonprofit), the gift should be declined.

Recognizing, Acknowledging, and Reporting Gifts

Once a donor has made a gift, cultivation can move to a new and higher level. A sincere expression of gratitude shows the human warmth of an institution. It goes without saying that every gift should be acknowledged when it is received; the donor is expecting acknowledgment. If in fact the gift has played a part in strengthening the institution, then the real opportunity to give thanks will come in six months or a year, when the effect of the gift is more fully known. In the interim period, keep in close contact with the donor, and never fail to follow up and provide the information that will tell the donor what the full positive effect of the gift has been.

Whether or not people say they want to be recognized, the plain fact is that 99 percent of all people love recognition. Because recognition is often a major motivation for giving, any successful development program must provide a means of recognizing key donors.

It is important that the right people thank those who have given. In each case, an individual determination of who should do the acknowledging should be made. There should also be continuing recognition for key donors. If they are properly handled in the recognition process, they are likely to make even greater investments in the future.

From the beginning of the campaign, all gifts should be promptly acknowledged, and each donor should be properly thanked:

- Thank them accurately.
- Thank them promptly.
- Thank them gratefully.
- Thank them publicly.
- Thank them privately.
- Thank them frequently.
- Thank them appropriately.
- Thank them innovatively.

Each donor should receive a personal letter of appreciation from the institution, as well as an official gift receipt. The thank-you letter should be personal, informative, and meaty. It should tell the donor about what is happening, the total amount raised, progress on the project, and other important information. This is one of the details that needs to be thought about in advance. Who will sign the letters? At what minimum level will institutional administrators and campaign leaders sign? $100? $500? $1,000? More? Does the plan call for the institution to ask each volunteer to thank each donor and send the institution a copy of the thank-you letter? It should. For larger gifts, the chief executive officer should certainly provide a personal acknowledgment. The key volunteer working on the solicitation may also choose to communicate with the donor, as may the chair of the board and the chair of the campaign. Gifts are made individually, and their acknowledgment should be considered individually. If more than one acknowledgment is to be sent, the staff should make certain that the acknowledgments complement and reinforce each other.

Acknowledging gifts is a time-consuming task. Therefore, to enable prompt preparation of the letters, there may be a need for additional secretarial staff or word processing capability. This is an important detail: long delays in acknowledging and thanking donors for gifts are unprofessional and make a bad impression. Be certain that everyone—donors and volunteers—is thanked as quickly as possible.

The Children's Museum of Indianapolis thanks all of its donors from the smallest to the largest in a timely fashion using the following format:

$1–$99

- Thank-you letter from the chief executive officer within one week of gift
- Invite to the donor open house
- Invite to donor shopping day

$100–$249

- Everything in the previous category
- Recognition in *Tributes* (a newsletter) for new donors
- Copy of *Tributes*
- Copy of *Newseum* (newsletter)
- Recognition in the annual report
- Copy of the annual report
- A telephone thank-you call from the donor relations officer (within one week of the gift)

$250–$999: Polar Bear Level and Rex Level

- Everything in the previous categories
- Corresponding benefits sent with a letter from the donor relations officer (within two weeks of the gift)

$1,000–$2,499: President's Club Level

- Everything in the previous categories, except that the thank-you letter is from the chair of the board
- Corresponding benefits sent with the letter from the major gifts officer (within two weeks of gift)
- A telephone thank-you call from the major gifts officer (within one week of gift)

$2,500–$4,999: Water Clock Society Level and Reuben Wells Society Level

- Everything in the previous categories except that the thank-you letter is from the chief executive officer
- Corresponding benefits sent with the letter from the major gifts officer (within two weeks of the gift)
- A telephone thank-you call from the major gifts officer (within one week of the gift)

$5,000+: Carousel Society Level

- Everything in the previous categories except that the thank-you letter is from the chair of the Carousel Society

- Corresponding benefits sent with the letter from the major gifts officer (within two weeks of the gift)

Another major consideration is reporting gifts, both internally and to volunteers and the public. As part of campaign planning, the institution must build internal recording and reporting systems that will enable it to handle gifts correctly and with dispatch. These systems must be able to compile the gift data to formulate reports showing the number, sources, and amounts of the gifts received and, more important, the purposes for which the gifts were received. This is essential not only for practical reasons, such as reporting periodically to campaign leaders and workers, but also for internal audit controls. The staff must be able to report daily where the campaign stands; the staff will certainly be asked for such information almost daily.

The staff should also consider preparing a weekly or monthly campaign report to be mailed to all volunteers and others important to the success of the campaign. Formats of such reports vary widely and can be determined by individual institutions. In some campaigns, a monthly report is all that is required. It helps to keep the focus on the campaign and can be used to energize volunteers who are not performing up to expectations. Each volunteer leader should review the division or team's effort at each report session. The bandwagon effect is important in an annual fund campaign.

According to the campaign's organizational structure, the staff may want to be able to report in a number of ways—by division, team, area, class, source, amount, fund, or all of these. Certainly a breakdown of this nature will be desirable in the institution's final report of the campaign, so why not plan it in advance and have this capacity during the campaign? Most institutions now use technology to make this a simple task if it is programmed carefully. If an institution still uses a manual system, multipart copies can do the trick.

Stewardship

An essential component of any follow-through program is the thoughtful, systematic organization of a stewardship effort. Stewardship, the ongoing process of saying thank you, giving attention, and expressing appreciation, effectively begins before the first gift is received—when the board establishes policies regarding the acceptance, handling, management, and investment of gifts. Once a gift is received, stewardship encompasses a variety of activities, including recognition, appreciation, and reporting. It also includes the wise and prudent financial management of the investment.

Stewardship is designed not only to recognize past support, but also to be a part of the cultivation program that leads to the donor's next gift. Its frames of reference are both the past (what has already been done) and the future (what might still be done), but its setting is the present (what can be done now to achieve the goals of thanking for the past and cultivating for the future simultaneously).

Every organization should prepare a written stewardship plan for its best donors and then follow it. Among the elements of a good program are these:

- Survey donors to discover their preferences and adhere to their wishes.
- Remember birthdays and anniversaries.
- Respect religious holidays, observances, customs, and dietary restrictions.
- Stop by when you are "in the neighborhood" and say hello; make sure you are occasionally "in the neighborhood."
- List names in the annual honor roll of donors.
- If your organization has an electronic reception desk, add a menu choice for donor recognition by listing donors' names at this site.
- List donors' names on your Web site.
- Call occasionally just to say hello and check in.
- Clip and send to donors articles of interest to them.
- Send an annual donor statement to those with named and endowed accounts; accompany it with a thank-you letter.
- Provide advance notice of upcoming events and activities; offer to assist with tickets or to provide transportation as appropriate.
- Offer appropriate courtesies and amenities. A parking pass for use while on campus or in your building is always appreciated.
- Send flowers occasionally and candy too (except to diabetics).
- Ask donors how they are doing. Ask too how they think *you* are doing.
- Always try to find ways to say thank you, to show appreciation, to remember people, to let them know they are valued (see Exhibit 11.5).

Conclusion

Treat special donors in a special way. Use best practices from the for-profit sector, such as high-end merchandisers like Nordstrom or Neiman-Marcus, which specialize in personal attention and attention to detail or like the airline industry that caters to its frequent flyers by knowing their preferences and satisfying them. You cannot say thank-you enough. However, it is very important that you say thank-you in appropriate ways that please donors. Not every donor is the same. Do not attempt a one-size-fits-all approach to stewardship and donor relations. Make your program flexible enough to fit your donors' needs, individually and collectively.

EXHIBIT 11.5. DONOR RECOGNITION AT VARIOUS GIVING LEVELS.

Gift Levels	$100	$500	$1,000	$2,500	$5,000	$10,000	$25,000	$50,000	$75,000	$100,000
Acknowledgment/receipt	X	X	X	X	X	X	X	X	X	X
Information (newsletters, e-mails)	X	X	X	X	X	X	X	X	X	X
Mementos	X	X	X	X	X	X	X	X	X	X
Holiday card		X	X	X	X	X	X	X	X	X
Special events (cultural, academic, athletic, black tie)			X	X	X	X	X	X	X	X
Holiday gift				X	X	X	X	X	X	X
Birthday card				X	X	X	X	X	X	X
Personal letter/phone call from key volunteers or staff					X	X	X	X	X	X
Personalized site visit(s)					X	X	X	X	X	X
Personal letter or phone call from the chief executive officer						X	X	X	X	X
Reception with chief executive officer and key volunteers						X	X	X	X	X
Letter from recipient of endowed fund						X	X	X	X	X
Personal report on endowment						X	X	X	X	X
Personal report on annual giving amounts and cumulative lifetime giving								X	X	X
Publicity								X	X	X
Personal visit from chief executive officer								X	X	X
Personalized donor recognition event(s)										X

CHAPTER TWELVE

CLOSING THE CAMPAIGN AND MOVING FORWARD

The annual cycle that defines each nonprofit's budget year and annual giving program necessarily faces closure. One cycle ends and another begins. However, before one set of books is closed and another opened, there invariably will be loose ends that need to be tied up. These include expressing appreciation one last time to those who worked and contributed and analyzing the year's performance and preparing written reports documenting both achievements and areas to be improved. It also requires culling from the ranks those who have failed to perform or moved on and finding a place for the fresh new faces that represent the requisite source of constant renewal that keeps any organization fresh and vibrant.

Success on Schedule

Ideally success on schedule will be the annual campaign's good fortune, and it is important to plan the victory celebration carefully in the event that this good fortune does come about. Continue to feature the campaign's leaders. All the credit and limelight should be theirs, not the staff's. Be certain that each person who has had a major campaign responsibility or did an outstanding job is appropriately recognized. Encourage the attendance of key donors who made success possible. Be certain that all volunteers are invited and recognized too. The celebration should be a well-organized, happy occasion.

Recognize key donors who will agree to be recognized. How they are recognized depends on the institution and the individual donor. Being recognized from the dais is enough for some; others like certificates, plaques, or some other imaginative, tangible symbol of their generosity. The institution may want to honor some donors at smaller occasions—perhaps private affairs. Each situation should be examined separately. But by all means, do give recognition, no matter how you choose to do so. Maintain friendly contact with donors, and use direct mail, the telephone, and face-to-face opportunities to report on what their gifts have accomplished. This contact reinforces the organization's appreciation and gives the institution an opportunity to keep donors aware of continuing needs. Additional gifts are often a by-product of the pleasure derived from being recognized and receiving information.

It is equally important to honor campaign workers. In all campaign announcements, reports, and news releases, praise the volunteers for their efforts, and invite them to special events along with donors and prospects. Maintain contact with and seek advice from important workers, as well as from major donors.

Prepare media handouts concerning what the campaign gifts have accomplished and will accomplish, and recap the highlights of the campaign. Once again, feature leaders and key donors if they will permit you to do so. If media representatives attend the victory event, a larger audience will be informed of the campaign's triumph, and that will help develop public relations for the institution. The size of the campaign goal, the prestige of the organization, the size of the media market, and the level of influence and affluence its key players have will all affect the organization's ability to access mass media outlets. Realistically, attracting such attention can be out of the reach of many smaller organizations.

Whatever the celebration program, however, it should be carried out in a thorough but light and entertaining way, leaving everyone feeling good about what has been accomplished. Go first class! Everyone wants to be recognized for accomplishments, and everyone wants to be on a winning team. When these factors are recognized in plans for the victory celebration, volunteers will be more likely to say yes when the organization asks for their assistance in future fundraising activities.

Donors should not be forgotten after the victory is celebrated. They should be invited to special occasions at the institution—lectures, research symposiums, special luncheons or dinners, plays or musical productions, gallery openings. Whatever brings them on site is sound cultivation. This is common sense, but sometimes institutions get so involved in daily activities that they overlook these possibilities for continued cultivation.

If you ask volunteers to do something today, do not forget them tomorrow. Workers and donors have the right to expect to be remembered forever for what they have done. Responsibility for remembering them belongs to the public relations and development departments. All past good deeds should be regarded as promises for the future. The best way to remember your volunteers and donors is to give them further opportunities to serve the institution. Never write anyone off as a future prospect—at least not until the day the will is probated.

Saving the Victory

If victory on schedule should elude an institution, it is important to do two things. First, be candid. Announce the results to date, and indicate that all gifts have not been received. Continue in a quiet, determined way to push for a successful conclusion as soon as possible. Second, have leaders call or visit every key prospect in their divisions or on their teams to ask that the prospects keep the campaign in mind until the work is finished, and offer assistance to particular leaders or staff members. For example, if certain volunteers have not been effective, perhaps some reassignment of prospects is called for. It does not take long for a campaign to die, so push harder than ever. This is the point when the campaign leaders must be aggressive. Review the status of the key prospects, and look for new approaches that may be needed. Have the campaign leadership consider going back to key prospects for a second gift; rarely does the initial gift tap out a donor. While the volunteers are making this final push, staff should return to the matter of uncollected telemarketing pledges or yet to be received proceeds from special events. Any loose gift that can now be secured needs to be.

Final Reports

At the conclusion of each annual fund year, two types of final reports should be prepared: the internal report (see Resource 27) and the public document (see Resource 28).

Internal Report

At the end of the campaign, the institution should internally analyze its effort. This analysis should be geared to answer the following questions:

- Was the goal achieved?
- Was the annual campaign well received?

- What was the best method of solicitation?
- Which expenditures proved the most beneficial and which the least effective?
- What promotional materials and special events were the most effective?
- Which efforts should be repeated, which ones altered, and which ones abandoned?
- Was key leadership developed during the campaign? If so, who were they?
- What key prospects appeared?
- Were key volunteers or donors lost during the campaign? If so, who and why? Can they be reinvolved?
- Has the institution recorded all the data obtained during the campaign?
- How well did the campaign leaders, volunteers, staff, and consultants, if used, perform?
- Did any individuals identify themselves as prospective board members during the campaign?
- Did others who might serve on important institutional committees surface?
- Did the success of the campaign create a need for increased staff and greater budget to support the development effort in the future?

The internal report should include a cover letter from the chief development officer to the chair of the annual fund, with a copy to the chair of the board, summarizing the campaign's major accomplishments and the problems that were encountered. This report should also include any recommendations or suggestions that the chief development officer would like to make. It should provide a plan for stewardship, describing activities that can be developed to recognize donors and keep them informed about the benefits being derived from their contributions. It may also include other suggestions designed to prepare the institution for a more fruitful long-range development program. The report should contain a brief plan for approaching those prospects who can still be solicited and a report on the volunteers, indicating the assignments they have taken, the assignments they have completed, and the assignments they must finish. It should also include a suggested collections procedure for any outstanding pledges to the campaign, along with a cash flow projection, indicating the amount already received and income projections. It may also provide a list of the named and memorial gift pledges that were recorded during the year.

Another part of this report should be a statistical review of the campaign, listing the annual fund goal, the total subscribed by particular donor groups (corporations, foundations, individuals, the total number of donors), and the number of volunteers involved with the project. In larger and more complex campaigns, there may also be an analysis of the prospects by campaign division. The report should contain an expense summary, showing expense accounts, budget allocations, and expenditures made against budget allocations.

One of the most important parts of the internal final report is a scrapbook that will serve as a visual record of campaign activity. It should be organized chronologically and show how the campaign and all its aspects were built. Early in the preparation for the campaign, the institution should prepare a file folder so that materials can be automatically collected in the scrapbook file as they are generated. The responsibility for preparing the scrapbook is usually assigned to a member of the office staff. It is important to understand that this scrapbook should be compiled as the annual fund year goes along; the materials should not be reconstructed and assembled at the end of the campaign.

Public Document

The second kind of final report is circulated widely to donors, workers, key constituents, and, according to the circumstances, prospective donors and workers as well. If this type of report is used, it can be designed as part of the transition from the current campaign to the next one if the organization is in an annual campaign model or from the capital campaign to the ongoing fundraising effort if that is the case. This report, which can take infinite shapes and formats, should include a list of all donors unless the list of donors is very long. In this case, the organization may opt to list only donors of a certain amount—say, $1,000 or more. It is equally important to consider segregating listings of donors, especially if the campaign has encompassed several separate objectives under a total goal or has been run in several separate divisions and to provide recognition according to the size of the donation. Obviously more attention will be given to donors of $10,000 than to donors of $1,000. Give recognition to key volunteers and workers as well as to donors. A campaign cannot succeed without both groups. The report should also provide an adequate amount of financial detail—amounts pledged and amounts collected—to satisfy donors and volunteers alike that their efforts are providing the benefits that the campaign aimed to provide.

Most organizations routinely publish annual reports. However, there is sometimes a temptation to eliminate this report or eliminate development information and include only financial statements. The rationale is typically that the annual campaign is over, the next campaign is already under way, and the report represents an additional expense that can be avoided. Do not be rationalized out of preparing this report. Whatever the institutional investment required, it assuredly will be returned in full and plentiful measure in the future.

Only the Beginning

The institution may think that the conclusion of its annual campaign marks the conclusion of its intensive work. Actually, its work should just be beginning. The end of the annual campaign is the time for the institution to capitalize on its success and move its development efforts to a new and higher level. It is the time to establish and begin to sustain an ongoing major gifts program. Conducting an assessment to find answers to the important questions just listed is a vital step in this process. Even more vital is taking action once the answers have been obtained.

Even as an institution concludes its current campaign, it is planning the next. The ongoing program to secure annual gifts never ends. The methods and contacts developed must sustain the institution and prepare it for its next annual campaign or special effort. Workers who develop in one campaign are the leaders of the next. They need to be continually developed through active, meaningful, appropriate, and increasingly responsible involvement from the time one effort ends until the next one begins.

Ask volunteers to continue serving. Many will now be ready and able to solicit top gifts, either on a face-to-face basis or through telephone solicitation programs, during the next annual campaign. Find a niche for each one, and use them—or risk losing them, possibly to the organization down the street.

The cultivation of prospects needs to continue, and weaknesses in the annual campaign need to be identified and corrected as part of the continuing development effort. It is also important to maintain the abilities of the staff beyond the current campaign period as the institution looks to the future.

In many cases, as much as 80 percent of the dollar objective will come from 20 percent of the constituency. This fact makes it vitally important that the institution treat its potential and actual donors with extreme care. When a campaign has been successful and celebration is at hand, it is time to begin a new period of cultivating current donors and to continue cultivating the prospective key donors to future annual campaigns. Chances are that the institution will have found new top prospects for continued support because of their gifts to the current campaign. A number of key donors may also have disappointed the institution and will need special attention. What will emerge is a new listing of the top 10 to 20 percent of the institution's constituency, and those prospects are the key to future fundraising success, as well as a major source of future institutional leadership.

How this new list is treated is important. First, it must be acted on, not just drawn up. Second, room must be made in the organization to accommodate these people. It is often hard to effect the succession of leaders or make room for new faces, but it is important that this be done, and that it be done in creative, enthusiastic, energetic ways so as to let everyone, old and new, feel wanted and welcome.

The key is involvement, which begets investment. The secret to involving volunteers and donors, old and new alike, is simple, well known, and timeless: give them something meaningful to do, and earnestly seek their counsel, advice, and support. What is most important is that the institution proactively and systematically go about involving its key donors and volunteers. *Do not leave involvement to chance.* There should always be a place in the organization for someone who is willing to work and who agrees to give. Furthermore, outstanding volunteers will have come to the light during the campaign because of their excellent performance. Do not overlook or forget them. Be certain they are brought into the institution's planning and that they have a voice in its future activities, and make this a certainty as soon as possible. Name them to committees; nominate them for positions on the board. By following through to tie up all the loose ends, the institution will have prepared a neat package for its future activities.

The annual fund is a continuous, forward effort. It is the sustaining lifeblood of virtually every nonprofit organization. It is the base on which all other fundraising activities are built. The wise institution is the one that lays an annual fund foundation strong enough to support its loftiest expectations.

PART TWO

THE ANNUAL FUND RESOURCE GUIDE

RESOURCE GUIDE CONTENTS

Preparing for the Annual Campaign

1. Stanford Law School Direct Appeal Program   207
       FY99 Operating Plan—Initial   208
       FY99 Operating Plan—Third Quarter Assessment   211

2. Annual Fund Solicitation Calendar   215

3. Web Site Examples   219
       Stanford University Web Site—The Stanford Fund   220
       British Columbia Children's Hospital Foundation Web Site   221

Elements of the Annual Campaign

4. Annual Fund–Capital Campaign Combined Strategic Goals
   and Calendar   223
       Strategic Goals for Institutional Advancement, 1999–2003   224
       Outline, Unified Campaign for Institutional Advancement,
           1999–2003   225
       Detail, Unified Campaign for Institutional Advancement,
           1999–2003   226
       Gift Range Chart, Unified Campaign for Institutional
           Advancement, 1999–2003   227

5. Corporate Campaign Plan   229

    The Adventure, Indianapolis Zoological Society Brochure   230

    Indianapolis Zoo Team Member Manual—1999 Corporate
       Campaign   236

6. Corporate Matching Gift Companies   243

    A List of Companies with Matching Gift Programs   244

7. Corporate Matching Gift Guidelines and Application Form   257

The Annual Fund in Action

8. Membership Program with Benefits   265

9. University Annual Fund Analysis   273

    Executive Overview: Sample University Undergraduate
       Annual Giving   274

10. Annual Fund Survey   277

    Lapsed-Donor Survey Letter   278

    Annual Giving Alumni Survey   279

11. Direct Mail Solicitation Package   281

12. Gala Event Invitation and Program   291

    Invitation   292

    Response Card   294

    Courtesy Reply Envelope   295

    Program   296

13. Sales and Raffle Event Promotion   301

14. "A-Thon" Event Packages   305

    Letter to Friends and Family   306

    Donor Form   307

    Letter to Church Friends   308

    Letter to Coworkers   309

    Thank-You Note from Volunteer   310

    Thank-You Note from Organization   311

15. "A-Thon" Team Captain's Kit and Supplies   313

    Team Captain Handbook   315

Team Recruitment Information   316

Sample Corporate Media Release   •   Sample CEO Recruitment Memo   •   Sample Article for Employee Newsletter   •   Sample Recruitment Press Release

Team Planning Information   320

Tour de Cure Team Roster   •   Tour de Cure Team Prize Order Form   •   Sample Team Goal Memo   •   Team Goal Form   •   Welcome Packet Information

Advertising Pieces   331

Poster   •   Brochure

Post-Event Follow-Up   333

Pledge Turn-In Party Poster   •   No-Show Pledge Chase Mailing   •   Thank-You Pledge Chase Mailing

16. Entertainment and Show Publicity Pieces   337

Antique Show Advertisements   338

Amethyst House Comedy Show   340

Poster   •   Program   •   Advertisements   •   Press Clippings   •   Sample Newspaper Article

17. Outing Registration Letter and Materials   349

Registration Letter   350

Registration Form   351

Information Brochure   352

18. Special Events Planning Checklists   355

Room Setup Checklist   356

Equipment Checklist   358

Audiovisual Checklist   360

Catering Checklist   363

Bar Checklist   365

Florist and Decor Checklist   366

Program Checklist   368

Program Participant and VIP Checklist   370

19. Sample Telemarketing Script for Lapsed Donors   375

20. Telemarketing Objection Packet   379

Sample Objection Responses   380

21. Code of Ethics Samples   381

Association of Professional Researchers for Advancement
(APRA) Statement of Ethics   382

Association of Fundraising Professionals (AFP)
Code of Ethical Principles and Standards of Professional
Practice   385

Council for Advancement and Support of Education (CASE)
Mission and Statement of Ethics   388

22. Fundraising Guidebook   391

23. Case Statement Examples   409

The United Way of Central Indiana Brochure   410

The Amethyst House Brochure   416

24. Newsletter Sample   421

25. Gift Receipt Templates   431

Backstreet Missions, Inc.   432

Children's Hospital Foundation, Vancouver   433

American Red Cross—Monroe County Chapter   434

Indiana University Foundation   436

26. Gift Agreement Template   439

27. Post-Campaign Assessment Report   443

Development and Membership Year-End Report
for 1998—Indianapolis Museum of Art   444

Contributions and Membership Activity
Report—December 1998   446

A Recommendation for Corporate Support from the
IMA Corporate Advisory Committee to the IMA Board
of Governors   450

28. Final Report   451

RESOURCE 1

STANFORD LAW SCHOOL
DIRECT APPEAL PROGRAM

FY99 Operating Plan—Initial   208
FY99 Operating Plan—Third Quarter Assessment   211

FY99 Operating Plan—Initial

BACKGROUND

Fiscal year 1997–98 was the first year during the Campaign for Stanford Law School with a focused direct appeal program. An outside consultant firm, Mal Warwick & Associates, was hired to review the direct appeal program and all alumni communications and to recommend a comprehensive direct marketing plan. The plan focused on personalization and an integrated, consistent message with all communications from the Law School, especially in solicitations. Mr. Warwick also suggested using generational segments in mailings, as well as class-based segments.

The ambitious direct marketing plan was not completely realized during the past year. Due to technical limitations, solicitations were not fully segmented using a generational focus, and the high level of direct mail personalization (i.e., past giving and targeted ask amount) was not implemented. These problems should be resolved in the coming year. A true completion and expansion of the direct marketing plan will occur during Year Five and post-Campaign.

GOALS

To involve as many alumni as possible with the Campaign for Stanford Law School via five-year pledges while sustaining continued growth in the Law Fund.

- **Law Fund Dollar Goal: $3.25 million**, an increase of 8% over FY98.
- **Law Fund Participation Goal: 40%.** With an alumni base of approximately 7,447, a 40% participation goal translates into 2,979 donors.

OBJECTIVES

- **Telemarketing Program Pledge Goal: $250,000**, an approximate 14% increase over FY98. With a 70% fulfillment rate, I expect $175,000 in realized donor gifts.
- **Telemarketing Donor Goal: 730**, an approximate 20% donor increase.
- **Direct Mail Program Dollar Goal: $400,000**, an approximate 10% increase.
- **Direct Mail Donor Goal: 1,430**, an approximate 20% increase.

Resource 1

OVERALL STRATEGIES

To create a comprehensive and coordinated effort between the direct mail and telemarketing program. All mailings should be personalized (using name, address, past giving, and specific ask amount) and stamped (first class preferred).

Action Plan

September 1998	Pre-call postcard to renewals & SYBUNTs

October 1998	1999 Reunion mailing #1
	Fall telemarketing begins
	  Renewals (excluding those who gave in June, July, and August)
	  1999 Reunions
	  1998 Reunion wrap-up (calling not to start until after AW98)
	  SYBUNTs
	Telemarketing refusal letters to be mailed on a bi-monthly basis

November 1998	Calendar year-end mailing
	  Renewals
	  1999 Reunion mailing #2
	  1998 Reunions
	  SYBUNTs
	  Severely lapsed
	  Nondonors
	  Friends/Parents
	Telemarketing refusal letters to be mailed on a bimonthly basis

December 1998	Fall telemarketing ends

January 1999	1999 Reunion mailing #3
	Winter telemarketing begins
	  Renewals (including those who gave in June, July, and August)
	  Nondonors
	  1999 Reunions
	  Friends (solicitable only)

	Parents (only donors since the beginning of the campaign) Telemarketing refusal letters to be mailed on a bimonthly basis
February 1999	Telemarketing refusal letters to be mailed on a bimonthly basis

March 1999	Winter telemarketing ends
	Winter mailing
	    LYBUNTs
	    1999 Reunion mailing #4
	    Nondonors

April 1999	Spring telemarketing begins
	    Reminder calls to fall pledges
	    LYBUNTs
	    SYBUNTs and Nondonors
	    1999 Reunions (business phone)
	Telemarketing refusal letters to be mailed on a bimonthly basis

May 1999	Telemarketing refusal letters to be mailed on a bimonthly basis

June 1999	Spring telemarketing ends
	Fiscal year-end mailing
	    LYBUNTS
	    1999 Reunion mailing #5
	    Severely lapsed
	    Nondonors

July 1999	Staff calls to LYBUNTs $1,000+

FY99 Operating Plan—Third Quarter Assessment

Bullet points contain the results, assessments, and recommendations for the direct appeal program. All other text is the original direct appeal operating plan for fiscal year 1999 created in August 1998.

GOALS

To involve as many alumni as possible with the Campaign for Stanford Law School while sustaining continued growth in the Law Fund.

Law Fund Dollar Goal: $3.25 million, an increase of 8% over FY98.

- Progress as of July 15, 1999 has the Law Fund dollars at $2,664,050, or 82.0% of our goal. This is an increase of $134,972 over last fiscal year at this time, which was 84.3% of its FY98 goal.
- We are slightly behind schedule in reaching our $3.25M goal.

Law Fund Participation Goal: 40%. With an alumni base of 7,449, a 40% participation goal translates into 2,980 donors.

- As of July 15, 1999, there are 2,493 donors to the Law Fund, or a 33.5% overall participation rate. This is 83.7% of our FY99 goal. Last year at this time, the Law Fund had 2,304 donors, or a 31.5% overall participation rate, which represented 78.7% of its FY98 goal.
- We are approximately 219 donors, or 7.3%, behind where we should be at this time to reach our 40% participation goal.
- Sources of FY99 Law Fund dollar and participation totals:
  - FY98 Telemarketing gifts = $11,623
  - FY98 Direct Mail gifts
    - 1997 CYE letter = $9,325
    - 1997 AROG = $875
    - Campaign Briefs #5 & #6 = $6,550
    - Lawyer Magazines #52 & #53 = $8,125
  - 1998 Reunion mailing gifts = $68,545

  - FY99 Telemarketing gifts = $175,501
  - FY99 Direct Mail gifts
    - Brochure mailings = $149,355
    - 1998 AROG = $21,425
    - Campaign Brief #7 = $11,975
  - 1999 Reunion mailing gifts = $109,468

OBJECTIVES

Telemarketing Program Pledge Goal: $250,000, an approximate 14% increase over FY98. With a 70% fulfillment rate, $175,000 is expected in realized donor gifts.

- Pledges for the fall, winter, and spring telemarketing quarters total $229,326, or 91.7% of our goal. This is an increase of $42,538 over last year at this time.
- We are slightly behind schedule in reaching our goal of $250,000. The summer telemarketing quarter must generate $20,674 in pledges in order to reach our goal.
- As of July 15, 1999, total realized gifts for FY99 are $175,501. Last year at this time, the Law Fund had total dollars in the door of $140,220, showing an increase of $35,281.
- The success of the telemarketing program thus far is due to several factors:
  1. A pre-call postcard mailed in November 1998, giving advance notice to alumni that they would be receiving a phone call from a student caller before the end of the calendar year.
  2. A comprehensive training session for the student callers, which includes listening to the dean or law student speak about the Law School, providing the student callers with a chance to see the School and some of its facilities, and including tips for handling Law School alumni and their objections to giving.
  3. Efficient and talented student callers who know the needs of the Law School and can articulate them clearly to alumni. Also, many of our students are now experienced callers who have called Law School alumni for at least one quarter.

- The spring quarter has poor results for a couple of reasons:
  1. The student callers had difficulty reaching prospects at home; there were a lot of "no answer" results.
  2. Most of the Law renewals were contacted during the fall and winter quarters; this is very different from what happened last fiscal year, when most renewals were contacted during the spring quarter.

Telemarketing Donor Goal: 730, an approximate 20% donor increase.

- As of July 15, 1999, the number of donors this fiscal year through the telemarketing program is 685, or 12.4% of the telemarketing population. This is an increase from last year at this time, which had 642 donors, or 12.0% of the telemarketing population.

Direct Mail Program Dollar Goal: $400,000, an approximate 10% increase.

Direct Mail Donor Goal: 1,430, an approximate 20% increase.

Direct Mail Solicitation Pieces

- As of July 15, 1999, the brochure mailings have generated the following gifts:
  CYE brochure (December 1998): $123,530 from 249 donors
  Spring brochure (March 1999): $21,520 from 51 donors
  FYE brochure (June 1999): $4,305 from 20 donors
- Last year at this time, the calendar year–end solicitation resulted in $118,182. Unfortunately, there are no records of a spring or fiscal year–end mailing last year, so comparisons are not possible. However, the brochure mailings have been successful because they have generated strong dollar figures, and they also have attracted 40 alumni to give who had never given to the Law School previously.

1999 Reunion Mailings

- Mailing #1 (December 1998): As of July 15, 1999, the first Reunion mailing has resulted in gifts totaling $36,750 from 64 donors. This is an increase from last year's Reunion mailing at this time, which generated $34,610 from 54 donors.
- Mailing #2 (February 1999): As of July 15, 1999, the second Reunion mailing has resulted in gifts totaling $38,805 from 43 donors. This is an increase from last year's Reunion mailing at this time, which generated $20,791 from 63 donors.
- Mailing #3 (April 1999): As of July 15, 1999, the third Reunion mailing has resulted in gifts totaling $23,688 from 44 donors. This is an increase from last year's Reunion mailing at this time, which generated $20,925 from 53 donors.
- Mailing #4 (June 1999): As of July 15, 1999, the fourth Reunion mailing has resulted in gifts totaling $10,225 from 21 donors. This is an increase from last year's Reunion mailing at this time, which generated $5,705 from 26 donors.

OVERALL STRATEGIES

To create a comprehensive and coordinated effort between the direct mail and telemarketing program.

- The third quarter continued to maintain strong cohesion between direct mail and telemarketing. For example, the scripting for the 1999 Reunion telemarketing population referenced the most recent letter that had been mailed to classmates and included updated news about *Celebration '99.*

Have three brochure mailings with one unified message of student needs and the importance of receiving gifts regardless of size.

- This has been accomplished to date with the wonderful assistance of the designer and writer we hired in September 1998.
- The final brochure mailing dropped on its own with no other publications mailed in the same time frame, thereby maintaining its effectiveness.

Have all Reunion mailings be personalized (using name, address, past giving, and specific ask amount) and stamped (first class preferred).

- The Reunion mailings have been personalized using the individual's name and address. There has not been a discussion about the integration of past giving and specific ask amounts in the letters, in part because it took a significant amount of time to coordinate the personalizing process internally and also externally with the mailing house. In addition, only one of the Reunion letters has a primary gift message; the remaining letters focus more on the social side of the Reunion weekend with only a few brief words about giving to the Law School. This is a topic that should be discussed with the Director of Reunion Giving in the coming months.
- A huge success with the Reunion mailings was personalizing the letters with salutations. An alumnus now receives a letter about his Reunion with his address at the top and his first name or nickname as the salutation. This was achieved through fantastic teamwork between Reunion staff people, the Reunion chairs, stewardship, and postgrads.
- All Reunion letters have been mailed stamped first-class and will continue to be done in that manner. A topic that will need to be discussed with the Director of Reunion Giving and the Director of Alumni Relations is the cost of each Reunion mailing. As the process has become more refined and sophisticated, the incremental cost has slowly increased. It must be determined what parts of the process are most effective, both in terms of cost and outreach to alumni.

RESOURCE 2

ANNUAL FUND SOLICITATION CALENDAR

United Way of Central Indiana
Resource Development Division

2000 Annual Campaign
Proposed Master Calendar

Month	Activity or Event	Date
January	Campaign Planning Meeting: Cabinet Structure and Volunteer Identification	Thursday, 1/6, 3:30–4:30, Parkwood 4
	Recruitment of Campaign Cabinet	Complete 1/31
February	Campaign Cabinet Meeting: Presentation and Discussion of Campaign Strategy Plans	Friday, 2/4, 3:30–5:00 P.M., UWCI
	UWCI Board Meeting	2/16
	Calls on Strategically Selected Individuals or New Business Prospects	Ongoing
March	Campaign Team Meetings	2/28–3/3
	Meeting of Metro 1-C Chairs (Baltimore)	3/9, 10
	Joint Campaign Cabinet and Team Meeting: Campaign strategies, time frames and desired outcomes	Wednesday, 3/21, 7:30–8:30 A.M., UWCI
	Calls on Strategically Selected Individuals or New Business Prospects	Ongoing
	United Way Annual Meeting	3/23, 12 Noon, Indiana Roof
April	CEO Call Planning Meeting	Tuesday, 4/4, Parkwood 4, 3:30–4:00 P.M.
	Calls on Strategically Selected Individuals or CEOs	Ongoing
	Campaign Team Meetings	4/3–7

Resource 2

	Leadership Giving Council I Orientation Meeting	4/15
	Youth Day of Caring	4/15, 16
May	Campaign Cabinet Meeting: Progress reports from all teams: volunteer recruitment and company calls	Wednesday, 5/23, 7:30–8:30 A.M., Goodwill Industries
	Calls on Strategically Selected Individuals or CEOs	Ongoing
June	Alexis de Tocqueville Reception POSTPONED	6/4
	Leadership Giving Council I Results Meeting	6/15
	Wine, Art, and Roses CANCELLED	6/25
	Calls on Strategically Selected Individuals or CEOs	Ongoing
	Campaign Team Meetings	6/19–23
	UWCI Executive Committee: Goal discussion	Wednesday, June 28, 7:30 a.m., UWCI
	Campaign Cabinet: Establish recommended goal	Thursday, June 29, 7:30 a.m., TBA
July	Pacesetter Kickoff	Wednesday, July 12, 12 noon, Colts Complex
	Present Proposed Goal to UWCI Board	Wednesday, July 26, 4:00 P.M., UWCI
August	Loaned Associates Welcome Reception	Wednesday, August 9, 5:00–6:30 P.M., Location TBA
	Campaign Kickoff & Cabinet Meeting	Wednesday, August 30, Meeting 3:00 P.M., Kickoff 4:00 P.M., Location TBA

Resource 2

September	Leadership Giving Council II Orientation Meeting	9/1
	Day of Caring	9/15, 16
	Campaign Team Meetings	9/4–8
October	Campaign Cabinet: Mid-campaign progress reports	Wednesday, October 11, 7:30–8:30 A.M., Location TBA
	UWCI Board Meeting	10/18
	Campaign Team Meetings	10/2–6
November	Final Campaign Team Meetings	11/13–15
	Leadership Giving Council II Results Meeting	11/15
	Campaign Cabinet Meeting: Final push activities	Thursday, 11/16, 9:00–10:00 a.M.
	Final Staff Projections	11/20
	Meeting of Board Chair, Campaign Chair, President, VP, and Campaign Director to approve final projection	Tuesday, 11/28, 9:00 a.m., UWCI
	Final Campaign Cabinet Meeting: Final Projected Total Announcement; Reception to follow	Wednesday, 11/29, Meeting 3:00 P.M., Reception 3:30 P.M.
December	Chair's Final Summary Report to UWCI Board	Wednesday, 12/13, 4:00 p.m., UWCI

Resource 2

RESOURCE 3

WEB SITE EXAMPLES

Stanford University Web Site—The Stanford Fund   220
British Columbia Children's Hospital Foundation Web Site   221

Stanford University Web Site—The Stanford Fund

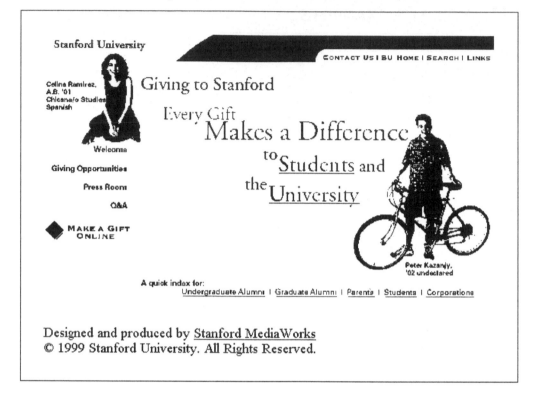

British Columbia Children's Hospital Foundation Web Site

helpingkidsvictoria.org

THE VICTORIA COMMUNITY FOR BC'S CHILDREN'S HOSPITAL

British Columbia's
Children's Hospital
FOUNDATION • Victoria

Established in 1982, **B.C.'s Children's Hospital Foundation** (link to BCCH FOUNDATION) is responsible for raising funds to support initiatives at **BC's Children's Hospital** (link to BCCH) that do not receive government funding such as research, education and equipment. Like the children cared for at Children's Hospital, the province is growing in leaps and bounds. That growth means an increasing demand for the very best child health care, making children's Hospital need for support greater with each passing year.

Through a wide range of **fundraising events and activities** (link to Victoria's Comm. fundraising activities page), Children's Hospital Foundation encourages members of the community to support the work that the foundation does. Every contribution goes directly toward helping provide the best care possible for children. At Children's Hospital, we are fortunate to have a global community that goes beyond medicine and academics; our global partners provide the special support we receive to make our work possible.

ANNUAL FUND–CAPITAL CAMPAIGN COMBINED STRATEGIC GOALS AND CALENDAR

Resource 4

Strategic Goals for Institutional Advancement, 1999–2003   224
Outline, Unified Campaign for Institutional Advancement, 1999–2003   225
Detail, Unified Campaign for Institutional Advancement, 1999–2003   226
Gift Range Chart, Unified Campaign for Institutional Advancement,
      1999–2003   227

Strategic Goals for Institutional Advancement, 1999–2003

Mission

To provide recreational learning experiences for the citizens of Indiana through the exhibition and presentation of natural environments in a way to foster a sense of discovery, stewardship and the need to preserve the Earth's plants and animals.

Goal

To provide adequate human and financial resources to support the organizational mission—this goal to be accomplished through a stabilization of resources strategy while continuing to position the Society for future growth.

Fundraising Goal

To merge all fundraising efforts of the organization into a unified strategy. Focus will be on raising capital and endowment funds ($69 million) while continuing effective growth of operational support ($16 million and 10,000 new donors).

Resource 4

Outline, Unified Campaign for Institutional Advancement, 1999–2003

Goal	Fundraising Goal	Fundraising Objectives
To provide adequate human and financial resources to support the organizational mission—this goal to be accomplished through a stabilization of resources strategy while continuing to position the Society for future growth.	To merge all fundraising efforts of the organization into a unified strategy. Focus will be on raising capital and endowment funds ($69 million) while continuing effective growth of operational support ($16 million and 10,000 new donors).	*Year 1(a):* Conduct campaign feasibility research. Launch 100,000 piece donor acquisition test mailing. *Year 1(b):* Secure lead gifts of $40 million for campaign. Mail 300,000 letters to recruit 2,000 new donors. *Year 2:* Secure $25 million in additional leadership or major gifts. Mail 500,000 to recruit 4,000 new donors. *Year 3:* Secure $15.25 million in major and mid-level gifts. Mail 1 million letters to recruit 6,000 new donors. *Year 4:* Launch public campaign for last $4.75 million. Mail 600,000 letters to recruit 4,000 new donors lost to attrition. *Year 5:* Reach campaign goal. Mail appropriate lapsed and acquisition pieces to revitalize and access new donors lost to attrition.

Detail, Unified Campaign for Institutional Advancement, 1999–2003

Fundraising Goal[a]	Deadline
Subdivide projects and units available	Jan. 15, 1999
Completion of gift range charts	Jan. 15, 1999
Establish feasibility of plan and structure	Jan. 19, 1999
Identify staff impact and responsibility	Jan. 19, 1999
Identify leadership	Feb. 15, 1999
Committee development	Feb. 15, 1999
Completion of cash flow projections	Feb. 15, 1999
Development of theme and campaign materials	Mar. 15, 1999
Development of recognition opportunities	Mar. 31, 1999
Development of reporting procedures	Mar. 31, 1999
Development of event strategies and activities	Mar. 31, 1999
Committee and solicitation training	Apr. 15, 1999
Kickoff—board	Apr. 30, 1999
Kickoff—staff	May 30, 1999
Kickoff—leadership gifts	June 15, 1999
Solicitation of resources	Apr. 1999–Dec. 2002
Recognition begins	Aug. 1, 1999
Campaign celebration activities	Oct. (each year)
Annual review process	Dec. (each year)

Note: [a]Staff responsible and project status would ordinarily be indicated for each activity as the campaign progresses.

Gift Range Chart, Unified Campaign for Institutional Advancement, 1999–2003

Range	Number of Gifts	Number of Prospects	Total per Range
$20,000,000	1	5:1 = 5	$20,000,000
$10,000,000	2	5:1 = 5	$20,000,000
$5,000,000	2	5:1 = 5	$10,000,000
$2,500,000	2	5:1 = 5	$5,000,000
$1,000,000	10	4:1 = 40	$10,000,000
$500,000	10	4:1 = 40	$5,000,000
$250,000	10	4:1 = 40	$2,500,000
$100,000	40	3:1 = 120	$4,000,000
$50,000	50	3:1 = 155	$2,500,000
$25,000	50	3:1 = 150	$1,250,000
$10,000	150	2:1 = 300	$1,500,000
$5,000	250	2:1 = 500	$1,250,000
$2,500	350	2:1 = 700	$875,000
$1,000	500	2:1 = 500	$500,000
Under $1,000	2,500	2:1 = 5,000	$575,000
Totals	3,927	7,560	$85,000,000

RESOURCE 5

CORPORATE CAMPAIGN PLAN

The Adventure, Indianapolis Zoological Society Brochure   230
Indianapolis Zoo Team Member Manual—1999 Corporate Campaign   236

Resource 5

The Adventure, Indianapolis Zoological Society Brochure

[front]

The mission of the
Indianapolis Zoological Society, Inc.,
is to provide recreational learning
experiences for the citizens of Indiana
through the exhibition and presentation of
natural environments in a way that fosters
a sense of discovery, stewardship, and the
need to preserve the earth's
plants and animals.

INDIANAPOLIS
ZOOLOGICAL
SOCIETY

1200 W. Washington St., P.O. Box 22309
Indianapolis, IN 46222-0309
(317) 630-2001 Fax (317) 630-5153

[back]

Corporate Partner Program

The Indianapolis Zoological Society, Inc., relies on the corporate community of Indiana to achieve and further its mission of connecting animals, plants and people. As one of only two percent of zoos in the country that receives no state tax support, the Indianapolis Zoo and White River Gardens must depend on support for general operating funds from corporations like yours that are committed to making Indiana a better place to live, work and raise a family.

Involvement of the corporate community is extremely important to the Indianapolis Zoological Society. Your help enables us to provide unique recreational learning experiences for our visitors. Corporate gifts allow us to serve more than 1,000,000 visitors annually, including over 150,000 school children, through educational programs, distance learning, camps, lectures and other related activities.

With the help of corporations, our institution has reached many milestones since opening in White River State Park in 1988. The Indianapolis Zoo has grown into a world-renowned facility that was the first to be accredited as a zoo, an aquarium and a botanical garden. It is home to almost 4,000 animals, including 16 species that are endangered and six that are threatened. Because of corporate support, we can be involved in remarkable conservation programs and a number of ongoing research projects.

This is your opportunity to enable the Indianapolis Zoological Society to continue its success. One way to develop a partnership with our institution is to give to the annual Corporate Campaign. Contributions to the campaign help with the general day-to-day operating expenses of running the institution, including the care and feeding of animals, upkeep of the facilities, utility expenses and all of the exciting programming mentioned above.

Benefits exist for corporations seeking more opportunities. There are many ways to become involved through underwriting of special exhibits or educational projects, or by giving gifts-in-kind. Benefits for corporate underwriters are determined on a project-by-project basis.

Join the pride by becoming a corporate partner with the Indianapolis Zoological Society, Inc., today.

Resource 5

Corporate Partner Program

CORPORATE CAMPAIGN BENEFITS TABLE

	Amigo ($35–$74)	Amigo + ($75–$249)	Associate ($250–$499)	Contributor ($500–$999)	Subscriber ($1,000–$2,499)	Patron ($2,500–$4,999)	Benefactor ($5,000–$9,999)	Partner ($10,000 +)
Special Animal/Plant Choices	X	X	X	X	X	X	X	X
Animal/Plant Fact Sheet	X	X	X	X	X	X	X	X
Certificates	X	X	X	X	X	X	X	X
Newsletter	X	X	X	X	X	X	X	X
Photo of Animal/Plant		X	X	X	X	X	X	X
Quarterly Zoosletter			X	X	X	X	X	X
Listing in Annual Report			X	X	X	X	X	X
$10 Zoo/$5 Gardens Membership Discount for Employees				X	X	X	X	X
Admission Tickets			10	20	30	50	75	100
Company Name on Honor Roll List on Grounds (1 year)				X	X	X	X	X
Special Invitations					X	X	X	X
Acknowledgment at Zoo Entrance Throughout the Year					X	X	X	X
Lowell Nussbaum Society Acknowledgment/Invitations						X	X	X
Plaque/Plate						X	X	X

Corporate Campaign

Corporate Underwriter

Animals

ENCOUNTERS

Giant Cockroach
Cow
Sicilian Donkey
African Pygmy Goat
Red-Tailed Hawk
Norwegian Fjord Horse
Percheron Horse
Llama
Screech Owl
Reindeer
Sheep
Yak

DESERTS

Egyptian Spiny-Tailed Agama
Starred Agama
Diamond Dove
Cuban Ground Iguana
Desert Iguana
Rhinoceros Iguana
Great Plated Lizard
Haitian Curly-Tailed Lizard
Jeweled Curly-Tailed Lizard
Yellow-Throated Plated Lizard
Aldabra Tortoise
Desert Tortoise
Ricord's Iguana

FORESTS

American Bald Eagle
Chilean Flamingo
White-Handed Gibbon
Kodiak Bear
Spectacled Langur
Collared Lemur
Ring-Tailed Lemur

Pygmy Marmoset
Reeves Muntjac
Asian Small-Clawed Otter
Red Panda
Raven
Black-Necked Swan
Golden Lion Tamarin
Amur (Siberian) Tiger

WATERS

Anaconda
Anemone
Polar Bear
Emerald Tree Boa
Clownfish
Cuttlefish
Dolphin
Electric Eel
Green Moray Eel
Queen Angel Fish
Scarlet Ibis
Giant Sea Bass
Pacific Giant Octopus
King Penguin
Rockhopper Penguin
Piranha
Puffin
Harbor Seal
California Sea Lion
Black-Tipped Reef Shark
Podocnemis Turtle
Walrus

PLAINS

Topi Antelope
Guinea Baboon
Salmon-Crested Cockatoo
East African Crowned Crane
African Wild Dogs

White-Faced Whistling Duck
African Elephant
Thomson's Gazelle
Reticulated Giraffe
Red Kangaroo
African Lion
Blue-Neck Ostrich
Princess Parrot
European White Stork
Maribou Stork
Black Swan
Bennett's Wallaby
Tammar (Dama) Wallaby
Zebra

Plants

TREES

Persimmon Tree
Fringetree
English Oak
Yellowwood
Princeton Sentry Ginkgo
Japanese Larch
Kentucky Coffeetree
Golden Raintree

SHRUBS & PLANTS

Bottle Brush Buckeye
Long Stalk Holly
Elderberry
Lily
Clematis/Vines
Ornamental Grasses
Ferns

FLOWERS

Summer Annuals
Fall Bulbs

Pledge Card
[front]

_____

Company Name (as you wish to be recognized)

_____

Contact Person   Title

_____

Address

_____

City, State, ZIP

_____

Phone

_____

E-Mail Address

Your investment today supports the Society's mission
of connecting animals, plants and people!

Donor Category		**Contribution**
Partner	$10,000 or more	$_____
Benefactor	$5,000–$9,999	$_____
Patron	$2,500–$4,999	$_____
Subscriber	$1,000–$2,499	$_____
Contributor	$500–$999	$_____
Associate	$250–$499	$_____
Amigo +	$75–$249	$_____
Amigo	$35–$74	$_____
Other		$_____

Animal/Plant we would like to
support _____

Signature _____

Date _____

Resource 5

Pledge Card [back]

IZS
INDIANAPOLIS
ZOOLOGICAL
SOCIETY

☐ Yes! We are pleased to make a pledge to the Corporate Campaign. Please invoice on (date) _____ .

☐ Yes! Please send additional information on membership discounts for my employees.

Contact name _____

☐ We are interested in additional underwriting and/or in-kind opportunities.

Contact name _____

Please make checks payable to The Indianapolis Zoological Society, P.O. Box 22309, Indianapolis, IN 46222-0309. The Indianapolis Zoological Society is a not-for-profit corporation exempt from law under the IRS code 501(c)(3).

☐ No, we do not wish to accept tickets. We want to enjoy the total tax benefit of our contribution.

☐ Yes, we wish to order the maximum number of tickets allowed for our giving level.

☐ Yes, we do wish to receive tickets. However, please send only _____ (number) tickets for our use _____ Zoo Tickets or _____ White River Gardens Tickets

Tax information effective January 1, 1994: IRS legislation requires donors to deduct the retail value of all benefits received by charitable organizations. Effective January 1, 1998, each ticket received as a benefit for a corporate contribution is valued at $9.75, the price of regular admission to the Zoo, or $6.00, the regular price of admission to the White River Gardens. The Society will note the tax-deductible portion of your gift on your receipt.

For more information, please contact Kim Luppino at (317) 630-2018 or kluppino@mail.indyzoo.com

Indianapolis Zoo Team Member Manual—
1999 Corporate Campaign

The Indianapolis Zoo Corporate Campaign will celebrate its 23rd year in 1999. Through the years, this fund raising effort has grown to be one of the largest and most successful in the city. In 1998, 153 corporate volunteers representing 15 corporations participated in the corporate campaign.

Themes and Goals from the Past

Year	Theme	Goal	Funds Raised
1988	White River Zoolympics	$75,000	$101,715
1989	The Great Cetacean Race	$150,000	$158,395
1990	Desert Trek Checks	$175,000	$178,000
1991	Zooming for Corporate Sponsors	$190,000	$180,000
1992	On a Zoofari for Corporate Sponsors	$205,000	$231,000
1993	Call for the Wild	$210,000	$188,000
1994	A Koala-fied Corporate Campaign	$210,000	$250,000
1995	Exploration of the Wild	$260,000	$275,000
1996	Invest in the Pride	$300,000	$304,000
1997	Exhibit A-Mazing Pride	$310,000	$235,630
1998	Growing Together	$230,000	$195,000+
1999	**The Adventure Continues . . .**	**$205,000**	

1999 Corporate Campaign Time Line

August 12, 1998	Campaign Committee Meeting
September 2, 1998	Campaign Committee/Captain Meeting
September 11, 1998	Fall C-Vol letter to mail
November 12, 1998	First Captain's Meeting at 8:00 A.M.
December 1, 1998	Prospect Selection Forms Due
December 1, 1998	Training Session #1 at the Zoo at 3:00 P.M.
December 9, 1998	Training Session #2 at the Zoo at 3:00 P.M.
January 7, 1999	Training Session #3 at the Zoo at 3:00 P.M.
January 11, 1999	January C-Vol letter to mail
January 13, 1999	Kickoff Party at 5:30 P.M. at the Zoo. Kickoff vols may begin calls on January 25

Resource 5

February 10, 1999	First Captain's Reporting Meeting at 8:00 A.M.
March 31, 1999	Second Captain's Reporting Meeting at 8:00 A.M.
March 31, 1999	End 1st phase Corporate Campaign
March 31, 1999	<u>All Completed Action Call Sheets are due by 5:00 P.M.</u> (send copies of incomplete call sheets to Corporate Development Coordinator)
April 5, 1999	Spring C-Vol letter to mail
July 5, 1999	Summer C-Vol letter to mail
August 31, 1999	Follow-up Captain's Meeting at 8:00 a.m.
September 1, 1999	Follow-up/Fall C-Vol letter to mail (this is also the "Put us in Your Budget for 2000" letter)
September 8, 1999	Follow-up begins—follow-up vols may start calls
November 1, 1999	Final Captain's Reporting Meeting at 8:00 A.M. New captains for 2000 also invited. <u>All call sheets are due by 5:00 P.M.</u>
November 17, 1999	Victory Party—River Room at White River Gardens

1999 Corporate Campaign Committee

[Identify committee members by function: chair; vice-chairs for such things as special events, team recruitment, follow-up campaign, and operations; and staff contacts.]

Introduction

Your time and involvement as a corporate volunteer are truly appreciated. This notebook contains the following information you will want to know about the 1999 Corporate Campaign:

 I. Campaign Outline and Schedule
    A. Mechanics of the Campaign
    B. Theme
    C. Goal
    D. Case for Support
 II. Scoring Information
    A. The Point System
    B. How to Earn Points
    C. How Points Are Calculated
 III. Sample Prospect Data Form

I. Mechanics of the Campaign

Step-by-Step Process

1. Team members select companies they would prefer to contact (preferences due at zoo December 15).
2. Put-us-in-your-budget letter mailed in September and the Pre-sell letter will mail in January to all 1998 donors, lapsed donors, and prospects. If we receive donations in the mail, we will notify the team member assigned to that company.
3. Each team member contacts at least eight (8) assigned companies. We will assign new companies according to the team member's preference list as much as possible.
   - Team members may also select additional calls, either new or renewals.
   - **Captains are to insure that all assigned renewals from last year's campaign are contacted.**
   - Prior to contacting any companies not assigned, please clear any additional assignment(s) with the zoo to avoid duplication of effort.
4. Team members should study the corporate call sheets *before* making the call. A sample copy of a call sheet is included in this notebook. Each call sheet will contain all contact information needed.
5. Team members write notes or telephone prospects immediately and make appointments to see them personally if necessary.
6. Team members record details of phone calls or appointments on call sheets.
7. Team members get reports to captains on time (prior to the report due dates).
8. Second or third calls made as necessary—keep captains informed. Continue to record details on call sheets.
9. The zoo and follow-up team members will coordinate all follow-up work; (e.g. invoicing, calling later in year). **Be sure to document all new information on the call sheets** so that the information can be added to the zoo's database for next year's campaign.
10. Team members and team captains attend the Victory Party on November 17, 1999—at White River Gardens—River House. Festivities, food, drink, prizes, and awards.

Theme

The theme for 1999 is: "The Adventure Continues . . ." Our theme was chosen by the Institutional Advancement Department at the Zoological Society from many suggestions provided by zoo staff members. This theme represents the continuing growth of the institution and lets prospects know that new things are happening. We are no longer the Indianapolis Zoo but the Indianapolis Zoological

Society, Inc.—which houses the Indianapolis Zoo, the White River Gardens, and the future Indiana State Aquarium. This theme also highlights and continues the "Passport to Adventure" title given to the 1997 Society annual report.

Goal
The 1998 Corporate Campaign goal was set at $230,000. The 1999 goal has been set at $205,000. This will be generated from new corporate support, corporate renewals, and miscellaneous corporate gifts. Companies may wish to provide gifts or services in kind to the zoo (free advertising, printing, etc.). Contact the Corporate Development Coordinator if a company expresses an interest. Please do not ask for or accept an in-kind gift unless you have coordinated it with the zoo.

The Case for Support
1. The Indianapolis Zoo receives *no direct tax support* from any city, state, or federal sources; it is supported entirely by private funds. Over 50% of the operating budget is provided by earned income through admissions and concessions. The remainder comes from contributions of individuals, businesses, and foundations. All money raised by the corporate campaign helps fund general operating expenses.
2. The Indianapolis Zoo draws nearly 900,000 visitors each year and serves as a magnet for tourist dollars. On a national basis, more people visit zoos every year than attend all professional baseball, football, basketball, and hockey games combined.
3. More than 90% of the zoo's income is returned to the community through payroll, purchased goods, and services.
4. The zoo is a 501(c)(3) corporation, and contributions to the Indianapolis Zoo are tax deductible as allowed by law.

II. Scoring

How Are Points Awarded?
Each year all teams compete for the prestigious "Lion's Pride" and "Golden Cub" trophies by accumulating the most points. Congratulations to the 1998 winners: AON Risk ("Golden Cub") and Eli Lilly and Company ("Lion's Pride"). This year the scoring will be based on three categories:

- Team participation
- Dollars raised
- Information obtained

We encourage each team to actively participate in the meetings and parties, which will make the campaign fun for all. The kickoff party provides you with the opportunity to meet other teams and some of the zoo staff. You won't want to miss the victory party, where you and your teammates will enjoy your success! Individuals will receive awards and prizes based on their own efforts.

How Do I Earn Team Points?

By attending all the meetings, parties, and the team orientation, you will help earn your team points toward the first awards! Here's how:

Attend the team orientation	10 points per person
Attend the January 13 Kickoff Party	10 points per person
Raise $2,000—your individual goal	10 points per person
Have written or verbal contact with the decision maker of a company	1 point per company contacted

Captain's Role

Attend Team Captain Meetings on 9/2/98, 2/10/99, 3/31/99, 8/31/99, 11/1/99	10 points each
Return initial prospect selection forms to the zoo on 12/1/98 by 5:00 P.M.	5 points
Return all first-phase reports to the zoo on 3/1/99 by 5:00 P.M.	5 points
Raise $2,000—help lead your team to success!	10 points

Points will be awarded only if team members turn in reports on ALL contacts assigned to them. A corporate gift may be given during the duration of the campaign or pledged for later payment. However, a pledge card signed by the appropriate corporate contact must be submitted for points to be awarded.

How Are Points Calculated?

1. After the points you earn for participation are calculated, they are added to the points awarded for dollars raised.
2. Each team goal for dollars raised for the zoo is based on the number of team members times $2,000 (including team captains).

   Example: 5 members x $2,000 = $10,000 team goal!

3. When your team goal is reached, you earn 100 points; you can earn additional points when you raise more than your goal.

> Example 1: $10,000 goal
>
> $11,250 total dollars raised
>
> 100 points awarded for reaching the $10,000 goal
>
> 13 additional points earned ($1,250 over goal = 12.5%)
>
> Take the % over goal; this is equivalent to your additional points.

> Example 2: $8,000 goal
>
> $7,250 total dollars raised
>
> Your team earns points for the % of the goal reached or 91% = 91 points.

4. Bonus points are awarded for new gifts: 10 points (regardless of the amount)
5. Bonus points are awarded for increased gifts: 5 points (regardless of the amount)
6. Bonus points are awarded for renewals: 3 points (regardless of the amount)
7. Bonus points are awarded for obtaining the name of the human resource director of each company contacted for a gift for the zoo: 2 points
8. Bonus points are awarded for obtaining the name of the president/owner/CEO (whichever is appropriate) of each company contacted for a gift to the zoo: 2 points
9. Bonus points are awarded for adding new companies to the zoo's prospect list: 2 points

Traditional Prizes
- Lion's Pride Award—First place, based on most team points earned by a company with 200 or more employees
- Golden Cub Award—First place, based on the most team points earned by a small business (200 or less employees)
- Second- and third-place teams based on team points earned
- Outstanding Team Award—The team who shows the most enthusiastic and total team effort (campaign committee will vote)
- Team Member of the Year Award—The volunteer who raises the most dollars
- Rookie of the Year Award—The first-year volunteer who raises the most dollars
- Courageous Cub Award—The volunteer who contacts the most corporations
- Volunteer of the Year Award—Team captains submit names to the Corporate Development Coordinator (campaign committee will vote)

Individual prizes
- Elephant paintings
- Others to be announced!

Team Prizes
- First-, second-, and third-place teams will receive special behind-the-scenes opportunities.

GOOD LUCK!
SEE YOU AT THE VICTORY PARTY!

RESOURCE 6

CORPORATE MATCHING GIFT COMPANIES

A List of Companies with Matching Gift Programs   244

A List of Companies with Matching Gift Programs

Abbott Laboratories
ABC, Inc
ACF Industries, Inc.
Acuson
Adams Harkness & Hill, Inc.
Addison Wesley Longman
Adobe Systems, Inc.
Advanced Micro Devices
AEGON USA Inc.
Aetna Inc.
AG Communication Systems
Air Products and Chemicals
Alabama Power Co.
Albany International Corp.
Albemarle Corp.
Alberta Energy Co., Ltd.
Albertson's Inc.
Alcan Aluminum Corp.
Alexander & Baldwin, Inc.
Alexander Hass Martin & Partners
Allegheny Ludlum Corp.
Allegiance Corp. and Baxter International
Allegro MicroSystems W.G. Inc.
Allendale Mutual Insurance Co.
Alliance Capital Management, LP
Alliant Techsystems
AlliedSignal Inc.
Allstate Corp.
Aluminum Co. of America
Amcast Industrial Corp.
Amerada Hess Corp.
American Electric Power
American Express Co.
American General Corp.
American Home Products
American Honda Motor Co. Inc.
American International Group Inc.

American Investment Advisory Service
American National Bank
American National Bank & Trust Co. of
    Chicago
American National Can Co.
American Optical Corp.
American Standard Inc.
American States Insurance Co.
American Stock Exchange
American United Life Insurance Co.
Ameritech Corp.
Amerus Group
Amgen Inc.
AMP Inc.
AmSouth BanCorp.
AMSTED Industries Inc.
Anadarko Petroleum Corp.
Analog Devices Inc.
Anchor/Russell Capital Advisors Inc.
Andersen Consulting, LLP
Andersons Inc.
Anheuser-Busch Cos. Inc.
Aon Corp.
Appleton Papers Inc.
Aqua Alliance Inc.
Aquarion Co.
ARAMARK Corp.
Archer Daniels Midland
ARCO
Argonaut Group Inc.
Aristech Chemical Corp.
Aristokraft Inc.
Arkwright Mutual Insurance Co.
Armco Inc.
Armstrong World Industries Inc.
Armtek Corp.
Arrow Electronics Inc.

Arthur Andersen, LLP

Ashland Inc.

Aspect Telecommunications

Associates Corp. of North America

Astra Merck Inc.

AT & T

Atlantic City Electric Co.

Augat Inc.

Autodesk Inc.

Automatic Data Processing Inc.

Avon Products Inc.

Axel Johnson Inc.

Ball Corp.

Baltimore Gas & Electric Co.

Bancroft-Whitney

Bank of America Corp.

Bank of California, NA

Bank of Montreal

Bank of New York

Bank One, NA

Bank South Corp.

BankBoston

Bankers Life and Casualty

Bankers Trust Co.

Banta Corp. Foundation Inc.

Barber-Colman Co.

Barclays Capital Inc.

C.R. Bard Inc.

Barnes Group Inc.

Barnett Associates Inc.

Barrett Technology Inc./
   Barrett Communications Inc.

BASF Corp.

Bass, Berry & Sims, PLC

Bay Networks

Bechtel Group Inc.

Becton Dickinson and Co.

Belden Wire and Cable Co.

Bell Atlantic Corp.

BellSouth

Bemis Co. Inc.

Bergen Record Corp.

L.M. Berry and Co.

Bestfoods

Bethlehem Steel Corp.

BF Goodrich Co.

BHP Minerals International Inc.

Binney & Smith Inc.

Bituminous Casualty Corp.

Black & Decker Corp.

Blount Foundation Inc.

Blue Bell Inc.

BMC Industries Inc.

BOC Group Inc.

Boeing Co.

Bonneville International Corp.

Borden Family of Cos.

Boston Edison Co.

Boston Gear

Boston Mutual Life Insurance Co.

Bowater Inc.

BP Amoco Corp.

Bridgestone/Firestone Inc.

Bristol-Myers Squibb Co.

Bronco Wine Co.

Brooklyn Union

Brown & Williamson Tobacco Corp.

Brown Group Inc.

Brown-Forman Corp.

BTR Sealing Systems Group

Buell Industries Inc.

Buffalo Color Corp.

Burlington Industries Inc.

Burlington Northern Santa Fe Corp.

Burlington Resources

Business & Legal Reports Inc.

Butler Manufacturing Co.

Cabot Corp.

Cadence Design Systems Inc.

Calex Manufacturing Co. Inc.

CambridgeSoft
Campbell Soup Foundation
Canadian Pacific Railway
Capital Group Inc.
Capital One Services Inc.
Carolina Power & Light Co.
Carpenter Technology Corp.
Carson Products Co.
Carter-Wallace Inc.
Castrol North America
Caterpillar Inc.
CBI
CBS Foundation Inc.
Central and South West Corp.
Central Illinois Light Co.
Certain Teed Corp.
Chamberlain Manufacturing Corp.
Champion International Corp.
Charles River Laboratories Inc.
Chase Manhattan Corp.
ChemFirst Inc.
Chesapeake Corp.
Chesebrough-Pond's USA
Chevron Corp.
Chicago Title and Trust Co.
Chicago Tribune Co.
Chrysler Corp.
Chubb and Son Inc.
Church & Dwight Co. Inc.
Church Mutual Insurance Co.
CIBA Specialty Chemicals Corp.
CIGNA Corp.
Cincinnati Bell Inc.
Circuit City Stores Inc.
Cisco Systems Inc.
CITGO Petroleum Corp.
Clariant Corp.
Clark Construction Group Inc.
Cleveland-Cliffs Inc. and Associated Cos.
Clopay Corp.

Clorox Co.
CNA
Coats North America
Coca-Cola Co.
Colgate-Palmolive Co.
Collins & Aikman Corp.
Colonial Management Association Inc.
Colonial Parking Inc.
Colonial Penn Group Inc.
Columbia Gas System Inc.
Columbus Life Insurance Co.
Comerica Inc.
Commercial Intertech Corp.
Commonwealth Edison Co.
Commonwealth Energy System
Commonwealth Fund
Community Bank System Inc.
Compaq Computer Corp.
Computer Associates International Inc.
Computer Network Technology Corp.
ComputerWorld
COMSAT Corp.
ConAgra Inc.
Congoleum Corp.
Connecticut Natural Gas Corp.
Conoco Inc.
CONRAIL Inc.
CONSOL Inc.
Consolidated Edison Co.
    of New York Inc.
Consolidated Natural Gas Co.
Consolidated Papers Inc.
Consumer Programs Inc.
Consumers Energy/CMS Energy
Co-Op Banking Group Cos.
Cooper Industries
Cooper Tire & Rubber Co.
Copley Press Inc.
Copolymer Rubber and Chemical Corp.
CoreStates Financial Corp.

Corning Inc.

Corporate Software and Technology

Covington & Burling

Crane Co.

Cranston Print Works Co.

Cray Research Inc.

Credit Agricole Indosuez

Crestar Financial Corp.

Crompton & Knowles Corp.

Crowe, Chizek, and Co.

Crown Central Petroleum Corp.

Crum & Forster Insurance

CSC Index

CSX Corp.

Cummins Engine Co. Inc.

CUNA Mutual Life Insurance Co.

Cyprus Amax Minerals Co.

Dain Rauscher

Dana Corp.

Danforth Foundation

Datatel Inc.

David L. Babson and Co. Inc.

Dean Witter Discover

DEKALB Genetics Corp.

Deloitte & Touche

Delta Air Lines Inc.

Delta Dental Plan of Massachusetts

Deluxe Corp.

Demont & Associates Inc.

Avery Dennison Corp.

Deposit Guaranty National Bank

Detroit Edison Co.

A.W.G. Dewar Inc.

Dexter Corp.

DFS Group Ltd.

Diebold Inc.

Difco Laboratories

Digital Sciences Corp.

Direct Marketing Technology

Dole Food Co. Inc.

Donaldson Co. Inc.

Donaldson, Lufkin & Jenrette

R.R. Donnelley & Sons Co.

Dow AgroSciences, LLC

Dow Chemical Co.

Dow Corning Corp.

Dow Jones and Co. Inc.

Dresser Industries Inc.

Dresser-Rand Co.

DSM Engineering Plastics Inc.

DTE Energy

Duff-Norton Co.

Duke Power Co.

Dun & Bradstreet Corp.

Duquesne Light Co.

Duracell International Inc.

Eastern Enterprises

Eastern Mountain Sports

Eaton Corp.

Eaton Vance Management

Eckerd Corp.

Ecolab Inc.

Eddie Bauer

Edison International

Educators Mutual Life Insurance Co.

El Paso Energy Corp.

Elf Aquitaine Inc.

ELF Atochem North America Inc.

Eli Lilly and Co.

Elizabethtown Water Co.

Emerson Electric Co

Engelhard Corp.

Enron Corp.

ENSERCH Corp.

Equifax Inc.

Equistar Chemicals, LP

Equitable Life Insurance Co. of Iowa

Equitable Resources Inc.

ERE Yarmouth

Erie Insurance Group

Ernst & Young, LLP
ESSTAR Inc.
Esterline Corp.
Ethyl Corp.
European American Bank
Exxon Corp.
Exxon Education Foundation
Fannie Mae
Federal Home Loan Mortgage Corp.
Federal-Mogul Corp.
Federated Department Stores Inc.
Feingold & Feingold Insurance
Ferro Corp.
Fidelity Investments
Fiduciary Trust Co., Boston
James and Marshall Field Foundation
Fifth Third Bancorp
FINA Inc.
Fingerhut Corp.
Fireman's Fund Insurance Co.
First Allmerica Financial Life Insurance Co.
First Data Corp.
First Energy Corp.
First Maryland Bancorp
First National Bank of Hudson
First Union Corp.
First Virginia Banks Inc.
Flavorite Laboratories Inc.
Fleet Financial Group
Fleming Cos. Inc.
Fluor Corp.
FMC Corp.
Follett Corp.
Ford Motor Co.
Ford Motor Co. of Canada, Ltd.
Fort James Corp. and Subsidiaries
Fortis Woodbury
Fortis Health
Fortune Brands Inc.
Foster Wheeler Corp.

Foundation for Educational Funding Inc.
Foxboro Co.
FPL Group Inc.
Freddie Mac Foundation
Frederic W. Cook & Co. Inc.
Freeport-McMoRan
Fuji Bank, Ltd.
H.B. Fuller Co.
Fulton Financial Corp.
Galileo Corp.
E. & J. Gallo Winery
Gannett Co. Inc.
Gap Inc.
Gartner Group
Gary-Williams Co./Piton Foundation
GATX Corp.
GenCorp Inc.
General Accident Insurance Co. of
    America
General Cable Co.
General Cable Co.
General Defense Corp.
General Electric Canada Inc.
General Electric Co.
General Mills Inc.
General Motors Corp.
General Re Corp.
M. Arthur Gensler Jr. and Associates Inc.
Geon Co.
Georgia-Pacific Co.
Georgia Power Co.
Gerber Products Co.
Gilbane Building Co.
Gillette Co.
Gilman Paper Co.
Glaxo Wellcome Inc.
Glenmede Corp.
Globe Newspaper Co. and Subsidiaries
Gnat Inc.
Golden Books Publishing Co. Inc.

Goldman, Sachs & Co.

Good Value Homes Inc.

Goodyear Tire & Rubber Co.

Gould Electronics Inc.

Goulds Pumps Inc.

Government Employees Insurance Co.

GPU Inc.

W.R. Grace & Co.

Graco Inc.

W.W. Grainger Inc.

Grant Thorton, LLP

Grantham, Mayo, Van Otterloo & Co., LLC

Graphics Controls Corp.

Graybar Electric Co. Inc.

Great West Casualty Co.

GreenPoint Bank

Greenwood Mills Inc.

Gregory Poole Equipment Co.

Grenzebach, Glier & Associates Inc.

Grinnell Mutual Reinsurance Co.

GTE Corp.

Guardian Life Insurance Co. of America

Guidant Corp.

Guide One Insurance

H & R Block Inc.

Haemonetics Corp.

Halliburton Co.

Hallmark Cards Inc.

Hambrecht & Quist, LLC

Hampton & Harper Inc.

M.A. Hanna Co.

Hanover Insurance Co.

Harcourt General Inc.

Harleysville Mutual Insurance Co.

Harrah's Entertainment Inc.

Harris Corp.

Harris Trust & Savings Bank

Hartford Insurance Group

Hartmarx Corp.

Hasbro Inc.

Hawaiian Electric Industries Inc.

Haworth Inc.

H.J. Heinz Co.

Heller Financial Inc.

Henry Luce Foundation

Hercules Inc.

Herold & Associates

Hershey Foods Corp.

Heublein Foundation Inc.

Hewitt Associates, LLC

Hewlett-Packard Co.

Hibernia National Bank

Higher Education Publications Inc.

Hillman Co.

Hoechst Marion Roussel Inc.

Hoffman-La Roche Inc.

Holmes & Narver Inc.

Holyoke Mutual Insurance Co. in Salem

Home Depot

Homestake Mining Co.

Honeywell Inc.

Hormel Foods Corp.

Houghton Chemical Corp.

Houghton Mifflin Co.

Household International Inc.

HRTek Corp.

HSB-Industrial Risk Insurers

Hubbard Milling Co.

Hubbell Inc.

J.M. Huber Corp.

Huffy Corp.

Hughes Electronics Corp.

Hunt Corp.

ICI Americas Inc.

IDEX Corp.

IES Industries Inc.

IKON Office Solutions

IKOS Systems

Illinois Tool Works Inc.

Inco United States Inc.

Resource 6

Independence Investment Associates Inc.
Industrial Bank of Japan, Ltd.
Information Technology Systems
Ingersoll-Rand Co.
Instron Corp.
Integon Corp.
Intel Corp.
Interlake Corp.
International Business Machines
International Flavors and Fragrances Inc.
International Multifoods Corp.
International Paper
International Student Exchange Cards Inc.
Intuit Inc.
IPALCO Enterprises Inc.
ITT Corp.
J. Walter Thompson Co.
Jefferies Group Inc.
Jefferson-Pilot Communications Co.
Jefferson Pilot Financial
John Brown Inc.
John Hancock Advisers Inc.
John Hancock Mutual Life Insurance Co.
John Wiley & Sons Inc.
Johns Manville Corp.
Johnson Controls Inc.
Johnson & Johnson Family of Cos.
S.C. Johnson & Son Inc.
Jones, JA Inc.
Jostens Inc.
JSJ Corp.
Kansas City Southern Industries Inc.
Karmazin Products Corp.
Kearney-National Inc.
Keefe, Bruyett & Woods Inc.
Kellogg Co.
W.K. Kellogg Foundation
M.W. Kellogg Co.
Kemper Insurance Cos.
Kennametal Inc.

Kerr-McGee Corp.
KeyCorp
Keystone Associates Inc.
Kimberly Clark Foundation
Kingsbury Corp.
Kiplinger Washington Editors
Kmart Corp.
KN Energy Inc.
Knight-Ridder Inc.
H. Kohnstamm & Co. Inc.
Korte Construction Co.
KPMG Peat Marwick, LLP
Laboratory Corp. Of America TM
Lam Research Corp.
Lamson & Sessions Co.
LandAmerica Financial Group Inc.
LaSalle National Bank
Law Co. Inc.
Law Cos. Group Inc.
Lehigh Portland Cement Co.
Leo Burnett Co. Inc.
Levi Strauss & Co.
LEXIS-NEXIS
Lexmark International Inc.
Libbey-Owens Ford Co.
Lincoln Financial Group
Link Engineering Co. Inc.
Thomas J. Lipton Co.
Litton Itek Optical Systems
Liz Claiborne Inc.
Lockheed Martin Corp.
Loews Corp.
Lone Star Industries Inc.
Lotus Development Corp.
Louisiana Power & Light Co.
Lubrizol Corp.
Lucent Technologies
Lucky Stores Inc.
Lukens Inc.
M/A/R/C Group

John D. and Catherine T. MacArthur
  Foundation
MacLean-Fogg Co.
Josiah Macy, Jr. Foundation
Madison Mutual Insurance Co. (NY)
Mallinckrodt Group Inc.
Marathon Oil Co.
Maritz Inc.
Marley Co.
Marsh & McLennan Cos. Inc.
Massachusetts Financial Services
  Investment Management
Massachusetts Port Authority
MassMutual-Blue Chip Co.
MasterCard International Inc.
Mattel Inc.
Maxus Energy Corp.
May Department Stores Co.
Maytag Corp.
Mazda (North America) Inc.
MBNA America Bank, NA
McCormick & Co. Inc.
McDonald's Corp.
McGraw-Hill Cos.
McKesson HBOC Inc.
McQuay Inc.
Mead Corp.
Mebane Packaging Corp.
Medical Consultants Network Inc.
Medtronic Inc.
Mellon Bank Corp.
Menasha Corp.
Merck & Co. Inc.
Meredith Corp.
Meridian Insurance Co.
Merit Oil Corp.
Meritor Savings Bank
Merrill Lynch & Co. Inc.
Metropolitan Life Insurance Co.
Mettler-Toledo Inc.

Michigan Mutual Insurance Co.
Micron Technology Inc.
Microsoft Corp.
Midland Life Insurance Co.
Miehle-Goss-Dexter Inc.
Milgard Matching Gift Program
Milliken & Co.
Millipore Corp.
Milton Bradley Co.
Milwaukee Electric Tool Corp.
Minerals Technologies Inc.
Minnesota Mutual Life Insurance Co.
Mississippi Power & Light Co.
Mitsubishi Electric America
Mitsubishi International Corp.
Mobil Oil Corp.
Moen Inc.
Monroe Auto Equipment Co.
Monsanto Co.
Montana Power Co.
MONY Life Insurance Co.
MOOG Inc.
Morgan Construction Co.
J.P. Morgan & Co. Inc.
Morgan Stanley Dean Witter & Co. Inc.
Morrison & Foerster, LLP
Morrison Knudsen Corp.
Mortgage Guaranty Insurance Corp.
Morton International Inc.
Motorola Inc.
Charles Stewart Mott Foundation
MSI Insurance
MTS Systems Corp.
Murphy Oil Corp.
Mutual of America
Mutual of Omaha Cos.
NACCO Industries Inc.
Nalco Chemical Co.
National City Bank of Pennsylvania
National City Corp.

National Computer System
National Gypsum Co.
National Semiconductor Corp.
National Starch and Chemical Co.
National Steel Corp.
NationsBank Corp.
NationsCredit Corp.
Nationwide Mutual Insurance Co.
NCR Corp.
NEES Cos.
Neles-Jamesbury
Nellie Mae
Network Associates
New Century Energies
New England Business Service Inc.
New England Electric System Cos.
New England Financial
New Jersey Bell Telephone Co.
New Jersey Natural Gas Co.
New York Life Insurance Co.
New York State Electric & Gas Corp.
New York Stock Exchange Inc.
New York Times Co.
Newmont Mining Corp.
Niagara Mohawk Power Corp.
Nicor Gas
Nielsen Media Research
NIKE Inc.
Nissan North America Inc.
Nordson Corp.
Norfolk & Dedham Group
Norfolk Southern Corp.
Northern States Power Co.
Northern Telecom Inc.
Northern Trust Co.
Northwestern Mutual Life Insurance Co.
Norton Co.
W.W. Norton & Co. Inc.
Norwest Corp.
Novartis Corp.

Novell Inc.
John Nuveen & Co. Inc.
NVEST Cos., LP
Occidental Petroleum Corp.
Ohio National Life Insurance Co.
Oklahoma Gas and Electric Co.
Olin Corp.
Ontario Corp.
Openaka Corp. Inc.
OppenheimerFunds Inc.
Oregon Portland Cement Co.
Orion Capital Corp.
Osmonics Inc.
OSRAM SYLVANIA
Otter Tail Power Co.
Outboard Marine Corp.
Owens Corning
Owens-Illinois Inc.
Oxford Industries Inc.
PACCAR Inc.
Pacific Enterprises
Pacific Life Insurance Co.
Pan-American Life Insurance Co.
PanEnergy Corp.
Parker Hannifin Corp.
Paul Revere Cos.
Pella Corp.
PCL Constructors Inc.
Penn Mutual Life Insurance Co.
J.C. Penney Co. Inc.
Pennsylvania Power & Light Co.
Pennzoil Co.
Pentair Inc.
People's Bank
Peoples Gas Corp.
PepsiCo Foundation
Perkin-Elmer Corp.
Peterson Consulting Ltd. Partnership
Pew Charitable Trusts
Pfizer Inc.

PG&E Corp.
P.H. Glatfelter Co.
Pharmacia & Upjohn Inc.
Phelps Dodge Corp.
PHH Corp.
Phillip Morris Cos. Inc.
Philips Electronics North America Corp.
Phillips Petroleum Co.
Phoenix Home Life Mutual Insurance Co.
Pioneer Hi-Bred International Inc.
Pioneer Group Inc.
Pitney Bowes Inc.
Pittston Co.
Pittway Corp.
PLATINUM technology inc.
Playboy Enterprises Inc.
Plum Creek Timber Co., LP
Plymouth Rock Foundation
Plymouth Bank
PNC Bank Corp.
Pogo Producing Co.
Polaroid Corp.
Pope & Talbot Inc.
Potlatch Corp.
PPG Industries Inc.
PQ Corp.
Preformed Line Products Co.
Premark International Inc.
Price & Pierce International Inc.
PricewaterhouseCoopers, LLP
Principal Financial Group
Procter & Gamble Co.
Proskauer Rose, LLP
Protection Mutual Insurance Co.
Provident Cos. Inc.
Provident Mutual Life Insurance Co.
  of Philadelphia
Providian Corp.
Providian Financial
Prudential Insurance Co. of America

Public Service Electric and Gas Co.
Purolator Products Inc.
Quaker Chemical Corp.
Quaker Oats Co.
Quaker State Corp.
Ralston Purina Co.
Rand McNally
Rayonier Foundation
Raytheon Co.
Reader's Digest Association Inc.
Reebok International Ltd.
Reliable Life Insurance Co.
Reliance Insurance Cos.
ReliaStar Financial Corp.
Republic National Bank of New York
Research Institute of America Inc.
Revlon Inc.
Rexam Inc.
Rexnord Corp.
Reynolds Metals Co.
Rhodia Inc.
Rhone-Poulenc Rorer Inc.
Riviana Foods Inc.
RJR Nabisco Inc.
RJR Nabisco Foundation Inc.
RLI Insurance Co.
Robert Wood Johnson Foundation
Rochester Midland Corp.
Rockefeller Brothers Fund Inc.
Rockefeller Family & Associates
Rockefeller Group
Rockwell
Rohm and Haas Co.
Rohr Inc.
RONIN Development Corp.
Ross, Johnston & Kersting Inc.
Royal & SunAlliance Insurance
Rubermaid Inc.
Ryco Division, Reilly-Whiteman Inc.
Ryder System Inc.

Safeco Corp.
St. Paul Cos.
Sallie Mae
Samuel Roberts Noble Foundation Inc.
Sanwa Bank California
Sara Lee Corp.
SBC Communications Inc.
Schering-Plough Corp.
Charles Schwab and Co. Inc.
    and Subsidiaries
Scientific-Atlanta Inc.
Scientific Brake & Equipment Co.
Scott, Foresman and Co.
E.W. Scripps Co.
Joseph E. Seagram & Sons Inc.
Sealed Air Corp.
Sealright Co. Inc.
G.D. Searle & Co.
Sedgwick Inc.
Sentry Insurance Foundation Inc.
Service Merchandise Co. Inc.
Seton Co.
SGL Carbon Corp.
Shaklee Corp.
Shearson Lehman Brothers Inc.
Sheldahl Inc.
Shell Oil Co.
Shenandoah Life Insurance Co.
Sherwin-Williams Co.
Showa Denko Carbon Inc.
Siemens Corp.
Sierra Health Foundation
Sierra Pacific Resources
Sifco Industries Inc.
Signet Banking Corp.
Silicon Graphics Inc.
SKF USA Inc.
Smith International Inc.
SmithKline Beecham
SNET

Sonat Inc.
Sonoco Products Co.
Sony Corp. of America
Spiegel Inc.
Springs Industries Inc.
Sprint Corp.
SPS Technologies Inc.
SPX Corp.
Square D Co.
Sta-Rite Industries Inc.
A.E. Staley Manufacturing Co.
Staley, Robeson, Ryan, St. Lawrence Inc.
Standard Insurance Co.
Standard Products Co.
Stanhome Inc.
Stanley Works
Star Enterprise
State Farm Insurance Cos.
State Street Corp.
Stauffer Communications Inc.
Steel Heddle Manufacturing Co.
Steelcase Inc.
Stone & Webster Inc.
Stop & Shop Cos. Inc.
STREM Chemicals
Stride Rite Corp.
Subaru of America Inc.
Summit Bancorp
Sun Life Assurance Co. of Canada
Sun Microsystems Inc.
Suntrust Bank, Atlanta
SUPERVALUE Inc.
Susquehanna Investment Group
Swank Inc.
Swedish Match
Swiss American Securities Inc.
Swiss Bank Corp.
SYSCO Corp.
20th Century Insurance Co.
3Com Corp.

3M
Tandy Corp.
TCF Financial Corp.
Teagle Foundation Inc.
Technimetrics Inc.
Tektronix Inc.
Telcordia Technologies
Teledyne Inc.
Tellabs Inc.
Temple-Inland Inc.
Tenet Healthcare Corp.
TENNANT
Tenneco Inc.
Tesoro, Hawaii
Tesoro Petroleum Corp.
Tetley USA Inc.
Texaco Inc.
Texas Instruments Inc.
Texon International
Textron Inc.
THAT Corp.
Thomson Financial Services
Tietex International, LTD
Time Warner Inc.
Times Mirror Co.
Times Publishing Co.
Tomkins Corp. Foundation
Toro Co.
Torrington Co.
Towers, Perrin, Forster, & Crosby
Toyota Motor Manufacturing,
    Kentucky Inc.
Toyota Motor Sales, U.S.A. Inc.
Transamerica Corp.
Transtar Inc.
Travelers Express Co. Inc.
T. Rowe Price Associates Inc.
TRW Inc.
TTX Co.
Turner Corp.

Tyco International, Ltd.
UAM Charitable Foundation Inc.
UGI Corp.
Unibase Direct
Unilever United States Inc.
Union Central Life Insurance Co.
Union Electric Co.
Union Mutual Fire Insurance Co.
Union Pacific Corp.
Unisource Foundation
United Fire & Casualty Co.
United Parcel Service
United Services Automobile Association
United Technologies Corp.
Unitrin Inc.
Universal Foods Corp.
Universal Studios
Unocal Corp.
UNUM Corp.
U.S. Bancorp
U.S. Borax Inc.
U.S. Trust Corp and Affiliates
US West Inc.
USA GROUP Inc.
USG Corp.
USLIFE Corp.
UST Inc.
USX Corp.
Utica National Insurance Group
Valero Energy Corp.
Vanguard Group Inc.
Victaulic Co. of America
Virginia Power/North Carolina Power
Vulcan Materials Co.
Wachovia Corp.
Wal-Mart Stores Inc.
Wallace & Wallace, Ltd.
Warnaco
Warner-Lambert Co.
Washington Dental Service

Washington Mutual

Washington Post Co.

Waters Corp.

Watkins-Johnson Co.

Wausau Insurance Cos.

C.J. Webb Inc.

Welch Foods Inc., a Cooperative

Wells Fargo Bank, NA

Western Resources Foundation

Westvaco Corp.

Weyerhaeuser Co.

Whirlpool Corp.

White Consolidated Industries Inc.

Whitman Corp.

Whittaker Corp.

Willamette Industries Inc.

Williams

Williams Gas Pipeline/Transco Energy Co.

Winn-Dixie Stores Inc.

Winter Wyman & Co.

Wiremold Co.

Wisconsin Energy Corp.

Wisconsin Gas Co.

Wisconsin Power & Light Co.

Witco Corp.

Wolverine World Wide Inc.

Words At Work Inc.

WordsWorth Books

Wyman-Gordon Co.

Xerox Corp.

Xtra Corp. Charitable Foundation

Young & Rubicam Inc.

Zurich-American Insurance Group

Zurn Industries Inc.

Source: Adapted from Council for Advancement and Support of Education, Washington, D.C.

CORPORATE MATCHING GIFT GUIDELINES AND APPLICATION FORM

THE MATCHING GIFTS PROGRAM

Eli Lilly and Company recognizes the importance of individual support for nonprofit organizations. Through the Matching Gifts Program, the Lilly Foundation assists many nonprofit institutions by combining the generosity of employee giving with corporate resources.

The Eli Lilly and Company Foundation's Matching Gifts Program is designed to encourage your participation and promote your personal support of those qualifying institutions that are important to you.

While many nonprofit organizations are directly supported by the company and the foundation, the Matching Gifts Program allows you to help determine how to spend a portion of the company's philanthropic resources. This brochure describes the program and the procedures for obtaining matching funds for your donations. The attached form is for use in making a contribution. Additional forms may be obtained from receptionists in all plant lobbies, personnel areas at all plant sites, and the retirement area and credit union office at corporate headquarters or by contacting the Matching Gifts Program at (317) 276-2663.

PROGRAM TERMS

The Eli Lilly and Company Foundation will match personal contributions of eligible contributors to qualified educational institutions, cultural organizations, and health care organizations subject to the guidelines of the program.

- Because of the voluntary nature of the program, matching gift requests must originate with the contributor.
- Gifts must be paid (not merely pledged) in cash, check, credit card, or in negotiable securities with an established market value determined by the average price on the day the gift is made.
- Original completed forms must be received within six months of the date of the donor's gift.
- Payments to a school or organization will be made quarterly, and the donor will be notified by the foundation at the time the gift is matched.
- An employee may give personal gifts of $25 or more but not exceeding $30,000 in each of the following qualified categories:
    EDUCATIONAL INSTITUTIONS: $25 MINIMUM, $30,000 MAXIMUM
    CULTURAL ORGANIZATIONS: $25 MINIMUM, $30,000 MAXIMUM
    HEALTH CARE ORGANIZATIONS: $25 MINIMUM, $30,000 MAXIMUM

- A retiree or retired board member may give personal gifts of $25 or more but not exceeding $2,500 in each of the following qualified categories:
  EDUCATIONAL INSTITUTIONS: $25 MINIMUM, $2,500 MAXIMUM
  CULTURAL ORGANIZATIONS: $25 MINIMUM, $2,500 MAXIMUM
  HEALTH CARE ORGANIZATIONS: $25 MINIMUM, $2,500 MAXIMUM

All eligible gifts will be matched by the foundation $1 for $1.

- For your gift to an individual college or university to qualify for matching, you must have a personal affiliation with the institution: you or a member of your immediate family (spouse or child) must have received a degree from, attended, or currently be attending the institution or have been or currently be a member of its administration, faculty, or governing board (i.e., its board of trustees).

Eligible Participants

- Current regular employees of Eli Lilly and Company working full-time or more than 20 hours part-time
- Retirees of Eli Lilly and Company
- Members of the board of directors of Eli Lilly and Company

Not Eligible to Participate

- Spouses and surviving spouses of employees, retirees, or members of the board of directors

ELIGIBLE INSTITUTIONS

Educational Institutions

- Graduate and professional schools
- Four-year colleges and universities
- Two-year junior and community colleges and technical institutes
- Public and private, primary, and secondary schools offering a four-year program at least equivalent to a high school curriculum and granting a diploma upon satisfactory completion of such program
- All schools must be accredited by a nationally recognized nonsectarian, regional, or professional association or a state department of education
- Tax-exempt educational funds (e.g., United Negro College Fund, American Indian College Fund, Hispanic Association of Colleges and Universities, and Foundations for Independent Higher Education) if the sole purpose is to raise money for constituent member colleges that individually are eligible under the program

Gifts made to support intercollegiate athletic programs, athletic scholarships, booster clubs, sororities, and fraternities do not qualify.

Cultural Organizations

- Museums
- Art councils
- Cultural centers
- Botanical or zoological societies
- Public broadcasting systems
- Libraries
- Symphony orchestras
- Historical associations
- Performing arts companies (dance, theater, orchestras, opera, etc.)

Health Care Organizations

- Affirming the concerns of our employees, the Matching Gifts Program supports organizations that serve patients who are fighting diseases for which we offer or are searching for pharmaceutical treatments and positive outcomes.
- For a listing of eligible organizations, please see the reverse side of the Matching Gift Applications Form, Card A.
- For ease of processing, gifts must be made to the organization's national headquarters. Donors may designate that their gift be directed to a local chapter if desired.
- Ineligible gifts include payments for medical treatment or any gift not intended to further the general program of the organization.

All eligible educational institutions, cultural organizations, and health care organizations must:

- Be located within the United States, its possessions, or the commonwealth of Puerto Rico.
- Be recognized by the Internal Revenue Service of the United States Department of Treasury as a tax-exempt organization and listed in the Cumulative List of Organizations, IRS Publication 78, gifts to which are deductible under the United States Internal Revenue Code
- Be able to make available audited financial statements upon request.

INELIGIBLE ORGANIZATIONS AND GIFTS

The following are not eligible for a matching gift:

- Gifts made more than six months before receipt of the completed form
- Gifts made with funds given to the donor in whole or in part for donation purposes by other individuals, groups, or organizations
- Gifts entitling the donor to some personal benefit, e.g., payment for tickets, subscription fees, or fundraising dinners or events; tickets for athletic, cultural, or other events; auction items; publications
- Gifts intended to fulfill a person's pledge, tithe, or other church-related financial commitment
- Community foundations
- Private foundations
- Conservation, environmental, and ecological organizations
- Fraternities, sororities, honor societies, educational associations, and campus organizations
- Nonaccredited educational institutions
- Preschools and day care centers
- Pledges not paid
- Gifts made by surviving spouses of employees, retirees, or directors
- Volunteer hours
- Bequests, pledges, tuition payments, or payments in lieu of tuition or other student fees
- Athletic activities, scholarships, and facilities
- Scholarships or financial aid that benefits specific individuals
- Programs that operate under the sponsorship of a religious organization that are not separately incorporated as independent, nonreligious, tax-exempt organizations
- Life income plan gifts, trust funds, and insurance policies
- Bequests or in-kind (noncash) gifts of real estate or personal property (other than securities)
- Alumni foundations unless they support the primary academic objectives of the institution
- Health care organizations other than those listed as being eligible
- Political parties
- Political advocacy, lobbying, or action organizations
- Organizations engaging in illegal activities
- Community fundraisers, such as walk-a-thons, that raise money by soliciting sponsors.

Photocopies of forms are not eligible for consideration.

APPLICATION PROCEDURE

1. Contributor—Completely fills in Card A of the attached form and sends it with his/her gift to the organization. The donor must sign the form—typed signatures are not acceptable. (Incomplete forms cannot be processed and will be returned to the contributor.)

2. Gift Recipient—Upon receipt of the gift and form, the designated financial officer of the institution reviews the contributor's information, completes Card B of the form, and signs. Facsimile signatures are not acceptable. The entire form must be mailed to:

> Matching Gifts Program
> Eli Lilly and Company Foundation
> Drop Code 1618
> Lilly Corporate Center
> Indianapolis, IN 46285

3. Lilly Foundation—Upon verification of the eligibility of the donor, gift, and the organization, the foundation will issue a matching gift check and will send a receipt to the donor indicating that payment has been made. Processing will occur on a quarterly basis.

4. If you have indicated a specific department or purpose for your contribution, the matching gift will be designated for that same use.

The Eli Lilly and Company Foundation may suspend, change, revoke, or terminate this program at any time but only with respect to gifts made after such action.

The program will be administered by the contributions committee of the Eli Lilly and Company Foundation, and its interpretation of the program will be final.

It is the policy of the Eli Lilly and Company Foundation not to furnish names, addresses, or other employee information to any organization or solicitation agent.

Requests for additional forms or for information concerning the program should be sent to:

> Matching Gifts Program
> Eli Lilly and Company Foundation
> Drop Code 1618
> Lilly Corporate Center
> Indianapolis, Indiana 46285

Attention: New Recipient Institutions

If you have not previously received matching gifts from the Eli Lilly and Company Foundation, it will be necessary to attach the following to the Matching Gifts form:

- A brochure describing the organization's activities and programs offered to the public
- A copy of your IRS 501(c)(3) tax-exempt certification and foundation classification under Section 509(a)
- A statement signed by a financial officer of your institution that your operations are as stated in the determination letter and that there have been no changes in your purpose, character, or method of operation
- A list of the members of the current board of directors of your organization.

MEMBERSHIP PROGRAM WITH BENEFITS

Note: Due to space considerations, only the *Sustaining America's Heritage* brochure is reproduced in full (see p. 266), by permission of the Museum of Fine Arts, Houston. See the copyright page for more credits.

Sustaining America's Heritage: 1999–2000
Bayou Bend Annual Fund Drive

Bayou Bend Collection and Gardens
The Museum of Fine Arts, Houston

Your gift to the Bayou Bend Annual Fund Drive supports

* a full range of tours of the collection and gardens, making Bayou Bend accessible to visitors of all ages

* innovative education programs, including free Family Days, student workshops, and outreach programs that welcome ever-increasing audiences to Bayou Bend

* continued research on the acclaimed collection

* essential, state-of-the-art conservation and maintenance of the collection of 4,600 masterworks

Your gift brings you

* complimentary admission to Bayou Bend, all year long

* *The Intelligencer* newsletter, published three times a year, bringing you the latest intelligence about the collection, programs, and events at Bayou Bend

* discounts on tickets for the Bayou Bend Lecture Series, which presents an unparalleled opportunity to hear prominent scholars speak on topics of special interest to lovers of the decorative arts

* invitations to social events, behind-the-scenes activities, and travel opportunities for Friends of Bayou Bend only

Tucker porcelain factory,
Fruit Basket
(one of a pair), 1827-38,
porcelain with gilding,
gift of Miss Ima Hogg.

To support Bayou Bend's Annual Fund Drive, please note the special benefits for each level, then complete and return the enclosed response card. For further information regarding benefits and the Annual Fund Drive, please call (713) 639-7712. For information on Bayou Bend tours and events, call (713) 639-7750.

Friend $60
- Complimentary admission to Bayou Bend Collection and Gardens, valid through December 31, 2000
- Subscription to *The Intelligencer* newsletter, published three times a year
- Discounted tickets to the Bayou Bend Lecture Series: October 21, November 18, January 20, February 17, and March 16
- Two bonus lectures for Friends of Bayou Bend only: November 10 and April 5
- Holiday wine-and-cheese reception at Bayou Bend on December 9
- A visit to the conservation lab for a demonstration by Bayou Bend conservators (limited space available)

Contributing Friend $125
- All Friend benefits, plus:
- Guided tour of the Bayou Bend Collection for you and one guest

Supporting Friend $300
- All Contributing Friend benefits, plus:
- Guided tour of the Bayou Bend Collection for you and three guests

Patron $500
- All Supporting Friend benefits, plus:
- Guided tour of the Bayou Bend Collection for you and five guests
- Acknowledgment in the Annual Report of the Museum of Fine Arts, Houston

Founder $1000
- All Patron benefits, plus:
- Private tour of the Bayou Bend Collection with a curator

*Designed by Benjamin H. Latrobe, **Pair of Side Chairs**, c. 1808, painted and gilded wood, museum purchase with funds provided by the Agnes Cullen Arnold Endowment Fund.*

Resource 8

The Chillman Parlor

- A fall cocktail reception in the home and collection of a Bayou Bend Founder
- Holiday reception at Bayou Bend on December 8
- A spring cocktail reception in the home and collection of a Bayou Bend Founder
- Invitations to other special events for Founders

Gallery/Founder $2,000
- All Founder benefits, plus:
- Membership in The Gallery, a special donor group of the Museum of Arts, Houston. Membership in The Gallery includes Patron-level membership to the MFAH, invitations to social and educational activities, discounted tuition on Glassell School of Art classes, and discounts at the MFAH Shops

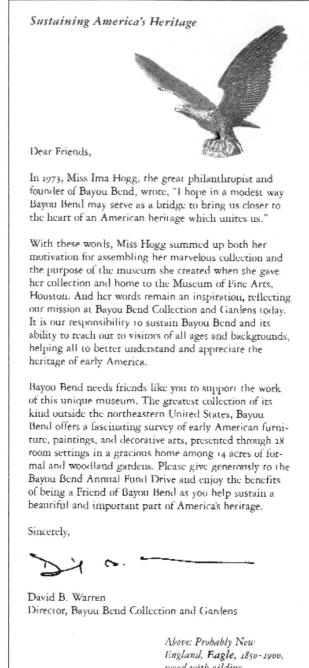

Sustaining America's Heritage

Dear Friends,

In 1973, Miss Ima Hogg, the great philanthropist and founder of Bayou Bend, wrote, "I hope in a modest way Bayou Bend may serve as a bridge to bring us closer to the heart of an American heritage which unites us."

With these words, Miss Hogg summed up both her motivation for assembling her marvelous collection and the purpose of the museum she created when she gave her collection and home to the Museum of Fine Arts, Houston. And her words remain an inspiration, reflecting our mission at Bayou Bend Collection and Gardens today. It is our responsibility to sustain Bayou Bend and its ability to reach out to visitors of all ages and backgrounds, helping all to better understand and appreciate the heritage of early America.

Bayou Bend needs friends like you to support the work of this unique museum. The greatest collection of its kind outside the northeastern United States, Bayou Bend offers a fascinating survey of early American furniture, paintings, and decorative arts, presented through 28 room settings in a gracious home among 14 acres of formal and woodland gardens. Please give generously to the Bayou Bend Annual Fund Drive and enjoy the benefits of being a Friend of Bayou Bend as you help sustain a beautiful and important part of America's heritage.

Sincerely,

David B. Warren
Director, Bayou Bend Collection and Gardens

*Above: Probably New England, **Eagle**, 1850–1900, wood with gilding. gift of Miss Ima Hogg.*

Bayou Bend Collection and Gardens

mailing address:
P. O. Box 6826
Houston, Texas
77265-6826

location address:
1 Westcott Street
Houston, Texas 77007
(713) 639-7750

Support the Bayou Bend Annual Fund Drive, and help sustain America's heritage.

Estimated fair-market values of contributions:
Friend $0;
Contributing Friend $25;
Supporting Friend $30;
Patron $45;
Founder $70;
Gallery/Founder $155.

Photographs by Thomas R. DuBrock, Rick Gardner, and Jud Haggard, for the Museum of Fine Arts, Houston.

The Newport Room

Front cover: Joseph Hiller, Sr., after Charles Willson Peale, **His Excellency George Washington Esqr.** *(detail). c. 1776, hand-colored mezzotint, museum purchase with funds provided by the Houston Junior Woman's Club.*

RESOURCE 9

UNIVERSITY ANNUAL FUND ANALYSIS

Executive Overview: Sample University Undergraduate Annual Giving   274

Executive Overview: Sample University Undergraduate Annual Giving

	FY 92	FY 93	FY 94	FY 95	FY 96	FY 97	FY 98	FY 99	FY 00	Percent Change		
										95–00	98–00	99–00
Giving Profile												
Donors	25,162	26,048	26,144	28,641	28,422	28,689	30,314	31,668	31,094	8.6%	2.6%	-1.8%
% Women	33.2%	34.3%	34.6%	34.8%	34.0%	35.0%	35.8%	36.8%	36.9%	6.2%	3.3%	0.3%
% Men	66.8%	65.7%	65.4%	65.2%	66.0%	65.0%	64.2%	63.2%	63.1%	-3.3%	-1.8%	-0.2%
Active Alumni									163,997			
Total Revenue	$4,192,605	$4,152,107	$4,877,824	$5,043,157	$5,438,684	$5,461,538	$6,597,256	$7,454,176	$9,065,131	79.8%	37.4%	21.6%
Revenue per Donor	$166.62	$159.40	$186.58	$176.08	$191.35	$190.37	$217.63	$235.39	$291.54	65.6%	34.0%	23.9%
Gifts per Donor	1.20	1.25	1.26	1.28	1.32	1.34	1.32	1.28	1.31	2.9%	-0.5%	2.2%
TAG Participation Rate												
% New Donors	15.3%	14.0%	14.4%	14.1%	13.4%	11.5%	13.5%	13.6%	11.5%	-18.7%	-15.0%	-15.7%
% Retained Donors	66.9%	66.4%	68.0%	65.1%	70.1%	69.3%	67.1%	67.5%	71.0%	9.0%	5.9%	5.2%
% Donors Giving 2 Cons. Years	20.6%	15.9%	16.1%	14.6%	16.6%	13.3%	13.3%	13.9%	14.7%	0.4%	10.2%	5.3%
% Donors Giving 3–4 Cons. Years	17.2%	22.1%	20.7%	16.5%	17.0%	17.8%	15.8%	14.4%	15.6%	-5.7%	-1.5%	7.8%
% Donors Giving 5+ Cons. Years	29.1%	28.4%	31.2%	34.0%	36.4%	38.2%	38.0%	39.1%	40.8%	19.8%	7.4%	4.2%
% Reactivated Donors	17.9%	19.7%	17.6%	20.7%	16.5%	19.2%	19.4%	18.9%	17.5%	-15.5%	-9.8%	-7.4%
% Donors $0–$49	44.1%	46.1%	44.8%	44.4%	44.2%	42.0%	43.4%	39.2%	36.6%	-17.5%	-15.6%	-6.5%
% Donors $50–$249	46.0%	44.4%	45.2%	45.2%	45.3%	47.2%	42.6%	46.6%	47.0%	-4.0%	10.4%	0.9%
% Donors $250–$999	7.4%	7.2%	7.6%	7.8%	7.9%	8.0%	11.1%	11.0%	12.6%	62.3%	14.1%	14.8%
% Donors $1000–$4999	2.1%	1.9%	2.0%	2.2%	2.3%	2.3%	2.4%	2.6%	3.0%	35.0%	21.7%	12.9%
% Donors $5000–$24999	0.3%	0.4%	0.4%	0.3%	0.4%	0.5%	0.4%	0.5%	0.6%	81.8%	39.5%	17.6%
% Donors $25000+	0.1%	0.0%	0.1%	0.1%	0.1%	0.1%	0.1%	0.1%	0.2%	142.9%	54.5%	54.5%
% Revenue $0–$49	6.4%	6.8%	5.8%	6.0%	5.6%	5.4%	4.9%	4.1%	3.0%	-49.7%	-37.4%	26.6%
% Revenue $50–$249	24.8%	25.5%	22.2%	23.2%	21.6%	22.7%	17.2%	17.6%	15.0%	-35.1%	-12.8%	-14.5%
% Revenue $250–$999	18.0%	18.4%	16.6%	18.0%	16.9%	16.9%	19.4%	18.2%	17.2%	-4.4%	-11.3%	-5.5%
% Revenue $1000–$4999	21.4%	21.1%	19.1%	22.2%	21.2%	21.1%	20.9%	20.4%	18.7%	-16.0%	-10.6%	-8.5%
% Revenue $5000–$24999	18.6%	20.4%	20.5%	14.8%	18.9%	21.1%	18.5%	21.2%	22.5%	51.8%	21.6%	6.1%
% Revenue $25000+	10.8%	7.9%	15.9%	15.7%	15.9%	12.7%	19.1%	18.5%	23.5%	49.6%	23.3%	27.5%

New Donors

Number of New Donors	3,840	3,647	3,766	4,043	3,816	3,299	4,093	4,311	3,571	-11.7%	-12.8%	-17.2%
New Donor Revenue	$173,604	$163,528	$230,030	$216,269	$178,432	$238,236	$266,577	$276,748	$291,799	34.9%	9.5%	5.4%
Revenue per New Donor	$45.21	$44.84	$61.08	$53.49	$46.76	$72.21	$65.13	$64.20	$81.71	52.8%	25.5%	27.3%

Donor Retention

Donor Retention Rate	70.3%	68.7%	68.3%	71.4%	69.5%	70.0%	70.9%	70.5%	69.7%	-2.3%	-1.6%	-1.1%
Revenue Retention Rate	106.0%	84.0%	94.0%	84.0%	92.0%	86.0%	102.0%	94.0%	100.0%	19.1%	-2.0%	6.4%
Revenue per Retained Donor	$209.42	$204.87	$220.15	$219.49	$232.56	$234.64	$272.99	$288.87	$399.05	54.5%	24.2%	17.4%
Rev. % Chg: Retained Donors	26.8%	0.9%	12.0%	0.7%	10.7%	2.8%	19.7%	11.5%	20.6%	2,845.7%	4.6%	78.7%
% Donors Upgrading	27.5%	28.9%	32.0%	31.8%	30.2%	32.5%	42.2%	34.7%	36.2%	13.7%	-14.3%	4.2%
% Donors Same	54.5%	49.5%	46.1%	46.2%	47.8%	47.5%	40.7%	42.7%	43.2%	-6.6%	6.0%	1.0%
% Donors Downgrading	18.0%	21.7%	22.0%	22.0%	22.0%	20.1%	17.1%	22.6%	20.7%	-6.0%	21.2%	-8.4%
Upgrade Revenue Variance	$1,103,359	$756,341	$1,104,085	$1,119,190	$1,356,050	$1,234,858	$1,982,814	$2,177,552	$2,710,925	142.2%	36.7%	24.5%
Downgrade Revenue Variance	-$358,218	-$724,256	-$683,936	-$1,090,648	-$910,073	-$1,107,959	-$1,069,064	-$1,538,821	-$1,431,567	31.3%	33.9%	-7.0%
Overall Revenue Var. for Ret. Donors	$745,141	$32,085	$420,149	$28,542	$445,977	$126,899	$913,749	$638,732	$1,279,358	4,382.4%	40.0%	100.3%
1st-Year Retention Rate	45.4%	40.2%	39.4%	39.9%	35.3%	35.0%	34.3%	32.0%	33.7%	-15.6%	-1.8%	5.1%
Rev. % Chg: 1st-Yr. Ret. Donors	17.7%	7.8%	-3.3%	-5.8%	3.3%	28.1%	-10.4%	10.8%	30.9%	95.7%	-396.0%	185.3%
Multi-Year Retention Rate	75.1%	73.8%	73.0%	76.7%	75.2%	75.4%	75.6%	76.5%	75.4%	-1.7%	-0.3%	-1.4%
Rev. % Chg: Multi-Year Ret. Donors	27.1%	0.8%	12.4%	0.4%	10.8%	2.4%	20.4%	11.6%	20.4%	4,646.5%	0.3%	76.6%

donorCentrics Copyright 2000 Target Analysis Group, Inc.   11/16/00   Gift Cap: $50,000   File Start Date: 1963   Executive Overview

RESOURCE 10

ANNUAL FUND SURVEY

Lapsed-Donor Survey Letter   278
Annual Giving Alumni Survey   279

Resource 10

Lapsed-Donor Survey Letter

April 1, 1998

[inside address]

Dear [recipient's name]:

I would like to take this opportunity to thank you for your past support of Indiana University.

The Indiana University Foundation works hard to raise badly needed support for the University. We realize how very important your participation and support of our efforts is to our students and to the University's future. I was sorry to learn that you did not renew your gift in 1997 and am curious as to the reasons why.

In an attempt to evaluate our fundraising program, the Annual Giving staff has decided to conduct an alumni survey. Your participation in the survey is important, as we value your input.

We would greatly appreciate it if you would complete and return the enclosed survey at your earliest convenience. Your answers and comments will be read with interest and will contribute to improving our development program and future fundraising efforts.

Please do not hesitate to contact me if you have questions. Thank you for your assistance in this effort.

Sincerely,

Carolyn Madvig
Director of Annual Giving
Indiana University Foundation

Resource 10

Annual Giving Alumni Survey

INDIANA UNIVERSITY FOUNDATION

APRIL 1998

1. Are you a current member of the IU Alumni Association? ☐ Yes ☐ No

2. Do you have an alumni club within 50 miles of your residence? ☐ Yes ☐ No

   If yes, do you attend the activities sponsored by the club? ☐ Yes ☐ No
   If so, why? If not, why not?

   _____

   _____

   _____

3. Have you attended an IU-sponsored event in the last year? ☐ Yes ☐ No

   _____

   _____

   _____

4. Have you ever visited the IUF Web site (www.iuf.indiana.edu)? ☐ Yes ☐ No

   _____

   _____

   _____

5. Were you involved with extracurricular activities as a student? ☐ Yes ☐ No
   Which ones?

   ☐ Marching Hundred   ☐ IU Student Foundation
   ☐ Singing Hoosiers   ☐ Student Athletic Board
   ☐ Fraternity/Sorority   ☐ IU Student Association
   ☐ *Indiana Daily Student*   ☐ Other (please identify) _____

Resource 10

6. Are you more interested in supporting these activities
   or your school of graduation?   ☐ Activity   ☐ School

7. Is there a specific reason that you decided not to give to IU
   again this year?   ☐ Yes   ☐ No

   Please explain: _____

   _____

   _____

8. What solicitation method do you most prefer: ☐ Mail   ☐ Telephone call

9. Are you satisfied with the current number and quality of
   contacts you receive from IU?   ☐ Yes   ☐ No

   Please explain: _____

   _____

   _____

10. What factors would positively influence you to give in the future?

    _____

    _____

    _____

11. Do you have any additional comments and/or suggestions?

    _____

    _____

    _____

THANK YOU FOR YOUR PARTICIPATION IN THIS SURVEY!

(Please return this survey in the enclosed postage-paid envelope.)

DIRECT MAIL SOLICITATION PACKAGE

MAKING DREAMS COME TRUE

1999 - 2000
Wish List of Gifts

Children's
Mercy
HOSPITALS
& CLINICS

Kids Say Thanks!
Thank you for healing us children. Allison Age 10
Thank you for giving the baby beds to Childrens mercy. It helped my new baby brother to stay safe and warm. Kelly age 8
Thank you for the Nintendo. I played with my friend in the hospital Age 4
Thank you for the cot bed so my mom and dad can stay with me in my room at nite. from Pasquali age 11

Children's Needs

At Children's Mercy, we are committed not only to providing the highest quality medical care, but also to meeting children's and families' emotional and social needs. There are a wide variety of items needed to help make a child's hospital stay more comfortable and less frightening.

	Cost Each	Number Needed
CABBAGE PATCH DOLL (specially designed) demonstrates kidney treatment for those children undergoing dialysis or transplants	$25	**UNLIMITED**
WAGON replaces wheelchairs when transporting little ones	$160	50
CONVENTIONAL HEARING AID brings the joy of sound to a child's silent world and gives the child an opportunity to learn to speak	$350	100
PROGRAMMABLE HEARING AID adjusts to the individual needs of children with severe to profound hearing loss	$500	50
WALKIE-TALKIE allows clear communication between the Security personnel and the main office thus providing for quick responses to hospital needs	$700	8
WHEELCHAIR assists a child in the hospital in learning how to maneuver before they get their own	$1,000	1
STRETCHER transports a patient in a comfortable and timely manner	$3,200	1
INFANT WARMER provides a warm, open bed for infants allowing caretakers easy access to the baby while maintaining the baby's body temperature	$10,000	6

CHILDREN'S MERCY VOLUNTEERS have fun! If you're interested in volunteering daytime, evenings or weekends, give us a call at (816) 234-3496. Come share in the fun while making a difference in a child's life!

CHILD LIFE provides hospitalized children with developmentally appropriate play opportunities.

DISTRACTION ITEMS (glitter, wands, rain sticks, bubbles, etc., which are used to help patients cope through medical procedures)	$2–$15
BOOKS (for all ages, including search and find and pop-up books which are used for distraction)	$2–$15
GAMES (card, board and electronic games)	$5–$30
PLAYROOM ACTIVITY SUPPLIES (paints, crayons, paper, etc. for play sessions offered to all inpatients on a daily basis)	$5–$30
TOYS (to supply playrooms and play areas throughout the hospital)	$5–$50
MUSIC (radios, tapes and tape players, CDs and CD players, for use by patients for relaxation and enjoyment)	$10–$40
INFANT TOYS (mobiles, crib mirrors and music boxes, exersaucers, bouncy seats, etc.)	$20–$50
VIDEO GAMES & SYSTEMS (for purchase of video game systems and appropriate games)	$30–$200
PLAYROOM FURNISHINGS (tables, chairs, toy and book shelves, playmats, etc.)	$100–$400

PLAY THERAPY uses specialized techniques to assist children and adolescents in expressing their feelings through interactive play.

Markers	$5
Play Doh	$5
Go Away Big Green Monster Book	$15
Multi-Ethnic Flexible Family	$16
Go Away Big Green Monster Storytelling Kit	$17
Snail Started It! Book	$19
One-Step Polaroid Film (20 exposures)	$20
Therapeutic Games	$20–$50
Giant Food Pyramid Puzzle	$30
Sentence Building Cubes	$30
Space Link Starter Sets	$30
Duplo Vehicles	$32
Soft and Still Block Sets	$40
Hardwood Furniture Sets	$50
Portable Doll Houses	$90
Duplo Homes	$95

PHYSICAL AND OCCUPATIONAL THERAPY encourages children to use inactive muscles through playtime activities.

SWITCH OPERATED TOY entices children to move	$25–$100
WATER VEST keeps children safe while undergoing water therapy	$100
MIRROR rolls where it is needed in the physical and occupational therapy area	$300
COMPUTER PROGRAM AND CD ROM teaches keyboard skills to children with disabilities	$500
HEAVY DUTY SEWING MACHINE adapts clothing for disabled children and makes straps for splints	$500
WHEELCHAIR ROLLER increases strength, endurance and cardiovascular fitness of children who use wheelchairs	$600
WEIGHT SET strengthens muscles	$700
TREADMILL provides aerobic conditioning for children with special needs following a prolonged illness	$2,300

SPECIAL GIFT ACCOUNT allows special items to be purchased or special events to be held to help brighten a hospitalized child's stay.

Sharing in Care

The physicians, nurses and staff at Children's Mercy have an important partner— our generous donors—who make it possible for us to offer a comprehensive range of services to meet all of the health care needs of the children of our region.

	Cost Each	Number Needed
DIGITAL THERMOMETER takes temperature readings rapidly	$250	3
BREAST PUMP expresses mother's milk for babies born with cleft palate who are unable to nurse	$550	2
WIRELESS PHONE allows quick and easy communication between doctors and nurses on changing patient condition	$600	4
PORTABLE OTOSCOPE/OPHTHALMOSCOPE examines ears/eyes	$1,000	1

	Cost Each	Number Needed
PORTABLE SUCTION UNIT transports care to infants and children with breathing difficulties	$1,200	1
SERVO ULTRANEBULIZER provides continuous aerosol nebulization of medication for patients with severe asthma	$1,300	2
MANNEQUIN simulates traumatic injuries to help nursing personnel and physicians to benefit from hands-on training	$1,325	1
BLOOD WARMER heats the blood as it is administered through the Hemofiltration Machine	$2,000	1
SYRINGE PUMP delivers crucial dosages of medication accurately over several minutes or several hours	$2,250	13
PATIENT LIFT lifts burn patients in and out of whirlpool treatment tub before and after treatment	$4,000	1
ENDOSCOPIC SINUS EQUIPMENT aids the doctors in performing surgeries on patients with chronic sinus diseases	$5,000	1
WHIRLPOOL provides care to Burn Unit patients at least once a day	$9,000	1
BILEVEL VENTILATOR provides therapy and additional support for young patients having difficulty breathing	$9,040	4
NURSING SCHOLARSHIPS enable any Children's Mercy staff person to pursue a nursing degree or enable current nurses to expand their abilities through additional education. These nurses provide expert pediatric health care, compassion and comfort so needed by the children and the families we serve.	**INVESTMENT IN CARE**	

FAMILY SUPPORT FUND assists families with limited income to be able to find lodging, meals, transportation so that they can stay with their hospitalized child.

Special Gifts

As Children's Mercy enters the 21st century, it is essential that we maintain the most up-to-date equipment and sophisticated services in caring for children. This list of state-of-the-art equipment will help us continue to provide the highest level of care for our patients in the future.

	Cost Each	Number Needed
WEIGH IN		
INFANT SCALE weighs the youngest of patients so that a fraction of an ounce shows progress	$1,795	3
DIGITAL STANDING SCALE weighs toddlers to adolescents	$1,800	4
INFANT BED WITH SCALE enables staff to weigh infants and small children who are too sick to be taken out of bed and weighed on an infant scale	$4,824	1
MONITORS		
OXYGEN SATURATION MONITOR measures the percentage of oxygen circulating in the blood	$1,950	1
BLOOD PRESSURE MONITOR measures a patient's blood pressure and pulse electronically and provides frequent readings during a procedure	$2,190	6
TRANSPORT MONITOR allows patients to receive necessary monitoring during sedation procedures, during transport and recovery	$7,219	1
COMPUTERS & PROGRAMS THAT HELP		
TRAUMA REGISTRY tracks types of injuries, locations and other vital information that assists in preventing future pediatric injuries	$1,500	1
COMPUTER, MONITOR & KEYBOARD assists the clinic staff with lab follow up and patient inquiries	$11,000	1

Resource 11

DIAGNOSIS	Cost Each	Number Needed
SPIROMETRY UNIT measures the function of the lungs	$2,400	1
FIBEROPTIC LARYNGOSCOPE assesses the upper airways	$5,800	1

RESULTS AT A GLANCE

	Cost Each	Number Needed
LCD PROJECTOR assists our physicians and nurses in education of other professionals by directly transmitting computer-based materials and by eliminating the need to produce slides	$8,000	1

Major Gifts

Every gift from the community is valued at Children's Mercy, but there are some unique individuals who have the capability—and the care and commitment—to provide a significant gift which can have a major impact on the lives of children well into the next century.

	Cost Each	Number Needed
PORTABLE OTOACOUSTIC EMISSION MACHINE screens the hearing of newborn babies while they are still in the hospital nursery	$11,000	2
TRANSCUTANEOUS MONITOR continuously displays the oxygen and carbon dioxide level in infants who are on ventilators	$12,000	4
PUPILOMETRY MACHINE attaches to the Compact Ultrasound	$15,000	1
COMPACT ULTRASOUND measures the eyes of children who have cataracts for intra ocular lens placement and helps confirm retinal detachment	$16,000	1
AUDITORY BRAINSTEM RESPONSE MACHINE tests the hearing of babies and handicapped children by measuring the electricity that goes up the hearing nerve to the brain	$16,000	1

	Cost Each	Number Needed
SURGICAL LIGHT illuminates the operating area and is vitally needed in two of the operating rooms	$17,000	2
BRAINTREE BASE SYSTEM AND LASER JET PRINTER records and maps brain waves to detect seizures	$18,995	1
VIDEO GASTROSCOPE looks into the stomach and small intestines	$19,000	1
DIALYSIS HEMOFILTRATION MACHINE – Replaces the function of the kidney temporarily so the kidney can rest and heal itself and therefore prevent permanent kidney failure	$23,500	1
VENTILATOR provides life support for neonates and infants who are unable to breathe on their own	$25,000	5
MICROSCOPE assists the physicians in surgeries performed on the ears, nose or throat	$30,000	1
HEMATOLOGY ANALYZER counts white cells and red cells in blood samples and is used in diagnosing and treating infections, leukemias, sickle cell, etc.	$38,000	1
ARTHROSCOPY TOWER AND SCOPE repairs knee and wrist injuries through a very small puncture site providing a quicker recovery	$40,000	1
VIDEO ENDOSCOPY CART assists in evaluation and education of patients and their families	$40,000	1
VIDEO LIGHT SOURCE illuminates the intestines so that diagnosis can be made	$45,000	1
DNA SEQUENCER analyzes the molecules that provide the chemical instructions for life (DNA) thus detecting genetic mutations that are responsible for cancer and inherited diseases	$55,000	1

Resource 11

Resource 11

I want to help the children at Children's Mercy Hospital.

☐ Enclosed is my/our (please circle one) gift/pledge of $ _____

☐ Please apply my/our gift toward the following item(s):

_____

_____

☐ Please use my gift to purchase priority medical equipment.

(In case of duplicate donations, your gift will be used toward the purchase of an equally needed piece of equipment.)

☐ Please send me information on how I can help the children at Children's Mercy in the future through planned giving.

☐ I work for a matching gift company. (My form is enclosed.)

CREDIT CARD INFORMATION

Please charge my

☐ Visa ☐ MasterCard ☐ American Express ☐ Discover in the amount of $ _____

Card Holder Name _____ Account Number _____
(PLEASE PRINT)

Signature _____ Exp. Date _____

☐ My/our check is enclosed (made payable to Children's Mercy Hospital).

          ☐ Individual Gift (Please check one)   ☐ Corporate Gift

          ☐ Mr. ☐ Ms. ☐ Mr. & Mrs. ☐ Other _____ Company _____

Name _____ Title _____

Address _____

City _____ State _____ Zip _____

Day Phone (____)_____ Evening Phone (____)_____

Note: The *Making Dreams Come True* solicitation package is reprinted with permission from Children's Mercy Hospital.

RESOURCE 12

GALA EVENT INVITATION AND PROGRAM

Invitation   292
Response Card   294

Courtesy Reply Envelope   295
Program   296

Invitation

[front]

The Empress will open its Ballroom,

Tea Lobby and Bengal Lounge

exclusively to the guests of

visions
1999

JOIN US AT OUR CHAMPAGNE RECEPTION

DANCE TO THE SOUNDS OF

THE SWINGIN' BACHELORS

COMPETE FOR OVER 150 UNIQUE

ITEMS IN OUR AUCTIONS

INDULGE YOUR APPETITE WITH

OUR SUMPTUOUS BUFFETS

BETTER DIAGNOSIS MEANS BETTER CARE.

[back]

THE GREATER

VICTORIA

HOSPITALS

FOUNDATION

PRESENTS

visions 1999

DATE: SATURDAY, NOVEMBER 6, 1999

PLACE: THE EMPRESS, 721 GOVERNMENT STREET

RECEPTION: 7:00 PM   **DINNER:** 7:30 PM

DRESS: BLACK TIE OPTIONAL

TICKETS: $125 PER PERSON
(A PORTION OF WHICH IS TAX DEDUCTIBLE)

RSVP: COMPLETE AND RETURN
THE ENCLOSED REPLY CARD,
CALL (250) 414-6688 OR FAX (250) 414-6687

GREATER
VICTORIA
HOSPITALS
FOUNDATION

Response Card

YES!
I WISH TO ATTEND visions 1999
AT THE EMPRESS
SATURDAY, NOVEMBER 6, 1999

☐ Please send me _____ tickets at $125 each
   (a portion of which is tax deductible)

☐ I am with _____ party.
   (Please print host's name if applicable.)

☐ Please reserve _____ table(s) (of 10) at $1,250 each
   in the name of _____

I have enclosed a cheque for $ _____

I prefer to use my ☐ Visa ☐ MasterCard

Number _____ Expiry Date _____

Signature _____

Name _____

Address _____

City _____Postal Code _____

Home Phone _____ Bus. Phone _____

Please provide the names of each of your guests:
(Attach list if necessary.)

_____

_____

_____

☐ In addition to my tickets, I would like to make an
   additional gift of $

☐ Unfortunately I am unable to attend. Please
   accept this donation as a gift. (Tickets and
   charitable tax receipts will be mailed.)

FOR MORE INFORMATION, CALL THE
GREATER VICTORIA HOSPITALS FOUNDATION
AT (250) 414-6688 OR FAX (250) 414-6687.

Courtesy Reply Envelope

visions 1999

GREATER VICTORIA HOSPITALS FOUNDATION

NOOTKA COURT

SUITE H304, 633 COURTNEY STREET

VICTORIA BC   V8W 1B9

Program

Dear Guest,

Welcome to Visions '99. I am very pleased that you are here with us this evening in support of diagnostic care at Victoria's hospitals.

This year we are especially proud to raise money for an important cardiac ultrasound for the Royal Jubilee Hospital. This ultrasound will benefit patients and families on Vancouver Island.

Visions '99 will entice you with gourmet cuisine, dancing and our very special live and silent auctions. Every dollar you spend tonight will directly impact patient care in our hospitals.

I would like to thank the Visions '99 Steering Committee, the generous sponsors, auction donors, the great volunteers, and you, our guest of Visions. All of us have come together to make this evening a memorable one to benefit patients in our community hospitals.

Enjoy!

Sincerely,

Leslee Farrell
Chair, Visions '99

VISIONS 1999 COMMITTEE

Leslee Farrell *Volunteer Chair*	Muriel Kovitz
	Walter Nicholson
Deedrie Ballard *Auction Chair*	Kelly Patterson
Glen Colwill	Alison Rippington
Marsha Crawford	Vickki Spievak
Sue Iles	Anna Thomson
Rob and Waffa Jennings	Monika Tomaszewski

THIS EVENING'S PROGRAM

7:00   Champagne Reception

EMPRESS TEA LOBBY/BENGAL LOUNGE
Dining

TEA LOBBY
Silent Auction—Red Section

RETAIL LOBBY
Silent Auction—Black Section
Chocolate Fondue, Compliments of
    Bernard Callebaut Chocolaterie

Diamond Millennium Pendant Raffle
    Brought to you by Paul Mara
    Jewellers—Tickets $100

Canine Capers
    Raffle Tickets $100

Chris Millington Quartet—
BENGAL LOUNGE

Muriel Wellwood—CRYSTAL BALLROOM

Victoria Conservatory of Music—
TEA LOBBY

8:30   Formal Announcements—
       CRYSTAL BALLROOM

8:40   Live Auction—CRYSTAL BALLROOM

9:15   Swingin' Bachelors—PALM COURT

9:30   Silent Auction Closes—BLACK SECTION

9:45   Silent Auction Closes—RED SECTION

10:00 Raffle Prizes are drawn—
       CRYSTAL BALLROOM

10:15 Bank Opens—CONSERVATORY
       (Beside Coat Check)

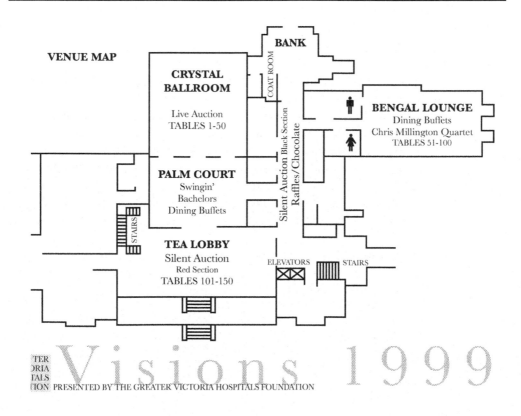

VENUE MAP

BANK

CRYSTAL BALLROOM
Live Auction
TABLES 1-50

COAT ROOM

Silent Auction Black Section
Raffles/Chocolate

BENGAL LOUNGE
Dining Buffets
Chris Millington Quartet
TABLES 51-100

PALM COURT
Swingin'
Bachelors
Dining Buffets

STAIRS

TEA LOBBY
Silent Auction
Red Section
TABLES 101-150

ELEVATORS   STAIRS

Silent Auction Red Section

Visions 1999

PRESENTED BY THE GREATER VICTORIA HOSPITALS FOUNDATION

SILENT AUCTION

The Greater Victoria Hospitals Foundation would like to thank all donors for their generosity in donating gifts for tonight's event. Without their continued support this event would not be possible.

SILENT AUCTION PROCEDURE

- Please use your name and ticket number when bidding on an item.
- Please note the minimum bid and bid increments to avoid disappointment.
- At closing time the successful bidder will be circled on the bid sheet. Bidders may pay for their item(s) starting at 10:15 p.m. at the Bank.
- The Bank will issue a proof of payment, which you will need to pick up your item(s).
- Items will remain on their original tables for pick up.
- Items must be paid for and collected this evening.
- Visa, MasterCard, Cheques and Cash will be accepted.
- For auction closing times please read the "Evening's Program" section of this pamphlet.

THE SMALL PRINT

- All sales are FINAL and items are sold "AS IS." Upgrades, extensions, exchanges and returns are not permitted.
- Decisions of the Greater Victoria Hospitals Foundation staff will be final.
- GVHF makes every effort to properly describe the auction items and in no event shall be responsible for the correctness of the descriptions of the items made orally, at the auction or elsewhere, nor shall there be deemed to be a warranty, representation or assumption of liability.
- Participation in the auction constitutes acceptance by the bidder of all the rules and conditions as set out in this program. GVHF reserves the right to withdraw any auction item.
- Due to Revenue Canada Guidelines, items for auction are not considered tax receiptable, nor can tax receipts be issued for the difference between the value of the item and the amount paid for the item.

Resource 12

VISIONS 1999 IS PROUDLY SPONSORED BY

PLATINUM

[platinum sponsors listed here]

GOLD

Berkshire Group/AIC
Bernard Callebaut Chocolaterie
Centra Gas
Jennings Florist
Monk Office Supply
Nationwide Carpet Cleaning
Paul Mara Jewellers
RE/MAX ports west
Three Point Motors

SILVER

Amazing Balloons

BRONZE

Carfre & Lawton
Empress Taxi
George and Jane Heffelfinger
Stay 'n Save Motor Inns Inc.
Western Tuxedo Sales & Rentals

SPECIAL THANKS TO . . .

Chintz & Co.
CHR Transport
CHR Staff Volunteers
Island Displays
Gregg Eligh
Ted Grant
Lexmark
LRM Rush
Staff of CIBC
Victoria Conservatory of Music

RESOURCE 13

SALES AND RAFFLE EVENT PROMOTION

Saturday, May 22, 1999

(raindate: Sunday, May 23)

Water Balloon Toss

Jump Rope Contest

Treasure Hunt

Harmony Extravaganza

Carnival-style BOOTHS & GAMES

RACES

Face-Painting

12:30 - 5:00 p.m.
909 E. 2nd Street

Co-sponsored by The Bloomington Independent

Live Entertainment with MC **BRAD WILHELM** and

12:30 to 12:50	Chris Clark
1:00 to 1:30	Yup Natok
1:40 to 2:20	Bloomington Quarry Morris Dancers, May Pole
2:20 to 3:00	Yuba Singers with Janiece Jaffe
3:10 to 3:40	David Christman with Alice Platz,
	Carrie Platz and Leah Beebe
3:50 to 4:20	Jason Wilber
4:30 to 5:00	Grey Larsen
5:00	Raffle

Special performance of "English Longsword Dance" by Harmony students

ELM HEIGHTS NEIGHBORHOOD CELEBRATION

Visions of Place Project volunteers will be on hand to copy old photographs and audiotape oral histories related to memories of the old school, the and the neighborhood.

BINGO

Basketball Contest

Cake Walk

...and more!

RAFFLE at 5 P.M.

Need not be present to win.
Prize - Donated By

One Year Family Membership
YMCA
Bird Feeder & A Year's Supply
of Deluxe Bird Seed
Wild Birds Unlimited
A Year's Supply of Bagels
(1 dozen/month)
Bloomington Bagel Company
A Year's Supply of Coffee
($5/month)
Capuccino's
A Year's Supply of Ice Cream
(1 sundae/month)
White Mountain Ice Creamery
Lithograph - Bruce David
Full Body Massage - Jan Hayes

Bicycle Tune-up and Helmet
Bicycle Garage & Bikesmiths
Pottery - Barb Lund
Pottery - **Karen Green Stone**
Happy Birthday Cake & Balloons
**Eileen's Catering &
The Flower Bowl**
$30 Gift Certificate
**Stranger's Hill Farm &
Greenhouse**
$25 Gift Certificate
Boca Loca Beads
$20 Gift Certificate
Red Chair Bakery
Family Hair Cuts - Great Clips
A Special Gift - Goods

Performance Sponsor
Plum Creek Cabinets

Booth Sponsors
Bloomington Office Supply
Ekimae Japanese Restaurant
ONB Bloomington
HoosierNet
K&S Country Market

Game Sponsors
Arby's
Ben Franklin Crafts and
Frame Shop
Bloomington Hardware
Bloomington Professional
Carpet Cleaners
Lynn Weddle Insurance Sales
Photo Solutions
Schnaible Service & Supply

Other Supporters
General Sign
Oliver Winery
Squire Boone Village
Sue Westhues
Zimmer Enterprises

Kids Raffle
Athena
25th Century Five and Dime
Boca Loca Beads
Classic Bowling Lanes
IMU Catering
Pygmalion's
Wendy's

Source: Harmony School Education Center. Printed with permission.

Resource 13

RESOURCE 14

"A-THON" EVENT PACKAGES

Letter to Friends and Family   306
Donor Form   307
Letter to Church Friends   308
Letter to Coworkers   309

Thank-You Note from Volunteer   310
Thank-You Note from
     Organization   311

Letter to Friends and Family

February 17, 2000

[inside address]

Dear Friends and Relatives,

Our son was diagnosed with **Crohn's disease** the year before his graduation from college. Two hospitalizations during this time (one of which was emergency intestinal surgery) added an extra challenge to graduating on time. He graduated and has been making his own way in the field of meteorology but with the extra knowledge that this disease will always be a part of his life.

For those of you who don't know what Crohn's disease is, it is the most severe of the irritable bowel disorders. Crohn's disease and ulcerative colitis attack the digestive system. These diseases cause intense pain and can lead to serious complications. **Most new diagnosed cases are children, teenagers, and adults under 35**, young people struggling to reach their potential while facing a chronic disease. Although the illness is not talked about very often, it's amazing how many of our friends and acquaintances know someone who is or has been afflicted with Crohn's; perhaps you do too.

We now have the opportunity to personally help raise funds for the **Crohn's & Colitis Foundation of America (CCFA)** by walking in this year's **Indianapolis Life—500 Festival Mini-Marathon**. We hope to provide not only moral support for our son and other persons who are living with this disease but also badly needed funds for research to help find a cure for this horribly debilitating disease. (And this effort is indeed a challenge for us. Training has started. My wife is definitely a "fish out of water," and I am recovering from surgery that removed all the "hardware" from the ankle I broke in January 1999.)

Each member of the **"TEAM WITH A DREAM"** is hoping to raise **$1,000** for CCFA. The funds raised will help the foundation achieve the dream of a future world without Crohn's disease. (Only individual, foundation, and corporate donations support CCFA. **More than 82 cents** of every dollar donated goes **directly** into **research and educational programs.**)

Please help us reach our goal by supporting our walk with a donation by **March 30, 2000**. Just complete one (or both) of the enclosed forms and mail it to us directly. All checks should be made out to **CCFA–Indiana Chapter**, and **no amount is too small**. All donations are tax deductible. If you have questions, please do not hesitate to contact us by telephone or e-mail.

Thank you in advance for your support.

[signature]

Resource 14

Donor Form

TEAM
WITH A DREAM
a future without Crohn's disease & colitis

CCFA
CROHN'S
&
COLITIS
FOUNDATION
OF AMERICA

Yes! I will help CCFA find a cure on behalf
of _____ **Name of individual** _____
Team With a Dream member

☐ I will donate $_____ for each mile of the
   13.1-mile mini-marathon, for a total donation
   of $_____

☐ Flat donation of $_____
☐ Check enclosed
   (please make payable to CCFA–Indiana Chapter)

☐ MasterCard   ☐ Visa
☐ American Express   ☐ Discover

Card No: _____

Expiration Date: _____

Signature: _____

PLEASE PRINT

Name: _____

Address: _____

City: _____ ST:_____ ZIP: _____

Phone: _____

*I have set a personal goal to raise a minimum of $1,000
for the Crohn's & Colitis Foundation of America and to
finish the 13.1-mile mini-marathon. I am helping CCFA
achieve its dream of a future without Crohn's disease
and colitis.*

Thank you for your support!
Mail your tax deductible donation to:

Resource 14

Note: This form accompanies all three letters featured in this
Resource.

Letter to Church Friends

Dear Friend at Trinity,

Our son was diagnosed with Crohn's disease the year before his graduation from college. Two hospitalizations during this time (one of which was emergency intestinal surgery) added an extra challenge to graduating on time. He graduated and has been making his own way in the field of meteorology but with the extra knowledge that this disease will always be a part of his life.

For those of you who don't know what Crohn's disease is, it is the most severe of the irritable bowel disorders. Crohn's disease and ulcerative colitis attack the digestive system. These diseases cause intense pain and can lead to serious complications. Most new diagnosed cases are children, teenagers, and adults under 35, young people struggling to reach their potential while facing a chronic disease. Although it is not talked about very often, it's amazing how many of our friends and acquaintances know someone who is or has been afflicted with Crohn's.

We now have the opportunity to personally help raise funds for the **Crohn's & Colitis Foundation of America (CCFA)** by walking in this year's **Indianapolis Life–500 Festival Mini-Marathon**. We hope to provide not only moral support for our son and other persons who are living with this disease but also badly needed funds for research to help find a cure for this horribly debilitating disease.

Each member of the "**TEAM WITH A DREAM**" is hoping to raise **$1,000** for CCFA. The funds raised will help the foundation achieve the dream of a future world without Crohn's disease. (Only individual, foundation, and corporate donations support CCFA. More than 82 cents of every dollar donated goes directly into research and educational programs.)

Please help me reach my goal by supporting my walk with a donation by **March 30, 2000**. Just complete the donor form and mail it to me directly. All checks should be made out to **CCFA–Indiana Chapter**, and no amount is too small. All donations are tax deductible. If you have questions, please do not hesitate to contact me via telephone or e-mail.

Thank you in advance for your support.

[signature]

Letter to Coworkers

Dear Fellow *Primerica PFAs* from Indiana and Kentucky,

Our son was diagnosed with **Crohn's disease** the year before he graduated from college. Two hospitalizations during this time (one of which was emergency intestinal surgery) added an extra challenge to graduating on time. He did graduate and has been making his own way in the field of meteorology—but with the extra knowledge that this disease will always be a part of his life—it knows no social, ethnic, or financial boundaries.

For you *PFAs* who don't know what Crohn's disease is, it is the most severe of the irritable bowel disorders. Crohn's disease and ulcerative colitis attack the digestive system. These diseases cause intense pain and can lead to serious complications. **Most new diagnosed cases are children, teenagers and adults under 35**, young people struggling to reach their potential while facing a chronic disease. Although the disease is not talked about very often, <u>it's amazing how many of our friends and acquaintances know someone who is or has been afflicted with Crohn's—perhaps you do too</u>.

My wife and I now have the opportunity to personally help raise funds for the **Crohn's & Colitis Foundation of America (CCFA)** by walking in this year's **Indianapolis Life–500 Festival Mini-Marathon**. We hope to provide not only moral support for our son and other persons who are living with this disease but also badly needed funds for research to help find a cure for this horribly debilitating disease.

Each member of the **"TEAM WITH A DREAM"** is hoping to personally raise **$1,000** for CCFA. These funds will help the foundation achieve the dream of a future world **without Crohn's disease**. (Only individual, foundation, and corporate donations support CCFA. More than **82 cents of every dollar** donated goes directly into research and educational programs.)

Please help me reach my goal by joining me in support of my walk with a donation by **March 30, 2000**. Complete the donor form and mail it to me directly. All checks should be made out to **CCFA–Indiana Chapter**, and **no amount is too small**. All donations are tax deductible. If you have questions, please do not hesitate to contact me by telephone or e-mail.

As always, thank you in advance for your support. Perhaps CCFA will become a project of *Primerica!* One day, we *will* have a cure! Take care and God bless!

GO-GO-GO!

[signature]

Thank-You Note from Volunteer

CROHN'S
&
COLITIS
FOUNDATION
OF AMERICA

February 24, 2000

Dear [name],

On behalf of the Indiana Chapter of the Crohn's & Colitis Foundation of America, I want to thank you for your generous [amount] donation toward my walk in this year's Mini-Marathon. I have listed your gift amount and name under "[name]" on my Donor chart toward the $1,000 I hope to raise toward the cure for Crohn's.

We have been training hard for the Mini. We walked 5 miles with the other members of the "Team With a Dream" last Saturday. We'll be walking 3 miles every day this week. We'll be "ramping up" our distance by 1 mile every Saturday until we reach that 13-mile goal. Once again [name], thanks for your support. One day soon we just might be free of Crohn's disease! Won't that be a fantastic day!

[signature]

Thank-You Note from Organization

CROHN'S
&
COLITIS
FOUNDATION
OF AMERICA

March 22, 2000

Indiana Chapter

931 East 86th Street, Suite 102

Indianapolis, IN 46240

Tel.: (317) 259-8071

Toll-Free: (800) 332-6029

Fax: (317) 259-8091

e-mail: indiana@ccfa.org

[inside address]

Dear [name]:

On behalf of the Indiana Chapter of the Crohn's & Colitis Foundation of America, thank you for your recent donation to the "Team With a Dream" Mini-Marathon.

CCFA is a nonprofit, research-oriented, voluntary health organization dedicated to improving the quality of life for persons with Crohn's disease or ulcerative colitis. Your support will allow us to continue to provide support to the estimated 1 million Americans who suffer from Crohn's disease and ulcerative colitis.

Our Indiana office sponsors support groups that meet regularly. We facilitate patient and physician education programs and provide ongoing support and referral to patients. Our various fundraising activities support national and local research programs.

If we can provide any additional information about Crohn's disease, ulcerative colitis, and the work of CCFA or our support groups, please do not hesitate to contact us at (317) 259-8071, and we will be happy to assist you. Again, thank you for your support.

Sincerely,

[signature]

National Headquarters:

386 Park Avenue South

New York, NY 10016

Tel.: (800) 932-2423

Fax: (212) 779-4098

e-mail: info@ccfa.org

www.ccfa.org

FOR YOUR RECORDS: This letter will serve as your receipt for tax purposes. We acknowledge your gift of $_____. No goods or services were received in exchange for this donation.

RESOURCE 15

"A-THON" TEAM CAPTAIN'S KIT AND SUPPLIES

Team Captain Handbook   315
Team Recruitment Information   316
    Sample Corporate Media
       Release   316
    Sample CEO Recruitment
       Memo   317
    Sample Article for Employee
       Newsletter   318
    Sample Recruitment Press
       Release   319
Team Planning Information   320
    Tour de Cure Team Roster   320
    Tour de Cure Team Prize Order
       Form   321
    Sample Team Goal Memo   322
    Team Goal Form   323
    Welcome Packet Information   324

Advertising Pieces   331
    Poster   331
    Brochure   332
Post-Event Follow-Up   333
    Pledge Turn-In Party Poster   333
    No-Show Pledge Chase
       Mailing   334
    Thank-You Pledge Chase
       Mailing   335

Resource 15

Team Captain Handbook

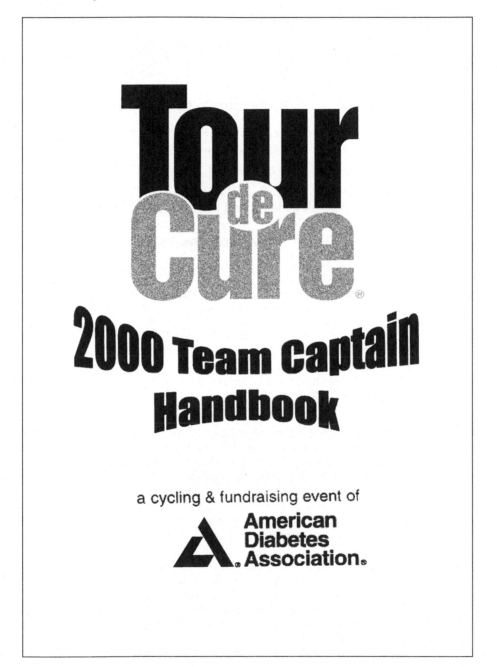

Team Recruitment Information

Sample Corporate Media Release

Tour de Cure & Fight Diabetes!

_____ IS FORMING A TEAM TO RIDE IN THE

2000 Tour de Cure

to benefit the American Diabetes Association
on Sunday June 4, 2000
And we need your help to make our TEAM a success! Do the Tour!
Team Captain: _____ Phone: _____
Join your colleagues, friends, and family for a great day of cycling.

Tour de Cure Facts

When?   Sunday, June 4, 2000
Check-In: 7:15–8:00 a.m.
Team Area for beverages & photos: 7:15–8:00 a.m.
Start: 8:15 a.m. sharp—the Tour will occur rain or shine!

Where?   The Start/Finish line is at Eagle's Crest, located in Eagle Creek Park in Indianapolis

How?   Fill out a registration form to ride or volunteer. You'll find one on the back of this flier, OR in the Tour de Cure brochure, OR you can get one from your team captain, OR call the Tour de Cure Hotline at (317) 352-9226 and we'll send you a brochure and registration form.

Why?   To benefit the American Diabetes Association in Indiana. Funds raised through your sponsors' donations support national research into the cause and cure of diabetes, as well as vital services for Hoosiers. One in every 20 individuals has diabetes. That is approximately 16 million Americans, one third of whom do not even know they have the disease! Complications include heart disease, stroke, kidney disease, blindness, nerve damage, and severe infections leading to foot and leg amputations. 798,000 people will be diagnosed with diabetes this year, and more than 180,000 will die.

You Get a Great Ride and Help Someone Else.
Think Big and Tour de Cure!

You can also win great prizes, like a week's vacation to places like the Great Smoky Mountains or Puerto Vallarta. You can even win a weekend getaway to New Orleans!

For More Information, Call (317) 352-9226

Sample CEO Recruitment Memo

(Use Your Company/Organization Letterhead)

TO: All (Company/Organization's Name) Personnel

FROM: (CEO or Executive's Name)

DATE:

RE: 2000 Tour de Cure for American Diabetes Association, scheduled (day & date)

Please join the _____ Team on June 4 for the 2000 Tour de Cure, a benefit for the American Diabetes Association. This is a monumental event that offers the challenge of "going the distance" and also does something very positive for the community in which we live and work. Besides doing something good for you and your health, you will be doing something good for people in [state or region] who have diabetes.

During this day of cycling, our team will begin its ride at Eagle's Crest in Eagle Creek Park and ride through beautiful Hendricks County. This is a route with incredible views you just won't see any other way. Don't you want to be part of this great effort?

Team contributions will support the work of the American Diabetes Association. Funds raised through your sponsors' donations support national research into the cause and cure of diabetes, as well as vital services for Hoosiers with diabetes. One in every 20 individuals has diabetes. That is approximately 16 million Americans, one-third of whom don't even know they have the disease! Complications include heart disease, stroke, kidney disease, blindness, and severe infections leading to foot and leg amputations. 798,000 people will be diagnosed with diabetes this year, and more than 180,000 will die. The Tour de Cure offers us the opportunity to truly change the world.

_____ is the Tour de Cure Team Captain for (company/organization) and will help you register as a team member. If you have any questions about the Tour, feel free to call (him/her) at _____.

Please register today and help us reach our goal of recruiting ten team members for this year's team. If you can't join us, please sponsor our team by pledging a donation. You can also volunteer at the Tour. Many thanks for helping our team make the Tour de Cure successful.

Sample Article for Employee Newsletter

Think Big . . . Tour de Cure

(Company/organization) is pleased to announce we are forming a team to participate in the 2000 Tour de Cure. Our team will join more than 25,000 cyclists, including 1,500 teams nationwide, who will raise more than $5,000,000 in the fight against diabetes in support of the American Diabetes Association. (Team Captain name) is confident our team will capture top team honors in 2000.

Our team will begin its ride at Eagle's Crest in Eagle Creek Park and will ride throughout Hendricks County. This exciting event offers (company/organization name) the opportunity to do something positive for the community.

Our team's contributions will support the work of the American Diabetes Association. Funds raised through your sponsors' donations support research into the cause and cure of diabetes and diabetes education programs here in Indiana. One in every 20 individuals has diabetes. Complications of diabetes include heart disease, stroke, kidney disease, blindness, and severe infections leading to foot and leg amputations. 798,000 people will be diagnosed with diabetes this year, and more than 180,000 will die.

By collecting donations from family and friends, team riders can qualify for valuable thank-you prizes including official Tour de Cure T-shirts and gift certificates. All employees, along with their families and friends, are encouraged to join the 1999 Tour de Cure. Please contact (team captain name) at (team captain's phone number), or call (317) 352-9226, or send e-mail to (team captain's e-mail address). Anyone wanting diabetes information or education materials can call (317) 352-9226.

Resource 15

Sample Recruitment Press Release (for internal use)

(Use Your Company/Organization Letterhead)

TO: All (Company/Organization's Name) Personnel

FROM: (Executive's Name)

DATE:

RE: 2000 Tour de Cure for American Diabetes Association,
            scheduled (day & date)

Please join the _____ Team on June 4th for the 2000 Tour de Cure, a benefit for the American Diabetes Association. This is an enjoyable event that offers the challenge of "going the distance" and also does something very positive for the community in which we live and work. Besides getting a good ride, you will be doing something great for people in [state or region] who have diabetes.

Challenge yourself to a day of cycling beginning at Eagle's Crest in Eagle Creek Park and going through Hendricks County. This is a route with incredible views you just won't see any other way.

Team contributions will support the work of the American Diabetes Association. Funds raised through your sponsors' donations support national research into the cause and cure of diabetes, as well as vital services for Hoosiers with diabetes. One in every 20 individuals has diabetes. That means approximately 16 million Americans have the disease and one third of them don't even know it! Complications include heart disease, stroke, kidney disease, blindness, and severe infections leading to foot and leg amputations. 780,000 people will be diagnosed with diabetes this year, and more than 180,000 will die. The Tour de Cure offers us the opportunity to truly change the world.

_____ is the Tour de Cure Team Captain for (company/organization) and will help you register as a team member. If you have any questions about the Tour, feel free to call (him/her) at _____.

We look forward to welcoming you to our team. If you can't join us, please sponsor our team by pledging a donation. You can also volunteer at the Tour. Many thanks for helping our team make the Tour de Cure successful.

Team Planning Information

Tour de Cure Team Roster

Company Name: _____   Team Captain: _____ Phone: _____

Address: _____   City: _____ State: _____ ZIP: _____ Fax: _____

E-Mail: _____   Does your company have a matching gift program? Yes or No

Please attach form for each qualified participant.

Name	Address	City/State/ZIP	In Case of Emergency Contact* Name	Phone	Signature**	Money Collected

Total Riders	Team Goal	Total Money Collected

*I hereby waive all claims against the American Diabetes Association, sponsors or any personnel for any injury I might suffer in this event. I grant full permission for organizers to use photographs of me in legitimate accounts and promotions of this event.

**Parent or Guardian must sign if participant is less than 18 years of age.

Tour de Cure Team Prize Order Form

Bring this completed form with you when you turn in your team's pledges.

Team Name: _____   Team Captain: _____

Team Member Name	Amount Collected	Prize Desired	Size (if applicable)

Sample Team Goal Memo

Date: (March xx, 2000)

TO: (Team Member's Name)

FROM: (Team Captain's Name)

RE: (Team Name) Team's Fundraising and Recruitment Goal

Thank you for signing up as part of the _____ Team. It's important for us to set a team fundraising goal and an individual team member goal so we can work toward these goals in the upcoming weeks.

The average rider last year raised _____. We don't want our team to be just average. We need to challenge ourselves to make a difference.

As a team we hope to raise $_____ and recruit _____ team members. Please try and recruit your coworkers, friends, cycling buddies, and family to join us. Thanks in advance for raising funds and for recruiting more members of our team. The chart below will illustrate our progress over the next five weeks.

Thanks again for joining our Team. Together we can make a difference and be part of the effort to change the world and find a cure for diabetes. See you on June 4!

Thanks for participating in Tour de Cure to benefit the American Diabetes Association

Team Goal Form

SETTING THE GOAL

Company _____

Address _____

City _____ State _____ ZIP _____

Captain_____ Phone _____ Fax _____

Team Committee Members:

_____ Phone _____

_____ Phone _____

_____ Phone _____

Number of Employees _____

C.E.O./President_____

Team Profile	1998 Results	1999 Goal
Number of Riders		
Rider Pledge Average		
Corporate Sponsorship		
Matching Gifts		
Pinup Stars		
Other Fundraising Activities:		
Total Team Dollars		

Welcome Packet Information

American
Diberica
Diabetes
Association.

7363 East 21st Street, Indianapolis, IN 46219

American Diabetes Association.

Mission
to prevent and cure diabetes
and to improve the lives of all
people affected by diabetes

You are officially registered
for Tour de Cure on
Sunday, June 4, 2000, at
Eagle Creek Park in Indianapolis!

Enclosed, please find...
- An extra pledge sheet for your to record additional pledges
- An extra brochure for you to give to a friend
- Your Welcome to Tour de Cure newsletter
- A Pledge Turn-in Party Reminder

Think about this...
- **Start now to recruit additional cyclists to join you!** Remember   If you have 5 or more friends, family members or co-workers participating in the event, you can be considered a team. This is great news because teams are eligible for additional exciting prizes!
- **Collect your money as people make pledges to your ride!** To receive a Tour de Cure T-shirt, you must turn in at least $100 in pledges, which is the minimum required to participate. But, shoot for a goal of $125! And remember   **your dollars DO make a difference!**

Between now and June, you'll receive additional newsletters and mailings updating you about day-of-event details. Please read over this information carefully so you'll be well prepared for the day's activities and festivities.

If you have any questions at all, please feel free to call us at the Indianapolis Tour de Cure headquarters. We are excited that you are joining us for this fun-filled event!

Tour de Cure – Indianapolis Headquarters
1-800-228-2897
(317) 352-9226
Fax: (317) 357-4288
online at www.diabetes.org/tour2000

Indiana/Northwest Ohio

2963 East 21st Street, Indianapolis, Indiana 46219   Tel: (317) 352-9226   1-800-228-7697 (Indiana only)
Fax: (317) 357-4288

For Diabetes Information Call 1-800-DIABETES • http://www.diabetes.org

The Association gratefully accepts gifts through your will

Sponsorship Form

Tour de Cure

Name _____

Address _____

City/State/Zip _____

Employer Name _____

Day Phone _____

Evening Phone _____

My Total Sponsor Goal $ _____

Team Name _____ Team Captain Name _____

Note: A matching gift by a company can help you reach your goals

Sponsor Name	Address	City	Phone	Amount Sponsored	Total Amount

MAKE CHECKS PAYABLE TO THE AMERICAN DIABETES ASSOCIATION

a cycling & fundraising event of
American Diabetes Association.

The Hero is in You!

WELCOME NEWSLETTER

Welcome To the Indianapolis Tour de Cure!

Everyone who participates in Tour de Cure will receive a day full of food, fitness, fun and festivities (all for a good cause). However, forming a team with five friends, family, and co-workers adds more excitement to Tour de Cure than you could imagine!

TEAMS RECEIVE:
Special recognition on event day by the emcee

Separate registration

Their own meeting spot at the start/finish line

Special team numbers.

The top fundraising team earns the right to showcase the Tour de Cure traveling Team Trophy.

Remember, it only takes five friends, family members or co-workers to form a team!

If you need additional information call 1-800-868-7888

www.diabetes.org/tour

Don't Forget

WHEN: Sunday, June 4
Check-in: 7:15 a.m.-8 a.m.

Start Time: 75K 8:15 a.m.
50K 8:30 a.m.
25K 8:45 a.m.

Where:
The start/finished line will be located at the Eagle's Crest at Eagle Creek Park in Indianapolis.

SEE YOU THERE!

Bring a Friend!

1-800-868-7888

Meet the Challenge

Make Fundraising Fun!

Remember, there is a $100 pledge minimum. It was originally printed as a $75 minimum…sorry for the confusion!

Big challenges bring big rewards. YOU can help 360,000 Hoosiers overcome their battle with diabetes by raising as much money as possible for this cause.

STEP ONE-SET A GOAL

Make your goal challenging. Your friends and family will want to help you meet you challenge.

STEP TWO-PLAN YOUR STRATEGY

- What is the best way to approach my family and friends?
- Send a letter to my church
- Send an e-mail to my co-workers

STEP THREE-SHARE YOUR PROGRESS

People will want to be a part of your success.

STEP FIVE- BEGIN WORKING YOUR PLAN TODAY!

Your Dollars at Work

In 1997, the ADA spent 77% of every dollar to fund diabetes prevention and research for a cure!

36.7% Information

Advocacy 26.8%

General Management 5.9%

Research Activities 14.2%

Fund-raising Activities 16.4%

1-800-868-7888

Directions to Eagle's Crest

The easiest way to get to Eagle's Crest in Eagle Creek Park is to take I-65. This interstate is accessible to everyone in the city, no matter which direction you will be traveling from. Take I-65 NORTH (or South depending on which side of the city you live in) to exit 121 – Lafayette Road. Turn North off the exit…that would be a RIGHT to those people traveling I-65 NORTH and a LEFT turn and under the bridge for those people traveling I-65 SOUTH. Go through two stop lights and turn LEFT at the stop light at 56th street. There is a Tuckman's cleaner's to the LEFT and a Super 7 Citgo to your RIGHT at this intersection. Travel approximately 3 miles - PAST the Colts building, PAST the main entrance to Eagle's Creek, PAST the golf course and you will eventually turn RIGHT at Raceway Road. There is a sign here pointing you into the direction of Eagle's Crest. Go one mile and turn RIGHT onto 700 N, there is also a sign here pointing you to Eagle's Crest. Continue on 700 N until you reach Eagle's Crest, which will be on your RIGHT. Turn into Eagle's Crest, park, and make your way to the registration area, located towards the back of Eagle's Crest. (Keep in mind that if you are traveling I-465, there is NO exit onto 56th Street, if you are traveling south from the north side of Indianapolis. That is why we recommend the I-65 route.)

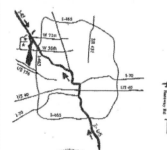

Diabetes: A Silent Killer

Nearly 16 million Americans have diabetes — or about one of every 20 people in America. Adults, teens, seniors and children — diabetes can affect anyone at any age.

It is projected that 180,000 people will die this year because of diabetes — more than from AIDS, breast cancer, or many other life-threatening diseases. The sixth leading cause of death by disease, diabetes has no known cure.

Often the disease is not detected until it causes other health complications such as blindness, kidney and heart disease, strokes, and amputations.

Who is at risk?

Anyone with a family history of diabetes should have regular tests to monitor their health. Other high risk categories include:

- Adults over 45 years of age and overweight.
- Women with high birth weight babies over 9 pounds.

Studies have identified certain ethnic groups to be at greater risk:

- Native Americans — 2.7 times as likely to have diabetes as the general population.
- Hispanics — 2 times as likely to have diabetes as the general population.
- African Americans — 1.7 times as likely to have diabetes as the general population.

For more information on diabetes, contact your physician or your local ADA.

www.diabetes.org/tour

Experience the Triumph

Pedal for a Prize!

We want to thank our participants by giving them a chance to win awesome prizes!

Win a 7 day resort condominium vacation! The Cyclist who turns in the most money for the 2000 Tour de Cure will chose between a vacation in Puerto Rico, The Great Smokey Mountains, Colorado or Williamsburg, VA. This vacation is compliments of RCI.

Turn in ALL your contributions before or on the day of the event and enter a drawing to win a night at Embassy Suites Downtown-Indianapolis.

Team Lilly Played a Huge Part in 1999 Tour de Cure

Team Lilly helped battle diabetes in 1999 by raising nearly $5,000.00 for Tour de Cure.

Thanks Team Lilly!

Fundraising Club

Silver Spokes Club - Individuals raising $500 to $1,249 will receive the following benefits
Subscription to the National Tour de Cure Champions newsletter
Silver Spokes certificate
Official Silver Spokes Jersey

Golden Gears Club - Individuals raising over $1,250 will receive the following benefits:
Subscription to the National Tour de Cure Champions newsletter
Golden Gears certificate
Official Golden Gears jersey
Recognition on Tour de Cure web page
Recognition from Volunteer leadership.

Tour of Champions – Individuals raising over $4,000 will travel to New Orleans October 6-8, 2000 for two days of cycling and French Quarter fun. Call your local ADA office for more information.

Calling all Volunteers

Do you know someone who wants to be part of Tour de Cure in a way other than cycling? We have just the opportunity for them...volunteer. Volunteers are needed the week of the event to assist with picking up supplies, stuffing rider packets, loading trucks, etc. Of course volunteers are needed the day of Tour de Cure to help with registration, drive accounting and gear vehicles. We promise a rewarding day! For more information, please call 1-800-868-7888.

$20,000 Club

Challenge your team to raise $20,000 and become a member of the exclusive Tour de Cure $20,000 Club. You can receive:
- Recognition in next years brochure
- Recognition in national ads
- $20,000 club team award
- $20,000 club team captain award

1999 Members

Bristol-Myers Squibb, Princeton, NJ ($63,189)

Bank of America, Los Angeles, CA ($42,258)

Team Sara, Napa Valley, CA ($33,403)

Team Firm, San Francisco, CA ($32,539)

LifeScan, Woodside, CA ($26,899)

Team Broken Wing, Morristown, NJ ($25,277)

Tidewater Bicycle Assoc., Outer Banks, ($22,928)

Cycling Connection, Riverside, CA ($22,000)

East-West Bank, Los Angeles, CA ($20,240)

Meet Our Pedal Pushers

Several cyclists pushed the limit by raising more than $300 each in our 1999 Tour de Cure. They are:

- Dewayne Boyer
- Melissa Brandt
- James Detty
- Bette J. Gumerson
- Karl Jacobson
- Elizabeth Kesling
- Mark D. Kesling
- J. Tyler Klassen
- Karl Kovach
- Roger Kuhn
- Mike Pasini
- James E. Pickett
- Bill Pullman
- Jim Wolfe

Prize Chart

Thank You Gifts!

If you raise at least $100, you'll receive an official Tour de Cure T-shirt.
Raise $150 or more and you'll also receive one of these great gifts...

Pledge Level		Plus
$4,000	$400 Gift certificate to L.L. Bean Golden Gears Top Fundraising Award	Golden Gears Membership & Jersey
$2,000	$200 Gift certificate to L.L. Bean or Tour Wind Shirt & Cycling Tights	Golden Gears Membership & Jersey
$1,500	$150 Gift certificate to L.L. Bean or Tour de Cure Wind Shirt	Golden Gears Membership & Jersey
$1,250	$125 Gift certificate to L.L. Bean or Tour de Cure Anorak Jacket	Golden Gears Membership & Jersey
$1,000	$100 Gift certificate to L.L. Bean or Tour de Cure Pouch Jacket	Silver Spokes Membership & Jersey
$750	$75 Gift certificate to L.L. Bean or Tour de Cure Cycling Shorts	Silver Spokes Membership & Jersey
$500	$50 Gift certificate to L.L. Bean or Silver Spokes Jersey	Silver Spokes Membership
$350	$35 Gift certificate to L.L. Bean or Tour de Cure Cycling Jersey	
$200	$25 Gift certificate to L.L. Bean or Tour de Cure Cycling Shorts	
$150	Tour de Cure Sweatshirt	
$100	Tour de Cure T-shirt	

To qualify for your gift, all money must be turned in within 4 weeks after day of event.

Tour Safety Tips

The route for the Tour de Cure has been chosen due to the beautiful scenery, but as well as the safety factors.

❑ Cyclists are expected to obey all directional arrows and remain on the marked route **at all times!**

❑ Rural Metro Ambulance has been notified and will be on stand-by should we need emergency medical support.

❑ **Helmets are required for this event!**

Special Thanks to our National Sponsors

[national sponsors listed here]

Our Sponsors

[corporate sponsors listed here]

Advertising Pieces

Poster

Brochure (cover)

Post-Event Follow-Up

Pledge Turn-In Party Poster

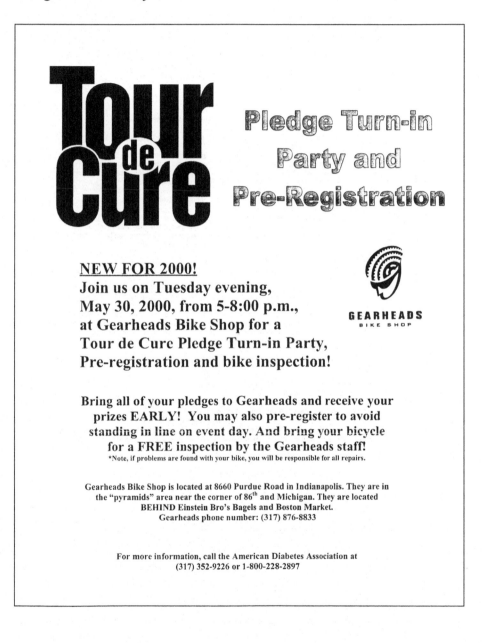

No-Show Pledge Chase Mailing

American Diabetes Association®

Mission
to prevent and cure diabetes
and to improve the lives of all
people affected by diabetes

April 30, 2000

IF...you were not able to join us at Feet to Beat Diabetes on Sunday, April 30th ...
- We missed you!
- You missed a fun day of fundraising, where we raised thousands of dollars to fund diabetes research and programs.
- We still need your help! To make your impact in the lives of over 360,000 Hoosiers who have diabetes, please mail your contribution or pledges in the enclosed envelope.
- If we receive your payment by May 30th, you are still eligible to receive the fundraising awards and prizes, including a T-shirt for a $50 or more contribution.

IF...you joined us at Feet to Beat Diabetes, but did not turn in pledges ...
- We hope you had a great time!
- We still need your help! To make your impact in the lives of over 360,000 Hoosiers who have diabetes, please mail your contribution or pledges in the enclosed envelope.
- If we receive your payment by May 30th, you are still eligible to receive the fundraising awards and prizes, including a T-shirt for a $50 or more contribution.

IF...you joined us at Feet to Beat Diabetes and turned in your pledge envelope...
- Fantastic! Your dollars are already at work, impacting the lives of over 360,000 Hoosiers who have diabetes. The money you turned in is:
  1. Sending a seven-year-old child with insulin-dependent diabetes to Camp John Warvel where he will learn to properly manage his disease, while finding out that he's not alone in dealing with it.
  2. Providing informational packets to remove the fear and uncertainty from a 50 year old woman who has just been diagnosed with diabetes. After reading these materials, she will feel more comfortable with managing her disease and following a proper diet.
  3. Funding research to ultimately remove diabetes from existence.

Many thanks in advance for your generous support of the American Diabetes Association. Your pledge dollars DO make a difference.

With renewed hope for a cure,

Cindy Bechman

Cindy Bechman
District Manager and Feet to Beat Diabetes Walk Coordinator

It's never too late to turn in a pledge! Fill out form and return in the envelope provided. Turn in $50 or more and you will receive a Feet to Beat Diabetes T-shirt! Questions? Call 317-352-9226.

NAME:_____ TEAM:_____

AMOUNT TURNING IN: $_____

(If $50 or over), T-shirt size: ❑Large   ❑X-Large

Address where T-shirt is to be sent:
Street:_____
City, State, Zip:_____

Indiana/Northwest Ohio

7363 East 21st Street, Indianapolis, Indiana 46219   Tel: (317) 352-9226   1-800-228-2897 (Indiana only)
Fax: (317) 357-4288

For Diabetes Information Call 1-800-DIABETES • http://www.diabetes.org

The Association gratefully accepts gifts through your will.

Note: Due to space considerations, the envelopes used for this and the following mailing are not reproduced here.

Thank-You Pledge Chase Mailing

American Diabetes Association.

Mission
to prevent and cure diabetes
and to improve the lives of all
people affected by diabetes

April 30, 2000

CONGRATULATIONS! YOU MADE IT!

Thank you for participating in the 2000 Feet to Beat Diabetes Walk at Conner Prairie! Your fantastic fundraising made a huge dent in our quest to find a cure for diabetes and to improve so many lives.

If you have not done so already, now is the time to take the next step and send in your pledges. Though pledges are due May 30, 2000 to be eligible for gift certificates and prizes, we would appreciate your sending your money in as soon as possible *in the enclosed envelope.*

This year, many of you turned in your pledge amount on event day. This was very much appreciated. If your balance is $0, then you're all set! Your dollars are already working to help people with diabetes in Indiana.

Remember, nearly 360,000 Hoosiers suffer from diabetes. By collecting pledges for this walk, you are:

1. Sending a seven-year-old child with insulin-dependent diabetes to Camp John Warvel where he will learn to properly manage his disease, while finding out that he's not alone in dealing with it.
2. Providing informational packets to remove the fear and uncertainty from a 50 year old woman who has just been diagnosed with diabetes. After reading these materials, she will feel more comfortable with managing her disease and following a proper diet.
3. Funding research to ultimately remove diabetes from existence.

Many thanks for your generous support of the American Diabetes Association.
Your pledge dollars DO make a difference.

With renewed hope for a cure,

Cindy Bechman
District Manager and Feet to Beat Diabetes Walk Coordinator

Indiana/Northwest Ohio

2451 East 71st Street, Indianapolis, Indiana 46220   Tel: (317) 352-9226   1-800-228-2897 (Indiana only)
Fax: (317) 941-8166

For Diabetes Information Call: 1-800-DIABETES (342-2383) • http://www.diabetes.org

RESOURCE 16

ENTERTAINMENT AND SHOW PUBLICITY PIECES

Antique Show Advertisements   338
Amethyst House Comedy Show   340
    Poster   340
    Program   341
    Advertisements   344
    Press Clippings   345
    Sample Newspaper
      Article   346

Antique Show Advertisements

Amethyst House Comedy Show

Poster

Program

COMEDIAN MARK LUNDHOLM

WHEEEEE!

I'M

..THE INSANITY REMAINS

An Amethyst House Benefit Performance
Saturday, 8 PM, April 1, 2000

After the comedy act,
Dance to the Dew Daddies!

. . . *the Insanity Remains*

an Amethyst House benefit performance
8 p.m., April 1, 2000

starring . . .

Comedian   MARK LUNDHOLM

Once upon a time in a former decade, Mark Lundholm traded his life as husband, father and employee for a home in a cardboard box on the streets of Oakland, California. The streets were the more attractive choice, because there Lundholm could chase his disease undisturbed.

Years have passed since Lundholm has taken drugs or guzzled booze. As part of his own recovery process he began doing volunteer comedy in drug rehabs, halfway houses and jails. In a few short years, he was headlining internationally in venues as diverse as Zanies in Chicago, the Comedy Connection in Indianapolis, the Funny Bone in Pittsburgh, a Russian jail, and the Betty Ford Center.

On most nights Lundholm performs a straight stand-up routine. But his favorite bookings will always be those for the recovery community. He's here tonight to share the common bond of having been through hell and back.

Master of Ceremonies   Eric Borders

Eric Borders serves as Treasurer of the Amethyst House Board of Directors. In his "spare time" he works professionally as a financial representative with Innovative Financial Solutions. Tonight he'll give you tips on how to save your tax dollars and benefit Amethyst House at the same time. He'll also provoke your participation in the "Name the Gargoyle" contest.

> Amethyst House provides transitional residential programs in separate houses for men and women, with their dependent children, to empower them in ways that give them dignity, hope and a healthier sense of themselves and their community as they recover from their addictions.

after the comedy act . . .
Dance to Bloomington band   the Dew Daddies

The Dew Daddies have played a hard-edged, traditional style of original and classic country music since the mid-1990s. Their self-produced CD *Makin' Good Time* received excellent reviews in national country music publications. In 1999 the Dew Daddies were featured on a Swedish CD compilation of contemporary American roots bands. For tonight's performance outstanding fiddle player Bret Raper joins the Dew Daddies. Bret played fiddle for Tom T. Hall and others before graduating from the IU Law School.

". . . the Insanity Remains" Event Sponsors

TEK Printing donated event tickets.

$1,700 has been donated by three local companies who wish to remain anonymous.

Note: Reprinted with permission by Amethyst House, Inc.

Advertisements

Press Clippings

Comic Pleases Sober Crowd 1 Joke at a Time

Rick Kogan, Chicago Tribune

"Lundholm comfortably and humorously examines the raucous, dangerous life of substance abuse and the rigors of recovery. . . . He's funny."

It Wasn't the Booze Laughing at Dry Set

Comic Mark Lundholm confronted his old demons with aplomb in a sold-out alcohol-free show

Hector Saldana, San Antonio Express-News

"Comedian Mark Lundholm delivered a performance to remember with an enthusiastic standing-room-only turnout.

"His sharp humor is not unlike that of comedy's supreme iconoclast, George Carlin, with its 'been there, done that' hipster swing. But where early Carlin gave a sweet peek into his hippy-dippy pot smoking, Lundholm navigates junkie and alcoholic hell. Somehow it works. Lundholm's natural comedic flair and clever premises are universally funny."

Comic Mark Lundholm Takes 12 Steps to New Level

Richard Toronto, Benicia Herald

"When people hear about Mark Lundholm's show—blatantly dealing with the pain and insanity of addiction—they invariably ask, 'You went to jail; you lost everything; you were a practicing alcoholic—how is that funny?' That's the crux of Lundholm's act: the irony of it all. And audiences everywhere love it."

Comic Zaps Audience with "12-Step" Humor

Steve Huddleston, Vacaville Reporter

"His return engagement concluded with another standing ovation, one habit that Mark Lundholm's sober audiences cannot kick. His 100-minute nonstop juggernaut slowed only twice during the evening. His powerful, healing humor is a product of going through hell and back. He avoids a return by poking fun at the insanity."

Stepping Lively

Mark Lundholm laughs about his road to recovery

Nicky Baxter, San Jose Metro

"The 36-year-old comic, whose only addiction these days is telling jokes, calls his act 'comedy for the "chemically challenged."' What makes his shows work is the fact that Lundholm doesn't turn a blind eye to the difficulties facing recovering addicts; he simply finds little verities and exposes them with a sharp twist of humor."

Sample Newspaper Article

Comedian Tells What's Humorous About Substance Abuse

Sandra Knipe, entertainment reporter

Mark Lundholm has a friend who smoked pot every day for 22 years, and he's still not addicted.

"If you don't believe me, just ask him," laughed Lundholm, who will present "An Evening of 12-Step Humor with Mark L." Monday at the Funny Bone Comedy Club.

Lundholm knows more than a little something about drug and alcohol addiction. His own addiction cost him his job, his family and his home. By the time he hit bottom, he was living in a cardboard box ("not the same cardboard box, different cardboard boxes at different times") on the streets of Oakland, Calif.

"There are 'high bottom' drug addicts and 'low bottom' drug addicts. . . Me personally, I was a very low bottom addict and alcoholic. I didn't 'get it' until I had lost everything, owed everything and had nothing."

So, as Lundholm himself asks rhetorically, what's so funny about substance abuse?

"Come see the show," he said. "There are things that will happen in the comedy club on Monday night that will not happen on HBO or in that particular room all year. That's a promise (pause for a drum roll) and, if I'm sober, I'll be there."

That wasn't really a joke. For all the dark humor and unrelenting honesty of "An Evening of 12 Step Humor," evident on a tape of Lundholm's show recorded live at the Luther Burbank Center for the Arts in Santa Rosa, Calif., Lundholm still deals with his own disease one day at a time. Monday's 8 p.m. show is chemical-free comedy, meaning no alcohol will be served—but this week, it's business as usual at the Funny Bone, where Lundholm is headlining with his regular stand-up act, starting tonight.

"The rest of the week, the normal people will just think I'm crazy. On Monday night, the audience will think I'm family," he said.

So how tough is it to get through a night when almost everyone else is drinking?

"I have days where I'm more vulnerable than others, but those are very, very few and far between. I don't eat macaroni and cheese either. So, if a whole roomful of people are eating it, it just means there's more for them," he said.

"A comedy club is a bar with a stage, and I realize that some nights, some nights only, I'm just a 60-minute distraction while people drink socially. I don't think alcohol is bad. I think Mark and alcohol is horrible. You would too if you watched me drink. The mistake a lot of recovering people make, especially early in their recovery, is to assume that everybody drinks like I did, and that's just not the case. Most people don't have a drinking problem, so they're allowed to drink socially. They'll have one to relax, and they won't drive drunk and they won't become abusive verbally or physically while they're drinking and they won't abandon their family and they won't miss weeks of work. That's what I did. You know, we addicts are all or nothing people. We either do it all or we can't do it at all."

Lundholm, 39, started drinking with friends at the age of 13.

"It progressed to the point where 'social' meant 'drinking.' It wasn't 'social drinking.' It was drinking in order to be social," he said. Next came marijuana, which "of course, back in the late '70s was not addictive—wink, wink." Eventually he progressed to "cocaine, speed, uppers, things like that."

"I was consuming drugs like breakfast cereal. I did it every day," said Lundholm, who said he became a dealer after it started taking too much energy to procure his own dope.

"It's a definite downward spiral, but it's like holding a book. It's hard to explain it to a normal person. Normal people would say, 'Why didn't Mark just quit?' You can see that because you're standing outside the circle. The closest analogy I can give is open up a paperback book and press it to the bridge of your nose. You can't read it. You don't know what the story is. You know the book is there, but you're not far enough away from it to be able to get the story. . . Distance was the only thing that allowed me to have a fresh perspective. A lot of this stuff I didn't know until way after I quit."

Lundholm said he "hated being sober early on" but decided at his lowest point when he lay on a hotel room bed with a gun in his mouth that it was better than being dead ("I guess").

"These days I have countless reasons to stay clean—so many that I can't count them all," said Lundholm, who headlines throughout the United States as a stand-up comic and continues to do the volunteer comedy in drug rehab centers, halfway houses and prisons which he began nine years ago as part of his own recovery process. Last November, he was the first non-alumnus to entertain at the Betty Ford Center.

"I really think I'm lucky to be doing this for a living instead of being a school teacher or a bus driver or a mechanic. It doesn't mean I have any extra credentials for survival, but I will say this—there were times early on in the first year of my recovery where doing these volunteer comedy shows at jails and rehabs was the only reason I had to stay sober. I knew if I got drunk, I couldn't do a show the next night. . .

"I've done shows in places where the inmates don't want visitors at all—let alone 'recovery comedy guy'—and 15 minutes into the show they are pounding on each other laughing. That's not about Mark. That's about humor and healing. I just happen to be there."

Tickets for "An Evening of 12-Step Humor with Mark L." are $8 in advance and $10 at the door of the Funny Bone at 68 N. Green River Road. For more information or reservations call 471-7171.

From *The Evansville Press,* Wednesday, April 8, 1999

RESOURCE 17

OUTING REGISTRATION LETTER AND MATERIALS

Registration Letter   350
Registration Form   351

Information Brochure   352

Registration Letter

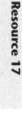

20th Anniversary

Gene Flander **2000** Harmony School

GOLF TOURNAMENT

February 17, 2000

Director
Steve Benchek, M.Ed.

Curriculum Coordinator
Daniel Baron, M.Ed.

Advisory Board
Mary Oliver,
Chairperson
Dan Berg, M.D.
Douglas R. Bridges, Esq.
Elizabeth Cosgray
Sandra Clark
Warren Henegar
Don Hollinger
Miles Kanne
Anthony Pizzo, M.D.
Jerry Ruff, M.D.
Henry Wahl
James Williams
Rod Young
Charlotte Zietlow

Tournament Committee
Annie Flander,
Honorary Chairperson

Miles Kanne
Jim Heckman
Joanna Henegar
Rod Young
Steve Bonchek
Elizabeth Cosgray
Mike Griggs
Lee Van Buskirk

Dear Golfer:

Mark your calendars now for **Sunday, May 7**, the date for the 20th Annual Gene Flander–Harmony School Golf Tournament. Once again, it will be on the beautiful course at Eagle Pointe Golf and Tennis Resort. Continental breakfast will be available starting at 7:30 a.m., and the shotgun start is scheduled for 8:30 a.m. In case of very inclement weather, we do have a rain date reserved for May 21.

Our Tournament is one of the earliest of the season, but we think the generous prizes make up for the changeable weather we often have in early May. The $400 per foursome covers green fees, carts, breakfast, and refreshments while on the course.

There will be three divisions to the Tournament again: open (low-handicap teams), special (higher-handicap teams), and women's. The prizes will be the same for each division (depending on the number of entries), starting with a **$275 gift certificate** for each member of the winning foursomes. As long as there are at least two teams in the women's division, they will receive the same prizes as the men.

Please return the enclosed registration form soon, even if you don't know all your players' names, so you can be sure of a place in the field and to save us a phone call later on! We are also looking for **sponsors**, and we hope you will consider including a tax-deductible sponsorship with your team fees. More details about sponsorship, tournament details, and a special **Golfers Raffle** are included in the enclosed brochure. If you want to know more about how your contributions will be used, see the back of the brochure for an outline of Harmony's work in Bloomington and around the country.

We hope to hear from you soon! Give us a call if you'd like to buy or sell some raffle tickets in advance of the Tournament or if you have any questions.

Sincerely,

Libby Cosgray

Resource 17

Registration Form

20th Annual GENE FLANDER–HARMONY SCHOOL GOLF TOURNAMENT
SUNDAY, MAY 7, 2000

☐ I will sponsor a team for $400 · · · · ☐ I will be a major sponsor for $300

☐ I will sponsor a tee for $100 · · · · · ☐ I will sponsor a team *and* be a major sponsor for $650

Division: · · · · · · ☐ Open · · · · · · ☐ Special · · · · · · ☐ Women's

TEAM NAME _____

Team Captain _____ Phone _____ E-mail _____

Address _____ Estimated Handicap _____

Player #2 _____ Phone _____ E-mail _____

Address _____ Estimated Handicap _____

Player #3 _____ Phone _____ E-mail _____

Address _____ Estimated Handicap _____

Player #4 _____ Phone _____ E-mail _____

Address _____ Estimated Handicap _____

Please mail this form with your check, made payable to Harmony School, to:
P.O. Box 1787, Bloomington, IN 47402

Information Brochure

Sign up now for
The 20th Annual

Gene Flander–
Harmony School
Golf Tournament

Sunday, May 7, 2000
(rain date: May 21, 2000)

Continental Breakfast: 7:30 a.m.
Shotgun start: 8:30 a.m.
Complimentary refreshments during the tournament

At Eagle Pointe Golf and Tennis Resort
Over $8,000 worth of prizes!

Last Year's Winners

Open	**Special**
NEW COMMUNITY BANK	*ROGERS GROUP, INC.*
Tom Risen	Robert Jones
Paul Gates	Mike La Grange
Larry Behme	Price Irving
Bob Hasty	Earl Brinker

Women's
LISA J. BAKER, D.D.S.
Lisa J. Baker, D.D.S.
Deborah Rumsey
Ruth Vallery
Dianne Porter

More About the Tournament

- **FEES** for a foursome: $400. This covers green fees, carts, breakfast, and refreshments while on the course
- **DIVISIONS:** open and handicap (based on team handicap). Identical prizes will be awarded in both divisions, depending on the number of teams in each division. (The Tournament Committee will make the final division assignment.)
- **WOMEN:** If two or more women's teams participate, there will be a women's division with similar prizes.
- **PRIZES:** Over $8,000 worth of gift certificates and prizes—something for everyone!
- **MULLIGANS** will be available for purchase again for $25 per team, maximum 2 per team. All four players must use the Mulligan on the same shot.

Sponsors Are Also Needed

Major sponsorship is $300; tee sponsorship is $100. Major sponsors will receive a free round of golf for two; tee sponsors will be given coupons worth 50% off a round of golf (for up to 4 people). All sponsors will be acknowledged by signs and will be thanked in the Harmony newsletter and the *Herald-Times*.

Special thanks to our 1999 Major Sponsors: Artifex, BBM Office Products, Lisa J. Baker, D.D.S., Cook Incorporated, Cook Urological, Indiana Energy, Inc., Monroe County Bank, Simanton Mechanical, Southside Rental, Terminix.

Gene Flander

Gene Flander was president of the Harmony School Advisory Board when he died in September 1987. Gene was also Chairman of the Board of Peck, Incorporated. He meant a great deal to Harmony School. He used to compare his eternal optimism toward Harmony School's never-ending quest for financial support to Boys Town founder Father Flanagan's philosophy of "Don't worry, God will take care of everything." This golf tournament is our way of assisting God in His providence and making Gene's optimism a reality.

Golfers Raffle

Raffle tickets will be on sale in a couple of weeks—tickets are $5 each or 3 for $10. The prizes are:

- *1st prize:* Ten (10) rounds of golf at Eagle Pointe (value $500)
- *2nd prize*: Two (2) 20-bucket passes at Tee to Green Driving Range (value $160)

Call the school if you want to buy yours ahead of time or sell some to your golfing friends. They will also be on sale at the Tournament.

Harmony School

Harmony School is a not-for-profit educational institution whose main objective is to offer an innovative choice in education to 185 students ages 3–18. Eighty percent of Harmony School students are on partial or full scholarships. Through events such as this Golf Tournament, Harmony must raise $300,000 annually to provide these scholarships. Scholarships to Harmony School allow young people to attend a school that

- Provides a full-time day school in a personalized, family-like atmosphere for learners ages 3–18
- Prepares young people for active citizenship by involving them in significant decision making affecting their school environment and curriculum
- Educates the whole person through an innovative curriculum that simultaneously emphasizes academics, social, emotional and physical development, and the learners' interconnectedness with the natural world
- Selects students regardless of family income and background

Harmony is also a leader in the movement to transform America's schools. The success of Harmony School has drawn the acclaim of researchers, educational foundations, and national publications. Harmony now serves as the national center for the National School Reform Faculty (NSRF), a network of 600 schools and 9,000 teachers and principals. Harmony is committed to supporting NSRF in a movement to find better ways to educate children as participants in a democratic society.

In addition, over the last nine years Harmony has provided on-site consultations and ongoing assistance to nearly 500 teachers in schools serving 20,000 students, helping teachers and students transform their own schools and resulting in dramatic increases in standardized test scores. In recognition of its leadership role, Harmony has been chosen by the Paul Foundation in New York City to influence the national discussion with policy-makers on education reform.

For more information, call the school at 334-8349.

Note: All materials in Resource 17 are reprinted with permission by Harmony School Education Center.

RESOURCE 18

SPECIAL EVENTS PLANNING CHECKLISTS

Resource 18

Room Setup Checklist   356
Equipment Checklist   358
Audiovisual Checklist   360
Catering Checklist   363
Bar Checklist   365

Florist and Decor Checklist   366
Program Checklist   368
Program Participant
      and VIP Checklist   370

Room Setup Checklist

Date: _____

Event title: _____

Date/time: _____

Institution sponsor: _____

Event planner: _____

Office phone: _____ Cellular phone: _____

Fax: _____

E-mail: _____

Address: _____

Facility name: _____

Address: _____

Facility manager: _____

Office phone: _____ Cellular phone: _____

Fax: _____

E-mail: _____

Rooms being used: _____

Caterer: _____

Contact person: _____

Office phone: _____ Cellular phone: _____

Florist: _____

Contact person: _____

Office phone: _____ Cellular phone: _____

Fax: _____

E-mail: _____

Specifications

Setups: _____

Stage: _____ Lights: _____

Sound: _____

Bandstand: _____

Podium: _____

Microphones (type needed): _____

Number needed: _____

Location of microphones: _____

Bars and serving areas

Bar needed: _____ Location(s): _____

Coat check room needed: _____ Location: _____

Registration area needed: _____ Location: _____

Floor plans

On a separate sheet, diagram the floor plan for each area to be used. Show setups for all areas; note traffic patterns and all entrances and exists. Attach.

Equipment Checklist

Date: _____

Event title: _____

Date/time: _____

Institution sponsor: _____

Event planner: _____

Office phone: _____ Cellular phone: _____

Fax: _____

E-mail: _____

Address: _____

Facility name: _____

Address: _____

Facility manager: _____

Office phone: _____ Cellular phone: _____

Fax: _____

E-mail: _____

Rooms being used: _____

Times being used: _____

Rental company/on-campus source: _____

Address: _____

Contact person: _____

Office phone: _____

Equipment needed and quantity: _____

_____

_____

_____

Color scheme: _____

Cost: _____

Deposit required: _____

Balance due: _____

Delivery and setup instructions: _____

_____

_____

_____

Pickup instructions: _____

_____

_____

_____

Resource 18

Audiovisual Checklist

Date: _____

Event title: _____

Date/time: _____

Institution sponsor: _____

Event planner: _____

Office phone: _____ Cellular phone: _____

Fax: _____

E-mail: _____

Address: _____

Facility name: _____

Address: _____

Facility manager: _____

Office phone: _____ Cellular phone: _____

Fax: _____

E-mail: _____

Rooms being used: _____

Equipment supplier:

Address: _____

Contact person: _____

Office phone: _____

Check equipment needed:

☐ **Slide projectors:**

No. needed: _____   For room: _____   Time: _____

☐ **Slide trays:**

No. needed: _____   For room: _____   Time: _____

☐ **Projector cart needed:**   ☐ yes   ☐ no

For room: _____   Time: _____

☐ **Extension cords:**   ☐ Length: _____

No. needed: _____   For room: _____   Time: _____

☐ **Spare bulbs:**   Size: _____

No. needed: _____   For room: _____   Time: _____

☐ **Screens:**

No. needed: _____   For room: _____   Time: _____

☐ **LCD projector:**

No. needed: _____   For room: _____   Time: _____

☐ **Video projector:**

No. needed: _____   For room: _____   Time: _____

☐ **Computer needed:**   ☐ yes   ☐ no

Kind: _____

Software requested: _____

☐ **Overhead projectors:**

No. needed: _____   For room: _____   Time: _____

☐ **Microphones:**   ☐ Type:

No. needed: _____   For room: _____   Time: _____

☐ **Tables:**   ☐ Size:_____

No. needed: _____   For room: _____   Time: _____

☐ **Chairs:**

No. needed: _____   For room: _____   Time: _____

☐ **Podiums:**

No. needed: _____   For room: _____   Time: _____

☐ **Televisions:**

No. needed: _____   For room: _____   Time: _____

☐ **VCRs:**

No. needed: _____   For room: _____   Time: _____

☐ **Flip charts:**

No. needed: _____   For room: _____   Time: _____

Miscellaneous (check all that apply and note special instructions below):

☐ **Laser pointer**   ☐ **Computer hookups**

☐ **Telephone**   ☐ **Hand truck**

☐ **Extra extension cords** (specify length) _____

☐ **Other:** _____

Estimated cost: _____ Amount of deposit: _____ Balance due: _____

Operator instructions: _____

_____

_____

Special instructions: _____

_____

_____

Equipment to be delivered on: Date: _____ Time: _____

Deliver to: _____

Equipment to be picked up on: Date: _____ Time: _____

Pickup instructions: _____

_____

_____

_____

Catering Checklist

Date: _____

Event title: _____

Date/time: _____

Institution Sponsor: _____

Event planner: _____

Office phone: _____ Cellular phone: _____

Fax: _____

E-mail: _____

Address: _____

Caterer: _____

Address: _____

Contact person: _____

Office phone: _____ Cellular phone: _____

Facility name: _____

Address: _____

Facility manager: _____

Office phone: _____ Cellular phone: _____

Rooms being used: _____

Time to serve: _____ Projected number of guests: _____

Date, time for final guarantee: _____

Cost per person: _____   Total projected cost: _____

Deposit required: _____   Paid on date: _____

Balance due: _____

Menu: _____

_____

_____

_____

Wines: _____   Toasting: _____

Linen colors: Napkins: _____   Tablecloths: _____

Uniform for wait staff: _____

Placecards: _____   Menu cards: _____

Programs: _____   Favors: _____

Cocktails: _____

Time to serve: _____   Time to close: _____

Location(s) of bar(s): _____

Equipment to be supplied: _____

_____

_____

_____

_____

Bar Checklist

A well-stocked bar should have these supplies:

Alcoholic beverages

☐ vodka   ☐ gin

☐ whiskey   ☐ scotch

☐ bourbon   ☐ rum

☐ beer, regular and light   ☐ white wine

☐ dry vermouth   ☐ red wine

Non-alcoholic beverages and mixes

☐ water   ☐ soda water

☐ tonic water   ☐ sparkling, flavored water

☐ tomato juice   ☐ orange juice

☐ selection of soft drinks (including diet drinks)

Garnishes

☐ lemon and lime wedges   ☐ cherries

☐ olives   ☐ cocktail onions

☐ Angostura bitters   ☐ sugar

Tools

☐ paring knife   ☐ measuring spoons

☐ pitchers   ☐ strainer

☐ jigger   ☐ towels

☐ shaker   ☐ can/bottle opener

☐ corkscrew   ☐ cocktail napkins

☐ bartender's guide of drink recipes   ☐ ice

☐ toothpicks   ☐ ice tongs

Resource 18

Florist and Decor Checklist

Date: _____

Event title: _____

Date/time: _____

Institution sponsor: _____

Event planner: _____

Office phone: _____ Cellular phone: _____

Fax: _____

E-mail: _____

Address: _____

Facility name: _____

Address: _____

Facility manager: _____

Office phone: _____ Cellular phone: _____

Rooms being used: _____

Florist: _____

Address: _____

Contact person: _____

Office phone: _____ Cellular phone: _____

Color scheme: _____

Type of flowers ordered for: _____

Tables: _____

Dais: _____

Reception area: _____

Foyer: _____

Corsages: _____ Boutonnieres: _____

Ushers/hosts/hostesses: _____

Other: _____

Time for deliveries: _____

Containers to be returned: _____

Rented equipment: _____

Return by: _____

Florist to pick up by: _____

Other decorations: _____

_____

Supplier: _____

Contact person: _____

Office phone: _____ Cellular phone: _____

Special instructions: _____

_____

Program Checklist

Date: _____

Event title: _____

Date/time: _____

Institution sponsor: _____

Event planner: _____

Office phone: _____ Cellular phone: _____

Fax: _____

E-mail: _____

Address: _____

Facility name: _____

Address: _____

Facility manager: _____

Office phone: _____ Cellular phone: _____

Rooms being used: _____

Program content: _____

Honored guests/VIPs: _____

Musicians/Band: _____

Contact person: _____

Office phone: _____

Address: _____

Time to begin: _____ Time to end: _____

Time to set-up: _____

Fee: _____ Deposit paid: _____

Check needed at performance: _____ Yes: _____ No: _____

Amount: _____ Pay to: _____

Master of ceremonies: _____

Office phone: _____ Cellular phone: _____

Address: _____

Speakers: _____

Name: _____ Name: _____

Address: _____ Address: _____

Office phone: _____ Office phone: _____

Audiovisuals to be used: _____

Equipment supplied by: _____

Contact person: _____

Office phone: _____

Address: _____

Program Participant and VIP Checklist

Date: _____

Event title: _____

Date/time: _____

Institution sponsor: _____

Event planner: _____

Office phone: _____ Cellular phone: _____

Fax: _____

E-mail: _____

Address: _____

Facility name: _____

Address: _____

Facility manager: _____

Office phone: _____ Cellular phone: _____

Rooms being used: _____

Participant's name: _____

Title/affiliation: _____

Office address: _____

Home address: _____

Office phone: _____ Home phone: _____

Fax: _____

E-mail: _____

Secretary's name: _____

Contact person: _____

Office (area code/phone): _____

Home (area code/phone): _____

Audiovisual requirements: (List equipment needed. If none, state "none.")

_____

_____

_____

Academic regalia:

☐ Will furnish own   ☐ Need to order:

Gown size: _____   Cap size: _____   Colors: _____

To receive: ☐ Award   ☐ Medal plaque   ☐ Citation   ☐ Honorary degree

☐ Other: _____

Presentation item ordered: _____ From: _____

Travel plans: _____

Arrival date: _____ Time: _____

Driving: _____

Flight (airport/airline/flight number and time): _____

To be met by: _____

Meeting place: _____ Time: _____

Accommodations:

Hotel name: _____

Address: _____

Phone: _____

Dates of reservations: _____

Special requests: _____

Departure:

Date: _____ Time: _____

Flight (airport/airline/number/time): _____

To be escorted by: _____ Phone: _____

Will meet for departure at: _____

Expenses:

☐ To be paid by participant   ☐ To be reimbursed, receipts required

☐ To be paid by: _____

Address: _____

Account number or billing information: _____

Honorarium to be paid: $_____ Budget: _____

Other needs:

Special diet: _____

Non-smoking accommodations: _____

Handicapped parking/seating: _____

Is spouse accompanying? _____ If so, name: _____

_____

Source: From *Special Events: Planning for Success* by April L. Harris. Council for Advancement and Support of Education 1998. Reprinted with permission.

SAMPLE TELEMARKETING SCRIPT FOR LAPSED DONORS

INTRODUCTION

Hello, is _____ in? Hi, my name is _____, and I'm a student calling from Penn State on behalf of the College of _____. How are you this evening? I'm with a group of other students calling to *thank you* for your previous support of academics, to answer any questions you may have, and to inform you about things going on at Penn State and in your College.

RAPPORT

- Prospect's major, occupation, location, student activities, etc.
- How did you choose Penn State?
- How's the weather in _____?
- How has your Penn State degree been helpful to you?

Remember to ask good open-ended questions!

FIRST ASK: $500—Stress Penn State

If prospect gave $500 or more last year, make your first ask higher!

Another reason I'm calling tonight is to talk with you about Penn State! Many exciting things are happening for Penn State this year. Once again, Penn State has maintained its status as one of the nation's best buys as listed in *Money Magazine.* This helps to attract top students from all over the nation as Penn State continues to receive more SAT scores from incoming freshman than any other school in the nation.

However, some 73 percent of Penn State students systemwide require some form of financial aid to be able to attend the University. Much of that aid is made possible through alumni contributions like yours in the past. Recognizing how important your contribution is to the continued strength of Penn State, can you support Penn State with a gift of $500 this year? And if it's easier for you, I can split that up into two monthly payments of $250 each.

If NO: I can understand that gift level may not be possible for you this year, but we only ask at that level as an indication of our need. Really, the important thing is to find a gift level you feel comfortable with.

SECOND ASK: $250—Stress the College

I would like to tell you a few things about your College of _____ and what types of programs you'd be supporting by getting involved with a gift this year. This year, thanks largely to Alumni support, these programs will be made possible:

Use the College fact sheets in your computer for information!

With your college's needs in mind, do you think that a gift of $250 to your college or any other academic program would be something you could consider this evening? Let me remind you that we can delay the billing on your pledge for up to one month.

THIRD ASK: $100—Stress Participation

One of the reasons we're calling you tonight is because you've already demonstrated your support for Penn State through your previous gifts, and we would hate to lose your support this year. Alumni dollars are always put to good use in areas where they are urgently needed, and your help is needed more than ever this year since we did not receive the level of funding from the state that we were hoping for and that we needed. Because of this, we are asking all of our previous alumni donors if they might be able to increase their last gift by $10 this year, as University costs increase each year, and we would like to see tuition increase as little as possible. Is this something you could consider this evening? *(If you do not get an upgrade, ask for a renewal or a minimum gift of $25.)*

CONCLUSION

1. Thank you very much! A gift of $_____ will really help out! Now, if we could ask you to extend that gift even further, at no cost to you, by putting that on a credit card, that would be great! The reason that I ask is that students like myself do not even receive their grades through the mail anymore. We have to call a toll-free number or get them from the Internet. The reason that Penn State does that is to save money on postage, and cutting back on paper also helps the environment. So we are asking alumni, whenever they help us out with a gift, to go along with that thinking by putting the gift on a credit card to help us cut down on administrative expenses. We have supervisors on hand who are authorized by Penn State to take your credit card information tonight, and in the next two weeks you will receive a receipt for your personal records and for tax purposes. We accept Visa, MasterCard, American Express, and Discover. Can I get a supervisor to put your gift on a credit card for you?

2. Where would you like your gift to be designated this year?

3. *If not on a credit card:* I will be recording that total pledge of $_____, and we'll mail a confirmation to you tomorrow.

4. Just to be sure that confirmation card arrives, I need to verify that your address is *(insert address here).*

Also, could you provide us with a business title and company name?

Offer Penn State Newswire—check for e-mail address and offer this service!

5. Do you happen to know if your company matches alumni contributions?

If YES: GREAT! Just pick up a matching gift form at your personnel office and mail it in with your payment.

ENCOURAGE THEM TO SEND THE MATCHING GIFT FORM IN WITH THEIR CHECK!

CHECKS SHOULD BE MADE PAYABLE TO PENN STATE.

6. Thank you very much for your commitment of $_____ to Penn State!

Note: Used with permission from Penn State University.

Resource 19

TELEMARKETING OBJECTION PACKET

INDIANA UNIVERSITY FOUNDATION TELEFUND

POINTS TO NEGOTIATE

$ ASK TOO MUCH
LOYALTY TO CHARITIES
PAYING BACK LOANS
BACK IN SCHOOL/STILL IN SCHOOL
I DON'T LIKE ANY INDIVIDUAL
ARE YOU A PAID SOLICITOR
SEND INFO
UNEMPLOYED
RETIRED
BOUGHT CAR, HOUSE/HAD BABY/NEW JOB/ETC.
LET ME THINK ABOUT IT
ONLY TIME I HEAR FROM I. U.
HOW MUCH GOES TO SCHOOL
LET ME CHECK WITH SPOUSE
NOT INTERESTED
DON'T WANT TO PLEDGE OVER THE PHONE
KIDS IN COLLEGE
BAD EXPERIENCE/PROBLEM
ANNUAL VS. SPECIAL PROJECTS/ALREADY GAVE

Sample Objection Responses   380

Sample Objection Responses

$ ASK TOO MUCH

That's no problem. That was just a suggestion and a starting point from which to discuss a pledge. I am sure you can appreciate that fact that we don't know the financial capabilities of each of our alumni—so the only way to find an appropriate pledge amount is to ask. How would you feel about a gift of $_____?

BACK IN SCHOOL/STILL IN SCHOOL

That's great! Where are you attending classes? What are you studying? *(Allow them to talk about school.)*

I have talked to others who are furthering their education, and they often view their IU degree as a part of their education as a whole, working together with the coursework they are doing now. They have felt comfortable something like $_____. It would be just great if you could come on board at this level!

ARE YOU A PAID SOLICITOR?

Yes, I am paid a small hourly wage. As an IU student, I see the impact of support from alumni like you. I'd just like to say thanks for that because if it weren't for some of the things alumni did years ago, we wouldn't have the scholarships, excellent faculty, and facilities that we do. *(Return to outline wherever you left off.)*

BOUGHT CAR, HOUSE/HAD BABY/NEW JOB/ETC.

That's great! Congratulations! *(Ask a positive question pertinent to the situation and build rapport.)*

You know, I have talked with a lot of alumni who are in a similar position. After we talked about how important the program is to the basic academic needs of the School of _____, they've found something they feel comfortable with. It's participation that makes this program so successful. It would be great if you would join us with a gift of $_____.

RESOURCE 21

CODE OF ETHICS SAMPLES

Association of Professional Researchers for Advancement (APRA) Statement
    of Ethics   382
Association of Fundraising Professionals (AFP) Code of Ethical Principles and
    Standards of Professional Practice   385
Council for Advancement and Support of Education (CASE) Mission and
    Statement of Ethics   388

Association of Professional Researchers for Advancement (APRA) Statement of Ethics

Association of Professional Researchers for Advancement (APRA) members shall support and further the individual's fundamental right to privacy and protect the confidential information of their institutions. APRA members are committed to the ethical collection and use of information. Members shall follow all applicable federal, state, and local laws, as well as institutional policies, governing the collection, use, maintenance, and dissemination of information in the pursuit of the missions of their institutions. APRA members shall respect all people and organizations.

Code of Ethics

Prospect researchers must balance the needs of their institutions to collect, analyze, record, maintain, use, and disseminate information with an individual's right to privacy. This balance is not always easy to maintain. The following ethical principles apply, and practice is built on these principles:

I. Fundamental Principles
   A. Confidentiality
      Confidential information about constituents (donors and non-donors), as well as confidential information of the institutions in oral form or on electronic, magnetic, or print media are protected so that the relationship of trust between the constituent and the institution is upheld.
   B. Accuracy
      Prospect researchers shall record all data accurately. Such information shall include attribution. Analysis and products of data analysis should be without personal prejudices or biases.
   C. Relevance
      Prospect researchers shall seek and record only information that is relevant and appropriate to the fund-raising effort of the institutions that employ them.
   D. Accountability
      Prospect researchers shall accept responsibility for their actions and shall be accountable to the profession of development, to their respective institutions, and to the constituents who place their trust in prospect researchers and their institutions.
   E. Honesty
      Prospect researchers shall be truthful with regard to their identity and purpose and the identity of their institution during the course of their work.

II. Suggested Practice

A. Collection

1. The collection of information shall be done lawfully, respecting applicable laws and institutional policies.

2. Information sought and recorded includes all data that can be verified and attributed, as well as constituent information that is self-reported (via correspondence, surveys, questionnaires, etc.).

3. When requesting information in person or by telephone, it is recommended in most cases that neither individual nor institutional identity shall be concealed. Written requests for public information shall be made on institutional stationery clearly identifying the inquirer.

4. Whenever possible, payments for public records shall be made through the institution.

5. Prospect researchers shall apply the same standards for electronic information that they currently use in evaluating and verifying print media. The researcher shall ascertain whether or not the information comes from a reliable source and that the information collected meets the standards set forth in the APRA Statement of Ethics.

B. Recording and Maintenance

1. Researchers shall state information in an objective and factual manner; note attribution and date of collection; and clearly identify analysis.

2. Constituent information on paper, electronic, magnetic or other media shall be stored securely to prevent access by unauthorized persons.

3. Special protection shall be afforded all giving records pertaining to anonymous donors.

4. Electronic or pager documents pertaining to constituents shall be irreversibly disposed of when no longer needed (by following institutional standards for document disposal).

C. Use and Distribution

1. Researchers shall adhere to all applicable laws, as well as to institutional policies, regarding the use and distribution of confidential constituent information.

2. Constituent information is the property of the institution for which it was collected and shall not be given to persons other than those who are involved with the cultivation or solicitation effort or those who need that information in the performance of their duties for that institution.

3. Constituent information for one institution shall not be taken to another institution.

4. Research documents containing constituent information that is to be used outside research offices shall be clearly marked "confidential."

5. Vendors, consultants, and other external entities shall understand and agree to comply with the institution's confidentiality policies before gaining access to institutional data.

6. Only publicly available information shall be shared with colleagues at other institutions as a professional courtesy.

III. Recommendations

1. Prospect researchers shall urge their institutions to develop written policies based upon applicable laws and these policies should define what information shall be gathered, recorded and maintained, and to whom and under what conditions the information can be released.

2. Prospect researchers shall urge the development of written policies at their institutions defining who may authorize access to prospect files and under what conditions. These policies should follow the guidelines outlined in the CASE Donor Bill of Rights, the AFP Code of Ethical Principles, and the Association for Healthcare Philanthropy Statement of Professional Standards and Conduct.

3. Prospect researchers shall strongly urge their development colleagues to abide by this Code of Ethics and Fundamental Principles.

Source: Association of Professional Researchers for Advancement (APRA), Sept. 30, 1998, http://www.aprahome.org/apra_statement_of_ethics.htm. Printed with permission from APRA.

Association of Fundraising Professionals (AFP) Code of Ethical Principles and Standards of Professional Practice

STATEMENT OF ETHICAL PRINCIPLES

Adopted November 1991

The Association of Fundraising Professionals (AFP) exists to foster the development and growth of fund-raising professionals and the profession, to promote high ethical standards in the fund-raising profession and to preserve and enhance philanthropy and volunteerism. Members of AFP are motivated by an inner drive to improve the quality of life through the causes they serve. They serve the ideal of philanthropy; are committed to the preservation and enhancement of volunteerism; and hold stewardship of these concepts as the overriding principle of their professional life. They recognize their responsibility to ensure that needed resources are vigorously and ethically sought and that the intent of the donor is honestly fulfilled. To these ends, AFP members embrace certain values that they strive to uphold in performing their responsibilities for generating philanthropic support.

AFP members aspire to:

- practice their profession with integrity, honesty, truthfulness and adherence to the absolute obligation to safeguard the public trust;
- act according to the highest standards and visions of their organization, profession and conscience;
- put philanthropic mission above personal gain;
- inspire others through their own sense of dedication and high purpose;
- improve their professional knowledge and skills in order that their performance will better serve others;
- demonstrate concern for the interests and well being of individuals affected by their actions;
- value the privacy, freedom of choice and interests of all those affected by their actions;
- foster cultural diversity and pluralistic values, and treat all people with dignity and respect;
- affirm, through personal giving, a commitment to philanthropy and its role in society;
- adhere to the spirit as well as the letter of all applicable laws and regulations;

- advocate within their organizations, adherence to all applicable laws and regulations;
- avoid even the appearance of any criminal offense or professional misconduct;
- bring credit to the fundraising profession by their public demeanor;
- encourage colleagues to embrace and practice these ethical principles and standards of professional practice; and
- be aware of the codes of ethics promulgated by other professional organizations that serve philanthropy.

STANDARDS OF PROFESSIONAL PRACTICE

Adopted and incorporated into the AFP
Code of Ethical Principles November 1992

Furthermore, while striving to act according to the above values, AFP members agree to abide by the AFP Standards of Professional Practice, which are adopted and incorporated into the AFP Code of Ethical Principles. Violation of the Standards may subject the member to disciplinary sanctions, including expulsion, as provided in the AFP Ethics Enforcement Procedures.

Professional Obligations

1. Members shall not engage in activities that harm the member's organization, clients, or profession.
2. Members shall not engage in activities that conflict with their fiduciary, ethical, and legal obligations to their organizations and their clients.
3. Members shall effectively disclose all potential and actual conflicts of interest; such disclosure does not preclude or imply ethical impropriety.
4. Members shall not exploit any relationship with a donor, prospect, volunteer or employee to the benefit of the member or the member's organization.
5. Members shall comply with all applicable local, state, provincial, federal, civil and criminal laws.
6. Members recognize their individual boundaries of competence and are forthcoming and truthful about their professional experience and qualifications.

Solicitation and Use of Charitable Funds

7. Members shall take care to ensure that all solicitation materials are accurate and correctly reflect the organization's mission and use of solicited funds.

8. Members shall take care to ensure that donors receive informed, accurate and ethical advice about the value and tax implications of potential gifts.

9. Members shall take care to ensure that contributions are used in accordance with donors' intentions.

10. Members shall take care to ensure proper stewardship of charitable contributions, including timely reports on the use and management of funds.

11. Members shall obtain explicit consent by the donor before altering the conditions of a gift.

Presentation of Information

12. Members shall not disclose privileged or confidential information to unauthorized parties.

13. Members shall adhere to the principle that all donor and prospect information created by, or on behalf of, an organization is the property of that organization and shall not be transferred or utilized except on behalf of that organization.

14. Members shall give donors the opportunity to have their names removed from lists that are sold to, rented to, or exchanged with other organizations.

15. Members shall, when stating fundraising results, use accurate and consistent accounting methods that conform to the appropriate guidelines adopted by the American Institute of Certified Public Accountants (AICPA)* for the type of organization involved. (*In countries outside of the United States, comparable authority should be utilized.)

Compensation

16. Members shall not accept compensation that is based on a percentage of charitable contributions; nor shall they accept finder's fees.

17. Members may accept performance-based compensation, such as bonuses, provided such bonuses are in accord with prevailing practices within the members' own organizations, and are not based on a percentage of charitable contributions.

18. Members shall not pay finder's fees, commissions or percentage compensation based on charitable contributions and shall take care to discourage their organizations from making such payments.

Amended October 1999

Resource 21

Council for Advancement and Support of Education (CASE) Mission and Statement of Ethics

MISSION

The purposes of CASE are to develop and foster sound relationships between member educational institutions and their constituencies; to provide training programs, products, and services in the areas of alumni relations, communications, and philanthropy; to promote diversity within these professions; and to provide a strong force for the advancement and support of education worldwide.

STATEMENT OF ETHICS

Institutional advancement professionals, by virtue of their responsibilities within the academic community, represent their colleges, universities, and schools to the larger society. They have, therefore, a special duty to exemplify the best qualities of their institutions and to observe the highest standards of personal and professional conduct.

In so doing, they promote the merits of their institutions, and of education generally, without disparaging other colleges and schools.

Their words and actions embody respect for truth, fairness, free inquiry, and the opinions of others.

They respect all individuals without regard to race, color, sex, sexual orientation, marital status, creed, ethnic or national identity, handicap, or age.

They uphold the professional reputation of other advancement officers and give credit for ideas, words, or images originated by others.

They safeguard privacy rights and confidential information.

They do not grant or accept favors for personal gain, nor do they solicit or accept favors for their institutions where a higher public interest would be violated.

They avoid actual or apparent conflicts of interest and, if in doubt, seek guidance from appropriate authorities.

They follow the letter and spirit of laws and regulations affecting institutional advancement.

They observe these standards and others that apply to their professions and actively encourage colleagues to join them in supporting the highest standards of conduct.

The CASE Board of Trustees adopted this Statement of Ethics to guide and reinforce our professional conduct in all areas of institutional advancement. The statement is also intended to stimulate awareness and discussion of ethical issues that may arise in our professional activities. The Board adopted the final text in Toronto on July 11, 1982, after a year of deliberation by national and district leaders and by countless volunteers throughout the membership.

Source: Council for Advancement and Support of Education 1982. Reprinted with permission.

FUNDRAISING GUIDEBOOK

Marathon Training Program

BECOMING A FUNDRAISER

As a member of **TEAM DIABETES**, you have made a personal commitment to train and prepare yourself to complete a 26.2-mile marathon.

In addition, you have been asked to make a commitment to help the American Diabetes Association in its fight to cure all forms of diabetes.

If you truly believe in and understand the critical importance of what you are doing, working to help cure diabetes . . . then fundraising will be enjoyable and will give you a great deal of satisfaction.

The purpose of this guidebook is to provide you with background information on diabetes and the American Diabetes Association's mission and to provide you with ideas and resources to support you in your fundraising efforts. In addition, our staff will be available to assist you in developing your fundraising plan and to provide fundraising "coaching" along the way.

To Be a Successful TEAM DIABETES Fundraiser

1. **Develop an understanding** of the devastation caused by diabetes.
2. **Communicate the successes** that the American Diabetes Association has experienced in its quest to cure diabetes and in improving the quality of life for patients and their families.
3. **Provide an assurance to donors** that all money given on your behalf will be used judiciously by the American Diabetes Association for information, research, and advocacy.
4. **Share your conviction** that every gift that you secure will make a difference in the battle against diabetes.
5. **Make a commitment** to ask everyone—friends, family and co-workers—to join you in supporting the lifesaving work of the American Diabetes Association.
6. **Thank your donors** in a heartfelt and timely fashion.

Your Fundraising Coach

We have provided a marathon coach to help you achieve your marathon goals; likewise, we are providing a fundraising coach to help achieve your personal fundraising goals.

Our staff is available to help you develop your personal fundraising plan and to offer ideas, suggestions, and encouragement to help you achieve your fundraising goals.

Please call your fundraising coach when you need advice and guidance on any of your fundraising initiatives.

The Golden Rule of Fundraising: Just Ask!

While Nike's slogan is "Just Do It!" the fundraising slogan for TEAM DIABETES is **"JUST ASK!"** Ask everyone you know. Raising money to conquer diabetes is a very worthwhile undertaking and one that should give you a great deal of pride.

The generosity of your family, friends, and acquaintances will amaze you. There is an old fundraising axiom that states, "People give to people." People will give because you ask—because they believe in and trust **you!**

Believe in yourself. **Share** your knowledge about the work and progress of the American Diabetes Association, and **ask** people to support you in your effort to help conquer diabetes.

Strategies to Raise Money

There are two basic strategies to raise money:

1. **Personal Appeals** (direct request for support to individuals, clubs, organizations, businesses, and corporations)
   - Face-to-face ask
   - Letter ask
   - Phone ask
   - A combination of the above

2. **Special Events/Activities** (conducted alone or with the support of a group)
   - Parties/get-togethers (with a variety of possible themes)
   - Sales (garage sale, bake sale, etc.)
   - "Fee for service" (contribution in return for services provided)
   - Door-to-door (a neighbor-to-neighbor campaign)
   - Club donations (gift from the treasury or through a club event sponsored on your behalf)
   - Store-front collection (support from patrons of the local bank, grocery tore, etc.)

Each will be covered in detail in the following sections.

PERSONAL APPEALS

The personal appeal is the most efficient and effective way to raise money. It is targeted, direct, and easy. Your personal approach will depend on your own style and your association with the prospect. Regardless of the approach you choose, the following steps will apply.

STEP ONE: Identify Your Prospects

Think big! During your life, you have made acquaintances with probably thousands of people. In developing your prospect list, think first in terms of groupings of people, not individuals. Think about the following groups of people and then identify individuals within each group. Consider:

- **Family and Relatives:** Immediate family, aunts, uncles, cousins, nieces, and nephews. People close to you will both admire and support your efforts.
- **School Acquaintances:** High school and college. Even if you have lost contact, do not underestimate the generosity of an "old" friend. A high school and/or college alumni directory is an excellent source of names.
- **Friends and Social Circle:** Pull out the holiday card list and you have your current circle of friends. Remember, "friends give to friends."
- **Work Associates:** Do not stop at your current position: think about the acquaintances you have made along the way, include individuals from other companies that you deal with in business.
- **Clubs and Organizations:** Individuals in clubs and organizations that you belong to are a solid source of potential donors (social clubs, service organizations, country clubs, etc.).
- **Neighbors:** People in your neighborhood. When they see you out training every day, they will know you are serious!
- **Church/Synagogue:** Saturday/Sunday acquaintances. These people can be very generous.
- **Community Businesses:** Places where you spend money (grocery stores, drugstores, corner deli, doctors, dentists, hair salons, etc.).
- **Anyone Who Owes You a Favor!** Think about this one—what a great way to call in your "chips"!
- **Companies and Corporations:** Direct company or corporate gifts can be a valuable source for larger contributions. Also, some of your individual donors may belong to a company or corporation that participates in a matching gift program; ask them. Does your own company or corporation have a matching gift program?

Working through this list will help you focus your fundraising efforts. **Quantity** is important. The more prospects, the more gifts. Use Attachment A to help you develop your personal prospect list.

STEP TWO: Select Your Approach

- Face to Face: Best approach for larger gifts or in situations where the opportunity presents itself.
- Letter: The most efficient way to reach a large quantity of prospects.
- Telephone: Effective as a follow-up to a mail solicitation.

HELPFUL TIP: The best approach is a personal mail appeal to all prospects, followed by a phone call or personal visit to individuals whom you feel have the greatest potential to contribute.

STEP THREE: Select the Style of the Message

- Serious, hard-hitting
- Light, humorous
- Combination of the above

STEP FOUR: Select the Format

- Form letter: Same letter to every individual
- Personal letter: Personalized on an individual basis
- Solicitation card: Provides opportunity for creative touch

HELPFUL TIP: If using a form letter, add a personal touch by writing a personal note or P.S. Also consider providing a self-addressed return envelope for ease of reply.

STEP FIVE: Suggest the Level of Giving

It is helpful for donors to know the level of contribution that you would like them to consider. Do not underestimate the donor's willingness to give. It will be easier to reach your fundraising goal if you have some larger gifts in your mix.

Do not be afraid to say, "Would you consider a gift of $25 or $50?" for the general audience. Also, do not be afraid to say, "Would you consider a gift of $100 or $200?" if you know that the individual is capable of giving at that level.

Some of you may want to tie your "gift ask" to the 26.2-mile marathon distance. This is an excellent approach and provides a good motivation to help you "go the distance."

NOTE: If using this approach, it is strongly recommended that you request payment at the time of the "ask." This campaign is not intended to be a "pledge" campaign.

See example below:

PER-MILE CONTRIBUTION
(Total Distance = 26.2 Miles)

$1/Mile	$2/Mile	$3/Mile	$4/Mile
$26.20	$52.40	$78.60	$104.80

SPECIAL EVENTS/ACTIVITIES

There are a number of ways to raise money through special events and activities, including:

- **Admission Fee or Donation** (cocktail party, dinner party, etc.)
- **Fee for Participation/Registration** (softball tournament, card tournament, Trivial Pursuit tournament, etc.)
- **Sale of Draw Prize Tickets** (weekend getaway, health club membership, etc.)
- **Auction** (gag gifts, sports memorabilia, weekend getaway, etc.)
- **Fee for Service** (serving a special meal, providing business services for a contribution)
- **Sale of Items** (garage sale, baked goods, etc.)

The key to a successful special event is good planning. In planning your event, determine all of the potential fundraising opportunities associated with the event and select the opportunities that represent the greatest potential for dollars.

Below is a listing of special events with a brief description of each. All of these are proven winners. This is not intended to be inclusive but rather represents a sampling of a variety of special events.

Let's Have a Party. What better excuse to have a party! Possible themes include:

- **Gourmet Dinner Party:** Treat your guests to the finest cooking or the finest your local restaurants have to offer.
- **Ethnic Food Sampler:** Let your friends sample the best from Italy, Greece, Mexico, China, etc.
- **Progressive Feast:** Ask your friends to commit to providing one stage of the meal at their homes (e.g., cocktails, hors d'oeuvres, dinner, dessert, nightcap).
- **Wine-Tasting Party:** Contact your local wine shop to see if it can provide a wine expert. Consider an auction or raffle for a bottle of premium wine.

Take Your Goal to Work. Your co-workers and company can be a wonderful source of support. Consider forming a fundraising campaign team within your workplace and conduct events throughout the training period. Consider:

- **Dress-Down Day:** This is a great promotion for people who work in a formal office environment. For a donation, (e.g., $5 or more), an individual has the "company OK" to dress down (jeans, no ties, etc.) for a specified day or days.
- **Covered-Dish Lunch:** Ask co-workers to bring a covered dish for a lunch party. Charge co-workers a lunch fee (typically what they would pay for a lunch at a local restaurant).
- **Company Silent Auction:** Ask co-workers to bring an item or two they have "laying around the house." Set up a silent auction at work and let it run for a day or two.
- **Company Matching Gift Program:** If your company has a matching gift plan, take advantage of it. If not, ask your manager if he or she will consider a matching company gift for your efforts.

Sales. What do you have that people may want to buy? "One man's junk is another man's treasure!" Consider:

- **Garage Sale:** Team up with neighbors and co-workers.
- **Bake Sale:** Works well at the workplace and at church after a service.

Fee for Service

- **Neighborhood Car Wash:** Good, wet fun!
- **Handyman Service:** Organize a handyman (or handywoman) service team and spend Saturday doing odds and ends for neighbors and friends, for a fee, of course.

Door-to-Door Campaign. Spend a Saturday or Sunday meeting your neighbors— let them know what you are doing and ask for their support.

Club Donations. Go on the speaking circuit at local clubs and organizations. Contact the local social and service clubs (Lions, Kiwanis, Elks, American Legion, Jaycees, etc.) and ask them if you can have a few minutes on the meeting agenda. These groups are very responsible and have a treasury set aside just for this type of request.

Store-Front Collections. Ask your local grocery store or bank if you can spend a Saturday asking patrons to support your efforts.

These are just a few ideas to get you thinking. Use one or more of these, or develop your own—be creative and have fun!

SET YOUR GOAL . . . DEVELOP YOUR PLAN

Every member of **TEAM DIABETES** is required to raise a minimum fundraising amount based on the marathon destination of choice. Many of you will choose to set a goal over and above the minimum. Set your sights high and develop a plan to get you there. (See Attachment B.)

GOOD LUCK!

Resource 22

Attachment A: Developing a Prospect List

List *as many people as possible* under each category.

Family and Relatives:

_____

_____

_____

_____

_____

School Acquaintances:

_____

_____

_____

_____

_____

Friends and Social Circle:

_____

_____

_____

_____

_____

Work Associates:

_____

_____

_____

_____

_____

Companies/Corporations:

_____

_____

_____

_____

_____

Clubs and Organizations:

_____

_____

_____

_____

_____

Neighbors:

_____

_____

_____

_____

_____

Church/Synagogue:

_____

_____

_____

_____

_____

Local Businesses:

_____

_____

_____

_____

_____

Anyone Who Owes You a Favor:

_____

_____

_____

_____

_____

Resource 22

Attachment B: Developing a Fundraising Plan

My goal is to raise $ _____

Personal Appeals

I have identified _____ potential individual contributors.
(See Attachment A)

I have identified _____ potential companies, businesses, clubs, and organizations contributors.

From this list, I anticipate raising $ _____

TOTAL REVENUE from PERSONAL APPEALS $ _____

Special Events/Activities

Name of Special Event/Activity	Date(s)	Projected Income
_____	_____	_____
_____	_____	_____
_____	_____	_____
_____	_____	_____
_____	_____	_____

TOTAL REVENUE from SPECIAL EVENTS/ACTIVITIES $ _____

GRAND TOTAL $ _____

Resource 22

Helpful Hints for Raising Money

PEOPLE GIVE MONEY TO PEOPLE WHO ASK THEM FOR IT!

Start Now . . . Here's How:

The American Diabetes Association will supply you with whatever fundraising support you require. If you develop a prospect list meeting the minimum requirements for a bulk mailing, the ADA will assist you with the mailing. It is suggested that you include an addressed return envelope so the sponsor forms can be mailed back to you, not the American Diabetes Association. *The results are much better.*

Sample letters are included to help you get started. Send them to anyone: clients, customers, suppliers, family members, neighbors, friends, business associates.

As Contributions and Responses Come Back to You

- Send a thank-you note.
- Forward the contributions and sponsor forms to your local ADA office.
- Send your collected contributions on a regular basis so they can be entered and your total can be kept up-to-date.
- The American Diabetes Association will deposit all checks and process credit card charges.

All proceeds benefit the American Diabetes Association's research, advocacy, and educational programs.

Prospective Donors to Ask for Sponsorship/Donations

- Aerobics/Fitness Trainer
- Attorney
- Banker
- Bridge Club
- Car Dealer/Mechanic
- Children's Teammates' Parents
- Clients
- Co-workers
- CPA
- Dentist
- Employer
- Eye Doctor
- Financial Advisor
- Florist
- Golf Partners
- Grocery Store Manager
- Hair Stylist
- Holiday Card List

- Insurance Agent (home, life, health, car)
- Interior Designer
- Lawn Service Company
- Manicurist
- Minister/Sunday School Class
- Neighbors
- OB/GYN
- Painter/Wallpaper Hangers
- Parent's friends
- Pediatrician
- Pharmacist

- Printer
- Professional Association Members
- Psychologist
- Realtor
- Relatives
- Service Organization you belong to
- Siblings' Friends
- Suppliers for your business (straight donation or small amount per case or item sold)
- Travel Agent
- Veterinarian

How to Raise $1,000 in Ten Days

Action	Running Total
Put in your own $50 contribution	$50
Ask two merchants to donate $30 each	$110
Ask four family members for $50	$310
Ask three friends to donate $50	$460
Ask two of your doctors for $100 each	$660
Ask two co-workers for $20	$700
Ask three neighbors for $30 each	$790
Ask three church/temple members for $20	$850
Ask another two friends for $50	$950
Ask your supervisor for $50	$1,000

The American Diabetes Association Fact Sheet

ABOUT DIABETES

- One of every 20 people in America has diabetes.
- 15.7 million people, or 5.9% of the U.S. population, have diabetes, and one-third of all people who have diabetes do not know it, which is the equivalent of 5.4 million people.
- Diabetes is the sixth leading cause of death by disease in the United States.
- Complications include heart disease, stroke, kidney disease, blindness, nerve damage, and severe infections leading to foot and leg amputations.
- Approximately 798,000 people will be diagnosed with diabetes this year.

SO WHERE DOES SPONSORSHIP MONEY GO?

The money you raise from TEAM DIABETES helps the American Diabetes Association search for a cure and improve the lives of all people affected by diabetes. Efforts focus on three key areas:

Research

- Learning more about the causes, treatment, factors leading to complications, and ultimately a cure

Information

- Improving the quality of life for people with the disease by providing diabetes programs and publications
- Informing the public about the seriousness of the disease
- Keeping health care professionals up-to-date on the latest developments in treatment

Advocacy

- Increasing public awareness, working for better health care, and improving the lives of all people affected by diabetes
- Influencing legislation in health care that affects the lives of people with diabetes

ARE YOU AT RISK FOR DIABETES?

You are at risk if

- You are over age 45
- You are overweight
- You do not exercise regularly
- You have a family history of diabetes
- You delivered a baby weighing over 9 pounds
- You are African American, Hispanic, or Native American

ABOUT THE AMERICAN DIABETES ASSOCIATION

- The American Diabetes Association is America's leading voluntary health organization supporting diabetes research and public education.
- The Association has invested more than $100 million in research.
- Other Association activities include serving as a clearinghouse for information and guides, public and community awareness campaigns, and advocacy activities.
- The American Diabetes Association writes standards of medical care for people with diabetes. These guidelines provide further tips on what to expect from your doctor. To get a copy, call the Association's Diabetes Information and Action Line (DIAL) at (800) DIABETES (800-342-2383).

Generic Letter Requesting Support

June 20_____

Dear _____:

When do printers, attorneys, homemakers, nurses, students, bankers, and executives join the same TEAM? When there is an opportunity to help raise funds that are needed to support diabetes research, education, and advocacy.

We have formed the *(local market)* TEAM DIABETES—a group of men and women who have made an extraordinary commitment to run or walk the _____ Marathon *(13.1 or 26.2 miles)* to raise money for this very worthwhile cause.

For a moment, think about what we hope to accomplish. None of us are professional athletes, and many of us are long-distance runners or walkers, but we understand and have accepted the discipline, the time, and the commitment necessary to be successful. Each member of the TEAM has accepted this challenge because we believe that the money raised will help find the cure for diabetes.

Our common goal, to help eliminate diabetes, has brought us together. We have set our sights high.

Please consider giving us your support by sponsoring the 20_____ TEAM DIABETES. A sponsor form, American Diabetes Fact Sheet, and return envelopes are enclosed for your convenience.

The Marathon is a celebration of the human spirit, physical ability, and mental endurance; but for members of TEAM DIABETES, it is also a celebration of life.

Thank you for helping us defeat diabetes.

Sincerely,

TEAM Member

Sample Letters for Written Solicitation

These can be adapted to businesses or individuals.

June 20___

Dear _____:

    On *(date)* 20_____, I will join many other runners and walkers from various parts of *(locality)* to run/walk the "_____ Marathon" for a reason much more important than the personal challenge the completion of 26.2 miles *(or 13.1 miles)* represents. As members of the American Diabetes Association's TEAM DIABETES, we will run or walk the event to assist the organization in its efforts to battle diabetes.

    My run/walk is dedicated to _____ *(name)*, a TEAM Ambassador who was diagnosed with the disease when he/she was _____ years old. Ever since the date of diagnosis, _____ has had to endure daily insulin shots and numerous painful finger pricks to test his/her glucose level. *(Ask your patient's family for additional information they feel comfortable about including in your letter. Type 1 and Type 2 diabetes are treated differently.)*

    The research advances that have helped _____ *(name)* and others continue to live productive lives were achieved as a result of contributions made by companies, foundations, and donations from the public at large.

    Sponsorship of my marathon by _____ *(company name or prospective donor)* would be greatly appreciated. Please complete the enclosed sponsor form and show your support.

    Thank you for considering sponsorship of my run/walk in the _____ Marathon. I look forward to hearing from you soon. Please call me at *(phone number)* should there be any questions about the American Diabetes Association's TEAM DIABETES training program.

    Sincerely,

(Name

Title)

October 20_____

Dear _____:

My training partner and I are preparing ourselves for a race that will test our strength, perseverance, and commitment to overcome a great challenge. My partner is *(name)*, who is, like me, committed to continuing the fight to find a cure for diabetes. The race I am running is a simple one to help in this fight—a 26.20-mile marathon scheduled for *(date and location of marathon)*. Through TEAM DIABETES, he/she and I have teamed together to fight this disease, which has, as yet, no cure. Together we hope to continue the struggle to combat this life-threatening disease.

My goal is to raise $4,000 for diabetes research so that the millions of people who have diabetes can be victorious in their race against it. The money raised through TEAM DIABETES and the American Diabetes Association helps fund research and educational programs. Anyone with diabetes will tell you that finding a cure through research is the top priority. Diabetes afflicts 16 million people, one-third of whom are undiagnosed, and causes an average of 180,000 deaths each year. Diabetes costs $91.1 billion each year in medical expenses. Even with these statistics, researchers believe that someday a cure will be found.

Please help *(name of partner)* and me by making a pledge or donation with the enclosed card and envelope and sending it to the American Diabetes Association, *(local office address)*, Attention: *(coordinator's name)*. In return, *(partner's name)* and I will keep you updated on our progress in our race for a cure. With your help, we can all win the race against diabetes!

Thank you for your support.

Sincerely,

(Participant's Name)

RESOURCE 23

CASE STATEMENT EXAMPLES

The United Way of Central Indiana Brochure   410
The Amethyst House Brochure   416

The United Way of Central Indiana Brochure

Together, we are . . .

The Caring Force

United Way brings our community together as a caring force of contributors, volunteers and proven programs to have the greatest possible impact on human challenges. It is the most powerful way to improve life throughout central Indiana.

Focusing on Solutions

United Way gets results by strategically using community assets to apply forward-looking solutions to human challenges.

Maximizing Your Impact

United Way offers the greatest return on philanthropic dollars.

- United Way's thorough research ensures resources are focused on central Indiana's greatest human challenges.
- Individual gifts are combined into one powerful resource.
- Dollars are invested in proven programs and services.
- Your company will be recognized as a leader in the community by clients, partners, employees and friends.

Please Join United Way's Caring Force and help more . . .
**children and youth succeed,
families and neighborhoods become healthy and safe,
people have a second chance,
seniors stay connected.**

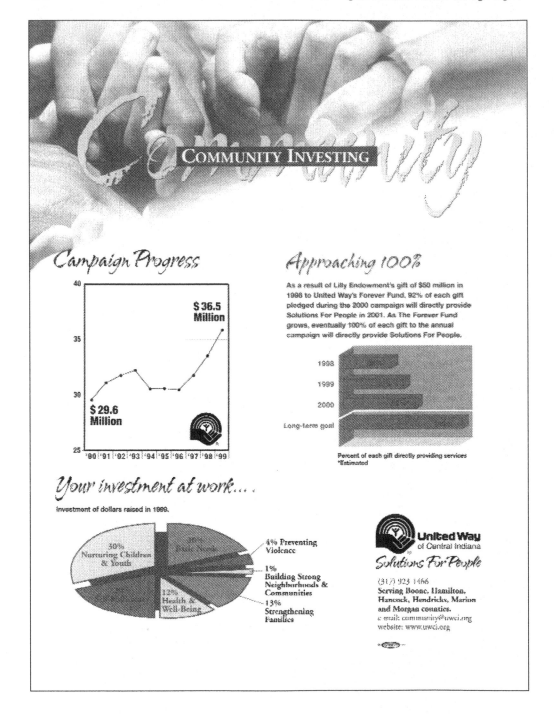

Campaign Progress

$ 36.5 Million

$ 29.6 Million

'90 '91 '92 '93 '94 '95 '96 '97 '98 '99

Approaching 100%

As a result of Lilly Endowment's gift of $50 million in 1988 to United Way's Forever Fund, 92% of each gift pledged during the 2000 campaign will directly provide Solutions For People in 2001. As The Forever Fund grows, eventually 100% of each gift to the annual campaign will directly provide Solutions For People.

1998
1999
2000
Long-term goal

Percent of each gift directly providing services
*Estimated

Your investment at work....

Investment of dollars raised in 1999.

30% Nurturing Children & Youth

4% Preventing Violence

1% Building Strong Neighborhoods & Communities

12% Health & Well-Being

13% Strengthening Families

United Way of Central Indiana

Solutions For People

(317) 923 1466
Serving Boone, Hamilton, Hancock, Hendricks, Marion and Morgan counties.
e-mail: community@uwci.org
website: www.uwci.org

GETTING RESULTS

1. Research

Before we ask you for a contribution, United Way does extensive research to determine the community's current and emerging human needs, along with the resources already in place to meet those needs. United Way is the only organization in central Indiana that does research of this kind.

6. Measuring Results

Reviewing outcomes achieved and their effect on the community is the important final step in ensuring United Way is being as effective as possible. Results are evaluated and reported to the community.

5. Investment

United Way strategically invests in proven programs and services that together achieve the outcomes that will best improve the community.

United Way
of Central Indiana

Solutions For People

2. Priorities

Once the needs and gaps in resources are known, expert volunteers help United Way determine the most critical needs and the outcomes that must be achieved to meet them.

4. Developing Resources

United Way invites you to join more than 100,000 other contributors in investing in the community. United Way's unique ability to combine resources and apply them to carefully planned strategies is the most powerful way to improve central Indiana.

3. Strategy

Expert volunteers and staff develop comprehensive strategies to change the trends causing the community's most urgent needs. This pro active approach serves to not just meet the needs, but eliminate them.

Resource 23

IMPACT

The following focus areas represent a strategic approach to finding solutions to central Indiana's human challenges. Each area is the responsibility of a council of volunteers who represent the diversity and expertise of the community. The charge of each council is to identify and find solutions to critical human need issues, enabling central Indiana to become a place where we are proud of the quality of life of all our citizens.

Nurturing Children and Youth

What?

Ensuring the successful development and transition to adulthood of children and youth.

How?

- Early childhood development
- Child care
- School readiness services
- Early identification and treatment programs
- Cultural and social awareness
- Civic engagement
- Recreation
- Leadership development
- Mentoring and preparation for adulthood

Self-Sufficiency for Adults, Seniors and People with Disabilities

What?

Helping adults achieve their potential in employment, living arrangements, mobility and community participation.

How?

- Maximizing skills and satisfaction through education and job training
- Supporting seniors in mobility or other daily living activities
- Accommodation and support so that persons with disabilities are not unnecessarily limited

Basic Needs

What?

Building and maintaining a safety net to meet people's basic needs.

How?

Providing access to services and information for people in poverty and those in crisis/emergency situations. Examples include food, clothing, shelter, energy assistance, homelessness prevention and intervention, migrant and refugee support, information, referral, mediation and disaster preparedness.

Strengthening Families

What?

Providing families with the tools they need to nurture and prosper.

How?

- Preventing and reducing the effects of child abuse and neglect
- Counseling and support services for families
- Juvenile justice programs
- Reunification, adoption and foster care
- Preventing teen pregnancy and support for pregnant teens

Health and Well-Being

What?

Improving the health of individuals, families and their communities.

How?

- Creating opportunities and providing resources to improve lifestyles and physical and social environments
- A healthy start for children; preventing and detecting chronic and communicable disease
- Building safe and healthy neighborhoods
- Support for the mentally ill
- Reducing substance dependency
- Improving access to and responsiveness of personal health care resources

Preventing Violence

What?

Helping people feel safe in their homes, neighborhoods and communities.

How?

- Preventing and reducing domestic violence
- Gang intervention
- Building skills so people can resolve conflicts and mediate crisis
- Support for victims of violence
- Fostering neighborhood safety

Building Strong Neighborhoods and Communities

What?

Involving residents and other stakeholders in ongoing and collaborative efforts to strengthen and improve the condition of neighborhoods.

How?

- Developing community/neighborhood leadership
- Fostering civic engagement and awareness
- Helping neighborhoods improve their quality of life
- Promoting diversity and improved race relations

United Way of Central Indiana

Solutions For People

(317) 923-1466
Serving Boone, Hamilton, Hancock, Hendricks, Marion and Morgan counties.
e-mail: community@uwci.org
website: www.uwci.org

Helpline: (317) 926-HELP

**Information and
Referral Network
Helpline:
(317) 926-HELP**

United Way
of Central Indiana

Solutions For People

United Way of Central Indiana
3901 N. Meridian Street
P.O. Box 88409
Indianapolis, IN 46208-0409
(317) 923-1466
**Serving Boone, Hamilton, Hancock,
Hendricks, Marion and Morgan counties**
e-mail: community@uwci.org
website: www.uwci.org

Hamilton County Service Center
942 N. Tenth Street
Noblesville, IN 46060-0678
(317) 773-1308

Hancock County Office
P.O. Box 734
One Courthouse Plaza
Greenfield, IN 46140
(317) 467-2346

Hendricks County Office
P.O. Box 701
Danville, Indiana 46122

United Way Center for Human Services

United Way of Johnson County

Member Agencies

Alpha Home Association of Greater
  Indianapolis, Inc.
* Alternatives Inc. of Madison County
American Cancer Society, Indianapolis
  Area, Great Lakes Division
American Heart Association
American Red Cross
Am. Rehabilitation Services
Annie Malone's Child Development
  Center, Inc.
Big Brothers of Greater Indianapolis, Inc.
Big Sisters of Central Indiana, Inc.
Boone County Cancer Society, Inc.
Boone County Senior Services, Inc.
Bosma Industries for the Blind, Inc.
Boy Scouts of America, Inc. Crossroads of
  America Council
Boy Scouts of America, Inc. Hoosier Trails
  Council
Boys & Girls Club of Hancock County
Boys & Girls Clubs of Indianapolis
Boys & Girls Club of Noblesville
Boys & Girls Club of Zionsville
* Camp Fire Boys & Girls, Indiana
  Heartland Council
Catholic Social Services of Central Indiana
Catholic Youth Organization
Child Advocates, Inc.
Children's Bureau of Indianapolis, Inc.
The Church Federation of Greater
  Indianapolis
Community Addiction Services of Indiana,
  Inc.
Community Centers of Indianapolis, Inc.
Community Service Center of Morgan
  County, Inc.
Coordinated Aging Services for Morgan
  County, Inc.
Crossroads Rehabilitation Center, Inc.
The Damien Center, Inc.
Day Nursery Association of Indianapolis,
  Inc.
Family Service Association of Central
  Indiana, Inc.
First Step, Inc.
Girl Scouts of Hoosier Capital Council
Girls Incorporated of Indianapolis
Goodwill Industries of Central Indiana,
  Inc.
Greater Indianapolis Council on
  Alcoholism, Inc. (NCADD)
Hamilton County Senior Services, Inc.
Hancock County Senior Services, Inc.
Happy Hollow Children's Camp, Inc.
Hendricks County Senior Services, Inc.
Heritage Place of Indianapolis, Inc.
Horizon House, Inc.
Independent Residential Living of Central
  Indiana, Inc.
* Indianapolis Neighborhood Resource
  Center
Indianapolis Senior Citizens' Center, Inc.
Indianapolis Speech & Hearing Center,
  Inc.
Indianapolis Urban League, Inc.
Information and Referral Network, Inc.

Janus, Inc.
Jewish Community Center of Indianapolis
* Johnson County Youth Service Bureau
The Julian Center, Inc.
Kaleidoscope Church and Community
  Partnership
Lebanon Area Boys & Girls Club
Legal Aid Society, Inc.-Indianapolis
Legal Services Organization of Indiana,
  Inc.
Little Red Door Cancer Agency
Lutheran Child and Family Services of
  INCKY, Inc.
Martin Center, Inc.
MCCOY, Inc. (Marion County
  Commission on Youth)
Meals on Wheels, Inc.
Mental Health Association in Boone
  County
Mental Health Association in Hamilton
  County
Mental Health Association in Hancock
  County
Mental Health Association in Hendricks
  County
Mental Health Association in Marion
  County
Mental Health Association in Morgan
  County
Mt. Zion Day Care Center, Inc.
Muscular Dystrophy Family Foundation
Noble of Indiana
PACE, Inc. Public Action in Correctional
  Effort
Perry Senior Citizens Services, Inc.
Pleasant Run, Inc.
Reach for Youth, Inc.
St. Elizabeth's Home
St. Mary's Child Center
The Salvation Army
Social Health Association of Indiana, Inc.
  Training Inc.
Tulip Trace Council of Girl Scouts, Inc.
United Cerebral Palsy Association of
  Greater Indiana, Inc.
USO Council of Indianapolis, Inc.
* The Villages of Indiana, Inc.
Visiting Nurse Service, Inc.
Volunteers of America of Indiana, Inc.
YMCA of Greater Indianapolis
Barbara B. Jordan YMCA
Youth Works, Inc.
YWCA of Indianapolis, Inc.

United Way Programs/Services

Bridges to Success
Hamilton County Service Center
Nonprofit Training Center
United Christmas Service
United Way/Community Service Council
United Way Center for Human Services
Volunteer Action Center
Youth as Resources

* New member agency

The Amethyst House Brochure

Foundations for Sober Living

AMETHYST HOUSE

Providing Dignity and Hope

Amethyst House: A Local Solution

Amethyst House is a nonprofit agency. We aim to empower men and women in ways that give them dignity, hope, and a healthier sense of themselves and their community as they recover from their addictions.

We are currently involved in developing an extensive database that links criminal justice and treatment data on individuals involved in drug and alcohol abuse. This database will give treatment providers and criminal justice officials information on the kinds of treatments provided and their outcomes in order to make more effective and efficient treatment plans.

Services at Amethyst House

We run a transitional residential program in separate houses for men and women with their dependent children. Experienced case managers and support staff ensure an alcohol- and drug-free environment and provide a structured setting.

The Program Works!

In the past year:

- We provided residents 4,756 days in a safe and supportive environment.
- More than half of Amethyst House residents leave our houses earning a living wage and having support in the community.

We Need Your Financial Support

- In the new managed care environment, Indiana has reduced payments to all providers of addictions services.
- The rent we charge does not cover the cost of services we provide.
- Help us tap into additional federal funds. *HUD gives us $4 for every dollar donated.*

For more information about Amethyst House, please call (812) 226-2570.

Hope

is the thing with feathers—
That perches in the soul—
And sings the tune without words—
And never stops—at all—

Emily Dickinson

Please help us provide Amethyst House residents the opportunity to build new lives full of promise and optimism for the future.

Name _____

Address _____

_____

Phone _____

E-mail_____

Please accept my tax-deductible donation of:

☐ $25   ☐ $50   ☐ $75   ☐ $100

☐ $250   ☐ $500   ☐ Other amount _____

☐ I would like to donate the following goods or services to Amethyst House:

_____

☐ I can volunteer my time:

_____

Amethyst House

P.O. Box 11
Bloomington, IN 47402

Resource 23

Alcohol and Drug Addiction

A National Problem

- Burdens society with $150 billion in social, health, and criminal costs each year.

- Plays a role in one out of three failed marriages.

- Costs employers up to $100 billion in lost time, accidents, health care and workers comp costs and plays a role in 65% of all workplace accidents.

- Plays a role in 50% of all traffic fatalities, 86% of murders, and 72% of assaults and robberies.

Here in Monroe County

- More than 80% of jail inmates are behind bars for substance-related offenses.

- 65% of the homeless people served by Shelter, Inc., have chronic drug or alcohol addiction problems.

Helping People Rebuild Their Lives

Amethyst House offers:

Experience from playing a vital role in the Bloomington area community for over 17 years.

Strength from our partnership with the Center for Behavioral Health and United Way.

Hope of recovery from drug and alcohol addiction through our supportive living environment and program.

Resource 23

Note: Reprinted with permission by Amethyst House, Inc.

RESOURCE 24

NEWSLETTER SAMPLE

Fairfield Country Day School

SPRING 1999 · a l u m n i   n e w s l e t t e r

INSIDE THIS ISSUE:

Page 2
Building Better Men
Page 3
Latin Then & Now
Page 4-5
What's New at FCDS
Page 6
Alumni News
Page 7
In Memoriam

COMING EVENTS AT FCDS

May 26:
Sixth Annual Scholarship Golf Tournament at the Country Club of Fairfield

May 28:
Dedication of Lawrence W. 'Pope' Gregory Classroom; Ninth grade homeroom

June 7:
Prize Night; Ninth Grade Dinner at FCDS

June 9:
Commencement

CAPITAL CAMPAIGN CLEARS $6.2 MILLION MARK

We're so close! Capital campaign co-chairs Lin Christie and David Rosow have announced recent commitments totalling $400,000 from FCDS trustees and others which bring the total raised to $6,260,000 toward the total campaign goal of $7 million. Although the Fairfield Country Day School campus has been transformed by the current renovation project – with most of the work completed – donors are still needed to help FCDS fulfill the project's financial obligations. Many beautiful spaces within the new facility are yet to be named, including the new gymnasium. Here's how the donations break down, as of May 1, 1999:

Capital renovations	$5,800,000
Goal:	$6 million
Endowment	$ 460,000
Goal:	$1 million

The endowment portion of the campaign will allow FCDS to create endowed funds that will support faculty development in perpetuity. Faculty development funds are critical to Country Day's ability to attract the finest faculty, ensuring that funds are always available for professional conferences, graduate work, and academic research.

"This campaign represents the coming together of many people for whom Country Day has been a wonderful influence – parents, grandparents, alumni, and friends," says Headmaster Bob Vitalo. "The renovation of the building allows us to look forward to the future, confident in the knowledge that we are providing our students with a state-of-the art educational facility. Endowed faculty development funds will ensure that the teaching in those facilities reaches the very highest academic standards."

It's just a little further to finish line to reach these two worthy goals. Please keep that support coming! For further information or to make a pledge, please contact the Development Office.

Currier Family Challenge Will Match Alumni Gifts: $100,000 Goal Set

The hallmark of any great school is its faculty, and FCDS has had truly gifted teachers in its 63-year history. Among them was Jim Currier (above), who taught at FCDS for 25 years, from 1953 to 1979. Many students remember Mr. Currier leading the school in singing 'Green the Fields,' giving extra help in his 'Dungeon,' or proctoring '3:10' in his 9th grade homeroom.

Jim's widow, Dorothy 'Dodo' Currier, has stepped forward to present a challenge to past parents and friends who remember Jim, and to alumni who attended Jim's classes during his tenure at Country Day. Mrs. Currier has pledged a $25,000 matching gift to encourage others either to make their first gift or to increase their gift to the capital campaign. All new or increased gifts to the capital campaign will be matched with the Currier gift on a 1:3 basis.

The goal is to raise $100,000 from alumni and friends of Jim Currier and to name the rotunda of the entrance of FCDS in his memory. The names of every donor will be listed with the plaque honoring Mr. Currier.

It's simple to make this match. Just write a note to credit your donation to the Currier Campaign Match on the memo line of your check and forward it to FCDS. Gifts of securities and corporate matching gifts are also welcome.

MEET PRESIDENT AND CEO ROB MACINNIS '99

Rob MacInnis '99 had his moment in the sun when he was profiled in the Winter 1999 issue of the Toshiba Corporation's Notebook for Schools Quarterly. Featured was his own web and computer design company, OCR Design, which Rob runs out of his home. According to the article, Rob has "international partners in Canada and Sweden... we're working on a web site for an international medical group. They work out of the rain forests in Peru. I'm also finishing a header logo for a company called Check Six."

The article goes on to ask Rob about the importance of computers in his life: "(The computer) is an amazing help for studying, but beyond that, these notebooks have brought new light to the word organization. No longer are there 'the dog ate my homework' excuses. The common reply of teachers now is, 'why didn't you back it up on floppy?' ...I believe that most kids will have laptops in place in a few years...computers will aid in everything from attendance to study hall monitoring. They are amazing tools and can and will be utilized for almost everything in the foreseeable future."

BUILDING BETTER MEN: PROJECT ADVENTURE AND INSIDE/OUT

Inside/Out, now in its seventh year, and Project Adventure, which began this year at Fairfield Country Day School, are two courses in the FCDS curriculum designed to enhance students' self-esteem and respect for others.

Inside/Out, offered to boys in grades 5-9, is designed to create a dialogue on important issues such as drug abuse, ethics, and morals. Classes meet by grade level.

The sixth grade group, for example, is working with Headmaster Bob Vitalo to explore the topic "leading an ethical life" by discussing the importance of acting in ways that uphold important, internal values. The culmination of the program for sixth-graders is an essay detailing their own personal set of values or "laws of life."

Under the direction of Dean of Students Joe Isola, seventh-graders are focusing on drug education, while Dean Isola's eighth grade groups are working on topics including the FCDS Honor Code, rule models, resolving conflicts, and respect for individual differences.

Project Adventure, designed for students in grades 6-8, builds cooperative and group skills, including communication, trust, loyalty, perseverance, patience, the ability to give and take constructive criticism, and the acceptance and delegation of authority. All activities take place in a group setting and participants learn to be part of a group that is working towards a common goal. The boys are also taught to recognize the importance of the individual within the group, as well as the power of groups to transcend the individual's limitations.

Project Adventure presents challenges for boys to overcome as part of a cooperative group (left) and individually (below).

in the classroom

LATIN: THEN AND NOW

Andrew Holmgren discusses the fine points of Latin with student Robert Moriarty, Jr.

Were Mrs. Oros (see sidebar, right) to visit a Latin class at Fairfield Country Day School today, chances are she would find much that is familiar. Latin remains a required subject for all 5th and 6th graders, and is an elective course for grades 7 - 9. Our Latin teacher, Andrew Holmgren, uses what he calls "traditional methods" for teaching the fundamentals. Fifth grade Latin provides the student with a basic understanding of Latin's grammatical structure, while at the same time introducing the culture and politics of the ancient world. The class stresses the similarities and differences between Latin and English. In the second half of the year the students begin to apply their knowledge to simple translations, while also continuing their study of Latin grammar.

The 6th grade Latin class introduces more complex translations, including a simplified version of the Aeneid. In the 7th grade, mythology is introduced and the boys publish a monthly newsletter covering history, myth and grammar. This course aims to both educate the student in the fundamentals of the Latin language and to instill in the boys a sense of mental discipline.

"There are several obvious benefits of studying a classical language: the clarity of grammar, economy of expression, and etymology, to name a few," says Andrew Holmgren. "I believe that Latin also instills a love of learning in a young student."

Mr. Holmgren started his Latin education in 7th grade, and went on to receive his B.A. in Medieval History from the University of Notre Dame's noted Institute of Medieval Studies in 1995. He earned his M.A. in 1997 from Fordham University's Institute of Medieval Studies, concentrating in codecology (manuscript studies) and Latin paleography (the study of scripts).

MRS. OROS CELEBRATES CENTISIMUS DIES NATALIS

On January 4, 1997 retired FCDS Latin and Math teacher Mrs. Marie Oros, celebrated her 100th birthday and was honored by her family with a reception at her home in Fairfield. Born in Saugatuck, she attended school there and following high school attended Columbia University teachers College in New York. She was the first principal of McKinley School and also taught in other Fairfield schools, including many years at Fairfield Country Day School, from which she retired in 1964. She speaks often and kindly of her students and teaching career.

John Payne '55 remembers Mrs. Oros's Latin classes very well. John writes, "How could I ever forget Mrs. Oros? Impossible! She didn't have to tell us more than once why we were in her eighth grade Latin class. We were there to learn. No one made a sound in her class unless called upon and she quickly stopped any attempt at foolishness. Most importantly, Mrs. Oros was a tough and fair teacher who prepared my classmates and me well for Latin II with Mr. Ely. She always expected and received our best effort. Happy Birthday, Mrs. Oros. Thank you for helping me and many other students – understand the mysteries of Latin."

Congratulations to Marie Oros, photographed recently at her home in Fairfield, on her landmark birthday!

OK, Class: How much Latin do you remember?

On a recent visit to a fifth grade (first year) Latin class, students were composing short stories of four or five sentences, first in English, then translating their stories into Latin. See if you can translate Michael Sueto's '03 story from Latin back into English.

Agricola ambulabat ad villam.
Filius portabat gladium ad agricolam.
    Navigabat ad bellum.
    cras natto. Amabat puellam.

FCDS people

HEADMASTER'S MESSAGE

Dear Friends,

In April we held our annual Grandparents' and Special Friends' Day. On that occasion we were very happy to host over two hundred visitors to our school. Of all the special events we have at Country Day, it is this one that is most popular with the boys. The opportunity to spend time with people so important to them really excites our students.

In addressing our visitors at the start of the day I expressed my hope that they would take away with them three important messages about our school.

The first message has to do with renewal. Country Day is a 63 year-old school. While we have been very successful in the past, we have demonstrated that we are not content to stand still. We are constantly reviewing our curriculum, updating technology and developing as teachers. Our building project is an example of analyzing our goals and working to meet them. In so many ways we are a better school than we were just two years ago. We are meeting the challenge of growing, learning and adapting in a changing world.

The second message about our school has to do with the importance of family. The grandparents have done a wonderful job of raising children who have become our dedicated group of parents. We structure our school to take advantage of the kinds of relationships that occur in families. Our boys receive a great deal of attention and lots of love. We count on the effectiveness of positive role models to teach our boys good lessons. We often joke that if a parent asks a boy to do something, it will sometimes get done; if a teacher asks a boy to do something, it will usually get done; but if a ninth grader asks a boy to do something, it will always get done.

The final message that I hoped our visitors left with was to appreciate boys. At Country Day we have boys with all kinds of talents and all different interests. We give them the space to learn in ways that are comfortable for them and we support their growth in becoming fine young men. Boys need all of the encouragement we can provide to creatively and effectively meet the challenges they confront as they grow up.

Country Day is a vital and growing institution, we are proud of our rich history and we eagerly anticipate what the future holds.

Sincerely,

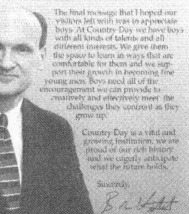

Robert D. Vitalo
Headmaster

COMMENCEMENT ADDRESS

John Steinbreder '71 delivering FCDS commencement keynote address.

John Steinbreder '71 delivered the keynote address at FCDS's 61st commencement exercises on June 10, 1998. A professional journalist, he has worked at Fortune Magazine and Sports Illustrated and contributes to The New York Times Magazine, Golf Digest, Forbes FYI and other publications. After graduating from FCDS, Mr. Steinbreder continued his education at Choate Rosemary Hall; received an associate's degree from Franklin College in Lugano, Switzerland; studied at the University of Nairobi; and graduated from the University of Oregon with a B.A. in journalism. The following words are from his commencement address:

"While Country Day did give me my start in writing, it taught me so much more. I learned about the necessity of being organized, of putting forth my best effort in whatever I did and of remembering that we would always be 'judged by our works.' It was that sense of commitment that Bill Fly and others taught us week after week, and their lessons have carried me through my life and career.

It hasn't always been easy following my dreams. There were enormous pressures from parents and peers to pursue more conventional careers. And finances have long been an issue because the publishing industry is not known for overpaying its people. But I wanted to make a living doing something I truly loved, and I would urge all of you to consider the value of that as you continue your education and begin to think about the things you will do once you have your college degrees...Don't be afraid to pursue an occupation simply because it is not as glamorous or lucrative as some others. Certainly, there is nothing wrong with being famous or making a lot of money. But make sure that reaching those goals doesn't come at the expense of everything else that can be good in your life...Be successful but be true to yourself as well. And always remember that at the end of the day, it is your self worth, and not your net worth, that is most important because that is what will bring you the greatest joy."

FCDS people

MEET BOB MORIARTY

It's not every day that you meet someone who is connected in as many ways to Fairfield Country Day School as is Bob Moriarty (right). He is an alumnus (Class of 1970); his sons, Michael '00 and Robert, Jr. '03 are current students; and he serves on the board of trustees. If that weren't enough, he agreed to serve as chairman of the 1998-99 Annual Fund, a job he has taken on with relish.

Bob's commitment to FCDS is evident – and it is reflected in the results of this year's Annual Fund campaign, setting a record for the number of gifts received (384 as of May 1). Bob has set his sights on breaking the school record from two years ago of $200,533 total dollars raised.

But what really motivates Bob is his enthusiasm about the quality of his sons' educational experience, and the continuum he sees between his days at Country Day and theirs.

"FCDS is quite simply the best KG-9 boys' school around and it keeps getting better," he comments. "I am proud to have gone to this school, and to see my sons thriving academically and emotionally here. It has become an important bond between us."

Bob has stayed close to his roots in Fairfield. He and Barbara, his wife of 16 years, are never far from FCDS. Bob has enjoyed the chance to touch base with alumni from former years through the many Annual Fund letters he has written.

"Bob has been great to work with," says Barbara Price Monahan, director of development. "He understands fundraising, he understands FCDS and he has a keen desire to see the Annual Fund and FCDS succeed. The next Annual Fund chairman is going to have a tough act to follow!"

NEW DEVELOPMENTS IN THE DEVELOPMENT OFFICE

Two new faces can be seen in the development office at FCDS these days. Barbara Price Monahan joined Country Day on October 1, 1998 as director of development, succeeding Audrey Edmonds Stone, who relocated to North Carolina. Barbara moved to Connecticut from Indiana, where she was director of development for the Indiana University School of Music. Joining her as development assistant is Marianne O. Harrison, who brings to Country Day extensive experience in the 'for profit' world, most recently as assistant to the president of SolTec International, Inc. in Southport, CT.

Barbara Monahan, left, and Marianne Harrison are enjoying their new jobs in the FCDS development office.

ADD 'EM UP!

These are but a few ways your Annual Fund gift improves just one "day in the life" of an eighth grader, Paul Fenner.

8:20 a.m.   Mr. Fallon's homeroom: window treatments to filter the early morning sunlight.

8:30 a.m.   Assembly: sound system for the auditorium.

9:00 a.m.   English: overhead projector and LCD panel for sharing work on the big screen.

9:48 a.m.   Math: Scholastic "Classroom Dynamath Magazine" to supplement textbook work.

10:31 a.m.   History: Rand McNally Continent Map Set & new globes. For each student: Quick Reference Atlas & Map Study Guide set.

11:14 a.m.   Inside/Outside Program with Mr. Isola: Community Intervention, Inc. videos and activity kits.

11:57 a.m.   Spanish: interactive CD and textbook series "Dime UNO" and "Dime DOS".

12:46 p.m.   Lunch: New dining room furniture that provides a warm, comfortable place in a busy day.

1:30 p.m.   Computer Lab: Quick Cameras, Hewlett Packard CD Writer, Tektronix Color Printer, digital camera.

2:11 p.m.   Study Hall: Tablet arm chair with larger surface to accommodate the laptop computer.

3:00 p.m.   Cross Country practice: Shuttle bus to Ludlow Field.

Your gift to the 1998-99 Annual Fund will enrich Paul's education – and that of more than 250 boys at Fairfield Country Day School – each and every day.

Contact: Barbara Price Monahan
Director of Development
(203)259-2723, ext. 311
bmonahan@fcds.pvt.k12.ct.us

5

F C D S   A l u m n i   N e w s

1940

Donald McGloon has retired from pharmacy, but has taken on the job as consultant pharmacist to the South Texas Health Corp.

1953

George B. Longstreth, MD and his wife Betsy made a long-awaited trip to Haiti where George volunteered his services for two weeks at the Hôpital Albert Schweitzer in Deschappelles. They had volunteered there for two months in 1982-83, and were longing to return to "give back for some of the blessing God has given us." Betsy and George spent two grueling weeks of what Dr. Longstreth described as an "overwhelming workload" during which time George saw patients with a variety of pathologies including malnutrition. Dr. Longstreth wrote movingly about their experiences in a two-part article for the Fairfield Citizen-News, published in January.

1956

Marion W. Smith has a new address in Savannah: 5 Marsh Island Lane, Savannah, GA 31411.

1964

James B. McKinney, Jr. has sent us his new address: 2065 Knox Road 850E, Wataga, IL 61488-9417.

1965

Edward Paige (above) was named managing editor of Westport magazine in November, 1998. He has served as managing editor at World Tennis Magazine and the Cable Guide for Paragon House Publishers; written for the Village Voice and Sport magazine; and edited for publishers including St. Martin's, McGraw Hill and Times Mirror with the Stratford Advocate. He also has taught editing and feature writing at New York University. Edward majored in English at the University of North Carolina at Chapel Hill and attended a master's program in English at Middlebury College.

1971

Tucker Crolius writes: "I am now the Ski Patrol Director at Wintergreen Resort in Virginia. I am keeping my "real" job as a financial consultant working for a company out of Charlotte, North Carolina (I have a very understanding boss!)."

Sean McManus and Tracy Torre were married at the Church of the Assumption in Westport this past summer. After graduating from FCDS, Sean attended Fairfield Prep and Duke University, where he graduated cum laude. He is currently president of CBS Sports. His bride attended Hofstra University. The couple divides their time between New Canaan and New York City.

1974

"Your picture brought back memories," writes Jon Goss about the old track team photo that was published in the 1997-98 Annual Report. He correctly identified several of those in the photo. Jon just passed the 10-year mark of living in Idaho. He is currently into his third year of teaching in a small, rural, one building K-12 school. His son Nathaniel, 5, is in kindergarten and daughter Claire, 3, has started pre-school. Jon's wife, Maria, just completed the Idaho teacher certification program. Jon can be reached at jmgoss@micron.net, or snail mail: P.O. Box 122, Bliss, ID 83314. He also sent news of twin brother Tom Goss, who recently received a masters in school counseling and is currently working in northern Vermont. He has two boys, Ethan, 5, and Tuy, 2. His wife, Linda, is a nurse at St. Johnsbury Hospital.

Ed Fiddler is living in Brookfield, CT. He is a senior vice president at Sedgwick Group (insurance brokers). Ed and his wife Terry have a son, Timothy, who is four years old.

John T. Curtis II continues to live in London with three little ones: Morgan, 7, Austin, 4, and Silas, 3. John writes that he has just taken the plunge on a thatched cottage on the Isle of Wight "to provide a weekend escape for all of us."

1980

Michael Licamele and wife Stephanie have a new address in Easton: 5 Ferndale Drive, Easton, CT 06612. Their son Michael Joseph is two.

1984

Christian Katzenbach and wife Greta have a new son, Clark Francis Katzenbach, born in August, 1998.

1985

Peter Nickowitz has been appointed as adjunct professor of English at New York University, where he is completing the requirements for a Ph.D. in English. Peter graduated from Brandeis University summa cum laude in 1992, specializing in contemporary American poetry. In addition to teaching at NYU, Peter has also taught recently at Long Island University and the New School for Social Research.

Kiliaen Van Rensselaer writes that he is in New York City working as a brand manager for Colgate-Palmolive, and starting a virtual reality hardware company in his spare time. He still visits Fairfield County some weekends.

1986

Elliot Gray writes that he is "living and working in Burlington, VT."

1987

Stephen Robert Jones (above) was married July 25, 1998 to the former Mary Theresa Varilla. Stephen is a 1990 graduate of the Hopkins School and a 1994 graduate of Rensselaer Polytechnic Institute. He is presently employed as a senior associate at Price Waterhouse Coopers in New York City. His wife is a 1990 graduate of Greens Farms Academy and a 1994 graduate of

F C D S   A l u m n i   N e w s

Wesleyan University in Middletown. She is an assistant editor at Scholastic, Inc. in New York City. The couple took a wedding trip to the Turks and Caicos Islands and now live in Manhattan.

1992

Laurance J. Guido, Jr. writes that he is completing his junior year at Columbia (class of 2000). Last summer, he was a White House intern and worked for Vice-President Gore. This next year, he will enter a combined BA/MPA (Masters of Public Affairs) program at Columbia School of International and Public Affairs.

SPECIAL MESSAGES

Following the family's relocation to Massachusetts, Billy Glavin '01 is attending 7th grade at Belmont Hills School in Belmont, MA. He is playing football, hockey and lacrosse. He misses his friends at FCDS and would love to hear from them at 7 Lincoln Center, Wellesley, MA 02181-6116.

This short note accompanied the Annual Fund contribution of Graciela and Frank Cappelli of Philadelphia, grandparents of Darius' 04 and Gabriel '05 Cappelli: "We are voice teachers and former opera singers – our appreciation and gratefulness on the quality of education our beloved grandchildren are receiving from your wonderful school."

FACULTY NOTES

At the recent SchoolTech Expo in New York City, FCDS Technology Coordinator Cindy Abate was invited to display FCDS' computer technology program as part of the conference's "Showcase of Model Schools."

Congratulations and best wishes to fifth grade teacher Peggy Flaherty and Latin teacher Andrew Holmgren who are being married on May 22. Are they the first FCDS faculty couple to wed? Let us know!

Lower School science teacher, Steve O'Connell and his wife Elizabeth are the proud parents of a baby boy, Thomas Brennan O'Connell, (class of 2013!), born February 26, 1999.

IN MEMORIAM

Howard H. Burr '57 died November 25, 1998 at the age of 56. Born in Bridgeport, he was a lifelong Fairfield resident. He was an avid golfer and skier and was a member of the Professional Golfer's Association and the H. Smith Richardson Men's Club. He was an independent golf sales representative at the time of his death. He is survived by his four children and their families, John S. Burr, Julie J. Burr, Sven J. Burr, and Daniel I. Burr and two brothers and their families, Peter N. Burr and Todd J. Burr '72.

Described by a current Board of Trustees member as two of the most important Trustees the school has ever had, Eben M. Graves and Ann Adams Mandeville died in December of 1998 and March of 1999 respectively.

A Trustee of Fairfield Country Day School from 1977 to 1983, Eben Graves passed away on December 20, 1998 at the age of 95. Mr. Graves practiced law in New York City for nearly 50 years. He was a patent attorney and a senior partner in the firm of Brumbaugh, Graves, Donohue and Raymond. He was predeceased by a son, Eben Graves, Jr. 36 and is survived by his wife Marion of Southport; daughter Deborah Nolin of Neenah, WI; son James Graves '49 of Westport, and seven grandchildren.

Ann Adams Mandeville, Trustee of Fairfield Country Day School from 1973–1988, died on March 1, 1999 at her home. She is survived by her daughter, Meredith Hollis, and sons Christopher '64, Matthew '68, Kempton '71, Jonathan '74 and William Mandeville '76; a son-in-law, five daughters-in-law and seventeen grandchildren. A graduate of Dana Hall and Vassar College, she will be remembered for her loyal and effective hands-on service to many institutions.

Philip B. Lentini '79 died suddenly on January 30. He was a 1982 graduate of Staples High School in Westport. He attended Whittier College in California where he studied restaurant management. For ten years he was employed by restaurants in New York City, returning to Connecticut to team up with his sister, Carol Lentini Mojcher, in a catering and party planning business, "Along Came Carol."

Charles E. Oudin, Jr. passed away this past year. He was father to Chip '73 and John '74 Oudin, a friend to many on Greenfield Hill, and a strong supporter of what FCDS meant to a boy's education and character.

FCDS has been transformed by the construction funded by the capital campaign

from the FCDS archives

CREDITS

Editor:
Barbara Monahan

Assistant editor:
Marianne Harrison

Produced and
Designed by:
Goldberg & Sack
Creative
Communications

Photographs:
Sven Martson

Printer:
Phoenix Press,
New Haven

Published by:
FCDS Development
Office
(P) 203•259•2723
(F) 203•259•3249
bmonahan@fcds.pvt.k12.ct.us
mharrison@fcds.pvt.k12.ct.us

Thank you to those who have helped identify familiar faces in our 'mystery' team photo (a track team, we believe). Athletic director John Curtis and John Goss '74 were of great help. We still have some remaining question marks and if you can help us replace them with the correct names, please call the Development Office.

Front Row (L to R): Martin Schmidt '72, ?, David Frassinelli '74, ?, Jamie McPherson '74, Frankie Riccio '72, ?, ?.

Middle Row (L to R): Timmy Stone '72, ?, Duffy Glaser '75, ?, ?, ?, Bobby Delbuono '72, Perry Gillies '72, Blake Payson '72, Roger Risley '72.

Back Row (L to R): Coach Matt Huber, Tucker Crolius '71, ?, Geoff Wiswell '71, ?, John Lloyd '71, ?, ?, ?, Bobby Skinner '71, Coach Harry Salo.

PARENTS OF ALUMNI:
If your son no longer maintains a permanent address at your home, kindly notify the School of his new mailing address. Thank you!

June is "Leave a Legacy Connecticut Month".

LEAVE A LEGACY is a community collaboration to encourage people to make gifts from their estates to support causes they care about. The message is simple: Leave something in your will for a cause that is important to you. For information about how your bequest can benefit Fairfield Country Day School, please call or write: Barbara Price Monahan, Director of Development.

LEAVE A LEGACY CONNECTICUT

WE WANT TO HEAR FROM YOU!
Please keep us informed and send us news about yourself and your classmates, including changes of address, employment and schools attended, marriages, births, and more. Send your notes by e-mail to: bmonahan@fcds.pvt.k12.ct.us

Non-Profit Org.
U.S. Postage
Paid
Permit No. 2
Southport, CT

Address Correction
Requested

Fairfield Country Day School
2970 Bronson Road
Fairfield, CT 06430-2095

RESOURCE 25

GIFT RECEIPT TEMPLATES

Backstreet Missions, Inc.   432

Children's Hospital Foundation,
    Vancouver   433

American Red Cross—Monroe County
    Chapter   434

Indiana University Foundation   436

Resource 25

Backstreet Missions, Inc.

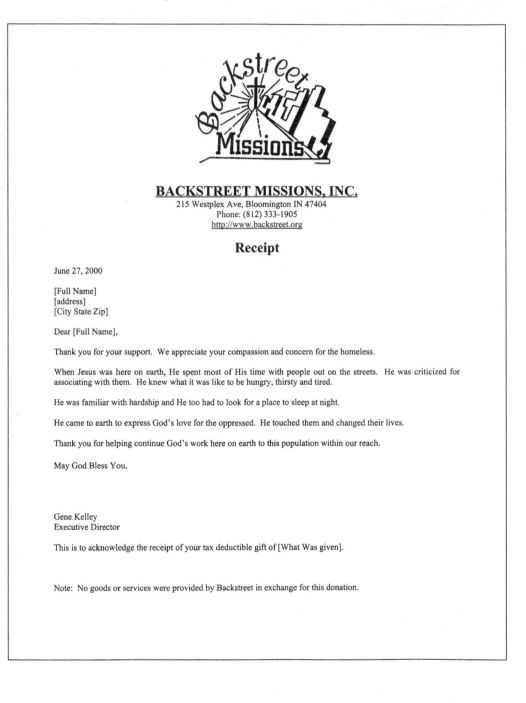

BACKSTREET MISSIONS, INC.
215 Westplex Ave, Bloomington IN 47404
Phone: (812) 333-1905
http://www.backstreet.org

Receipt

June 27, 2000

[Full Name]
[address]
[City State Zip]

Dear [Full Name],

Thank you for your support. We appreciate your compassion and concern for the homeless.

When Jesus was here on earth, He spent most of His time with people out on the streets. He was criticized for associating with them. He knew what it was like to be hungry, thirsty and tired.

He was familiar with hardship and He too had to look for a place to sleep at night.

He came to earth to express God's love for the oppressed. He touched them and changed their lives.

Thank you for helping continue God's work here on earth to this population within our reach.

May God Bless You,

Gene Kelley
Executive Director

This is to acknowledge the receipt of your tax deductible gift of [What Was given].

Note: No goods or services were provided by Backstreet in exchange for this donation.

Children's Hospital Foundation, Vancouver

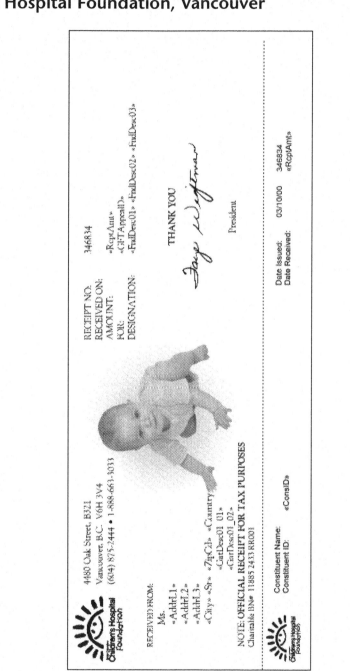

Children's Hospital Foundation

4480 Oak Street, B321
Vancouver, B.C. V6H 3V4
(604) 875-2444 • 1-888-663-3033

RECEIPT NO.: 346834

RECEIVED FROM:

Ms.

«AddrL1»
«AddrL2»
«AddrL3»
«City» «St» «ZipCd» «Country»

RECEIVED ON:
AMOUNT: «RcptAmt»
FOR: «GiftAppeal»
DESIGNATION: «FndDesc01» «FndDesc02» «FndDesc03»

THANK YOU

Doug Weltman

President

«GstDesc01 01»
«GstDesc01 02»

NOTE: OFFICIAL RECEIPT FOR TAX PURPOSES
Charitable BN# 11885 2433 RR0001

Children's Hospital Foundation

Constituent Name:
Constituent ID: «ConsID»

Date Issued: 03/10/00 346834
Date Received: «RcptAmt»

American Red Cross—Monroe County Chapter

American Red Cross—Monroe County Chapter
411 E. Seventh Street
Bloomington, IN 47408-3723

Sales Receipt

DATE	SALE NO.
07/21/2000	6609

SOLD TO

JOHN Q. PUBLIC
1234 ANYWHERE STREET
BLOOMINGTON, IN 47401

CHECK NO.	PAYMENT METHOD	PROJECT
9999	CHECK	

DESCRIPTION	QUANITY	RATE	AMOUNT
GENERAL DONATION	1	50.00	50.00

THANK YOU!

Total	$50.00

AMERICAN RED CROSS
MONROE COUNTY CHAPTER
411 E. SEVENTH STREET
BLOOMINGTON, IN 47408

Thank You for your donation of Books/In-Kind Items.
The items will be sold (books) or given (in-kind) to local victims of disaster.

Please retain this receipt for tax purposes.
Attach a list of your donated items.

Date: _____

Signature: _____

Indiana University Foundation

[FRONT]

Indiana University Foundation
P.O. Box 500
Bloomington, IN 47402

July 24, 2000

Indiana University Foundation salutes:
Hubert T. Steerherder
P.O. Box 12345
Fort Somewhere, TX 12345-6789

DONOR - INDIANA UNIVERSITY

999999-9999999
For your commitment and generosity to
Indiana University, the Officers and the
Board of Directors of the Indiana University
Foundation want to thank you for your gift
of $210.00 to Foundation Annual Giving.

Indiana University Foundation
P.O. Box 500
Bloomington, IN 47402

July 24, 2000

Indiana University Foundation salutes:
Hubert T. Steerherder
P.O. Box 12345
Fort Somewhere, TX 12345-6789

DONOR - INDIANA UNIVERSITY

999999-9999999
For your commitment and generosity to
Indiana University, the Officers and the
Board of Directors of the Indiana University
Foundation want to thank you for your gift
of $500.00 to Making Money Fund.

Under IRS guidelines, you received no benefit for your contribution, or the estimated
value of the benefit is not substantial; therefore the full amount of your gift is deductible.

Indiana University Foundation
P.O. Box 500
Bloomington, IN 47402

July 24, 2000

Indiana University Foundation salutes:
Hubert T. Steerherder
P.O. Box 12345
Fort Somewhere, TX 12345-6789

DONOR - INDIANA UNIVERSITY

999999-9999999
For your commitment and generosity to
Indiana University, the Officers and the
Board of Directors of the Indiana University
Foundation want to thank you for your gift
of $200.00 to Athletics Fund.

Benefit Received by Donor:
Dinner w/IU President
Value of Benefit Received: $100.00
Deductible Amount of Gift: $100.00

[BACK]

INDIANA UNIVERSITY FOUNDATION

Showalter House, Bloomington
(812) 855-8311, fax: (812) 855-6956
50 South Meridian Street, Suite 400, Indianapolis
(317) 673-4438, fax: (317) 274-8818

"People who have been touched by Indiana University have developed a strong loyalty and have expressed that in faithful support and generous gifts. . . . They help to make a difference for the future, building the foundation of one of the great universities for the twenty-first century."

Herman B Wells
University Chancellor

Thank you for your generous gift to Indiana University.

The many dollars in private support contributed each year by people like you add up to a wealth of opportunities for Indiana University to serve the citizens of the state, the nation, and the world. Your gift enables the University to provide greater access to quality educational opportunities, enhance Indiana's tradition of excellence in higher education, contribute to economic development, and conduct research that will change the quality of human life for the better.

Your support is gratefully acknowledged.

Curtis R. Simic
Curtis R. Simic, President
Indiana University Foundation

INDIANA UNIVERSITY FOUNDATION

Showalter House, Bloomington
(812) 855-8311, fax: (812) 855-6956
50 South Meridian Street, Suite 400, Indianapolis
(317) 673-4438, fax: (317) 274-8818

"People who have been touched by Indiana University have developed a strong loyalty and have expressed that in faithful support and generous gifts. . . . They help to make a difference for the future, building the foundation of one of the great universities for the twenty-first century."

Herman B Wells
University Chancellor

Thank you for your generous gift to Indiana University.

The many dollars in private support contributed each year by people like you add up to a wealth of opportunities for Indiana University to serve the citizens of the state, the nation, and the world. Your gift enables the University to provide greater access to quality educational opportunities, enhance Indiana's tradition of excellence in higher education, contribute to economic development, and conduct research that will change the quality of human life for the better.

Your support is gratefully acknowledged.

Curtis R. Simic
Curtis R. Simic, President
Indiana University Foundation

INDIANA UNIVERSITY FOUNDATION

Showalter House, Bloomington
(812) 855-8311, fax: (812) 855-6956
50 South Meridian Street, Suite 400, Indianapolis
(317) 673-4438, fax: (317) 274-8818

"People who have been touched by Indiana University have developed a strong loyalty and have expressed that in faithful support and generous gifts. . . . They help to make a difference for the future, building the foundation of one of the great universities for the twenty-first century."

Herman B Wells
University Chancellor

Thank you for your generous gift to Indiana University.

The many dollars in private support contributed each year by people like you add up to a wealth of opportunities for Indiana University to serve the citizens of the state, the nation, and the world. Your gift enables the University to provide greater access to quality educational opportunities, enhance Indiana's tradition of excellence in higher education, contribute to economic development, and conduct research that will change the quality of human life for the better.

Your support is gratefully acknowledged.

Curtis R. Simic
Curtis R. Simic, President
Indiana University Foundation

Resource 25

RESOURCE 26

GIFT AGREEMENT TEMPLATE

For Foundation Use Only

ACCOUNT NUMBER: _____

INDIANA UNIVERSITY FOUNDATION

GIFT AGREEMENT

[ACCOUNT NAME]

DONOR(s):_____ ("Donor(s)")

AUTHORIZATION: School of _____ ("School"), *[Department of _____* *("Department"),* Indiana University _____ *("IU_____," "Campus")]*

[If 32 account funded by transfer] SOURCE OF FUNDS: *[add source of money coming into the account]*

WHEREAS the Indiana University Foundation ("Foundation") receives, invests, administers, and manages private gifts for the benefit of Indiana University in an account designated for gifts (the "Account"); and

WHEREAS *[state any donor wishes (e.g., in honor or memory of someone) or information on how the account was created if known]*;

NOW, THEREFORE, IT IS AGREED:

1. This Account shall be used for *[**Choose one of the following account descriptions or modify as needed:**]*

faculty and staff development. Expenditures may include but are not limited to continuing education, research, departmental awards, travel expenses of faculty and staff, and faculty development.

     -or-

capital and equipment needs. Expenditures may include but are not limited to minor renovations to a building or rooms, improvements to the grounds, and purchase of equipment.

     -or-

awards, fellowships, or scholarships. The *[award, fellowship, or scholarship]* will be given out to *[spell out specific criteria here]*. The number, amount, and recipient(s) of the scholarship(s) will be determined by the Scholarship Committee of the School.

     -or-

representation funds. Expenditures from representation accounts shall meet four criteria: they must be of direct benefit to the University, be reasonable in amount, constitute a necessary expenditure that may or may not be made from University funds, and have the appearance of proper use. Expenditures may include employee goodwill, membership dues, meals and entertainment (when the purpose is conducive to conducting university business), and memorabilia given in recognition of support of the institution.

-or-

research. Expenditures may include but are not limited to faculty and staff travel, lodging and travel of visiting scholars, lecturers and research collaborators, supplies, and other items that may best serve the needs of the research program.

-or-

general purposes. Expenditures may include but are not limited to faculty and staff recruiting, faculty development, faculty travel, program promotion, and other expenses that may best serve the *[academic program or department]*.

2. The use of this gift will be authorized by the School [*or Department or Campus]* for the reasonable and customary requirements of authorized expenditures as indicated above in accordance with internal operating policies governing investments and administration as established by the Foundation, Indiana University, and the *[School, Department, or Campus]*. An annual report on the status of the fund will be provided to the Donor(s).

3. The Foundation will annually make available the Account balance for the purpose(s) stated above. The Board of Directors of the Foundation established a spending policy that provides for the distribution of both income and a portion of the capital appreciation resulting from investment activity. This policy is consistent with the Foundation's investment philosophy to maintain the purchasing power of the original gift so that the Account may keep pace with inflation. This Agreement is subject to the provisions of the Uniform Management of Institutional Funds Act (Indiana Code 30-2-12) ("UMIFA").

4. The officers and directors of the Foundation have the power, and final decision, to invest, to change investments, to accept property, to sell, to hold, or to reinvest all or any of the monies or property transferred to the Foundation under the terms of this Agreement in such manner as they deem proper, and any additional gifts received in support of this purpose are subject to the terms of this Agreement.

5. In the event that the original purposes stated here can no longer be fulfilled, the Foundation, through its Board of Directors, and in consultation with the Dean

[Campus Chancellor], shall review the circumstances and shall modify this Agreement to the extent necessary to enable the gift to be used in a manner that coincides with the Donor's *[Donors']* original intent as closely as possible and consistent with the provisions of UMIFA and the internal operating policies of the Foundation.

6. This Agreement will be terminated no later than one year after all funds received for this purpose have been expended according to the terms stated here.

7. The Agreement shall be governed by and interpreted in accordance with the laws of the State of Indiana.

Signed and dated this_____ day of _____, 20_____.

DONOR(s)

By: _____
         [Name(s)]

INDIANA UNIVERSITY SCHOOL OF

By: _____
         [Name, Dean/Chairperson/Chancellor]

INDIANA UNIVERSITY FOUNDATION

By: _____
         [Name, President]

RESOURCE 27

POST-CAMPAIGN ASSESSMENT REPORT

Development and Membership Year-End
Report for 1998—Indianapolis
Museum of Art   444
Contributions and Membership Activity
Report—December 1998   446

A Recommendation for Corporate
Support from the IMA Corporate
Advisory Committee to the IMA
Board of Governors   450

Development and Membership Year-End Report for 1998—Indianapolis Museum of Art

February 9, 1999

The Development and Membership staffs focused on bringing in new members and donors and upgrading current members and donors in 1998. To achieve these goals the staff integrated all of the development and membership functions into one unified program that was responsible to the museum event and marketing schedules. All renewal and acquisition projects were centered around the museum's main event for 1998—the King of the World exhibition and its marketing thrust. Additional emphasis was focused around the Ravine Garden and Lilly Pavilion renovations.

The members of the staff also strove to diversify the donor and members giving options by producing multiple appeals throughout the year to yield multiple gifts and offering restricted and unrestricted giving appeals to individuals, corporations, and foundations. This method is exemplified in the broader calendar spread of received gifts and the increase in giving amounts form previous donors caused by moving their gift appeal from unrestricted to restricted.

An ad hoc committee was used to prioritize the major grant initiatives, the curators to determine possible future incoming gifts of art, and a greater use of volunteers to help cultivate prospective donors and to plan cultivation events. Corporate volunteer groups basically took over the phonathons throughout the year with the help of some individual volunteers. The Corporate Advisory Council was instrumental in identifying new corporate contacts and following through with current corporate donors. The Trustee Development and Donor Relations Committees were used to direct donor cultivation and identification. This more directed use of volunteers and staff seemed to be more productive than using volunteers in the more traditional mode of team calling and follow up.

The prospect research efforts were heightened as a staff member was dedicated full time to the endeavor and computer support was provided. As a result, area entrepreneurs and corporate heads were identified for solicitation and restricted giving reports, and resources for current donor research were established.

The foundation base was broadened tremendously through increased research made possible by the on-site access to the Internet. Some 30 new funding sources were approached for funding, and others were asked for multiple gifts for the first time. This area really reaped the rewards of hiring a full-time Foundation Relations Coordinator in mid-1997 (a position that had been eliminated four years earlier).

Corporate funding for unrestricted gifts continued to be a challenge. A decision was made to continue seeking unrestricted support but to move more aggressively to sponsorships of existing and new programs, exhibitions, etc. A policy for sponsorship recognition was put into place with the help of the curatorial and marketing departments.

The staff was given a better computer software system and upgraded hardware to aid them. It took the entire year to make the transition to the point that policies and procedures can be determined in the first quarter of 1999.

Linda Hardwick

Note: Courtesy Indianapolis Museum of Art, Indianapolis, Indiana, USA.

Contributions and Membership Activity Report—December 1998

Campaign Progress Toward Goal

Annual Unrestricted

	Goal 1998	YTD 1998	YTD 1997
Individual gifts over $1,250	$490,000	$544,536	$524,386
Staff gifts	10,000	11,334	7,777
Individual gifts under $1,250	280,000	230,695	179,775
Corporate	430,000	371,317	427,605
Membership	454,940	343,476	367,701
Subtotal	$1,664,940	$1,491,358	$1,507,244
Satellite gallery	60,000	57,612	64,718
GOS Grants	132,000	278,327	137,725
Federal		56,240	
City/state		221,965	137,725
Private foundation	450,000	450,000	450,000
Total	$2,306,940	$2,277,297	$2,167,412

Annual Restricted

	Goal 1998	YTD 1998	YTD 1997
Corporate	$290,000	$422,831	$426,142
Individual	45,000	1,526,624	870,753
Grants	268,000	219,688	55,400
Total	$603,000	$1,949,455	$1,352,295
TOTAL ANNUAL GIVING	$2,909,940	$4,226,752	$3,407,207

Permanently Restricted

	Goal 1998	YTD 1998	YTD 1997
Operational endowment		$264,593	$983,901
Restricted endowments		140,602	1,419,014
Art endowments		20,560,682*	1,401,560
Undesignated			41,133,825*
Annuities			40,786
Total		$20,965,877	$43,977,016
TOTAL 1998 REVENUE	$2,909,940	$25,187,018	$45,730,677
Total memberships	9,500	9,036	8,408
Total new members	3,600	3,106	1,777
Value of donated art		$3,225,329	$4,453,890
TOTAL 1998 REVENUE PLUS VALUE OF DONATED ART		$28,412,347	

Note: *The art endowment figure for 1998 and the undesignated bequest for 1997

Development and Membership 1998 (Compared to 1997)

Second Century Society

- 24 new members and 40 upgrades
- 24 members not renewing
- Total membership 294 households
- 3 percent increase in revenue

Staff Giving

- 46 percent increase in revenue

Individual Giving to $1,250

- 25 percent increase in revenue
- 3 percent increase in the number of donors making multiple gifts
- Goal increased 81 percent over 1997's; 80 percent of increased goal received
- 2,969 gifts received (2,466 in 1997)
- 75 percent of gifts from museum members

Corporate Giving

- 49 new corporate donors
- 50 percent increase in number of corporate gifts
- Restricted giving revenue increased by 70 percent
- Unrestricted giving revenue down by 16 percent
- Average unrestricted gift decreased by 46 percent

Membership

- 3,108 new members joined—86 percent of total goal
- 7 percent growth in total membership over 1997
- 77 percent retention rate of current members
- 209 new Young Friends of Art members

Grants

- 100 percent increase in grant revenue (excluding Lilly Endowment's annual grant)
- 40 percent decrease in government restricted project giving
- 11 percent increase in private foundation restricted project support
- 66 percent increase in government unrestricted support

Summary

- 24 percent increase in revenue for all annual giving
- 99 percent of the unrestricted goal raised
- 44 percent increase in revenue for restricted giving (November figures)
- 223 percent of the restricted goal raised

General Observations

- Completion of first full year of new staff team
- Conversion to new computer system
- Completion of corporate sponsorship policy
- Integration of development and membership solicitations and donor/member cultivation with overall museum marketing, event, and exhibition calendars
- Implementation of use of the Internet for individual, corporate, and foundation prospect research

Trends in Fundraising

1. Collaborations, community service, and outreach are the most important cases currently for fundraising.
2. The new fundraising is donor-driven rather than methodology-driven
3. The institution that will survive will make continuous asks throughout the year.
4. There is more professionalism in the field and less use of volunteers.
5. Donor base is moving from an older, civic-minded generation to the baby boomers.
6. There is greater use of technology.
7. Corporate donations are turning almost entirely to restricted programs.

Trends in IMA Fundraising

1. Annual giving is relatively flat in all areas and is keyed directly to the number of new members acquired.
2. Increasing numbers of annual fund donors are inquiring about restricted gifts.
3. Membership retention is relatively flat, but new member growth is increasing.
4. Corporate giving is shifting to restricted projects with funds coming from marketing budgets rather than contributions budgets.
5. Grant income from private foundations is the area of fastest growth.
6. Cost to raise $1 is 36 cents.

How the Development and Membership Staff Is Responding to the Trends

1. Focus on IMA's community outreach and service programs as the cases for giving and the varied "lines of business" to create appeals.
2. Segment prospects and current donors for solicitations and cultivation.
3. Incorporate the museum's marketing plan and special exhibition calendars to drive appeals and events.
4. Begin to use more technological resources in procedures.
5. Survey membership to determine lapsing reasons.
6. Use the related trustee committees to identify and cultivate prospects.
7. Implement the Corporate Advisory Council's recommendation to shift the major focus of corporate giving to sponsorships.
8. Consider merging the financial goals for unrestricted and restricted annual gifts into one annual giving goal.

A Recommendation for Corporate Support from the IMA Corporate Advisory Committee to the IMA Board of Governors

January 19, 1999

The Corporate Advisory Committee has been reviewing the trends in corporate giving nationally and within the Indianapolis community since its creation in 1994. Many of its members are concurrently on the boards and committees of other nonprofit organizations and have seen similar trends in those organizations. Philanthropic allocations that provide unrestricted support are decreasing, causing corporations to structure their giving around projects that tie directly to their corporate mission, product, employee interests, or location.

To fulfill their role as community supporters and to align themselves with prestigious arts organizations for image building, corporations are looking to their marketing budgets as the resource pool for providing arts support. To justify the allocation of marketing resources on indirect expenditures, corporations are seeking sponsorship opportunities in which they receive at least a two-for-one return on their investment. For instance, if the arts organization requests a $50,000 sponsorship, the corporation is seeking $100,000 in tangible benefits as a direct result of its investment. In addition, many corporations are seeking specific demographic information regarding audience served and the direct impact their sponsorship had on revenue. They are most interested in working with arts organizations that are flexible enough to allow them to be a part of the sponsorship structure process—less client-driven and more customer-driven in approach.

Because of these trends, the Corporate Advisory Council recommends the following:

1. Shift development resources of time, budget, and effort into the development and maintenance of sponsorships.
2. Restructure museum policies to allow more flexibility and visibility regarding sponsor benefits.
3. Develop marketing plans when possible for major projects and exhibitions at least one year prior to the opening of the exhibition.
4. Investigate the possibility of using outside council to provide an in-depth look at the museum's assets and assist with the development of sponsorship proposal policies, procedures, and fee structures.
5. Endorsement from the museum to provide the support and resources necessary to build a sponsorship program.

FINAL REPORT

Table of Contents

Mission Statement . . . . [453]
Message from the Board President . . . . [454]
1999 Board of Directors and Committees . . . . [456]
Statement of Financial Position and Activities . . . . [459]
Message from the "Solutions for People" Campaign Co-Chairs . . [460]
Campaign Leadership . . . . [461]
Campaign Totals by Division . . . . [461]
Indiana University Campaign Team . . . . [462]
1999–2000 "Solutions for People" Campaign . . . . [463]
Vanguard Leadership Giving . . . . [468]
Strategic Marketing and Communications . . . . [469]
Campaign Highlights . . . . [470]
Week of Caring/Raise the Roof '99 . . . . [471]
Agency Highlights . . . . [472]
Community Connections . . . . [473]
Community Services: White River Central Labor Council . . . . [476]
United Way Member Agency Directory . . . . [478]

Resource 28

United Way of Monroe County, Inc.
Community Service Council
441 South College Avenue
Bloomington, IN 47403
(812) 334-8370 Fax: (812) 334-8387
uw@unitedway.monroe.in.us
www.unitedway.monroe.in.us

Mission Statement *(Approved October 17, 1995)*

THE MISSION OF UNITED WAY OF
MONROE COUNTY, INC. IS TO INCREASE THE
ORGANIZED CAPACITY OF PEOPLE
TO CARE FOR ONE ANOTHER.

WE WILL ACCOMPLISH THIS MISSION BY

- identifying, evaluating, and communicating service needs within our community
- encouraging efficient and effective collaboration among social service agencies
- supporting quality programs, information, and services to and through our membership
- providing information, referral, and training opportunities
- increasing financial, material, and voluntary resources

IN FULFILLING OUR MISSION, WE WILL

- operate in a manner that is consistent with our values of honesty, diversity, public service, and respect for the individual
- inspire trust in our organization by adhering to the highest professional standards of accountability and stewardship
- serve as leaders in our community and our profession

*United Way of Monroe County, Inc., is a member agency of
the Indiana Association of United Ways and United Way of America.*

Resource 28

Message from the Board President

I have had the privilege and responsibility of serving as United Way Board President for the past two years. It has been a challenging experience that has given me a unique perspective into a vibrant and valuable organization. It has been overwhelming, at times, as well as gratifying in demonstrating what hard work, dedication, and creativity on the part of staff and volunteers, can accomplish.

Some highlights of 1999:

- Expanded donor choice was implemented for this campaign, results of which will be examined closely.
- Work is in process on the strategic communication plan.
- The much-anticipated Giant Step technology grant report was published thanks to the CSC/UW Information and Communications Committee.
- Week of Caring grew in the number of projects and volunteers involved.
- The United Way and CSC Web sites were expanded and enhanced.
- Our United Way/AFL-CIO Community Services Liaison, Josh Cazares, has been busy with projects that included Resource Specialist Training, Pride at Work, and the state AFL-CIO Community Services and Labor Institute for Training conference this past November.
- Campaign highlights include: the Board's decision to work toward a goal of $2,000,000 in 2000; Carmen Odle's outstanding second year of leadership along with Christopher Simpson, who also co-chaired the Indiana University campaign with Dorothy Frapwell; IU's campaign exceeding its goal of $500,000; the "Solutions for People" theme, a regional effort that included the series of infomercials (one of which featured a Bloomington family); and a multicounty billboard project.

It is wonderful to enjoy our accomplishments, but we cannot overlook the enormous challenges we face: How can we best communicate United Way's mission and relevance to our community? How can we let the community know about the work that is happening on a day-to-day basis? Where does United Way fit into the new culture of philanthropy? These are not easy issues, but they are ones that we must deal with. United Way/CSC are seen as major players at the table when it comes to crises in our community, when it comes to creative problem solving around human needs, and when it comes to being the social service umbrella resource for our Monroe County citizens.

I would like to express my appreciation for the energetic and intelligent Board of Directors; an Executive Committee that was always ready to report, react, discuss, and advise; the dedicated staff that makes this organization thrive; and my family, who have supported my volunteer endeavors over the years. My special thanks to Executive Director Peg Stice, Community Service Council Director Beverly Calender-Anderson, CSC Board President Michael Shermis, and incoming United Way Board President Barry Lessow.

Kathryn Brown
1999 Board President

1999 Board of Directors and Committees

UNITED WAY BOARD OF DIRECTORS

Kathryn Brown,* *President*

Virginia Metzger,* *Treasurer*

Cassandra Brooks,* *Secretary*

Debby Allmayer,* *Vice President Personnel*

Brian Hall,* *Vice President Allocations*

Elizabeth Bridgwaters

Larry Brown, *WRCLC Representative*

Doris Burton, *CSC Representative*

Elizabeth A. Feitl, *WRCLC Representative*

Kenny Frazier

Lisa Hewes

Steve Howard

Karen Jones, *UWADA Representative*

Barry Lessow,* *CSC Representative*

Barbara Light

Jim Muehling

Susan Nelson

Carmen Odle,* *Campaign Co-Chair*

Sue Polsgrove

Ed Ryan

Michael Shermis, *CSC Representative*

Christopher Simpson,*
    Campaign Co-Chair

Kim Sutton

Jane Thoma

Carven Thomas

Mary Tschirhart

Judith Wertheim

Janice Wiggins

Carl Zeigler*

*Executive Committee

> *If you find it in your heart to care for somebody else, you will have succeeded.*
>
> —MAYA ANGELOU

COMMUNITY SERVICE COUNCIL BOARD OF DIRECTORS

Michael Shermis, *President*

Lynette Miller, *Vice President*

Barry Lessow, *Treasurer*

Courtney Hulce, *Secretary*

Doris Jean Burton, *Secretary*

Catherine Berg Stafford

Kathryn Brown, *United Way Representative*

Rev. Ernest Butler

James Cummings

Tom Doyle

Patrick Efiom

Lorraine Farrell

Jon Gant

Mark Hood

Nancy Howard

Christine Maguire-Hastings

Cheryl Monroe

Benjamin Olges

Joan Pong Linton

Peg Stice, *United Way Representative*

Steve Stroup

Mary Tschirhart, *United Way Representative*

> *You get the best out of others when you give the best of yourself.*
>
> —HARRY FIRESTONE

UW/CSC ACTION PLAN COMMITTEE

Barry Lessow, *Chair*

Kathy Aiken

Kathryn Brown

Christine Glaser

Christine Hoezee

Myra Kinser

Christine Maguire-Hastings

Jim Muehling

Michael Shermis

Laura Shoemaker

Phil Stafford

Mary Tschirhart

Judith Wertheim

AGENCY RELATIONS COMMITTEE

Cassandra Brooks, *Co-Chair*

Carl Ziegler, *Co-Chair*

Kathryn Brown

Elizabeth A. Feitl

Lisa Hewes

Steve Howard

Robin Jackson

Karen Jones

Barry Lessow

Barbara Light

ALLOCATIONS COMMITTEE

Brian Hall, *Chair*

Kathy Aiken

Carol Bentley

Robin Jackson

Barry Lessow

Jim Muehling

Susan Nelson

Deborah O'Brien

Sue Polsgrove

Doris Sims

> *The ultimate expression of leadership is service to others.*
>
> —Johnnetta B. Cole

AUDIT COMMITTEE

Cassandra Brooks, *Chair*

Steve Howard

Winston Shindell

FINANCE COMMITTEE

Virginia Metzger, *Chair*

Barry Lessow

Tony Mobley

Ed Ryan

CSC/UW INFORMATION AND COMMUNICATIONS COMMITTEE

Catherine Berg Stafford

David Ernst

Jon Gant

Courtney Hulce*

Barry Lessow

Lynette Miller

Cheryl Monroe

Michael Shermis*

Susan Tomlinson*

Shared leadership

> *Progress lies not in enhancing what is, but in advancing toward what will be.*
>
> —Kahlil Gibran

NOMINATING COMMITTEE

Michael Shermis, *Co-Chair*

Janice Wiggins, *Co-Chair*

Jim Ackerman

Larry Brown

Steve Howard

Jane Thoma

OUTCOMES MEASUREMENT PILOT PROJECT

Michael Shermis, *Chair*

Boys & Girls Club, *Deborah Elliott*

City of Bloomington Community and Family Resources Department, *Denise Abel*

Family Service Association, *Merrill Hatlen*

Hoosier Hills Food Bank, *Amy Robinson and Georgia Schaich*

Middle Way House, *Toby Strout*

Stone Belt ARC, *Elbert Johns*

United Way of Monroe County, *Michael DeNunzio and Peg Stice*

PERSONNEL COMMITTEE

Debby Allmayer, *Chair*

Kim Sutton

Judith Wertheim

PERSONNEL/LABOR COMMITTEE

Debby Allmayer, *Chair*

Larry Brown, *WRCLC*

Elizabeth A. Feitl, *WRCLC*

Kim Sutton

Judith Wertheim

Jackie Yenna, *WRCLC*

UNITED WAY AGENCY DIRECTORS ASSOCIATION (UWADA) EXECUTIVE COMMITTEE

Karen Jones, Girls Inc., *President*

Michael Reinke, Shelter, Inc., *Vice President*

Robin Jackson, Community Kitchen, *Secretary*

WHITE RIVER CENTRAL LABOR COUNCIL COMMUNITY SERVICES COMMITTEE

Jim Crabb, *Carpenters 1664*

Elizabeth A. Feitl, *CWA 4730*

Kenny Frazier, *IBEW 2249*

Roger Kent, *Laborers 741*

Rosie Ritchison, *UAW 440*

Jerry Sutherlin, *NALC 828*

Connie Voughn, *CWA 4730*

Jackie Yenna, *IBEW 2249*

UNITED WAY/CSC STAFF

Peg Stice, *Executive Director*

Zain Mackey-McGee, *Finance Director*

Josh Cazares, *AFL-CIO Community Services Liaison*

Michael DeNunzio, *Resource Allocations Director*

Beverly Calender-Anderson, *Director, Community Service Council*

Wendy Perrotta, *Communications Director*

Joshua Timmons, *Office Manager*

Brad Swanson, *Administrative Assistant*

Kathy Aiken, *IU/United Way Liaison*

VOLUNTEERS/INTERNS

Charles Aiken

Kelly Caufman

Elizabeth Kwai-Fong Chan

Karen Danielson

Iola Frame and the RSVP mailing team

Madlena Haikazi Hakobyan

Jean Joque

Denise Lessow

Eric Vance Martin

Fawzia Mirza

Joe O'Connor

Harriet Pfister

Margrit Rothmuller

Sandy Sfikas

Brent Van Bruane

Brian Weiss

Michael Westmoreland

Statement of Financial Position and Activities (December 1999 [unaudited])

I would like to thank Tony Mobley, Ed Ryan, and Barry Lessow for serving on the 1999 Finance Committee, and Zain Mackey-McGee and Peg Stice for their staff support. In addition, a special thank you goes to Cassandra Brooks, Steve Howard, and Winston Shindell for their work on the 1999 Audit Committee. Thank you also to Duane Vaught, CPA, Stampfli Associates, for conducting the 1998 audit and for preparing our tax returns, and Rebecca Robbins, Attorney-at-Law, for her legal advice.

Respectfully submitted,
Virginia Metzger
Treasurer, United Way of Monroe County, Inc.

ASSETS		LIABILITIES AND FUND BALANCE	
Checking: General—Monroe County Bank	$203,865.66	Accounts Payable	$(4,654.51)
Checking: Administration—Monroe County Bank	26,612.36	CFC/Crane 1998/1999 Payable	8,006.68
		Other County Designations	(95.00)
CD—Civitas Bank	77,031.07	Due to Administration from GSI	6,286.69
Money Market—IU Credit Union	88,761.44	Board-Designated Reserves	190,591.00
Money Market—Irwin Union	12,980.93		
Hilliard Lyons Investments	105,000.00	Total Liabilities	$200,134.86
Endowment—Community Care Fund	33,955.69		
Endowment—Pledge Receivable	7,500.00		
GSI Technology Grant—Irwin Union	42,505.51		
Pledges Receivable—1999/2000 Campaign	1,101,981.11	GSI Restricted Fund Balance	40,065.70
Pledges Receivable—1998/1999 Campaign	201,143.40	Unrestricted Fund Balance	1,463,618.31
		Year Revenue Overexpense	94,404.78
Allowance for Uncollectables—1998/1999	(116,418.75)		
Advance to Agencies	3,230.00	Total Fund Balance	1,598,088.79
Due from GSI to Administration	6,286.69		
Property & Equipment	30,523.99		
Accumulated Depreciation on Property & Equipment	(26,735.45)		
TOTAL ASSETS	$1,798.223.65	TOTAL LIABILITIES AND FUND BALANCES	$1,798,223.65

Resource 28

Message from the "Solutions for People" Campaign Co-Chairs

Dear Community Partners,

We are proud to acknowledge that the 1999–2000 United Way "Solutions for People" Campaign delivered on its promise to offer more people more opportunities to support more regional agencies, accomplished through a stronger unity between the Indiana University campaign and the Monroe County community campaign. This promise was well timed as Bloomington faced some of the greatest challenges ever.

Our shared leadership focused on the strong belief that our community needs to pull together like never before. Our previous sense of security was shattered by the tragedy of a graduate student gunned down on a Bloomington street, apparently for racist motives. We will all suffer, economically and socially, as several core industries announce major cutbacks and layoffs, affecting literally thousands of citizens and their families.

How do we as a community come together to overcome tragedy and address growing socioeconomic needs? There is no other organization that filters through the community more pervasively than the United Way. Our hope was that this year, the United Way would be the cornerstone of the network constructed by our citizens to bring our community closer together in good times and in bad. Thanks to all of you, this hope was realized.

For the first time, we had the Donor Choice option on every pledge card. This addressed each and every donor's desire to give where their dollars would best serve the community. We found that more donors participated as they enjoyed increased freedom to designate where their dollars go. Many others were more committed than ever to give undesignated dollars. These donors appreciate and rely on the Allocations Committee, a group of community volunteers that comes together to conduct an in-depth analysis of the outcomes produced by each of the 26 United Way agencies and then allocate the communitywide campaign dollars to best support the agencies' needs.

Now, six months after it officially began, we can point with great pride to a strong, successful campaign, thanks to the dozens and dozens of volunteers who, recognizing the need, joined together, rolled up their sleeves, and worked as a team to raise $1,717,341.

But the work doesn't stop now. Before we launch the 2000–2001 campaign, we'd like to take a moment to celebrate this year's success. Thanks to all of you who made it happen—campaign volunteers, United Way staff, agency directors and staff, and business and institutional workplaces that one by one conducted their own campaigns for the good of Bloomington and its extended family.

And to you—the donors—words cannot express our gratitude for your support. Without you, all of you, it would not have been possible.

That is the *United* Way.

Carmen Odle   Christopher Simpson
Senior Vice President, Human Resources   *Vice President, Public Affairs and Government Relations*
Monroe County Bank   *Indiana University*

1999–2000 *"Solutions for People"* Campaign Co-Chairs

Campaign Leadership

COMMUNITY CAMPAIGN
Carmen Odle, *Monroe County Bank*
Christopher Simpson, *Indiana University*

VANGUARD LEADERSHIP
Susan Nelson, *Andrews Harrell Mann*
   Chapman and Coyne
Jim Muehling, *Indiana University*
   Foundation

INDIANA UNIVERSITY
Christopher Simpson
Dorothy Frapwell

INDIANA UNIVERSITY ANNUITANTS
Harriet Pfister
Wain Martin
Doris Burton

INDIANA UNIVERSITY STUDENTS
Amy Choi
Josh Cooper

DOWNTOWN RETAIL
Denise Lessow

MEADOWOOD
Marian Battenhouse

NOT-FOR-PROFIT DIVISION
Robin Jackson

GOVERNMENT DIVISION
Elizabeth A. Feitl

FINANCIAL INSTITUTIONS
Brian Hall
Jane Thoma

RESTAURANT WEEK
Doris Jean Burton

Campaign Totals by Division

Division	Final 2/29/96 (Pledged in 1995–96)	Final 2/28/97 (Pledged in 1996–97)	Final 2/28/98 (Pledged in 1997–98)	Final 2/28/99 (Pledged in 1998–99)	Final 2/29/00 (Pledged in 1999–2000)
Major Firms	$748,569	$783,547	$831,551	$815,745	$738,090
Commercial	76,573	83,321	93,677	81,020	77,899
Retail	66,058	68,175	57,074	67,306	68,185
Professional	70,308	68,058	71,167	74,002	67,197
Indiana University	422,787	431,074	458,835	476,604	541,590
Government	57,922	58,625	70,451	65,596	102,023
Not for Profit	65,119	58,216	68,930	61,739	60,063
Personal	45,250	43,046	53,315	55,483	62,294
TOTAL	$1,552,586	$1,594,062	$1,705.000	$1,697.495	$1,717,341

Resource 28

Indiana University Campaign Team

Christopher Simpson*,
    Co-Chair
Dorothy Frapwell,
    Co-Chair
L.K. Alexander
Ted Alexander
Deborah Allmayer*
Alfred Aman*
Jill Argenbright
Jayne Averitt
JoEllen Baldwin
Stephanie Baxter
Richard Bier
Judy Boruff
Jo Anne Bowen
Myles Brand*
Melonee Bristoe
Dan Brown
Kathryn Brown
Trevor Brown*
Becky Bryant
Doris Jean Burton
Cary Buzzelli
Edda Callahan
Linda Campbell
Anita Chang-Vigo
Amy Choi*
Terry Clapacs*
Nancy Clensy
Shirley Colavito
Doreen Cole
Clay Collier
Wainona Collins
Josh Cooper*
Les Coyne
Terri Crouch
Cheryl Crouch*
Mike Crowe
Storme Day

Mollie Duckett
Chris Eakins
Suzanne Easter
Patricia Ek
Diana Embry*
Harriet Figg
Donna Fink
Lana Fish
Sherry Fisher*
Gregg Floyd*
Marilyn Franklin
Michael Friedman
John Gallman
Pam Garrett-Fawcett
Susan Gastony*
Heidi Gealt
Rosalind Gerstman
Kenneth Gros Louis*
Karen Hanson
Mike Hardesty
John Harner
Helen Harrell
Paul Hazel
Andy Heck
Jim Hertling
Hank Hewetson
Jeff Hoffman
John Hollingsworth
Doris Howard
Loyd Hudson
Helen Ingersoll
Sondra Inman
Karon Jamison
Ron Jensen
Edwina Johansen
Bill Jones
Kate Keen
Judy Kelley
Charnele Kennedy

Steve Keucher
Donna Klyn
Kevin Kneer
Mark Kuchefski
Nancy Lethem
Meg Lindeman
Ken Long
David Lovell
Wain Martin*
Jerry McCune
Robert Meier
Virginia Metzger
Joan Meyer
Marzell Milberger
Tom Mitchell
Wayne Mnich
Clarence Morrison
Lisa Moyers
Charlie Nelms*
Marilyn Norris
Kim Nunn
Patrick O'Meara
Kate O'Shea
Theresa Owens
Judy Palmer*
Jean Person
Harriet Pfister*
Joe Phillips
Suzanne Phillips*
Susan Platter
Sue Polsgrove
Joan Pong Linton
Doug Porter
Vella Price
Hope Ramirez Flores
Brenda Records
Laura Reed
Dan Rives
Tim Robbins

Christine Rodden
Jennie Russell
Kim Schulte
Becky Schum
John Scully
Jack Shelton
Michael Shermis
Barbara Shields
Janet Shirley
Martha Smiley
Cindy Smith
Ray Smith
Charlotte Smith*
Mardi Spence Leonard
Kathi Spicer
Nancy Stoute
Nancy Jane Talbott
Jill Taylor
Terence Thayer
Barry Thomas
Suzanne Thompson
Jordan Tillett
Linda Vaught
Derek Vint
George Walker*
Don Weaver
Fred Webb
Nnacy Werner
Judy Wertheim
Sara White
Kathy Wiegand
Christine Wilkinson
Tom Williams
Shirley Wines
Cindy Wise
Cornelius Wright
Carl Ziegler*
Margaret Zuckschwerdt
*TEAM CAPTAIN

1999–2000 "Solutions for People" Campaign

The United Way of Monroe County's Solutions for People Campaign was made possible through the generous help of many corporations, organizations, and individuals. While it would be impossible to list every donor on these pages, we want to thank everyone who has given valuable resources, money, and/or time to the 1999–2000 campaign.

MAJOR FIRMS DIVISION

Ameritech/CWA Local 4818

AT&T/CWA Local 4818

Bank One Bloomington, N.A.

Bloomington Hospital & Healthcare System

BMG Music

Carlisle Industrial Brake & Friction

Charities Funds Transfer/United Way of America

Cinergy, parent company of PSI Energy, Inc./IBEW Local 1393

Columbia House

COMARCO

Cook, Inc.

Cummins Employees Combined Charities

Federal Express

Fifth Third Bank (Civitas Bank)

General Electric Co/IBEW Local 2249

General Motors Powertrain/UAW Local 440

The Herald-Times*

Hershey Foods Corporation

IBM

Indiana Energy

Irwin Union Bank & Trust

IU Employees Federal Credit Union

Kerasotes Theatres/Lucasfilm/ 20th Century Fox

Key Bank

Lucent Technologies

M3Studio*

Microsoft Corporation

Monroe County Bank*

Old National Bank*

Pitney Bowes

PYA/Monarch, Inc.

Rockwell Automation/Dodge

Rogers Group/Teamsters Local 135/Carpenters Local 1664

Rogers Group Investments

Schneider National, Inc.

Sundstrand Corporation

Thomson Consumer Electronics

Union Planters Bank

United Airlines/I.A.M.

United Commerce Bank

United Technologies-Otis Elevator/IUE Local 826

UPS/Teamsters Local 135

XEROX Corporation

COMMERCIAL DIVISION

AAA Hoosier Motor Club

Akard Forestry Consultants

Allstate Insurance

American Express

American General Finance #00010134

American General Finance #14025080

Answer Indiana*

Anyetsang's Little Tibet Restaurant

A One Carpet & Upholstery*

Associates Financial Services

Avco Financial Services

Bardes Environmental Services

Bear's Place

Beijing Chinese Restaurant

Bill C. Brown Associates

Blast Off Balloons*

Bloomington Business Machines

Bloomington Independent*

Bloomington Iron & Metal

Bloomington Mini-Warehouses

The Brewpub @ Lennies

Bridgestone/Firestone Trust Fund

Burnham Rentals*

CACI, Inc.

Cafe Django

Chez Nous

Cassady's

Chapman's Restaurant & Banquet

Charles Steele & Associates

Colorado Steakhouse

Conseco Risk Management

Consolidated Products, Inc.

Curry-Buick-Cadillac-Pontiac-
GMC Truck, Inc.

Tim Ellis Realtor*

Encore Cafe

Equitable Life Assurance

Exmin Corporation

Expert Tire

Fazoli's

FC Tucker Realtors-L. Strickholm

Fine Print*

Flora Ristorante

General Sign*

Grayson Bernard Publishers

Great West Casualty Company

Hilliard Lyons, Inc.

Hoosier Energy REC, Inc./
IBEW Local 1393

Hoosier Outdoor Advertising*

Household International

Huse Food Group

IMI-Irving Materials Inc.

Inari Information Services, Inc.*

Interiors Inc./Carol Clendening
& Associates

Kirby Risk Electrical Supply Co.

Kocolene Sunoco

Kulwin Electric Supply Co.

La Rosa

La Torre, Inc.

Ladyman's Cafe

Limestone Grille

L.K. Hunter Excavating Co.

Luca Pizza

MCL Cafeteria

Meier Insurance Agency, Inc.

Memories

Michael's Uptown Cafe

O'Charley's Inc. Restaurant

Personnel Management Inc.

Pinnacle Properties

Pizza Hut

Prudential Insurance Co.

Puccini's La Dolce Vita

R&D Computer Hardware
Concepts*

Repp Associates Foundation

Rib Cage

Samira Restaurant

Don R. Scheidt & Co. Inc.

Shanti Indian Cuisine

Siam House

SiliconGraphics Computer
Systems

Soft Touch Moving & Storage*

Steak 'n Shake, Inc.

Stefano's Ice Cafe

Tasus Corporation

Terry's Banquets & Catering*

Textillery

Tinwistle Corporation*

Tortilla Flat

The Trojan Horse

Upper-Webb Interior
Design, Inc.

ValuComp Computers*

Village Deli

WBWB*

WFHB*

WFIU*

WTIU*

WTTS/WGCL*

Weddle Bros. Construction

Woodward Insurance, Inc.

Yogi's Grill & Bar

Zuchinni Prints*

RETAIL DIVISION

à propos*

ARAMARK Corporation

Bare Essentials*

Barnes & Noble Booksellers*

Eddie Bauer

Ben Franklin/
Moir Merchandising*

Big Red Liquors

Black Lumber Company

Bloomington Office Supply

Bloominton Antique Mall*

Bloomingfoods Market & Deli

Borders Books & Music*

The Chocolate Emporium*

Circuit City

Columbus Office Supply

Dee Aaron's Boutique*

Faris Bros. Market

Fossil Rain*

Fountain Fabrics*

Game Preserve*

Grant Street*

The Gap and GapKids, Inc.

General Housewares

H.H. Gregg Appliances

Howard's Bookstore*

J. C. Penney, Inc.

Kroger #91—Seminary
Square/UFCW Local 700

Kroger #928—Jackson
Creek/UFCW Local 700

Kroger #960—Highland
Village/UFCW Local 700

The Latest Glaze*

L. S. Ayres & Company

Lowe's Home Improvement Warehouse

Marsh Supermarkets

Melton's Orchard

Mondo*

Office Depot

Osco Drugs #873

Osco Drugs #459

Perennial Designs*

Pygmalion's Art Supplies, Inc.*

Rich's Lazarus Goldsmith's, Inc.

Roadworthy Guitar & Amp*

Sam's Club 18-6437

Sears Roebuck & Co.

JR Stallsmith & Co.*

Standex Electronics

Streetside Records*

Sullivan's

T & T Market

Talbot Studio

Talbots*

Target Stores

Tivoli*

Vance Music*

Wal-Mart Stores #6437

White Mountain Ice Cream*

Williams Jewelry

Zales

PROFESSIONAL DIVISION

Abbott Laboratories

Aegis Women's Health Care

Charles C. Aiken & Associates

Andrews Harrell Mann Chapman & Coyne

Barnhart Sturgeon & Spencer

Laurence Barnhill, Ph.D.

Bingham Summers Welsh & Spilman

Gary Bishop, DDS

M. Theresa Block, D.D.S., PC

Bloomington Convalescent Center

Bristol Myers Squibb

Barry S. Brown & Associates

Bunger & Robertson

Bynum Fanyo & Associates

Center for Informal Learning Solutions (CILS)

David Coverly/"Speed Bump"*

CVS Pharmacy, Inc.

Digestive Disease Center

DuPont Pharmaceutical Company

Eli Lilly & Company

Eye Center of Southern Indiana

Ferguson Law

Hoffmann-La Roche Inc.

C. Denise Howard, O.D.

Internal Medicine Associates

Intracorp-CIGNA

Johnson & Johnson

Jones McGlasson & Benckart, P.C.

D.J. Tony Kenworthy, DDS

Kinkead Law Office

Legal Services Organization of Indiana

Robert W. Linnemeier, DDS

LJM Enterprises

Mallor Clendening Grodner & Bohrer

Merck & Co.

Allan M. Miller, M.D., Inc.

Monroe County Bar Association

Monroe Shine & Co., Inc.

Olson & Company PC

Optiks

Pfizer, Inc.

Robert Rimstidt, D.D.S.

SIRA, Inc.

SmithKline Beecham

SMS-Shared Medical Systems

Southern Indiana Pediatrics

Margaret F. Squires, Ph.D.

Stampfli Associates

SuperValu

Town & Country Veterinary Clinic

Unity Physicians Group

Michael Wenzler, M.D.

INDIANA UNIVERSITY DIVISION

Greekfest*

*Indiana Daily Student**

Indiana Institute on Disability and Community*

Indiana Memorial Union*

IU Alumni Association*

IU Annuitants/Retirees*

IU Athletic Department*

IU Faculty and Staff*

IU Foundation*

IU Kelley School of Business*

IU Students*

IU Physical Plant*

IU Public Relations and Governmental Affairs*

IU School of Public and Environmental Affairs*

IU Vice President for Academic Affairs and Chancellor, Bloomington Campus*

Marriott*

Poynter Center*

AFSCME Local 832*

CWA Local 4730*

NOTE: Almost every department and organization at IU gets involved in community caring through the United Way campaign. Thank you!

GOVERNMENT DIVISION

American Postal Workers/ U.S. Postal Service/Union Branch 2122

Bloomington Township Trustee's Office

City of Bloomington Employees/AFSCME Local 2487*

Hoosier National Forest

Indiana State Employee Community Campaign

Monroe County Employees*

National Association of Letter Carriers/Branch 828

Naval Surface Warfare Center, Crane Division/AFGE Local 1415

Perry Township Trustee's Office

Rural Letter Carriers

Social Security Administration

MEADOWOOD DIVISION

Meadowood Residents and Staff

OFC Corporation dba Meadowood

NOT-FOR-PROFIT DIVISION

Abilities Unlimited

Agency for Instructional Technology

American Red Cross-Monroe County Chapter

Amethyst House

Area 10 Agency on Aging

Arlington Methodist Men

Big Brothers/Big Sisters of Monroe County

Bloomington Urban Enterprise Association

Borrowed Time Club

Boy Scouts of America, Hoosier Trails Council

Boys & Girls Club of Bloomington

Cambridge Square Senior Citizens

Carpenters Local Union #1664

Catholic Social Services— Bloomington

Center for Behavioral Health

Communications Workers Local 481

Community Kitchen

Community Service Council

Conversation Club

Eastside Senior Citizens Club

Ellettsville Senior Citizens

Environmental Fund for Indiana*

Family Service Association of Monroe County

First Presbyterian Church*

Girl Scouts of USA, Tulip Trace Council

Girls Incorporated of Monroe County

Greater Bloomington Chamber of Commerce

Harmony School

Hoosier Hills Food Bank

HoosierNet

IBEW #725

Indiana Association of United Ways

Ivy Tech State College

Laborers Int'l Local Union 741

Monroe County Community School Corporation

Mental Health Association, Monroe County Chapter

Middle Way House/The Rise

Monroe County Council for Older Americans

Monroe County Historical Society Museum

Monroe County Humane Association*

Monroe County Public Library

Monroe County United Ministries

Opportunity House

Pi Lambda Theta International

Planned Parenthood of Central & Southern Indiana

Public Health Nursing Association

Richland-Bean Blossom School Corporation

Rhino's Youth Center

Salvation Army

Senior Citizens Golden Age Club

Shelter, Inc.

Southern Indiana Center for Independent Living

St. Charles School

Stanford Community Seniors

Stone Belt ARC, Inc.

Unionville Senior Citizens

United Way of America

United Way of Bartholomew County, *Columbus*

United Way of Central Indiana

United Way of Chester County, *Exton, PA*

United Way, Crusade of Mercy, *Chicago, IL*

United Way of Daviess County, *Washington, IN*

United Way of Delaware, *Wilmington, DE*

United Way of Johnson County, *Franklin, IN*

United Way of Kenosha County, *Kenosha, WI*

United Way of King County, *Seattle, WA*

United Way of Lawrence County, *Bedford, IN*

United Way of the Metro Area, *Louisville, KY*

United Way of Monroe County

United Way of Palm Beach County, *West Palm Beach, FL*

United Way of The Tri-State Area, *New York, NY*

United Way of the Wabash Valley, *Terre Haute, IN*

Unity of Bloomington

Victim Offender Reconciliation Program*

White River Central Labor Council*

WonderLab*

YMCA Family Fitness Center

*Note: *Indicates that some portion of this gift was in-kind.*

Every effort was made to ensure the accuracy of the Annual Report. Please accept our sincere apologies for any errors or omissions throughout this report.

Resource 28

Vanguard Leadership Giving

Vanguard Leadership Giving recognizes donations of $1,000 and above. For the 1999–2000 campaign, we have received 309 generous contributions totaling $476,352, or 28% of the campaign total. Thank you.

Benjamin Harrison Society
($10,000 and above)

[Honor Roll of Donors names listed here]

Platinum ($5,000–$9,999)

[Honor Roll of Donors names listed here]

Gold ($2,500–$4,999)

[Honor Roll of Donors names listed here]

Silver ($1,000–$2,499)

[Honor Roll of Donors names listed here]

Strategic Marketing and Communications

A regional co-marketing grant from the Indiana Association of United Ways with funds from Lilly Endowment resulted in several billboards on I-65 and Highway 37. The billboards all featured the shared "Solutions for People" theme.

Another Indiana Association of United Ways/Lilly Endowment grant allowed us to participate in United Way of Central Indiana's television marketing project. Here, Catherine Sherwood-Puzzello, Paul Puzzello (with Sophia), and Olivia prepare to tape an informercial for distribution to all Indianapolis-area television stations. We are sincerely grateful to Catherine and her family for sharing their story so openly and for reminding us how important agency services can be to our lives.

The Agency Relations Committee, co-chaired by Cassie Brooks and Carl Ziegler, worked diligently during 1999 to create a Strategic Marketing and Communications Plan. Above, Cassie and 2000 Board President Barry Lessow discuss proposed marketing strategies.

The CSC/United Way Newsletter is published monthly with a circulation of approximately 3,000. All not-for-profits in the community are welcome to submit articles and events. With features that include agency profiles, fundraising events, campaign news, and a calendar of activities, the newsletter is one of our most powerful communication tools.

Resource 28

---

www.unitedway.monroe.in.us

The CSC/UW Information and Communications Committee went back to the drawing board to redesign the United Way Web site. The site includes general United Way information, member agency profiles, campaign updates, highlights and tools, a pledge card to download, and links to Community Service Council, White River Central Labor Council, IRIS, Bloomington Volunteer Network, Indiana University volunteer programs, and agency Web sites. Special thanks to Cheryl Monroe and Michael Shermis for their technical and design expertise.

Campaign Highlights

Thanks to the thousands of generous, caring people who donate time, materials, and dollars to make our efforts successful. The campaign is an exciting blend of creative special events like Restaurant Week, educational opportunities like agency tours, and new communication tools such as the weekly Web-based progress reports. Special thanks to those who personalized our "Solutions for People" theme by sharing their motivating stories.

Volunteer and Vanguard Marian Battenhouse prepares for the Meadowood campaign.

Employees of the Indiana University Paint Shop produced six progress signs for this year's campaign; four were displayed on the IU campus, one at City Hall, and one at the Courthouse Square downtown.

Week of Caring/Raise the Roof '99 *(October 16–23)*

More than 400 coworkers, students, members of the faith community and labor unions, corporations, retailers, and organizations rolled up their sleeves to provide much needed service to Bloomington's not-for-profit community during Week of Caring/Raise the Roof '99, October 16–23. Volunteers inspected and weatherized buildings, planted bulbs for spring gardens, conducted food drives, and much more. The event was a collaborative effort of United Way of Monroe County/Community Service Council, White River Central Labor Council, Bloomington Volunteer Network, Indiana University Student Activities Office, and the City of Bloomington Housing and Neighborhood Development Department. Financial and in-kind support was provided by Indiana University Foundation, Monroe County Bank, White River Central Labor Council, Monroe County Heating Contractors Association, Bloomington Hardware, InterArt Distribution, and the Bloomington Urban Enterprise Association.

Laura Brown and Kathy Connelly of Monroe County Bank process donor designations at the United Way/CSC office. Bank volunteers also helped with "Downtown Cares" contacts.

Resource 28

Agency Highlights

The excellent programs and dedicated service of United Way member agencies and donor choice affiliates motivate and inspire our volunteers and donors. Monthly meetings with agency representatives, board liaison linkages, workshops, trainings, resource sharing, special events, fundraisers, and regular communication via the CSC/United Way Newsletter all keep United Way/CSC closely connected to the agencies throughout the year.

Allie Welch and Kimberly Wrestler take a break during architecture class at Girls Inc.'s afterschool program.

Merrill Hatlen, Executive Director of Family Service Association, leads a children's activity at the Family Fun Fair in September.

Children from Boys & Girls Club of Bloomington at the annual pumpkin pick.

Resource 28

Community Connections

Study Circles are small, democratic, highly participatory discussions that provide a way for people to build community and address local issues. During 1999, more than 400 individuals in Monroe County took part in Study Circles on Race Relations and/or Diversity. The most recent session was based on the campus of Indiana University and involved groups of faculty, students, and staff.

Chaired by Michael Shermis, the Outcomes Measurement Pilot Project included the Hoosier Hills Food Bank, Boys & Girls Club, Family Service Association, Middle Way House, Stone Belt ARC, United Way, and the City of Bloomington Community and Family Resources Department.

Service and learning partnerships with Indiana University are extremely important to United Way/CSC and other local agencies. Through coursework, internship, and fundraising experience, students complement their degrees by participating in this not-for-profit management certification program. We also work closely with the Kelley School of Business Civic Leadership Development Program, the Office of Community Partnerships in Service and Learning, the Volunteer Students Bureau, and Collins Living Learning Center.

FEMA

The Monroe County allocation from the Federal Emergency Management Agency's (FEMA) Emergency Food and Shelter Program is used by local not-for-profits strictly for emergency housing assistance, utilities, and food. United Way of Monroe County administers this program for the county with the guidance of a local volunteer board, including representatives of city and county government, Salvation Army, Monroe County United Ministries, Beth Shalom congregation, Catholic Social Services, American Red Cross, a consumer representative, and the United Way. In 1999, $28,149 was distributed to Area 10 Agency on Aging, Hoosier Hills Food Bank, Community Kitchen, Middle Way House, Shelter, Inc., and Monroe County United Ministries.

FEMA Board

Denise Abel	Karen Brosius	Clark Morrison	Jodi Tobias	Frank Weinberg
Carol Bentley	Debbie Hawkins	Meri Reinhold	Peg Stice, *Chair*	Kirk White

Members of General Electric's Elfun Society complete a major volunteer project for not-for-profit agencies each spring and fall, as well as smaller projects throughout the year. In September 1999, the Elfun Society renovated and repaired Rhino's Youth Center and Big Brothers/Big Sisters.

CFC

The Combined Federal Campaign (CFC) is regulated by the Office of Personnel Management and is designed to allow federal employees the opportunity to make charitable donations to a wide variety of agencies through payroll deduction. In 1999, United Way of Monroe County once again served as the Principal Combined Fiscal Organization (PCFO) for the Crane Area CFC. Funds are distributed through a separate trust account at Bank One. Special thanks to Crane employees Vonda Smith, Marcia Hubler, JoAnn Blackwell, Lila Massa, and Carol Baldwin for their help.

Last year, United Way of Monroe County piloted the Donor Choice program at select workplaces to determine if Bloomington and Monroe County would react favorably to the increased options for their donations beyond the United Way Member Agencies. The answer was a resounding yes. So, for the 1999–2000 campaign, Donor Choice was available to everyone. United Way staff and volunteers compiled a list of more than 100 local and regional not-for-profits that met the criteria set forth by our Action Plan Donor Choice subcommittee. This list was distributed at workplaces, updated as new organizations were designated, and added to our Web site for easy access. We will continue to monitor the impact of the Donor Choice program on our local campaign over the next several years.

Several times a week, the United Way/CSC office receives calls from individuals and organizations wanting to donate used furniture, housewares, office equipment, clothing, computers—you name it! United Way/CSC staff then contact local service agencies that might be in need of such items. When the City of Bloomington upgraded their computers, United Way/CSC coordinated the distribution of the used equipment to local agencies.

Resource 28

Community Services: White River Central Labor Council

The local United Way/labor partnership is strong and productive. Coordination by our United Way/AFL-CIO Community Services Liaison, Josh Cazares, results in worker assistance and training, campaign planning and support, diversity initiatives, special events, volunteer projects, and outreach efforts.

Josh Cazares, AFL-CIO/United Way Community Services Liaison, Pat Muyskens, recipient of the Pride at Work AFL-CIO Humanitarian Award, and Dennis Schmidt, Co-Chair, Pride at Work AFL-CIO.

Shoppers hunt for bargains at the August 1999 yard sale sponsored by the White River Central Labor Council to benefit the United Way campaign.

During Week of Caring '99, volunteers repaired the wheelchair ramp at Middle Way House. Above is Jim Crabb of Carpenters 1664.

Resource 28

United Way Member Agency Directory

ABILITIES UNLIMITED
239 Winslow Rd./P.O. Box 1814
Bloomington, IN 47401
812/332-1620
abunlim@bloomington.in.us
Barbara Grissom Hillery, Executive Director
Provides advocacy, medical equipment loans, camperships, family support and casework to assist persons with disabilities in achieving their full potential.

AMERICAN RED CROSS, MONROE COUNTY CHAPTER
411 E. 7th St.
Bloomington, IN 47408
812/332-7292
redcross@bloomington.in.us
Carol Bentley, Chapter Director
Provides lifeline services, disaster relief, blood services, emergency assistance/ communication for military families, and training in CPR, first aid, and lifesaving.

AMETHYST HOUSE
1310 E. Atwater Ave./P.O. Box 11
Bloomington, IN 47402
812/336-3570
amethyst@bloomington.in.us
Janna Kosinski, Executive Director
Provides transitional residential services for men and women in recovery from chemical dependency.

AREA 10 AGENCY ON AGING
7500 W. Reeves Rd.
Bloomington, IN 47404
812/876-3383
area10@bloomington.in.us
Jewel Echelbarger, Executive Director
Through Assistance to the Homebound, provides escorted transportation, shopping and other services to help frail elderly live independently in their own homes.

BIG BROTHERS BIG SISTERS OF MONROE CO.
418 S. Walnut/P.O. Box 2534
Bloomington, IN 47401
812/334-2828
bbbs@bloomington.in.us
Liz Grenat, Director
Matches adult volunteers one-on-one with children primarily from single parent families, providing positive role models and promoting self-esteem.

BOY SCOUTS OF AMERICA, HOOSIER TRAILS COUNCIL
2307 E. 2nd St.
Bloomington, IN 47401
812/336-6809
htcbs145@bloomington.in.us
Randy Brown, Scout Executive
Volunteer leaders serve as positive role models for boys (6–20) and girls (15–20) as they develop leadership, citizenship, and personal fitness.

BOYS & GIRLS CLUB OF BLOOMINGTON
311 S. Lincoln/P.O. Box 1716
Bloomington, IN 47401
812/332-5311
bgclub@bloomington.in.us
Joe Stebbins, Executive Director
Gives boys and girls ages 6–18 a safe, healthy place for athletic programs, arts activities, tutoring, counseling, games, hobbies, leadership groups, camping, and field trips. Operates Crestmont and Henderson Court Boys & Girls Clubs for children ages 6–12.

CATHOLIC SOCIAL SERVICES—BLOOMINGTON
511 S. Madison St.
Bloomington, IN 47403
812/332-1262
css@bloomington.in.us
Karen Brosius, Executive Director
Enhances human dignity and functioning for the community at-large through education, social service delivery, and advocacy.

COMMUNITY KITCHEN OF MONROE CO., INC.
917 S. Rogers St.
Bloomington, IN 47403
812/332-0999
kitchen@bloomington.in.us
Robin Jackson, Executive Director
Directly addresses the problem of hunger in Monroe County by providing free,
nutritious meals to anyone who needs food.

COMMUNITY SERVICE COUNCIL
441 S. College Ave.
Bloomington, IN 47403
812/334-8370
csc@unitedway.monroe.in.us
Beverly Calender-Anderson, Director
Mission: To nurture interagency communication and collaboration in the Monroe
County human services family, to identify emerging community needs, and to be a
catalyst for meeting those needs.

FAMILY SERVICE ASSOCIATION OF MONROE CO.
441 S. College Ave.
Bloomington, IN 47403
812/339-1551
fsa@bloomington.in.us
Merrill Hatlen, Executive Director
Strengthens families and individuals through counseling and support groups.
Sponsors CASA, a court-supervised advocacy for abused and neglected children.

GIRL SCOUTS, TULIP TRACE COUNCIL, INC.
5488 E. State Rd./P.O. Box 5485
Bloomington, IN 47407-5485
812/336-6804
gscouts@tuliptrace.org
Deborah O'Brien, Executive Director
Helps girls (5–17) through a preventative approach to healthy youth development.
Programs include Joyous Garde for at-risk girls, substance abuse prevention, the
environment, and leadership training.

GIRLS INCORPORATED OF MONROE COUNTY
1108 W. 8th St.
Bloomington, IN 47404
812/336-7313
girlsinc@bloomington.in.us
Karen Jones, Executive Director
Gives girls (kindergarten–18) a place for recreation, education, and social activities to learn new skills, explore career possibilities, develop leadership, and build self-esteem.

HOOSIER HILLS FOOD BANK
615 N. Fairview
Bloomington, IN 47404
812/334-8374
hhfb@bloomington.in.us
Amy Robinson, Executive Director
Collects, stores, and distributes donated and surplus food to 105 not-for-profit agencies who feed the hungry in six counties.

MCCSC SCHOOL ASSISTANCE FUND
315 North Dr.
Bloomington, IN 47401
812/330-7700
Gary Plaford, Director
Provides clothing, eye care, dental care, group counseling, and short-term medical care for children of low-income families.

MENTAL HEALTH ASSOCIATION, MONROE COUNTY CHAPTER
407 S. Walnut St.
Bloomington, IN 47401
812/339-2803
mha@bloomington.in.us
Elaine Moore, Executive Director
Provides support to mentally ill clients and their families through support groups, advocacy, and information & referral. Sponsors the Listening Line at 332-6060.

MIDDLE WAY HOUSE, INC.
414 W. Kirkwood/P.O. Box 95
Bloomington, IN 47402
812/333-7404
mwhouse@bloomington.in.us
Toby Strout, Executive Director
Offers safe, temporary housing to abused women and their children, along with
advocacy, support groups, child care, education and training. Operates 24-hour
Rape Crisis Line at 336-0846.

MONROE COUNTY COUNCIL FOR OLDER AMERICANS
7237 N. Wayport Rd.
Bloomington, IN 47408
812/876-1246
Wilbert Williams, President
Supports 12 senior citizen clubs offering companionship, outings, hobbies, and
educational programs to prevent isolation.

MONROE COUNTY UNITED MINISTRIES, INC.
827 W. 14 St.
Bloomington, IN 47404
812/339-3429
mcum@bloomington.in.us
Meri Reinhold, Executive Director
Offers quality day care, emergency food/shelter, and financial counseling to
low-income families.

PLANNED PARENTHOOD OF CENTRAL AND SOUTHERN INDIANA, INC.
421 S. College Ave., Bloomington, IN 47403
3209 N. Meridian St., Indianapolis, IN 46208
812/336-0219 (clinic)
812/336-7050 (administration)
800/421-3731, ext. 101
ppcsi@bloomington.in.us
Delbert Culp, CEO
Provides comprehensive health care. United Way supports education services and
Pap and other lab tests for women and men.

PUBLIC HEALTH NURSING ASSOCIATION dba
BLOOMINGTON HOSPITAL HOME HEALTH SERVICES
333 E. Miller Dr., Bloomington, IN 47401
812/336-4492 (Business Office/Home Health Care)
812/332-2901 (CHAP Clinic)
812/334-0650 (WIC and Walk-in Clinic)
phna@bloomington.in.us
Eleanor Rogers, VP of Home Health Services
Provides "advanced home health care" and operates a community health services center.

RHINO'S YOUTH CENTER
325 1/2 S. Walnut St./P.O. Box 1727
Bloomington, IN 47402
812/333-3430
rhinos@bloomington.in.us
Brad Wilhelm, Services Director
Provides entertainment, recreation, and job training activities for adolescents in a safe, alcohol, drug, and smoke-free environment that is co-managed by the adolescents themselves.

RICHLAND-BEAN BLOSSOM SCHOOL ASSISTANCE FUND
7973 W. Main St.
Stinesville, IN 47464
812/876-2474
Bill Buxton, Director
Assists with dental, optical, medical, and clothing needs of students who might otherwise go without these services.

SALVATION ARMY
111 N. Rogers St./P.O. Box 2117
Bloomington, IN 47402
812/336-4310
salvarmy@bloomington.in.us
Major G. Wesley Green, Commanding Officer
Offers emergency assistance, food, clothing, furniture, and temporary shelter. Provides counseling, referrals, recreation, inspiration, and hope.

SHELTER, INC.
919 S. Rogers St./P.O. Box 1955
Bloomington, IN 47402
812/332-1444
shelter@bloomington.in.us
Michael Reinke, Executive Director
Provides shelter for homeless individuals and families, case management and networking with other social service agencies.

STONE BELT ARC, INC.
2815 E. 10th St.
Bloomington, IN 47408
812/332-2168
sbcarc@bloomington.in.us
Elbert Johns, Executive Director
Helps persons with disabilities attain independence through development education, sheltered and community-based employment, residential services, and other assistance in community living.

UNITED WAY OF MONROE COUNTY, INC.
441 S. College Ave.
Bloomington, IN 47403
812/334-8370
uw@unitedway.monroe.in.us
Peg Stice, Executive Director
Mission: to increase the organized capacity of people to care for one another.

FIRST CALL FOR HELP
812/334-8393

Resource 28

REFERENCES

American Association of Fundraising Counsel Trust for Philanthropy. *Giving USA, 1997*. New York: American Association of Fundraising Counsel Trust for Philanthropy, 1997.

Association of Fundraising Professionals (formerly, National Society of Fund Raising Executives). *Membership Survey Profile*. Alexandria, Va.: National Society of Fund Raising Executives, 1999.

Barth, S. "Finding the Needle in the Haystack: Using Computer Screening and Database Analysts to Discover the Hidden Major-Gift Prospects Among Your Alumni." *Case Currents*, June 1998, pp. 32–36.

Broce, T. E. *Fund Raising*. Norman: University of Oklahoma Press, 1979.

Campbell, D. A., Jr. "The Capital Campaign: Soliciting the Lead Gift(s)." Presentation at the annual conference of the Council for Advancement and Support of Education, District VI, St. Louis, Mo., Jan. 1985.

Conrad, D. L. *How to Solicit Big Gifts*. San Francisco: Public Management Institute, 1978.

Coulter, A. [acoulter@iquest.net]. Personal communication, Aug. 1999.

Dove, K. E. *Conducting a Successful Fundraising Program: A Comprehensive Guide and Resource*. San Francisco: Jossey-Bass, 2001.

Dunlop, D. R. "Suggestions for Working with Volunteers." Presentation at the Council for Advancement and Support of Education Summer Institute in Educational Fund Raising, Dartmouth College, Hanover, N.H., July 1981.

Fund Raising School. *Principles and Techniques of Fund Raising*. Indianapolis: Indiana University Center on Philanthropy, 1995.

Gallup Organization. *Patterns of Charitable Giving by Individuals*, Vol. 2. Washington, D.C.: INDEPENDENT SECTOR, 1982.

Gallup Organization. *An Analysis of Charitable Contributions by Upper-Income Households for 1986 and 1987.* New York: American Association of Fundraising Counsel Trust for Philanthropy, 1987.

Hale, E. E. Remarks made at the annual conference of the Council for Advancement and Support of Education, Atlanta, Apr. 1980.

Harris, A. L. *Special Events: Planning for Success.* Washington, D.C.: CASE Books, 1998.

INDEPENDENT SECTOR. *Giving and Volunteering in the United States, 1996.* Washington, D.C.: INDEPENDENT SECTOR, 1996.

Kughn, J. C., Jr. "Using Volunteers Effectively." Presentation at the annual conference of the Council for Advancement and Support of Education, Nashville, Tenn., Mar. 1982.

La Rocque, P. "More Precise Writing." Handout given with presentation at the Council for Advancement and Support of Education Writing Institute, Philadelphia, Dec. 1992.

Legon, R. D. *The Board's Role in Fund Raising.* Washington, D.C.: Association of Governing Boards of Colleges and Universities, 1997.

Livingston, H. J., Jr. "The Role of Trustees in a Capital Campaign." *Bulletin on Public Relations and Development for Colleges and Universities,* Mar. 1984, pp. 1–4.

Lyon, J. B. "Considerations in Respecting Donor Interests." *Trusts and Events,* Sept. 1998, pp. 108–120.

Picton, R. R. "Effective Follow-Through." Presentation made at the annual conference of the Council for Advancement and Support of Education, Nashville, Tenn., Mar. 1982.

Seymour, H. J. *Designs for Fund Raising.* New York: McGraw-Hill, 1966.

Stuhr, R. L. *Gonser Gerber Tinker Stuhr on Development.* Chicago: Gonser Gerber Tinker Stuhr, 1977.

Taylor, J. H. *Your Noncash Gift Questions Report, 1996.* New York: Conference Board, 1998.

Tillman, A. *Corporate Contributions Report, 1996.* New York: Conference Board, 1998.

Tri-Media Marketing & Publicity, Inc. [www.121marketing.com]. 2000.

Wasow, M. "Corporate Involvement in the Nonprofit Sector." *Giving USA Update,* no. 2, 1998.

INDEX

A

Account administration: and conditionality, 188; and documenting pledges, 187–188; and gift receipts, 185–186; and nonacceptance of gift, 188; and valuing noncash gifts, 186–187

American Association of Fundraising Counsel, Inc., 182; Trust for Philanthropy, 140

American College of Obstetricians and Gynecologists, 43

American Diabetes Association, 37

American Express, 43

American Health Foundation, 43

Amethyst House (United Way; Bloomington, Indiana), 73, 163

Annual fund: definition of, 8; in-house, 47; traditional, 7

Annual fund chair, duties of, 145–146. *See also* Volunteer campaign leaders

Annual giving plan: case statement for, 12; and continuous lifetime giving, 18–20; developing, 11–31; and ease of giving, 26–29; and

multiple gifts, 30–31; and partnerships, 20–22; planning solicitation calendar for, 22–24; and quality of prospects, 24–26; setting goals for, 12–15; and timing issues, 29; two types of gift tables for, 15–18

AFP. *See* Association of Fundraising Professionals

APRA. *See* Association of Professional Researchers for Advancement

Association of Fundraising Professionals (AFP), 125, 182; Code of Ethical Principles, 125; Standards of Professional Practice, 125

Association of Professional Researchers for Advancement (APRA), 125

Automation, and telemarketing, 121–122

B

Barth, S., 127

Barton, D. W., Jr., 174

Barton Gillet, 174

Bentz Whaley & Flessner, 127

Bloomington, Indiana, 37, 39, 40, 43, 73; Hospital Foundation, 166–167

Bonchek, S., 37, 39, 40

Bonus sheet, for callers, 112

British Columbia Children's Hospital Foundation, 29

Broce, T. E., 147

Budget: and annual campaign budget report, 181; gift administration and, 179–180; and sponsoring special events, 87–88

C

Callers: and advanced caller training, 120; bonus sheet for, 112; and calling session, 110, 112–113; choosing, for telemarketing, 97–98; motivation for, 112–113; and role playing, 109–110; sample fact sheet for, 100–102; script for, 103–105; statistics on (Indiana University Foundation), 116–117; training, for

telemarketing, 99–109; volunteer recruitment ads for, 99
Calling session, 110, 112–113
Campaign: capital, 35; closing of, 194–200; conclusion of, as new beginning, 199–200; corporate, 37–41; definition of, 11–12; direct mail, 60–86; in-house annual fund, 47; membership, 47, 49; and multiple gifts, 30–31; naming, 177–178
Campbell, D. A., Jr., 134
CASE. *See* Council for Advancement and Support of Education
Case statement, 12
Challenge gifts, 37, 38
Checklists, 93–94
Coaching, 113; evaluation form, 114
Communications: fundraising, 164–168; marketing and, 175–176; principles for, with volunteers, 155–157
Community Foundation, Bloomington and Monroe County (Indiana), 37, 39, 40
Community leaders, four main groups of, 142
Computerworld Smithsonian Award, 78
Conditionality, 188
Conference Board, 42
Connelly, T. A., 41
Conrad, D. L., 136
Consultants, 182
Contact report, 126
Continuous lifetime giving, 22; broad outline for, 19; definition of, 18; track for, 20
Corporations: and corporate matching, 42; researching, 46–47
Coulter, A., 89
Council for Advancement and Support of Education (CASE), 125

D

Demographic screening, 127
Design, publications, 174–175. *See also* Fundraising publications
Development: councils, 151–152; definition of, 18

Dialog, 46
Direct mail campaign: and avoiding errors, 76; and enclosures, 75; essential elements of, 61–76; and Internet, 75–76; and outer envelope, 68–70; reasons for wide use of, 60–61; and reply envelope, 75; and response device, 70–74; sample segmentation letter (Greater Victoria Hospitals Foundation) for, 64–65; and solicitation package for Fairfield Country Day School Annual Fund (sample), 77–82; and solicitation package for Penn State Library, 83–86; and solicitation piece, 62–63, 68
Directory of Corporation Affiliations, The, 46
Donor solicitation letter (sample), 39
Donors: and donor recognition at various giving levels, 193; and donor societies, 49; effective segmenting of, 34–35; and sample donor retention report, 59; and sample donor upgrade report, 58
Donors' Bill of Rights, 137–138
Dove, K. E., 187
Dun & Bradstreet, 46
Dunlop, D. R., 155
Dupree, R. K., 41

E

Econometrics, 127
EFT. *See* Electronic Funds Transfer fact sheet
Electronic Funds Transfer fact sheet, 27
Elli Lilly and Company, 43
Ellis Island, New York, 43
Emotion, 51
Envelope: outer, 68–70; reply, 75
Ethics, in solicitation, 125

F

Fact sheet, for telemarketers (Indiana University), 100–102
Fairfield Country Day School, 77–82
FCDS. *See* Fairfield Country Day School

Feedback, 58–59
Final reports: and internal report, 196–198; and public document, 198
Foundation boards: and board members as solicitors, 150–151; and characteristics of effective board fundraisers, 151; and development councils, 151–152; and early stages of planning, 148–149; and soliciting board members, 149–150. *See also* Volunteer boards; Volunteer campaign leaders
Fund Raising School, 63, 88, 89
Fundraising communications: and sample organization fact sheets, 165–167; types of, 164–165, 168
Fundraising publications: design and layout in, 174–175; elements of creative strategy for, 172; preparing, 172–176; writing style for, 173–174

G

Gallup Organization, 140
General Electric, 43
Gift administration: and account administration, 185–188; and annual campaign budget report (sample), 181; and budget, 179–180; and donor recognition at various giving levels, 193; and recognizing, acknowledging, reporting gifts, 188–191; and stewardship, 191–192; and use of report forms, 183–184; and use of unpaid solicitors and consultants, 182
Gift table: functions of, 13; standard of, for goal of $100,000 with less-proven prospect pool, 16; standard of, for goal of $100,000 with proven prospect pool, 17; standard of, for goal of $1 million with less-proven prospect pool, 16; standard of, for goal of $1 million with proven prospect pool, 17; two types of, 15–18; unworkable, 18; workable, 15–17

Gifts: challenge, 37–38; corporate matching, 42; and gift clubs, 49; and gift receipts, 185–186; in-kind, 42; kinds of, 41–42; multiple, 30–31; and nonacceptance of gift, 188; outright, 41; reporting, 188–191; and valuing noncash gifts, 186–187

Gill, J., 141

Gill, L., 141

Gill Foundation, 141

Girl Scouts, Inc. (Tulip Trace Council), 73

Giving chart, 13

Glamour magazine, 43

Go Direct Marketing, Inc., 36

Goals, setting: for annual fund, 12–15; at Indianapolis Children's Museum, 14–15

Gonser Gerber Tinker Stuhr, 147

Greater Victoria Hospital Foundation (Victoria, British Columbia), 64, 65, 69, 186

Grenzeback Glier & Associates, 127

H

Habitat for Humanity, 43

Hale, E. E., 154

Hanes, 43

Hanna House (Bloomington, Indiana), 43

Harmony School Education Center (Bloomington, Indiana), 37, 39, 40

Harris, A., 89, 93

Houston, Texas, 141; Museum of Fine Arts, 37

Huckleberry Finn (Twain), 174

I

Indiana University (IU), 41, 44, 54, 103, 112; Alumni Association, 22; Annual Fund, 48, 54, 55, 111; Bloomington, School of Law, 155; Continuous Lifetime Involvement Program (CLIP), 22; Foundation, 22, 44, 106, 116–117, 127, 172; Kelley School of Business, 41, 99, 100–102; Telefund, 99, 119

Indianapolis Children's Museum, 14–15, 189–191; goal-setting process at, 14–15

Information gathering, different levels of, 125

Internal Revenue Service (IRS), 47, 185–187

Internet: and delivering support materials, 171; direct marketing and, 75–76; prospect research on, 127–130; telephone and address information on, 120–121

K

Kimberling, J., 155

Kughn, J. C., Jr., 161

L

LaRocque, P., 173

Layout, publications, 174–175. *See also* Fundraising publications

Lead gift, 8

Leadership giving chair, volunteer job description for, 144. *See also* Volunteer campaign leaders

Legislation, and telemarketing, 121

Legon, R. D., 151

Letters: guidelines for writing better, 63, 68; and nondonor solicitation letters, 40; personalization *versus* nonpersonalization in (samples), 54–55; segmentation, 64–67

Lexis/Nexis, 46

Lilly Endowment, 37, 39, 40

Lists: buying, 32–33; cleaning up, 120–121

Livingston, H. J., Jr., 148

Locality, 45–46

LYBUNT, meaning of, 23

Lyon, J. B., 188

M

Major gift, 8

Marketing: cause-related, 42–45; developing realistic plan for, 175–176

Martin, V., 127, 128–130

Marts & Lundy, 127

McDonalds, 43

Media attention, variables for attracting, 176

Microsoft Access, 118

Microsoft Excel, 118

Mission, 51

Monroe County Bank (Indiana), 43

Motivation, caller, 112–113

Museum of Fine Arts, Houston, 37

N

National Cancer Institute, 43

National Football League, 43

National Heart Month, 29

Nieman-Marcus, 192

Nondonor solicitation letter (sample), 40

Nordstrom, 192

Nucleus gift, 8

O

On-line giving, 26–29; and Electronic Funds Transfer fact sheet (Penn State Transfer), 27; and Penn State's annual fund on-line form, 28

Organization fact sheets (samples), 165–168

Oversolicitation, 30

P

Partnerships, 20–22

Paterno, J., 83, 84

Paterno, S., 83, 84

Penn State Transfer, 27. *See also* Electronic Funds Transfer fact sheet

Pennsylvania State University, 83, 86, 177; Annual Fund, 66, 66–67, 71–72, 72; annual fund on-line form, 28; Library, 66, 85; Office of Annual Giving, 27; and Penn State Campaign, 84, 85

Personal touch, 9

Personalization, *versus* nonpersonalization, 54–55

Picton, R. R., 161

Pledges, documenting, 187–188

Positive dollar asks, 108

Pre-call notification mailing, 106

Pro bono services, 42

Promotions: and attracting media attention, 176; and designing response devices, 168–170; and developing realistic plan for marketing and communications, 175–176; and naming campaign, 177–178; and preparing fundraising publications, 172–175; and purpose of support materials, 171–172; and types of fundraising communications, 164–168

Prospects: and annual giving techniques, 25–26; critical variable for quality of, 24–26; definition of, 9; demographic screening of, 127; and estimating individual's giving potential, 132–133; internal ethics policy in research of, 125; principles of research of, 126; and prospect data form, 111; quality of current pool of, 24–25; rating, 131–132; three levels of, 124. *See also* Solicitation

Public Management Institute, 136

R

Report forms: campaign progress, 183; creating and using, 183–184; prospect status summary, 184

Response devices: Amethyst House sample of, 73–74; designing, 168–170; Penn State Annual Fund sample of, 71–72

Retention report, donor (sample), 59

Role playing, in telemarketing, 109–110

Ronald McDonald House, 43

Ruff, K., 163

S

Screening vendors, 127

Script, 103–105; pledge confirmation, 109

Segmentation letter: Greater Victoria Hospitals Foundation sample of, 64–65; Penn State Annual Fund sample of, 66–67

Segmenting: during capital campaign, 35; and cause-related marketing, 41–45; and challenge gifts, 37; and corporate campaigns, 37–41; and gift clubs or donor societies, 49; in-house, 47; and list buying, 32–33; and locality, 45–46; and membership campaigns, 47–48; and primary methods of giving, 41–42; and researching corporations, 46–47; and sponsorships, 45; and targeting for maximum effectiveness, 34–35; and timelines, 33–34; and University of British Columbia donor base comparison, 36

Seymour, H. J., 142, 157

Skidmore, M., 37

Smith, J., 14

Solicitation: determining prospect pool for, 124; and donor's bill of rights, 138; errors to avoid in, 136–137; estimating individual's giving potential for, 132–133; facilitating process of, 125–128; and making the ask, 133–136; overview of, 123; rating prospects for, 131–132

Solicitation calendar: Fairfield Country Day School sample of, 23; planning of, 22–24; timing issues for, 29

Solicitation letter (sample): donor, 39; faculty-staff, 48; nondonor, 40

Solicitation package, 61–68; for Fairfield Country Day School, 77–82; for Penn State Library, 83–86

Special events: budget for, 87–88; checklists for, 93–94; criteria for selecting, 88–89; as most versatile technique, 87; planning details for, 89–92; and sponsorship, 88

Sponsorships, 45, 88

Stanford University, 29; Law School, 12

Stewardship, 10, 191–192

Stuhr, R. L., 147, 148

Support: case for, 62–63, 68; purpose of materials for, 171–172

Surveys, 58–59

SYBUNT, meaning of, 23

T

Taylor, W. L., Jr., 46, 186

Team chair, volunteer job description for, 143. *See also* Volunteer campaign leaders

Telemarketing: advanced caller training for, 120; automated, 121–122; and calling session, 110, 112–113; choosing callers for, 97–98; and cleaning up lists, 120–121; coaching evaluation form for, 114; and fulfillment process, 113, 118; and legislation, 121; overview of, 95–96; planning program for, 96–97; positive dollar asks for, 108; precall notification mailing for, 106; role playing for, 109–110; and sample bonus sheet for callers, 112; sample fact sheet for (Kelley School of Business, Indiana University), 100–102; and sample pledge confirmation script, 109; sample prospect data form for, 112–113; sample reasons to give (Indiana University), 103; sample volunteer recruitment ads for, 99; script elements for, 104; tracking results of, 118, 120; training callers for, 99–109

Testing: and analysis of annual fund trends, 56–58; need for, 50–52; and other forms of analysis, 58–59; and tracking code systems, 53, 56

Thiede, J., 44

Tillman, A., 42

Timeliness, 29, 33–34

Tracking code systems, 53, 56

Training: advanced caller, 120; for telemarketing, 99–109

Trends, understanding, 56–58

Tri-Media Marketing & Publicity, Inc., 43

Twain, M., 174

U

United States Postal Service, 33

United Way, 20–21, 37, 43; Amethyst House (Bloomington, Indiana), 73, 74; of Central Indiana, 14, 143–144; menu reply card, 21

United Way-Lilly Endowment
Challenge Gift, 37
University of British Columbia, 36;
donor base comparison, 36
Unpaid solicitors, 182
Upgrade report, donor (sample), 58
USA Today, 172

V

Volunteer boards: and board members as solicitors, 150–151; and early stages of planning, 148–149; four main functions of, 147; populating, 146–148; and setting example for others, 148; and soliciting board members, 149–150. *See also* Foundation boards; Volunteer campaign leaders
Volunteer campaign leaders: characteristics of successful, 142; choosing, 141–145; importance of, 139–141
Volunteerism, 42
Volunteers: dealing with challenges of, 161–163; educating, 157–160; and peer-to-peer recognition, 163; principles for communicating with, 155–157; recruitment of, 153–155; recruitment ads for, 99; and staffing, 160–161; worker kits for, 159; working with, 153–163

W

Wasow, M., 43
White, J., 14–15
Wilson, J., 172
Wilson, K. K., 46
World Wide Web, 171. *See also* Internet
Writing style, 173–174. *See also* Fundraising publications

CPSIA information can be obtained at www.ICGtesting.com
Printed in the USA
BVOW09s0927120815

412898BV00009B/26/P